FROM JET PROVOST TO STRIKEMASTER

DAVID WATKINS

FROM JET PROVOST TO STRIKEMASTER

A DEFINITIVE HISTORY OF THE BASIC AND COUNTER-INSURGENT AIRCRAFT AT HOME AND OVERSEAS

GRUB STREET | LONDON

Published by
Grub Street
4 Rainham Close
London
SW11 6SS

Copyright © Grub Street 2017
Copyright text © David Watkins 2017

A CIP record for this title is available from
the British Library

ISBN-13: 9-781-910690-35-2

Cover and book design by Daniele Roa

Printed and bound by Finidr, Czech Republic

Previous page: Pre-delivery image of Strikemaster Mk.83 of the
Botswana Defence Force. It had previously served with the Kuwait
air force and been stored at Warton before its delivery to Botswana
in March 1988. The aircraft was eventually sold to a buyer in the
USA and registered as N4242T. (BAe Systems Heritage Warton-Per-
cival/Hunting Collection)

CONTENTS

ACKNOWLEDGEMENTS

I would like to thank everyone who provided the generous and enthusiastic support to enable me to complete this book. It is a great pity that both Hunting and BAC disposed of most of its historic material and images some years ago and I am, therefore, particularly grateful to Reg Stock for the archive reports and photographs from his time as the Jet Provost/Strikemaster project pilot, and for kindly agreeing to contribute the foreword; to Ray Deacon, who once again provided me with constant encouragement to complete this work, together with numerous images from his vast collection; and Kate Yates for generously making available a large number of original images from the BAe Systems Heritage Warton-Percival/Hunting Collection; this incredible collection is worthy of a book in its own right and it is with great regret that only a small number could be incorporated into this work. I would also like to thank those who responded to my seemingly endless requests and for making their photographic collections freely available; I have attempted to include a representative selection of these images within these pages. I have also tried to ascertain the original contributor of each image, which has proved particularly difficult in some cases and I therefore hope that anyone who has not received the rightful credit will please accept my sincere apologies.

My gratitude is also extended to the following: Alan Allen; Gp Capt Dick Allen; Tim Allen; James Baldwin; Laurie Bean; Sqn Ldr Dick Bell MBE; Derick Bridge; Sqn Ldr Rod Brown; Eric Bucklow; Mike Butt; Steve Carr; Ian Carroll; Rob Chambers; Sean Chiddention; Philip Clifford (Brooklands Museum, Weybridge); Neil Corbett; Sqn Ldr Allan Corkett; Capt Nigel Courtis; Brendan Cowan; David Croser; Ms Judith Cross (PA to Comdt CFS); Peter Curtin; Wg Cdr Eddie Danks; Wg Cdr Barry Dale; Paul Dandeker; John M Davis; Rod Dean; Mike Edwards; Gp Capt Tom Eeles BA FRAeS; Hywel 'Taff' Evans; Rod Farquhar; Sqn Ldr Mark Fielding RAAF; Mike Fox; Bob Garlick; Guy Gibbons; Norman Giffin; Dave Gledhill; Y. K. Goh; Dennis Grey; Gp Capt Brian Gubbins; Jacques Guillem; Anthony Haig-Thomas; Wg Cdr P. J. 'Curly' Hirst; Gp Capt Brian Hoskins AFC FRAeS; Jerry Hughes; Capt Bruce Hutton MRAeS RN; Capt Bill Jago; Wg Cdr Jeff Jefford; Peter Jennings; Martin Kaye; Jukka Keranen; Fredric Lagerquist; Sqn Ldr Dickie Lees; Flt Lt Darren Legg MBE; Paul Lewis; John Lloyd; Terry Lloyd; Noel Lokuge; Gordon Macadie; Wg Cdr Doug Marr AFC*; David McCann; Don McClen; Keith McCloskey; Sqn Ldr Bruce McDonald AFC*; Gp Capt Paul McDonald; Dave McIntyre; Frank Milligan; David Milne-Smith; Mike Napier; Terry Nash; Brett Nicholls; Alick Nicholson; Air Marshal Sir Peter C. Norriss, KCB CB AFC MA FRAeS; Charles O'Neill; Bill Perrins; Mark Petrie; Mike Phipp; AVM Les Phipps CB AFC; Patrick Vinot Prefontaine; Air Cdre Richie Profit OBE AFC MRAeS; Captain William Portes, FAV rtd; Sqn Ldr R. M. Pugh AFC/Anthony Pugh; Graham Rawlinson; Wally Rhodes; Sqn Ldr Colin Richardson; Sqn Ldr John Robinson AFC*; Gp Capt Nick Rusling; Wg Cdr Mick Ryan; Bob Screen; John Scutt; AVM Sir John Severne KCVO OBE AFC DL; Brian Shadbolt; Ian Sheppard; Tim Simpson; Art Stacey; 'Turbo' Tarling; Bob Thompson FRAeS; Nick Tillotson; Claudio Toselli; James Watts-Philips; Joe Whitfield; Paul Wiggins; Nick Wilcock; Gerald Williams; Steve Wilson; Keith Wilson-Clark.

01

FOREWORD

In his introduction, David Watkins regrets that despite training many generations of pilots throughout their long careers, the Jet Provost and Strikemaster have been largely overlooked. But obviously not by me, heavily involved as I was with both types for many years. My first connection with the company responsible for their gestation was during initial training as an RAF pilot on the Percival Prentice. Although aerobatic and 'spinnable' it was a rather lumbering beast. I remember whilst serving on a fighter squadron based in Celle, West Germany, it was required to transport our heavyweight boxer to Wildenrath for a boxing match. Being one of the few familiar with our Prentice, I was detailed for the flight. I naturally chose to take off in a westerly direction using the grass light aircraft strip, opened the throttle and away we trundled. It soon became obvious, when it was too late to stop, that we would not be able to clear the sergeants' mess, I initiated a turn to the south west as though it were normal procedure and managed to retrieve the situation. I was thus rather surprised to discover that in its latter days one of them was converted to carry no less than seven persons. Anyway, on return to Celle the following day, in a casual conversation in the mess bar, the senior air traffic controller asked, "By the way, why did you take off downwind?" I leave the reader to fashion a suitable reply. But not before they have read this incredibly detailed book about the Jet Provost and Strikemaster.

I was a flying instructor on the Piston Provost, then converted to the Jet Provost in the early stages of all-through jet training. My service in the RAF was nearing its end during this period when the chief test pilot of Hunting Aircraft (previously Percival and subsequently BAC) visited us at Syerston and asked for a likely person to do production testing. I was that lucky chap and subsequently on moving from Luton to Warton (I was given the option of joining Eric Trubshaw at Wisley – Concorde?! But preferred the more vigorous alternative) I became the project pilot for the Jet Provost and Strikemaster, and that is why I have been inundated with questions from David Watkins.

I have to say that his attention to detail has caused me endless recovery forays into my logbooks and other various documents fortunately not thrown away. Even so I am amazed at the wealth of information he has unearthed, knowing how much persistent digging is necessary. However, as David has written several other memorable aviation tomes, he knows what is involved and thus earns our admiration and thanks. He has of course thanked his many contributors and I would also like to mention all those observers, navigators and test pilots who flew with me. Two in particular, flight test observers Dave Croser and John Scutt were present during some trials which were far from comfortable. Looking back, I do not recall anyone ever saying, "Reg, are you sure we should be doing this?" I would have asked myself that same question had I been required to write a book about the Jet Provost and Strikemaster.

Reg Stock

01. 'Ready for Delivery to Saudi Arabia'. Brian McCann (navigator), Reg Stock (leader) and Alan Love pose for a company photograph prior to the delivery of the first Strikemaster Mk.80s, '901' and '902', for the Royal Saudi Air Force. (BAC via Reg Stock)

REG STOCK was born in Harrold, Bedfordshire. He joined the RAF in November 1951, initially as a National Service pilot, and was posted to RAF Celle in Germany in August 1953. Then he was posted to 94 Squadron, a day-fighter/ground-attack unit flying Vampire and Venom aircraft, and during the next four years he was a member of the squadron's rocket-firing and formation aerobatic teams. He returned to England in September 1957. Volunteering for an instructor's course at the Central Flying School in July 1958, he was then awarded the Hopewell best pilot and Clarkson aerobatic trophies, and graduated as a B1 instructor. Between November 1958 and July 1961, Reg instructed on Provost and Jet Provost trainers at No.2 FTS, RAF Syerston, and also gave solo, synchronised and formation aerobatic displays. Leaving the RAF in 1961 he was appointed jet training officer at Marshall's Flying School at Shawbury before joining Hunting Aircraft in March 1962 (later to become British Aircraft Corporation, Luton Division) as a test pilot.

At Luton, Reg became heavily involved with various aspects of test flying, including spin recovery and high Mach trials. In 1964 he transferred to BAC Warton when the Jet Provost was reassigned to the Military Division following the cancellation of the TSR.2 and became the Jet Provost/Strikemaster project pilot in 1967. He was in command of the first flights of both the Jet Provost Mk.5 (28 February 1967) and the BAC Strikemaster (26 October 1967). As well as the development flying of these two types Reg undertook most of the customer demonstration and aerobatic display flights, including the Farnborough air shows between 1962 and 1970 and the Paris Salon in 1969 and 1971.

Deliveries of various aircraft were also made to Iraq, Sudan, Ecuador and Saudi Arabia no fewer than fourteen times. He also tested Jaguar and Canberra aircraft from the production line. In 1973, Reg was deployed to Ecuador for two months to test rebuilt aircraft; he was also required to convert nine Ecuadorian pilots (subsequently reduced to four) on to the Strikemaster and include general handling, navigation, instrument and night flying plus bomb dropping, gunnery and rocket firing.

Together with his test flying, he was appointed senior communications pilot in 1978 and promoted to chief communications pilot in January 1983. During this time, Reg was awarded the Queen's Commendation for Valuable Services in the Air in the Birthday Honours List of 1981. He left the company in February 1989 to fly Boeing 727s with Dan Air until it was sold to British Airways for £1 in November 1992.

Following retirement, Reg maintained his interest in music and gardening, including the redesigning of a local pub garden – which requires regular visits to check growth rates. He first met his wife on a bus, in 1961, and they live in Penwortham, a few miles across the river from Warton.

02

03

INTRODUCTION

Originally designed by Percival Aircraft at Luton in 1951, the P.84 Jet Provost was developed from the company's Piston Provost primary trainer and built as a private venture in response to an RAF requirement for a jet-powered primary training aircraft. To reduce manufacturing costs and to speed up the development programme of the prototype, components from those of its predecessor were utilised, including mainplanes, tail surfaces and main undercarriage legs. The most significant change to the new design, however, included the replacement of the Alvis Leonides radial engine by an Armstrong Siddeley Viper jet turbine of 1,750-lb thrust, an expendable engine originally produced for the Australian Jindivik pilotless target drone. Also installed in the prototype was a nosewheel undercarriage leg; the tricycle undercarriage being pneumatically operated and retractable.

The constant debate as to the advantages of a jet-powered basic trainer to provide an all-through jet-training syllabus for the RAF eventually resulted in an announcement by the Secretary of State in March 1953 that an order for an initial batch of ten Jet Provost T Mk.1s (plus an eleventh airframe for use as a company demonstrator) would be placed with Percival Aircraft to enable a practical service evaluation to be carried out. The prototype first flew on 26 June 1954.

In August 1955, eight pre-production Hunting Percival Jet Provost T Mk.1s were delivered to No.2 FTS, RAF Hullavington, allowing the initial course of eighteen pupils to begin their training; two months later, on 17 October 1955, the first student, Fg Off Richard Foster,

02. Retaining many of the components from the piston-engine Provost, the prototype Jet Provost T Mk.1, XD674, was also fitted with temperature-sensing probe and control-position indicators. It is depicted during an early test flight from Luton. (BAe Systems Heritage Warton-Percival/Hunting Collection)

03. A formation of Jet Provost T Mk.1s from No.2 FTS. Between September 1955 and November 1957 three all-through training courses were carried out at RAF Hullavington to evaluate basic flying training on jet aircraft. (Author's Collection)

went solo after eight hours and twenty minutes of instruction. The subsequent results of the three evaluation courses conducted at Hullavington between August 1955 and November 1957, soon showed a 'significant' saving of flying hours during the advanced phase on Vampire aircraft, and an overall saving on the complete Wings course. The evaluation also successfully demonstrated the suitability of the Jet Provost basic trainer as a logical step in providing pupils with their entire flying instruction on jet aircraft.

There were those, however, who were slightly more cynical about the results of the evaluation of the Jet Provost at Hullavington, stating that, despite the savings that were achieved, the AFTSs and OCUs quickly noticed the degradation of the BFTS product with consequent extra flying hours required on more expensive aircraft, increased failure rates and the transfer of the initial students to the transport OCUs.

Meanwhile, work was progressing at Luton on a batch of four pre-production Jet Provost T Mk.2s, which had been jointly funded by Hunting and Armstrong Siddeley for development and demonstration work. The success of the Jet Provost service trials had resulted in a development programme which incorporated many refinements omitted in the Mk.1, including the installation of a 1,750 lb-thrust Viper 102 (ASV 8) turbojet. Also introduced was the hydraulic operation of flaps, brakes, undercarriage and airbrakes to replace the original pneumatic system, while the stalky undercarriage legs of the Piston Provost were substituted with much shorter and strengthened units. The result of these improvements culminated in the third pre-production Mk.2 becoming the prototype Jet Provost T Mk.3.

In February 1957 the RAF announced that it was to adopt the concept of all-through training on jet aircraft and that Flying Training Command would standardise on an improved Jet Provost basic trainer. The following August, an initial order for 100 Jet Provost T Mk.3s was placed with Hunting Aircraft, with the Central Flying School at RAF Little Rissington and No.2 FTS at RAF Syerston receiving its first aircraft in July and August 1959, respectively. Two months later the first

course of Jet Provost/Vampire syllabus students began their ab initio training at RAF Syerston and graduated in June 1960.

By early 1960, continued development work of the Jet Provost T Mk.3 at Luton resulted in the improved T Mk.4, which was fitted with a more powerful Viper 11 engine of 2,500-lb thrust, providing an increase in speed and a much greater rate of climb. Extended high-altitude training sorties in the T Mk.4, however, began exposing the instructors and students to a painful condition of the joints caused by repeated exposure to low atmospheric pressure called the 'bends', a problem exacerbated by the unpressurised cockpits of the early Jet Provosts.

The logical solution to this problem was to modify the Jet Provost to incorporate a pressurised cockpit, which resulted in the Jet Provost T Mk.5. Most of the design work of the new project had been completed at Luton, and modification work on two prototypes converted from production T Mk.4s began in 1965. Both airframes were transferred to Warton when the company was taken over by the British Aircraft Corporation and the first prototype, XS230 – officially designated as a T Mk.5 (Interim) – made an initial thirty-minute test flight on 28 February 1967.

Two major changes distinguished the T Mk.5 from the earlier Jet Provosts: a pressurised cockpit and 'export' wings with a greater fatigue life; the latter being fitted with hard points, capable of the possible carriage of external fuel tanks or underwing stores. The pressurised

05

cockpit, however, was a major design change to the Jet Provost airframe and the changed airflow altered the handling characteristics to such an extent that a flight test programme was required to re-examine the stalling and spinning characteristics of the aircraft.

It is also interesting to note that the standard of the elevators remained the same from the Piston Provost up to the Jet Provost Mk.3, after which a different standard was introduced for the Mk.4/Mk.5 and the Strikemaster which included revised full chord elevator balances. In addition, a revised 'thin' tailplane had been fitted to the prototype Jet Provost Mk.4 in 1960 for high Mach trials. This singular experiment was intended to improve longitudinal stability at high Mach numbers in preparation for the Jet Provost Mk.5 / Strikemaster but did very little to overcome the natural limitation of the Jet Provost wing. Trials were continued with the H 166 (XS231 fitted with an uprated engine) in various attempts to increase the Mach number limit to M 0.8, particularly for the Australian air force, but behaviour

at this speed was found unsuitable for Service release.

In July 1968, a one-off contract for 110 Jet Provost T Mk.5s was signed and deliveries to the CFS, Little Rissington, began in September 1969. Further improvements to the T Mk.5 included an improved canopy removal system and, to meet the latest air traffic control requirements, a large number of the RAF's fleet of Jet Provost Mk.3 and Mk.5 aircraft were upgraded with new radio and navigation equipment during a three-year modification programme at Warton; the modified aircraft being designated as the T Mk.3A and T Mk.5A, respectively.

Following the transfer of the Jet Provost design and manufacture from Luton, the BAC 167 Strikemaster became the first export version of a basic military trainer/ground-attack aircraft to come off the production lines at Warton. The Strikemaster was essentially an armed version of the Jet Provost T Mk.5, upgraded with a 3,140-lb Bristol Siddeley Viper ASV 20 engine and a built-in armament of two 7.62-mm machine guns. Further

04. The BAe sales team actively promoted the Jet Provost and Strikemaster to overseas buyers. This artist's impression of one of its products in the markings of the Swedish air force unfortunately failed to impress as they decided to acquire the SAAB 105 instead.

(BAe Systems Heritage Warton-Percival/Hunting Collection)

05. 141 Strikemasters were produced at Warton, with deliveries to eight overseas countries between 1968 and 1978. (BAe Systems Heritage Warton-Percival/Hunting Collection)

06

improvements to the wing design included a ground attack capability with pylons to which a varied combination of armaments and fuel tanks could be fitted, together with a revised fuel system and wing-tip tanks.

The prototype Strikemaster made its maiden flight from Warton on 26 October 1967 and a total of 141 airframes were built there, with the first contract for twenty-five Strikemaster Mk.80s for Saudi Arabia being placed in December 1965. Between 1968 and 1983, ten overseas air forces purchased the type, including South Yemen, Oman, Kuwait, Kenya, New Zealand, Singapore, Botswana, Ecuador, Saudi Arabia and Sudan.

Each mark of Strikemaster was unique in that the customer chose the communication/navigation systems, the armament configuration and other specific

enhancements to suit their own national requirements. In the case of Mk.82/Mk.82A aircraft supplied to Oman, cockpit pressurisation was omitted and the aircraft was fitted with armour plating (side of the fuselage, cockpit floor, base of the ejection seats and the fuel collector tank) to provide protection during low-level operations.

With the completion of Jet Provost and Strikemaster production at Warton in May 1978, it was decided to assemble a further ten Strikemasters at Hurn against possible future sales; the first airframe being transferred from Warton for the newly established production line at Hurn in November 1979. Sales of these aircraft proved slow, however, with the final three eventually being handed over to Ecuador in October 1988.

Together with production contracts for the RAF, Hunting Aircraft at Luton had also enjoyed some moderate export success with armed versions of the Jet Provost T Mk.3 and T Mk.4 – the T Mk.51 and T Mk.52, respectively – with sales to Ceylon, Iraq, Kuwait, South Yemen, Sudan and Venezuela for training and close-support duties. Both the Jet Provost and Strikemaster saw limited ground-attack operations in border disputes and internal wars in Ceylon, Ecuador, Nigeria and South Yemen. But it was the Strikemaster aircraft of the SOAF's Strike Wing which played a crucial part during the Dhofar War in Oman between 1968 and 1976,

07

08

operating in the close-support and counter-insurgency role against well-armed, Communist-backed guerrillas. Flown by contract and seconded officers, at least ten Strikemaster aircraft were either shot down or badly damaged in a conflict which has been largely forgotten by the outside world.

Between 1954 and 1983, some 723 Jet Provost and Strikemaster airframes were produced at Luton and Warton. By the time the Jet Provost was finally withdrawn from RAF service in July 1993 it had been responsible for the training of many generations of pilots as an ab initio, refresher and navigation training aircraft. During the later part of its Service career, the Jet Provost also provided instruction for trainee air traffic controllers at Shawbury and Forward Air Control students at Brawdy.

Despite going into the history books in July 1956, when the first course of students graduated from No.2 FTS at Hullavington as part of the evaluation of the RAF's all-through flying training programme – a concept which would eventually become accepted by leading air arms throughout the world – it is unfortunate that both the Jet Provost and Strikemaster have been overlooked by many as lacking the appeal associated with other aircraft types. There can be no greater recommendation for the aircraft, however, than HRH Prince Charles during a visit to Warton, who commented that the Jet Provost Mk.5 was a delightful aircraft to fly: "...... with nice tight controls and good response – I like to think of it as an MG as opposed to an Aston Martin."

Fortunately, many of the surviving airframes found further careers at various training schools as maintenance airframes, while others were acquired for preservation in museum collections. Between 1993 and 1997, a number of those put up for sale by the Ministry of Defence were also acquired by companies, such as Phoenix Aviation at Bruntingthorpe and Global Aviation at Binbrook, where they were stored and refurbished, before being sold to private enthusiasts for display on the Warbird air show circuit.

Finally, I make no excuse for including the coverage of the various RAF Jet Provost display teams, official and informal. Between 1958 and 1976, these teams delighted those who not only attended the SBAC Farnborough air shows, but also the numerous parochial and continental events. Despite lacking the excitement of the 'big' premier teams, they undoubtedly contributed to the good name of the Service, supplied a reserve of formation aerobatic pilots and provided an invaluable source of recruitment.

06. With eight 25-lb fragmentation bombs and four Mk.8 rockets fitted on the underwing hard points, Jet Provost T Mk.51, CJ701, formates with the camera ship before delivery to the Royal Ceylon Air Force in December 1959. (HAL via Terry Lloyd)

07. The Jet Provost final assembly line at Luton in March 1959. (BAe Systems Heritage Warton-Percival/Hunting Collection)

08. First batch of pre-production Jet Provost T Mk.3s for the RAF at Luton in July 1959. The nearest aircraft are XM356 and XM359, which were delivered to CFS. (Hunting via Norman Giffin)

Above: First prototype Jet Provost T Mk.1, XD674, prior to its roll-out and first flight at Luton in June 1954. (BAe Systems Heritage Warton-Percival/Hunting Collection)

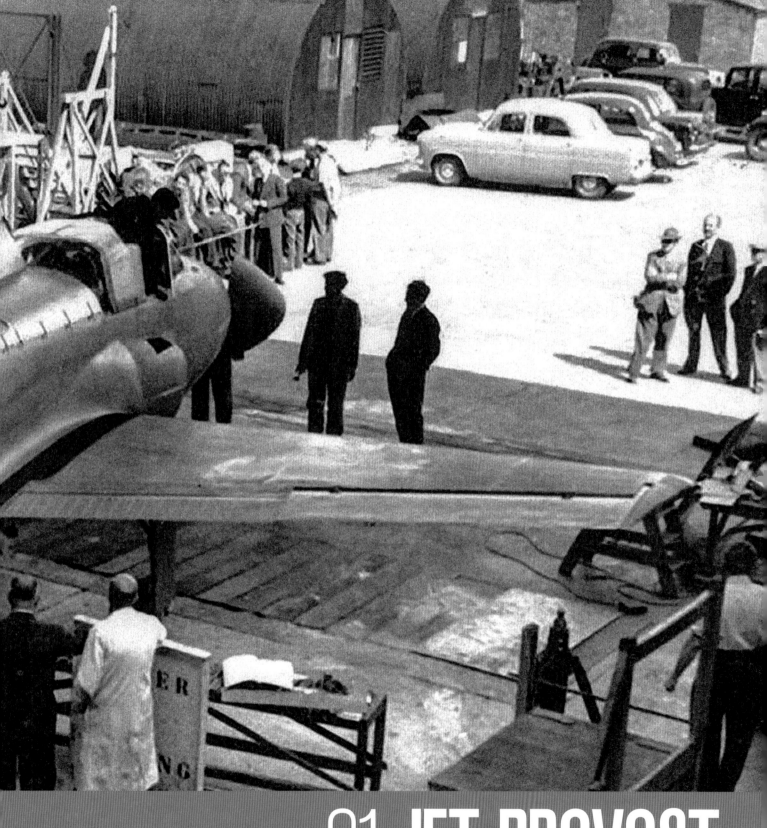

01 JET PROVOST

JET PROVOST T MK.1

In May 1953 the Percival Provost entered service as the standard basic trainer for the RAF. Powered by an Alvis Leonides radial engine, the two-seat Provost T Mk.1 became the first half of the new pilot training scheme known as the Provost/Vampire sequence.

The Piston Provost proved a popular aircraft, being powerful, strong and highly manoeuvrable, and had been developed through a close association between Percival Aircraft at Luton and RAF Flying Training Command. During the war the company had been subcontracted to build large numbers of Airspeed Oxfords and de Havilland Mosquitoes for the RAF, which was followed by a succession of communication and training aircraft of its own design, including the Percival Proctor, Prentice and Pembroke. As a result of this association, the company had been given a valuable insight into the RAF's concept of all-through jet training and design studies of a proposed 'basic jet trainer'.

Following the production of the Piston Provost, in April 1951 Percival Aircraft began internal discussions on the feasibility of a jet-powered trainer based on the Provost and took the decision to proceed with such a project on a private-venture basis, the following August. By September 1952, preliminary design work was so advanced that a model of the jet-propelled trainer was exhibited at that year's Farnborough show, attracting a great deal of interest.

On 27 May 1953 Specification T16/48 Issue 4, The Design and Construction of Provost Basic Jet Trainer to meet OR.321, was issued and was an extension of an original requirement released in 1948 to cover the design and construction of a single-engined basic trainer for the RAF. The specification included the following requirements: air brakes, provision for not less than 180 gallons of internal fuel for a typical sortie at 20,000 ft, and the installation of a Viper turbine engine. Although two other companies had also vied for the contract, the Air Ministry awarded it to Percival Aircraft on 8 June 1953:

These aircraft will be used to assess the advantages of using a jet trainer for basic flying training. The

Provost Jet Trainer has been chosen because of the easy and rapid conversion to a turbine-engined version, while retaining the excellent handling qualities of the piston-engined trainer.

The development work on the original Percival P.84 design concentrated on the safe handling characteristics necessary for primary training, with performance as a secondary concern. Several structural designs had been considered for the project, including an engine installed in the forward fuselage with air intakes beneath the cockpit and an engine fitted beneath the nose.

The company had worked closely with the Air Ministry on the new design and it was concluded that to reduce manufacturing costs and to speed up the development programme, many of the components could be utilised from those of the piston-engined Provost, including mainplanes, tail surfaces and main undercarriage legs. Principal changes included the wings which had been adapted to accommodate six bag-type fuel tanks, with a total capacity of 165 gallons, and the provision for mounting 45-gallon fuel tanks under the wing tips. Other changes included a modified and strengthened rear fuselage being extended by three feet to house the Viper 101 (ASV.5) axial-flow turbojet; a hinged nose cap allowing access to radio, oxygen and electrical control equipment; the Provost's side-by-side cockpit arrangement being retained and repositioned further forward to balance the weight of the engine; and the air intakes being placed next to the wing roots. While, to conform with modern

09

10

11

instruction techniques, a retractable tricycle undercarriage, oxygen system, airbrakes and a revised cockpit instrumentation panel was also incorporated.

The choice of the Armstrong Siddeley Viper turbojet for the Percival design project would also reflect the aircraft's continued use at present training airfields and give a fuel consumption which would enable the sortie duration of the training syllabus to be flown with comfortable reserves. The Viper turbojet had originally been designed by the Australian General Aircraft Factory in the early 1950s as a cheap expendable engine with only ten hours expected lifetime to power the Australian Jindivik pilotless target drone. A subsequent development programme resulted in a requirement for the turbojet to be installed in manned aircraft when it

became clear that an engine of similar weight, size and performance was required. It was therefore decided to modify the Viper as a more cost effective alternative to designing and developing a totally new engine. By 1953, Armstrong Siddeley Motors had been awarded the contract to develop and manufacture a 'long life' version of the engine – the Viper 101 (ASV.5) capable of developing 1,640 lbs of static thrust, which was jointly selected by Folland Aircraft for its Midge lightweight fighter and by Percival Aircraft for its P.84 design project.

On 12 March 1953, the Secretary of State for Air, Mr George Ward, announced in the House of Commons that he had signed a contract with Percival Aircraft, worth £85,000, for an initial batch of aircraft to conduct a service evaluation. Ten Jet Provost T Mk.1s (XD674-XD680

09. Cockpit of Jet Provost T Mk.1. (BAe Systems Heritage Warton-Percival/Hunting Collection)

10. The first prototype took to the air at Luton on 26 June 1954, flown by the company's chief test pilot, 'Dick' Wheldon. (BAe Systems Heritage Warton-Percival/Hunting Collection)

11. On 10 May 1955, the Jet Provost T Mk.1 officially entered RAF Service when XD677 was issued to the handling squadron at RAF Manby for the preparation of the pilots' notes. It subsequently served with the CFS and No.2 FTS before being scrapped in 1960. (BAe Systems Heritage Warton-Percival/Hunting Collection)

and XD692-XD694), were ordered against Contract 6/Aircraft/9265/CB.5(a), dated 24 March 1953. An eleventh airframe (G-AOBU) was also included in this contract for use as a company demonstrator, while XD694 became the prototype for the proposed T Mk.2.

The prototype Hunting Percival Jet Provost T Mk.1, XD674, (the company had changed its name during April 1954) made its first flight at Luton on 26 June 1954 in the hands of the company's chief test pilot, R. G. 'Dick' Wheldon. Following its public debut at the Farnborough air show in September, further test flights over the next few weeks resulted in a number of structural alterations. These included the replacement of the original dorsal fin (which was fitted to compensate for the increased side area of the rear fuselage caused by the re-positioning of the cockpit) and a ventral fin extending from the wing trailing edge to the tail bumper. In addition, a fillet was fitted at the leading edge wing roots to increase the low-speed handling qualities, which was found necessary because of the absence of airscrew slipstream. In May 1955, the prototype was transferred to Armstrong Siddeley Motors at Bitteswell for engine handling work and development of the Viper ASV.5 and ASV.8 engines. It was eventually allocated for ground instruction use in May 1958.

On 25 June 1955, Phase 'A' of the official Service trials began when two Jet Provost T Mk.1s, XD676 and XD679, (the latter being replaced by XD677 in August following a landing accident) were issued to the CFS, RAF South Cerney. During an intensive 111-hour flying programme, in which experienced basic and advanced flying instructors flew in pairs and gradually developed a programme to assess the behaviour of the Jet Provost as a potential ab initio trainer, formulate a basic training syllabus, and convert the first ten flying instructors. The CFS evaluation was completed in August 1955 and resulted in a favourable report in which the Jet Provost was strongly recommended for ab initio training; it also stated that the first course should be of twenty-three weeks, during which time a total of 160 hours were to be flown: eighty-five hours ab initio and seventy-five hours in the basic stage.

In 1955, No.2 Flying Training School at RAF Hullavington was selected to evaluate the first all-through jet training courses – Phase 'B' of the official Service trials. Primarily equipped with Piston Provost T Mk.1s, the unit received the first of its eventual establishment of nine Jet Provost T Mk.1s in August 1955.

The first course – No.113 (Jet) Course – began on 2 September 1955. The eighteen students on the course had not been specifically selected and all went solo in an average time of eleven hours and fifteen minutes for those without previous flying experience and nine hours and fifty minutes for those who had flown before; the corresponding times for those on the Piston Provost courses being fourteen hours and eight hours thirty minutes, respectively. In March 1956, seven students from the course were detached to No.8 FTS at Swinderby to investigate if they were suitable for advanced training on the Vampire at their present stage of instruction. During their time at Swinderby the students each flew between four to five hours on Vampires and returned to Hullavington in early April. The first Jet Provost course was completed in July 1956 and the students progressed to Swinderby for the advanced stage of their flying training.

With the conclusion of the third and final course in November 1957, the Jet Provost experiment had proved itself capable of taking the students from the beginning of their pilot training and through at least two-thirds of the pre-Wings syllabus, showing a saving in the overall flying time from 160 hours to 120 hours.

The evaluation had also been seen to remove an important training barrier – that of the transition from piston to jet. With correct techniques being acquired from the outset the students had formed no undesirable 'piston/propeller habits'; inadequate students had been removed at an earlier stage of their training; and there had been nothing to interrupt the smooth continuity of their training as jet techniques did not have to be learned on conversion to advanced trainers. As a result, the CFS Examining Wing assessed the student standard at Hullavington as 'high average' and issued a report, stating that:

> The student standard….reflects most favourably on the suitability of the aircraft as an ab initio trainer. Compared to the average student the jet-trained student has, in a shorter time, achieved a more dexterous and better mental approach to the art of modern flying.

To coincide with the official report, the manufacturers simultaneously released their own comprehensive account on the eighteen-month evaluation at Hullavington:

> Fifty RAF pupils have now been introduced into the Jet Provost in the last two years. Of these, thirty-five

had no previous flying experience; fifteen had flown light piston-engined types. Forty-nine of these pupils were sent solo: at least five from each course failed to make the solo stage and were transferred. The nine aircraft at RAF Hullavington flew 4,000 hours and made 11,000 landings. Engine reliability showed an increase between service from 100 hours to 300 hours, and with a saving of £3,000 on flying alone the Jet Provost has proved itself as the only jet trainer capable of such economical training.

The company's conviction that the Jet Provost was a practical and desirable proposition was backed by a strong section of opinion in the RAF, and in February 1957, a written parliamentary statement by Mr George Ward, Secretary of State for Air, confirmed that he was satisfied with the results of the initial flying training trials and intended to progress with the Jet Provost:

> The evaluation trials have shown that ab initio flying training on jet aircraft has definite advantages, and it has therefore been decided to establish this form of training on a larger scale. A production order is now being placed for the Hunting Percival Jet Provost, which I am satisfied is the best aircraft for the purpose.

It was further stated that the decision to proceed with the development of the Jet Provost was taken after consideration of the reports on the experimental courses at Hullavington, pupils from which had gained their Wings after flying Vampires at Swinderby. The official reports also confirmed that those found to be unsuitable for all-through flying training were discovered earlier, thereby saving wasted training time and resources.

In November 1957, seven of the surviving Jet Provosts (one had been written off in a flying accident during August 1956) were transferred to the CFS to provide jet conversion training and for the advanced phase of the

12. Typifying the RAF's Provost/Jet Provost flying training sequence at RAF Hullavington in 1957, Jet Provost T Mk.1 XD693:Q-Z and Provost T Mk.1 WV625:R-A of No.2 FTS. (Author's Collection)

13

student courses. The primary reason for the transfer of the aircraft to Little Rissington, however, was to form the basis of an aerobatic flight, 'The CFS Jet Aerobatic Team'. Led by Flt Lt Norman Giffin, and comprising four volunteer flying instructors, the display team was put together at the beginning of 1958 to represent the CFS at the prestigious SBAC Show at Farnborough the following September. The aircraft were repainted in an attractive red and white colour scheme and, despite being underpowered for formation aerobatics which resulted in a limitation of its routine, the team flew seventeen displays during the season.

With the arrival of the first batch of Jet Provost T Mk.3s to the CFS in July 1959, the T Mk.1s were withdrawn the following November and transferred to No.27 MU Shawbury for eventual scrapping.

Two airframes have survived: XD674 was presented to the RAF Museum at Cosford in November 1985, while the sixth production airframe, G-AOBU, which was retained by Huntings for use as a development aircraft and company demonstrator, is with Kennet Aviation at North Weald, repainted as XD693/Q-Z.

JET PROVOST T MK.2

The final airframe to be built from the original order for ten Jet Provost T Mk.1s, XD694, was removed from the Luton production line to become the prototype of four pre-production Jet Provost T Mk.2s,

which had been jointly funded by Hunting and Armstrong Siddeley for development and demonstration work.

XD694 The success of the Jet Provost service trials had resulted in a development programme which incorporated many refinements omitted in the Mk.1 in the interests of production speed and economy. The improvements included a 1,750-lb thrust Viper 102 (ASV 8) turbojet being installed in the Mk.2 version, which gave an extra 100 lbs of thrust. The Viper engine's slightly larger jet pipe necessitated a number of structural changes to the rear fuselage, including a refinement of the fin and rudder and the replacement of the ventral fin with a dorsal fin. The hydraulic operation of flaps, brakes, undercarriage and airbrakes to replace the original pneumatic system was introduced, while the stalky undercarriage legs of the Piston Provost were substituted with much shorter units which retracted into the wings rather than the fuselage.

In this form, XD694 made its first flight on 1 September 1955 and by the following December it had completed 143 hours of company test flying before being transferred to Boscombe Down for its service acceptance trials. In September 1956 it was issued to RAF Hullavington for a comparative evaluation with the Jet Provost Mk.1s at No.2 FTS, completing some 260 flying hours, and was subsequently loaned to Armstrong Siddeley at Bitteswell and Filton in June 1957 for further engine development flying. In July 1958, Flt Lt Tom Frost, the

14

chief test pilot for Armstrong Siddeley, delighted the crowds at the National Air Races, Coventry, when he demonstrated the aircraft in an exciting display of aerobatic flying, which included inverted turns around the airfield. With the completion of the engine trials, the airframe was passed to No.27 MU at Shawbury in December 1959 and eventually sold for scrap.

G-AOHD The Hunting development fleet was soon joined by a second aircraft, G-AOHD, which first took to the air in March 1956 and made its public debut at the British Lockheed International Aerobatic Competition at Baginton the following July, flown by test pilot, 'Dick' Wheldon.

With the conclusion of the brief trials at Luton, it was allocated as a company demonstration aircraft to prove the Jet Provost in a wide variety of climates and conditions. In February 1957, 'Dick' Wheldon demonstrated the aircraft to air force officers at Ljungbyhed in Sweden. The following month, he progressed to Helsinki for further demonstrations and operated from Malmi and Seutula, providing familiarisation flights to Finnish pilots during the week-long visit.

13. A line-up of the three Jet Provost prototype and demonstration aircraft operated by Hunting Percival at Luton in 1955, including Jet Provost T Mk.2 XD694, and Jet Provost T Mk.1s, XD674 and G-AOUS. (BAe Systems Heritage Warton-Percival/Hunting Collection)

14. The final aircraft to be built from the batch of production Jet Provost T Mk.1s for the RAF, XD694 was converted as the prototype T Mk.2. It first flew in September 1955 and incorporated

On 5 April 1958 the Jet Provost was crated and shipped to Trinidad as part of an ambitious sales tour of Latin America. Following its reassembly, on 28 April, company test pilot, 'Dicky' Rumbelow, flew the aircraft to Maracay, Venezuela, where the scene was repeated throughout the whole tour with selected groups of pupils given ab initio training up to solo standard. Moving on to Bogata, Colombia, in early May the tour then progressed to Quito, high in the Ecuadorian Andes mountains, Santiago in Chile, Lima and Chiclayo in Peru, and Cordoba and Buenos Aires, Argentina, where a series of demonstration flights and aerobatic displays were laid on for groups of senior officers.

Its arrival in Peru on 29 May was typical of the demonstration tour, where the Hunting team was informed that, in order to make a thorough evaluation of the aircraft, the Peruvian air force requested that it wanted to train six officers to solo standard; three of whom had never flown before and two had limited piston-engine experience. As the time was limited, Rumbelow provided five hours of highly concentrated conversion training to two pupils, and was assisted by a local air force officer, Capt Hernandez. Despite language difficulties, during the next fourteen days all five pupils reached solo standard with an average of between six

15

many of the structural refinements omitted in the Mk.1. (BAe Systems Heritage Warton-Percival/Hunting Collection)

15. Between February 1957 and August 1958, Jet Provost T Mk.2, G-AOHD, undertook extensive demonstration tours of Scandinavia and Latin America. The following year it was evaluated by the RAAF and placed into store at the RAAF Museum, Point Cook, Victoria, in 1985. (BAe Systems Heritage Warton-Percival/Hunting Collection)

16

and twelve hours without problems, which reflected much credit to all concerned.

With further demonstrations at various airfields in the country, the Jet Provost moved on to Montevideo, Uruguay, on 19 July, and Rio de Janeiro, Brazil, a week later. Here, the aircraft was given special permission to perform aerobatics over Copacabana Beach in front of thousands of excited spectators. The tour ended on 12 August 1958 when the aircraft was dismantled for shipment back to Luton.

The visit was considered a great success. In just over four months the Jet Provost had flown some 8,400 miles during the tour of nine South American countries, with a total flying time of 178 hours. Twenty-seven airfields had been visited, at which numerous demonstrations were given without an interruption to the flying programme.

In March 1959 the aircraft was shipped to Australia to take part in a six-month trial with the Royal Australian Air Force to evaluate all-through jet training. Following its re-assembly with the de Havilland Aircraft Pty. Ltd at Bankstown near Sydney, the aircraft's acceptance trials were carried out by flying instructor, Flt Lt John Paule, under the guidance of Hunting's chief test pilot, Stan Oliver. Allocated the military serial A99-001, the Jet Provost was flown to No.1 Basic Flying Training School, RAAF Point Cook, on 22 April, where two selected student pilots, cadets Brian Morgan and C. V. Smith of No.35 Pilot Training Course, were given ab initio training on the Jet Provost; the remainder of the course continued their training on the Winjeels and their comparative progress was closely monitored. After completing their basic training, the members of No.35 Course transferred to Pearce, WA, for advanced training on Vampires.

At the conclusion of the evaluation, the RAAF decided not to order the Jet Provost as a basic training aeroplane because of its limited role, deciding instead to continue operating the Vampire until it was eventually replaced by the Macchi MB-326 in 1967. At the end of the six-month trial, the Jet Provost was returned to de Havilland in November 1959 before being presented to Sydney Technical College in May 1961 as an instructional airframe. Since 1985 it has been stored at the RAAF Museum, Point Cook.

G-23-1 The third pre-production airframe was originally built as a T Mk.2 and scheduled to be registered as G-APVF. However the registration was quickly cancelled and it was re-issued with the 'B' class serial, G-23-1, and modified at Luton to become the prototype T Mk.3. In this form it became the first to have a rear-ranged cockpit with a single, central blind-flying instrument panel, and a single-piece, clear vision windscreen with a Mk.2 sliding cockpit hood. It was also fitted with standard production wings with wing-tip tanks, a Viper 103 (ASV.9) turbojet, but retained the original seating of the previous aircraft.

Following a brief period of company trials, the aircraft was issued to Boscombe Down in April 1958 for its preview handling and performance tests. The two test pilots responsible for the tests found the aircraft to be simple to operate and easy to fly; it was also found to have no inherent vices and carried out all the manoeuvres required by its role satisfactorily. However, it was considered that it had lost the crisp and powerful control of the Piston Provost and that the benign

17

18

out to Aden in a Beverley transport aircraft and re-assembled for the trials, which ran from 14-17 August 1958.

Operating from the airfields of Khormaksar and Riyan, the Jet Provost had been issued with a temporary military serial, XN117, and modified to carry machine guns and rocket and bomb carriers for the trial. Unfortunately, it was considered as a rank outsider from the beginning and, despite its low operating costs, the Jet Provost did not perform any of the operational tasks to the required standard and was subsequently eliminated. The Hunter eventually emerged as the clear winner of the trial.

From Aden, Stan Oliver flew the aircraft to India and Pakistan, giving air experience flights and aerobatic demonstrations at seven different bases during the tour; the principal evaluations being made at Mauripur and Risalpur by the Pakistan air force and at Jodhpur by the Indian air force. The ten-week tour was completed in October and the aircraft was returned to Luton, where it was converted to a T Mk.51 and became the first of a batch of six aircraft to be delivered to the Royal Ceylon AF as 'CJ701' in February 1960.

G-AOUS In August 1956, a fourth and final pre-production airframe, G-AOUS, took to the air and departed on a demonstration/sales tour of Canada and the USA, the following month. The RCAF wanted to replace its ageing Harvard aircraft with jet trainers and had demonstrated an interest in the Jet Provost when an evaluation team of four officers visited Luton the previous year to examine and fly the aircraft. A number of aircraft

characteristics of the aeroplane would allow marginal students to progress much further with their course before their lack of ability led to removal from training. The A&AEE report also criticised the aircraft's lack of ejection seats.

Returning to Luton, the aircraft was selected to take part in the Venom Replacement Evaluation Trial at Khormaksar, Aden. By mid-1958, a replacement for the RAF's de Havilland Venom ground-attack aircraft operating in the Middle East was considered to be urgent. HQ, British Forces Arabian Peninsula in Aden had been able to persuade the Air Ministry to lay on a competitive evaluation project to find a new ground-attack aircraft, which would involve three contrasting aircraft types, the Hawker Hunter, the Folland Gnat lightweight fighter and the Hunting Jet Provost trainer. Accordingly, the Venom Replacement Evaluation Trial was established at Khormaksar and while the two Hunters were flown direct from the UK, the Gnat and Jet Provost were flown

16. Following a sales tour of Latin America, G-AOHD was shipped to Australia in 1959 for an evaluation by the RAAF as a replacement for its Vampire trainers. Issued with the temporary serial, A99-001, it was later sold to the RAAF in 1961. (via Brendan Cowan)

17. Jet Provost T Mk.2, G-23-1, was the second of four private venture, pre-production aircraft built by Hunting Percival at

Luton and first flew in June 1956. It was modified at Luton to become the prototype Jet Provost Mk.3 and featured a revised cockpit arrangement, and a single-piece, clear vision windscreen with a sliding cockpit hood. It was also fitted with standard production wings, tip tanks and a Viper 103 (ASV.9) turbojet. (BAe Systems Heritage Warton-Percival/Hunting Collection)

18. Originally built as a T Mk.2,

G-APVF/G-23-1, was converted to the T Mk.3 prototype and issued with a temporary military serial, XN117, for the Venom Replacement Evaluation Trial at Khormaksar in August 1958. It later took part in a demonstration tour of India and Pakistan, and was subsequently converted to T Mk.51 standard and delivered to Ceylon as 'CJ701' in 1960. (Simon Watson/The Aviation Bookshop via Ray Deacon)

were selected for the evaluation, including the CM-170 Fouga Magister, Canadair CT-114 Tutor and the Jet Provost. Supported by the Hunting Percival demonstration team, Wg Cdr A. N. 'Bill' Kingwill, the Service liaison officer, Ron Brown, technical sales manager, and Stan Oliver, the company chief test pilot, the Jet Provost toured RCAF bases at Ottawa and Trenton, Ontario, before moving on to the USA, where it was inspected by representatives from the US Air Force and Navy in the Washington area. Despite completing a trouble-free schedule and being flown by over a hundred Service pilots, who spoke well of its handling characteristics, the RCAF eventually chose the Canadair CT-114 Tutor as it primary jet trainer.

Returning to the UK in October 1956 and a period with the RAE at Farnborough, the aircraft was fitted with the more powerful Viper ASV 11 engine in August 1958 and was unofficially referred to as 'Jet Provost T Mk.2B'. In between further engine development trials it took part in the *Daily Mail*-sponsored London-Paris Air Race on 13 July 1959 and also appeared at the Farnborough air show the following September with two other company products, a standard T Mk.3, XM370, and T Mk.51, CJ701, destined for Ceylon.

In October 1959 the aircraft took part in a further sales trip to Portugal when it was evaluated against the Cessna T-37 'Tweet', a twin-engine primary trainer. For the purposes of the evaluation it was allocated the Portuguese serial '5803' and was later involved in a slight accident after it suffered a wheels-up landing at Sintra AB.

On 16 November 1960, G-AOUS was written off during a routine test flight when the nose wheel lowered while the aircraft was recovering from a dive, opening the wheel bay doors, which then detached; this caused a nose-up trim change and severe over-stressing leading to a complete disintegration of the airframe. The aircraft crashed at Langford Common, three miles south of Biggleswade, Bedfordshire, killing company test pilot, Lt-Cdr J. R. S. 'Jack' Overbury RN.

JET PROVOST T MK.3

In February 1957, an announcement by the Secretary of State for Air confirmed that the Royal Air Force had decided to adopt all-through training on jet aircraft, which resulted in the first production order for 100 Jet Provost T Mk.3 aircraft being authorised under Contract 6/Aircraft/ 14157/CB.5(a), dated 9 August 1957.

Ordered against a further revision of the earlier specification, T MK.16/48 Issue 5, dated 21 May 1957, the third pre-production Mk.2, G-23-1, became the prototype T Mk.3 in early 1958. The principal structural differences between T Mk.3 and that of its predecessors included a sloped and strengthened rear cockpit bulkhead for the installation of two Martin-Baker Mk.4P ejection seats, a clear-view windscreen and rear fairing, with sliding hood, together with Rebecca 8 with DF and UHF radio equipment. Further refinements included the incorporation of hydraulic services instead of pneumatic and a reduction of the length of the undercarriage legs by 22 inches. A Viper Mk.102 (ASV.8) turbojet of 1,750-lb static thrust was also retained to provide a maximum level speed of 260 knots between sea level and 30,000 ft, and a climb to 30,000 ft in not more than twenty-five minutes.

The wings of the T Mk.3 remained structurally identical to those of the Mk.2 except for the installation of tip tank lugs for the attachment of two non-jettisonable, 45-gallon fuel tanks which, with the three internal bag-type tanks, provided a total usable capacity of 286 gallons. The fillet fitted at the leading edge of the wing

19

roots to increase the low-speed handling qualities was also retained on some of the early production aircraft.

In April 1958, the prototype was evaluated at Boscombe Down and the subsequent report considered it to be an "easy and pleasant aeroplane to fly and should make a good trainer". The first aircraft to roll off the lines at Luton, XM346, took to the air on 22 June 1958 and deliveries began six days later; the first batch of aircraft being issued to the manufacturers and the A&AEE for a series of handling and Service acceptance trials. Serviceability was found to be good during the various trials and the results indicated a favourable impression of the Jet Provost with its intended role.

On 26 June 1959 the first Jet Provost Mk.3s were handed over to the RAF during an informal ceremony at Luton Airport. The AOC-in-C Flying Training Command, Air Mshl Sir Hugh A. Constantine, took delivery of the first aircraft while the second was presented to AVM Colin Scragg, AOC No.23 Group. Further aircraft from the first production batch were accepted by Air Cdre J. N. H. Whitworth, commandant of the Central Flying School, and Grp Capt J. H. L. Blount, CO of No.2 FTS, Syerston.

On 31 July 1959, the first three of an eventual six pre-production aircraft (i.e. those retaining the wing leading edge fillets – XM355, XM356, XM357, XM359, XM360 and XM361) destined for the CFS were collected from RAF Lyneham. None of the pilots had previously flown the Jet Provost Mk.3 and found themselves in the peculiar position of having to familiarise themselves with the new cockpit layout before returning to RAF Little Rissington. The following November, six students of No.199 Course became the first to graduate as Jet Provost QFIs and were posted to RAF Syerston.

19. Fourth and final pre-production Jet Provost T Mk.2, G-AOUS, on the compass swing base at Luton. In September 1956 it took part in a demonstration/sales tour of Canada and the USA, and was later evaluated by the Portuguese. The aircraft broke up and crashed during a routine test flight in November 1960, killing the company test pilot. (BAe Systems Heritage Warton-Percival/Hunting Collection)

20. Armstrong Siddeley Viper ASV.8 axial turbo-jet installed in the Jet Provost T Mk.2 and T Mk.3.

1. Oil pump
2. Drain collector unit
3. Aircraft accessories drive connection
4. Fuel filter
5. Fuel pump
6. Trunnion
7. Atomizer
8. Igniter
9. Burner
10. Flow control unit
11. Tachometer generator mounting face
12. Nose bullet
(BAe Systems Heritage Warton-Percival/ Hunting Collection)

21

Deliveries to No.2 FTS at Syerston began in August 1959, with the first course of students beginning their training in October. By February 1962, a total of 201 Jet Provost T Mk.3s had been delivered to the RAF, equipping a further five schools for ab initio training. These included No.1 FTS at Linton-on-Ouse, No.3 FTS at Leeming/Cranwell, No.6 FTS at Acklington/Finningley, No.7 FTS at Church Fenton and the RAF College at Cranwell.

Once in service, the Jet Provost was considered to have reasonable spin characteristics. However, following the loss of three aircraft in spinning accidents between June 1960 and February 1961 and complaints from RAF flying instructors regarding students who found themselves in difficulties during disorientating spin situations, a series of tests was carried out at Boscombe Down with two aircraft, XM346 and XM456; the latter of which had developed a reputation of being difficult to recover from the spin and was loaned to the manufacturer for further investigation. On 22 August 1962, control of the aircraft was lost during a check of its spinning characteristics and it dived into the ground at Girton, Cambs; both RAF pilots successfully abandoning the stricken aircraft.

As a result of the accident, C(A) clearance for spinning with fuel in the wing-tip tanks was withdrawn until modifications had been embodied. Hunting test pilot, **Reg Stock:**

> Spin involves yaw – no yaw, no spin – and yaw is controlled by the rudder. I taught spinning for

three-and-a-half years as an instructor at RAF Syerston in both piston and the JP Mk.3, and neither I nor my pupils had any problems with recovery. Extensive trials were later carried out at Luton to find out why the RAF had problems. These involved recoveries from high rotation spins with various control inputs and 'rudder only' recoveries which took a little longer but were always successful.

It was considered that disorientation or failure to maintain anti-spin controls for long enough before trying something else was a probable cause of the complaints. We even checked one of the so-called 'rogue' aircraft together with its pilot but could find no fault with either.

The only time I personally had difficulty was when we deliberately loaded the aircraft with a completely unrealistic fuel imbalance (one tip tank full and the other empty). Even so, the aircraft was recovered, despite being ridiculously outside the allowable conditions.

The modification previously mentioned being a non-return valve fitted between the wing and tip tank to ensure no reverse fuel flow.

The Jet Provost T Mk.3 soon proved suitable for formation aerobatics and the first display teams to be formed were drawn from the Central Flying School and No.2 FTS in 1960, both of which went on to achieve notable success. The CFS had earlier gathered some experience with its Jet Provost T Mk.1 display flying during the

22

23

1958/1959 seasons, and the 1960 team appeared at the Farnborough air show in September, together with its first overseas show at Lorient in France and a visit to Ghana in October to take part in the Nigerian independence celebrations. By 1962 the CFS team was named as 'The Red Pelicans' and nominated as the RAF's premier aerobatic team for the 1964 season.

Other display teams to fly Jet Provost T Mk.3s included No.1 FTS 'Gin Section' at Linton-on-Ouse and the aerobatic team of No.3 FTS at Leeming. In 1963, the 'Cock's o' The North' from No.6 FTS at Acklington became the last team to display with the Jet Provost Mk.3, the remainder having re-equipped with the more powerful Mk.4.

Although the RAF did not require any armament to be fitted to its Mk.3s, space provision for machine guns and wing hard points for rockets and bombs were included in the basic design. Designated as the Jet Provost T Mk.51, the 'armed' export version was available with a variety of underwing weapons: a .303 calibre machine gun with 500 rounds of ammunition installed in each wing root, with a reflector sight fitted in the cockpit; a camera gun fitted in the nose was also available. Underwing armament included the option of eight 25-lb fragmentation bombs, four under each wing on standard bomb racks; six Mk.8 rockets with 60-lb heads, three under each wing; twelve Mk.5 rockets, six under each wing; eight 25-lb

21. Jet Provost T Mk.3, XM346, first flew in June 1958 and was used by Hunting for a variety of company trials. It was a pre-production aircraft with fillets fitted at the leading edge wing roots to increase the low-speed handling qualities and was delivered to the CFS in August 1960. Sadly, it ended its days on the fire dump at RAF Thorney Island. (Hunting via Norman Giffin)

22. In addition to the option of a .303 calibre machine gun with 600 rounds of ammunition installed in each wing root fairing, the Jet Provost T Mk.51 was also capable of carrying sixteen SURA rockets and eight 500-lb bombs. (Hunting/Percival via Reg Stock)

23. In January 1972, Jet Provost T Mk.3, XN629, was allocated as the prototype for the avionics upgrade of the RAF's fleet of Mk.3s and Mk.5s. Trials of the modification work began at Warton on 15 July 1973, with Reg Stock being handed the appropriate documentation by the flight shed foreman, Bert Goodwin. (BAe Systems Heritage Warton-Percival/Hunting Collection)

fragmentation bombs and four Mk.8 rockets, two under each wing; or eight 25-lb fragmentation bombs and eight Mk.5 rockets.

Three countries bought the Jet Provost T Mk.51 for use as a primary/weapons training aircraft, and twenty-two aircraft were exported to Ceylon (twelve aircraft), Sudan (four aircraft) and Kuwait (six aircraft) between December 1960 and January 1962.

By the early 1970s, a modification programme to install new radio and navigation equipment in the RAF's fleet of Jet Provost T Mk.3 and T Mk.5 aircraft to meet the latest air traffic control requirements was carried out by BAC Warton. Designated as the T Mk.3A, eighty-six Mk.3 aircraft were upgraded under Contract KA5(c)/466/CBA.5(c), introducing a greater measure of commonality between both aircraft. The revised instrument layout included the replacement of the Eureka DME receiver, the single UHF radio and G4 compass with a VOR instrument landing system, civil DME, VHF radio, Sperry CL6 compass and a standby Ferranti Attitude Indicator.

In January 1972, Jet Provost Mk.3, XN629 was allocated as the prototype for the modification work and delivered to Warton for survey and installation of the avionics fit. This was followed by a comprehensive evaluation to ensure the new equipment lived up to its specification and to check aircraft environment capability.

By the time BAC had begun validating the new equipment, the first of the Mk.3 aircraft to be upgraded had already been flown into Warton with the arrival of XM357 in June 1973. The three-year modification programme was finally completed on 9 August 1976, when XN510 was handed over to the station commander of RAF Leeming during a small ceremony at Warton. Airframes upgraded to Mk.3A standard included: XM349, 350, 352, 357, 358, 365, 366, 370, 371, 372, 374, 376, 378, 385, 387, 401, 403, 405, 412, 414, 419, 424, 425, 453, 455, 458, 459, 461, 463, 464, 465, 466, 470, 471, 472, 473, 475, 478, 479, XN459, 461, 462, 466, 470, 471, 472, 473, 494, 495, 497, 498, 499, 500, 501, 502, 505, 506, 508, 509, 510, 547, 548, 551, 552, 553, 574, 577, 579, 581, 582, 584, 585, 586, 589, 590, 593, 595, 598, 605, 606, 629, 634, 636, 640, 641 and 643.

By October 1990, the impact of the government's latest defence review saw a gradual decrease in the requirement for pilot training and the subsequent reduction in the number of flying training schools, leaving No.1 FTS at Linton-on-Ouse as the only school to provide basic training with the Jet Provost T Mk.3A. Although the unit had started to receive its replacement Short Tucanos in April 1992, it would be another year before the last Jet Provost course graduated from Linton due to a backlog of students in the system.

On 22 July 1993, the Jet Provost Mk.3A was finally retired from RAF service when the school's five remaining aircraft were flown to the MU at Shawbury for disposal; the formation being led by Linton's station commander, Gp Capt Tom Eeles.

A number of Jet Provost T Mk.3/T Mk.3As remain in an airworthy condition, including XM479/G-BVEZ, which was restored after a period of service as an instructional airframe and owned by Neil McCarthy. While in February 1983 XN637/G-BKOU was placed on the civil register and makes frequent appearances at air shows as part of the Classic Jet Preservation Group/Jet Provost display team, based at North Weald. In the USA, XM374/N374XM is still thought to be airworthy at Hemet, California, as is XM478/I-PROV at Museo Volante Vola Fenice, Reggio Emilia, Italy.

JET PROVOST T MK.4

Even as the Jet Provost T Mk.3 was entering service with the RAF, work was progressing at Luton on a high-powered successor in response to a requirement for increased upper air work in the student's syllabus – the Jet Provost T Mk.4. With an uprated Viper 202 (ASV11) turbojet of 2,500 lbs thrust installed, the T Mk.4's engine had been originally flight-tested in the pre-production T Mk.2, G-AOUS, in 1958 and demonstrated a forty per cent increase in power. This additional performance provided improvements, especially noticeable during take-off and climb, which resulted in the aircraft being able to reach the upper air work environment in less time.

24

With the exception of new engine bearers and slightly enlarged dorsal air ducts required for the Viper 202, the T Mk.4 retained the features of its predecessor, including two Martin-Baker Mk.4P lightweight ejector seats, a single centrally-placed blind-flying panel and the manually-operated rearward-sliding jettisonable canopy.

As with the Jet Provost T Mk.3, the Mk.4 featured an emergency canopy jettison system operated by a cartridge on top of the coaming behind the seats. The cartridges could be initiated by either the ejection seat occupant operating the face blind or seat pan ejection handle. This action essentially lifted the canopy rails off the cockpit allowing the airflow to get under the forward edge of the canopy, breaking the canopy jettison gun breech and main gun shear pins, enabling the slipstream to clear it away from the aircraft. The canopy could also be jettisoned independently by the canopy jettison handle in the cockpit and by an external jettison handle situated under a frangible Perspex cover on the port side of the front fuselage.

In July 1960, two Jet Provost T Mk.3s, XN467 and XN468, had been removed from the production line at Luton and fitted with the new Viper 202 engine to serve as prototype aircraft for the T Mk.4. The first aircraft (XN467) took to the air on 15 July 1960, flown by the company chief test pilot, Stan Oliver.

It was followed by the second prototype (XN468) in August and made its public debut in the flying display at that year's SBAC show at Farnborough, where it was joined by a Mk.3 (XN462) in the static park with a range of weapons available for the armed version.

Both prototypes subsequently joined the test and development programme at Luton, Boscombe Down and Filton, and, despite initial problems with the throttle system and cracks in the engine mounts, quickly

24. A factory-fresh Jet Provost T Mk.3, XN458, in August 1960. Following its service career with No.1 FTS it was relegated as an instructional airframe and restored to its original colour scheme at its present location, The Standard Public House, Northallerton. (BAe Systems Heritage Warton-Percival/Hunting Collection)

25

impressed the Air Ministry with their improved performance. An initial production order for 100 Jet Provost T Mk.4s to be built by Hunting Aircraft at Luton (the company being renamed the British Aircraft Corporation during January 1964) was signed, and between November 1961 and December 1962, a total of 185 Jet Provost T Mk.4s were eventually built and delivered to the RAF.

The first Jet Provost T Mk.4s – XP549 and XP550 – entered service with the CFS at Little Rissington on 23 November 1961. No.1 Flying Training School at Linton-on-Ouse followed suit with its first Mk.4 in April 1962, together with No.2 FTS at Syerston in May. Further units included Nos.3, 6 and 7 Flying Training Schools, the RAF College at Cranwell and the College of Air Warfare at Manby.

A further unit to operate the Jet Provost T Mk.4 was the Jet Provost Trials Unit (Far East), which was formed in August 1965 to examine Forward Air Control (FAC) operations in the jungle terrain in Malaysia and Singapore. Initially commanded by Sqn Ldr Mick Ryan and comprising three pilots and a team of scientists, the unit's three aircraft (XS221, XS223 and XS224) were transported to Seletar during August and re-assembled, with the first aircraft (XS224) being air-tested fourteen days after its arrival. Trials began with selected, transportable target areas in southern Malaysia before moving to the RAAF base at Butterworth in October to continue operations as the terrain was considered the most representative of the Borneo jungle. The original trials were completed in November but reinstated during

February 1966 to examine further FAC combinations and techniques; its existence being cut short following the tragic loss of XS221 on 5 February 1966, which crashed near Alor Star, Malaya, after hitting trees.

An armed, export version of the Jet Provost T Mk.4 was also made available and purchased by three countries as the T Mk.52, including Iraq (twenty aircraft), Venezuela (fifteen aircraft) and Sudan (eight aircraft). South Yemen also took delivery of eight refurbished, former RAF aircraft in August 1969. A further and much larger order for the South African Air Force in 1964, however, fell foul of the Labour government's imposition of armament exports to the country and was blocked. Instead, South Africa built the Macchi MB.326 for its air force, under licence.

By 1962, the current RAF flying training syllabus for student pilots consisted of around 230 hours, of which only 120 hours was devoted to basic training on the Jet Provost and the remainder on advanced training. With the introduction of the Jet Provost T Mk.4 to the second part of the students' courses, it was decided to extend the RAF's basic training syllabus by forty hours, thereby reducing the time spent on advanced training with the Vampire T11 or the Folland Gnat. This revised '160 hours to Wings' syllabus was considered as a significant saving in the training of students.

The Jet Provost T Mk.4's service life would prove to be relatively brief, however, due to the later, more demanding parts of the flying training syllabus where they encountered much higher airframe fatigue consumption. As a result, most of the Mk.4s were withdrawn from the various training establishments by 1971; the School of Refresher Flying at Leeming finally relinquishing its Mk.4s in October 1976. A small

26

number of the survivors continued to remain in service with the Tactical Weapons Unit at Brawdy and the Central Air Traffic Control School at Shawbury until March and July 1989, respectively, becoming the last units to operate the type.

RAF formation display teams had been quick to take advantage of the improved performance of the Jet Provost T Mk.4, with the CFS 'Red Pelicans', 'Gin Section' from No.1 FTS, the RAF College Cranwell and No.6 FTS all re-equipping with the type during 1962. Following the temporary ban on formation display flying following a mid-air collision in May 1966, restrictions were partially lifted with the formation of 'Viper Red 1967', a synchronised and formation aerobatic routine flown by Sqn Ldr 'Cas' Maynard and Flt Lt George Lee from No.2 FTS. In March 1968, the No.3 FTS synchronised aerobatic team – the 'Gemini Pair' – marked the first formal Jet Provost display team at Leeming for four years; comprising Flt Lts Mike French and Euan Perreaux, the formation of the team was partly in response to a MoD directive which called for a reduction in the number of four-ship display teams and became best known for its trademark 'mirror' formation manoeuvre.

In 1973, Flt Clive 'Bob' Thompson and Fg Off Graham 'Dusty' Miller became the last two pilots to fly as Leeming's display team and between May and October they appeared at forty-three air shows in the UK and Europe in front of an estimated audience of more than one million people. The last display team to operate with the Jet Provost Mk.4 was 'the Macaws' from the CAW at Manby, which made its final appearance at Luxeuil in France on 30 September 1973.

Following their retirement, at least thirteen airframes were sold to private owners between 1983 and 1995 and at the time of writing, eleven T Mk.4s are thought to remain in an airworthy condition: XR673/G-BXLO of Century Aviation at Gamston; XS228/G-PROV (actually a T Mk.52) of Swords Aviation at North Weald, painted in the markings of a South Arabian aircraft and coded '104'; XP547/N547XP located at San Juan, Puerto Rico; XP567/N8272M owned by Ricky Mantei of Zephyr Hills, Florida; XR679/G-BWGT/C-FDJP owned by Graham Rawlinson and operated by Jet Aircraft Museum, London, Ont, Canada; XR701/N204JP of the RAF Linton-Texas Squadron, Houston, SC; at Cheraw, South Carolina, USA as N8272Y; XR704 in North Carolina; XS178 in Texas, registered as N400KT; while XS219/N219JP is reportedly at Texarkana Regional Airport, Texas.

JET PROVOST T MK.5

As previously mentioned, extended training sorties above 20,000 ft began exposing the instructors and students to a painful condition of the joints known as the 'bends'. This was caused by repeated exposure to low atmospheric pressure and was a problem exacerbated by the unpressurised cockpits of the early Jet Provosts.

The logical solution to this problem was to modify the Jet Provost to incorporate a pressurised cockpit to allow extended, high-altitude training sorties. Although no official requirement was specified by the RAF at the time, in 1961 a proposal for a suitably modified Mk.4 airframe was submitted to the Ministry of Aviation by Hunting. A further proposal to design a new pressurised cockpit, which could be retrospectively fitted to T Mk.4 aircraft being returned to the manufacturers, was also discounted as being uneconomic as the aircraft were nearing the end of their airframe fatigue lives. It was therefore considered that the answer was to design and build a complete new aeroplane – the H 145 – which was officially announced at Farnborough in September 1962.

25. The first production Mk.4, XP547, took to the air in August 1961 and was fitted with a more powerful Viper 11 engine, providing an increase in speed and a greater rate of climb. This particular airframe is still airworthy in San Juan, Puerto Rico, registered as N547XP. (Ray Deacon Collection)

26. Jet Provost T Mk.4, XP554, seen on arrival at Little Rissington on 7 December 1961. With the exception of the larger air scoops on the top of the fuselage, the new mark was virtually indistinguishable from its predecessor. (Ray Deacon Collection)

27

Essentially a private venture, most of the design work of the H 145 project had been completed at Luton and by December 1964 it began to attract sufficient interest for a development contract to be issued by the Ministry of Aviation.

Two major changes were incorporated into the project. The fuselage forward of the rear wing spar was completely redesigned to include a pressure cabin for the two crew members; the nose section being slightly lengthened to provide a better streamlining and more space for the cockpit pressurisation and air conditioning system by transferring the batteries to the rear fuselage. The fully automatic pressurisation system was tapped off the engine compressor and commenced controlling at 8,000 feet; the differential and full pressure increasing uniformly with altitude until the maximum of about 3 lb/sq in was achieved at 38,000 ft. The new bulbous nose section also featured a redesigned, power-operated one-piece rearward-sliding cockpit canopy, which greatly improved the view for the crew members and reduced drag; while two Martin-Baker Mk.4 ejection seats with ninety-knot/zero height capability were retained for emergency egress.

During the design stage of the project it was recognised that potential export customers would require wings fitted with four hard points for the carriage of external fuel tanks or underwing stores. These 'export' wings, with a greater fatigue life, were not considered to be a necessity for aircraft supplied to the RAF, where underwing stores were not required. Although it was initially decided to produce two types of wings, eventually the RAF settled on the 'export' wings for its Jet Provosts, thereby reducing design and construction costs.

A group of four interconnected fuel tanks were located in each wing, three of which were bag-type in the outer-wing sections and the other being integral with the wing; each group of tanks being gravity refuelled through a filler point on the upper surface of the wing leading into the integral tank. The total internal fuel tankage of 263.5 gallons reduced the need for wing-tip tanks; the attachment lugs and wiring being retained for possible use for long-range navigation exercises or in the ferrying role. Finally, a Viper 202 (ASV 11) turbojet providing 2,500 lb static thrust, similar to that installed in the Jet Provost T Mk.4, was retained; during testing, however, it was found that an increase of installed thrust necessitated the installation of an increased diameter jet pipe, from fifteen inches to seventeen inches.

Two prototype aircraft for the H 145 project had been set aside at Luton during 1965. Originally constructed as Jet Provost T Mk.4s, the project was delayed by the transfer of both partially completed prototypes to Warton in August 1966 (where they subsequently became the BAC 145). The first aircraft, XS230 – officially designated as a T Mk.5 (Interim) – made an initial thirty-minute test flight on 28 February 1967, captained by Reg Stock with 'Jimmy' Dell acting as observer.

The second prototype, XS231, was modified to become the Viper 20 engine test bed, designated H 166, and first flew at Luton on 16 March 1965 with the company's senior test pilot, D. G. 'Dizzy' Addicott, at the controls. Two further flights were made later that day in spite of a two-hour delay due to weather and initial reports indicated that the performance estimates had been achieved and that handling characteristics remained unchanged from its predecessors. Following its brief career as the flight evaluation airframe for the BAC 167 Strikemaster project, it was modified once again with a pressure cabin as the second prototype T Mk.5 and flew at Warton on 12 July 1967, crewed by Reg Stock and Malcolm Ribchester.

Dave Croser was a flight test observer with both Hunting and BAC.

It was about March 1965 that a numerically out-of-sequence Jet Provost (XS231) was allocated for

28

flight testing with a Viper 20 engine, as a demonstration of the performance model of the proposed Jet Provost T Mk.5. It was in fact a Jet Provost T Mk.4 airframe with the increased power, and distinguished for company identity as the Hunting H 166. The first flight took place on 16 March 1965, flown by 'Dizzy' Addicott, with myself as observer. The inherent increased power was immediately apparent on performance, together with the fact that it was a hybrid aircraft, which impacted on the aircraft's handling.

Despite a company sales brochure for the Jet Provost Mk.5 being published in January 1965 which claimed that 'behaviour at the stall is innocuous and recovery is immediate', the flight test programme of the two prototypes soon ran into slight problems. Subsequent handling tests conducted by BAC with the first prototype had shown that the stall behaviour was unacceptable for basic

training – the stall itself being indeterminate with no nose drop on any configuration.

The enlarged nose structure had been a major aerodynamic modification to the fuselage of the T Mk.5: revised cockpit lines and larger intake ducting with diverter, together with the necessary refinement of the fairings, resulted in a changed airflow. This significantly altered the handling characteristics to such an extent that a flight test programme was required to re-examine the stalling and spinning characteristics of the aircraft to achieve a satisfactory clearance.

The RAF required the stall behaviour of its training aircraft to be clearly defined by a sharp nose-down pitch, with a minimum amount of wing drop, preceded by a natural warning in the shape of buffet. The earlier Jet Provosts had been developed by improvised testing to produce this characteristic, together with a spin which was regular, easily achieved and from which a clean recovery could be made.

27. Depicted with an underwing weapons load, an artist's impression of the proposed H 145 project which was featured on the early company sales brochures. (BAe Systems Heritage Warton-Percival/Hunting Collection)

28. The prototype Jet Provost Mk.5 (Interim), XS230, during its first flight on 28 February 1967, piloted by Reg Stock with 'Jimmy' Dell acting as observer. (BAC via Reg Stock)

The first prototype had been evaluated at Boscombe Down, during which the stalling, lateral and directional characteristics and oscillations at high Mach were found to be unsatisfactory. Whereas the spinning behaviour of the earlier Jet Provosts had been conventional, it was found that the Jet Provost Mk.5 had too much rotary damping, so the spin tended to become oscillatory. These oscillations in pitch gave a very uncomfortable and disorienting ride and had been isolated to flow separations at the wing root.

To improve the stall behaviour, two small slats were fitted to the leading edge of each wing root. The unacceptable oscillations during the spin were cured by the fitment of nose strakes which acted as spoilers at high incidence and also reduced body damping. At the same time the outer-wing leading edges were roughened to minimise the effect of any wing inconsistencies at high angle of attack. An improvement to directional damping was effected by fitting a small plate to the fuselage, below the rudder. **Reg Stock:**

Because of the aircraft's role it was necessary to demonstrate a clearly defined stall with a positive and fairly straight nose-down pitch preceded by natural warning buffet. Unfortunately, despite relatively small differences from earlier marks these characteristics were not present. Maximum lift was also low. Initial analysis pointed to the wing root as the critical area so considerable re-shaping was undertaken using balsa wood and suitable glue. The new shape had a powerful effect; it resulted in a greater Cl max airfoil than even the earlier marks, a nice little straight nose pitch-down but no warning whatsoever in any configuration. Basically the change involved making the wing root aft of the engine intake convex instead of concave and to cut a long story short, we found that there was a change-over point along the wing root aft of which a convex shape resulted in ideal behaviour with no warning, and a concave shape resulting in original behaviour with no compromise in between. The cure came eventually by fitting a very small slat over the leading edge wing root.

Of interest, during this dedicated phase of the flight testing carried out with the two Jet Provost prototypes between June and December 1968, Reg Stock and flight test engineer John Scutt established an unofficial record of an incredible ten sets of spins of eight turns each during one sortie on 12 December in XS230.

In July 1968, a sole order for 110 aircraft for the RAF to be built under contract KC/E/124/CB5(b) was formally placed by MinTech on behalf of the MoD. With the wings built at Hurn, construction of the fuselage and tail unit and final assembly of the airframes was concentrated at Warton. The first production aircraft, XW287, took to the air on 16 July 1969, crewed by Reg Stock and Dave Croser, and deliveries to the RAF began on 3 September 1969 when it was officially handed over to the commandant of the CFS, Air Cdre Ivor Broom.

In addition to the order for the RAF, five Mk.55s – an export version of the Mk.5, fitted with two machine guns in the wing roots and various underwing armaments and/or jettisonable fuel tanks – were also produced for Sudan; the first production aircraft took to the air at Warton on 10 January 1969 and were delivered between March and June 1969. A further order for thirty-five of this variant for the Greek air force was embargoed by the Labour government in 1974.

Following the completion of a revised flying training syllabus and conversion of the first instructors at Linton-on-Ouse, No.1 FTS became the first unit to equip with the Jet Provost T Mk.5 following the arrival of XW298 and XW299 in December 1969. With further deliveries to the school, the new aircraft had replaced the Jet Provost T Mk.4s at Linton by the following July, by which time No.3 FTS at Leeming had also taken delivery of its first T Mk.5 (XW315).

In December 1970, the RAF College at Cranwell became one of the last units to receive the Jet Provost Mk.5 when XW336 was delivered from Warton; No.99 Entry and No.1 Graduate Entry being the first courses to use the new aircraft for training. In December 1971 the College was allocated two further aircraft, XW322 and XW323, for the exclusive use of HRH Prince Charles during his five-month training course. The two aircraft were returned

29

to Cranwell in September 1972 when Prince Charles underwent a brief period of refresher flying.

At the same time as the stalling problems were being resolved, work on the canopy jettisoning system was still being carried out by BAC. The original intention of installing a similar system to that of the earlier aircraft where the canopy was jettisoned before ejection seat initiation soon ran into problems. In April 1968, early trials carried out on XS231 showed an unacceptable delay in the canopy jettison sequence and the RAF requested the development of a canopy removal system modified with a miniature detonation cord (MDC).

The MDC system comprised a 1.6-mm sheathed cord bonded to the inside of the Perspex canopy, two cartridge firing units, one at the rear of each ejection seat, and a detonator assembly; each cartridge being fired by removal of the firing pin sear, which directed gas pressure to a detonator block on the canopy frame, opening a striker pin to detonate the cord and shatter the canopy.

Dave Croser again:

The Jet Provost cockpit configuration was the standard T Mk.3/4 shape comprising a wind back hood on side rails, which in emergency could be jettisoned as part of the seat/canopy jettison auto sequence. This took, as I recall, about half a second between canopy gone and seat departure. Reshaping the cockpit/windscreen configuration was going to form part of the definitive T Mk. 5 design, and part of the line of thought for this was to jettison through the canopy, bearing in mind that the Martin-Baker Mk.4 ejection seat was designed for ground-level use. Therefore, the use of the seat as the means of

fracturing the canopy hood was not considered that trustworthy, so enter the separate MDC as an independent hood fracturing means. It wasn't until after the actual T Mk.5 (XS230) had flown, that the MDC pattern was designed and a ground test in a wind tunnel at Boscombe Down was carried out between December 1971 and July 1972.

In August 1972 a standard production T Mk.5, XW425, was issued to BAC at Warton for the trial installation and company evaluation of the MDC and canopy removal system. John Scutt was a flight test observer with BAC during this period: the Jet Provost T Mk.5 went into RAF service during 1969 without the MDC canopy removal system as there was no intention to fit it since the idea was fairly new. It was certainly never discussed during the basic development trials on XS230 and XS231.

We undertook a series of successful trials to ensure that the canopy cleared the fin at all airspeeds, including in the spin. However there was about a 0.5 second delay to allow the canopy to clear the fin before the seat could be fired. Although not long, 0.5 second was deemed too long to wait after pulling the handle as, in a critical situation, this could prove fatal. The MDC shattered the canopy in less than 0.1 seconds and seat firing was almost instantaneous after pulling the handle.

With the completion of the development and trials programme at both Warton and Boscombe Down, sixty-one aircraft were eventually modified with the MDC system by a working party at RAF Leeming between June 1975 and March 1976.

Further work to the T Mk.5 fleet included the upgrading with an improved avionics refit. With the completion of the previous work to install the MDC and canopy

29. Following its brief career as the flight evaluation aircraft for the BAC 167 Strikemaster project, the second prototype, XS231, was used for a variety of company trials. These included canopy jettison trials by Reg Stock over Morecambe Bay between April and November 1968. The nose section is currently preserved at Boscombe Down. (BAC via Reg Stock)

removal system in XW425 at Warton, its loan was extended to include the incorporation of the new radio and navigation equipment. The first modified aircraft took to the air again on 13 September 1973 to assess the new installation and work on the first RAF T Mk.5, XW473, began the following month. The upgrade of the ninety-three aircraft to T Mk.5A standard was finally completed in January 1976 and included: XW288, 289, 290, 292, 294, 295, 299, 301,303, 305, 308, 310, 312, 313, 314, 315, 316, 317, 318, 319, 320, 321, 322, 323, 325, 326, 327, 328, 329, 330, 332, 333, 334, 335, 336, 351, 353, 354, 355, 357, 358, 359, 360, 361, 362, 363, 364, 365, 366,367, 368, 369, 370, 371, 372, 373, 374, 375, 404, 405, 406, 407, 408, 409, 410, 411, 412, 413, 414, 415, 416, 417, 418, 419, 420, 421, 422, 423, 424, 425, 426, 427, 428, 429, 430, 431, 432, 433, 434, 435, 436, 437 and 438.

Between October and December 1975, a further batch of T Mk.5s was modified for use as long-range, low-level navigational trainers with No.6 FTS at Finningley. The work was undertaken by a civilian working party at Leeming to Mod No.1791, which included removing the nose strakes and fitting 48-gallon tanks to the wing tips to enhance training sorties. The thirteen aircraft involved in the modification included – XW287, 291, 293, 296, 298, 302, 304, 306, 307, 309, 311, 324 and 352. Deliveries began in October 1975. In 1988, the wings of some of the aircraft began to fail the structural fatigue tests and five 'low fatigue' airframes (XW322, 325, 429, 431 and 438) were modified at Scampton as replacements; the upgraded airframes retaining their wing-tip tanks and nose strakes.

By the early 1980s there was a move to replace the Jet Provost with a more economic aircraft. The CFS favoured a turboprop aircraft, as it believed the Jet Provost's handling was too docile for an introduction to jet flying; it was considered that students got through only to fail when introduced to the front-line fast jets, the most expensive stage of training. Their argument was that a trainer with high torque from the engine would be a more challenging aircraft whilst also being more economic than a pure jet. The CFS argument eventually won the day, and after a prolonged competition, in March 1985, Embraer and Short Brothers were awarded the contract to build the Tucano, a two-seat turboprop training aircraft, which entered service with the CFS in June 1988. With further deliveries of the Tucano to No.7 FTS at Church Fenton and No.3 FTS at Cranwell, No.1 FTS at Linton-on-Ouse became the final basic training unit to receive the new trainer in April 1992; its remaining Jet Provost Mk.5As being passed to RAF Shawbury for storage in September 1993.

Although the Jet Provost Mk.5 was never adapted for smoke-making equipment, it was considered by most display pilots to be much easier to fly in formation aerobatics than the earlier marks, possessing a considerably cleaner airframe and lacking wing-tip tanks. Between 1970 and 1976, five RAF aerobatic teams operated the type. In January 1970, the Red Pelicans, led by Sqn Ldr Eric Evers, became the first display team to be equipped with the type, and for the next three years the CFS Jet Provost teams displayed at venues throughout the UK, Germany, Belgium and Italy. The team was finally disbanded as part of the government's economy measures.

THE CRANWELL POACHERS Sqn Ldr John Robinson's leadership of the RAF College team coincided with the arrival of the first Jet Provost T Mk.5 at RAF Cranwell in December 1970. During the 1971 season, the team was restricted to displaying in the UK but this was followed by a very active programme of overseas shows, the following year. The team was temporarily disbanded in 1974, but in a surprise move it was officially reformed in March 1975 with OC Standards Squadron, Sqn Ldr Peter Curtin, appointed as leader of the team. On 5 September 1976, the team gave its final show at the Burma Star Day, Waterbeach, which not only marked the end of the season but also the RAF's last Jet Provost formation aerobatic display team.

THE LINTON BLADES The No.1 FTS display team was formed at Linton-on-Ouse in January 1970, led by Flt Lt Dave Waddington. The team's first public display was at RAF Church Fenton on 2 May 1970 and was followed by its first overseas show at Wiesbaden on 10 May.

THE GEMINI PAIR With the delivery of the first Jet Provost T Mk. 5 to No.3 Flying Training School at Leeming in July 1970, the Gemini Pair re-equipped with the new aircraft in readiness for the start of the new season. As in previous years, the Gemini Pair entertained the crowds with its 'mirror' formation routine at numerous air shows throughout the United Kingdom and Europe. The team's two pilots, Fg Off Ron Pattinson and Flt Lt Gordon Revell, made their debut at the Leicester Aero Club meeting; the name 'Gemini' on the fin being a feature of the team's Jet Provosts.

THE SWORDS As the 1974 the oil crisis began to take effect, the MoD decided to limit the number of formation display teams as an economy measure; the Blades, Macaws, Red Pelicans, Gemini Pair were all disbanded, with the Cranwell team being temporarily withdrawn. This left the Swords from No.3 FTS at RAF Leeming as the RAF's official Jet Provost aerobatic team, led by Flt Lt Clive 'Bob' Thompson. The team's existence would prove to be brief and made its last appearance at the Rolls-Royce Open Day at Filton on 12 October 1974.

Following retirement from RAF service, a number of the airframes were relegated for ground instruction at various training establishments. The Jet Provost was also eagerly sought after by enthusiasts who were keen to see the type displayed on the air show circuit, and between November 1993 and July 1994, at least twenty-eight Mk.5s (together with a further thirty-three T Mk.3As, four T Mk.4s and fifteen Strikemasters) were

acquired by Global Aviation at Binbrook for refurbishment and re-sale to private owners. These included:

UK – XS230/G-VIVM; XW289/G-JPVA; XW291/G-BWOF; XW310/G-BWGS; XW324/G-BWSG; XW325/G-BWGF; XW333/G-BVTC; XW355/G-JPTV; XW422/G-BWEB; XW433/G-JPRO

USA – XW287/N287XW; XW305/N453MS; XW306/N313A; XW317/N355A; XW334/N334XW; XW336/N8089U; XW354/N300LT; XW359/N400LT; XW368/N600LT; XW372/N399PS; XW415/N900LT; XW428/N4311M; XW429/N556A; XW435/N4XW; XW437/N80873

Australia – XW295/VH-JPV; XW362/VH-YZB; XW374/VH-JPE

30. Jet Provost T Mk.5A, 'XW295', at RAAF Point Cook in March 2014. The aircraft was exported to Australia in June 1993 and flew again after restoration in February 1999. Registered as VH-JPV, it retains its former RAF identity. (Brendan Cowan)

Above: The SBAC show at Farnborough in September 1964 would be the final year that the Red Pelicans would officially represent the RAF as its premier display team. (Bristol Siddeley via Terry Lloyd)

31

No. 26 SQUADRON

The squadron operated as a holding unit for the staff at HQ Training Command, RAF Brampton, and took delivery of its first two Jet Provost T Mk.3s in July 1974. On 31 March 1976 the unit was renamed as the Wyton detachment and transferred to the RAF College on 31 December 1976 as the Jet Provost detachment. The last Jet Provost was withdrawn from the squadron in October 1977.

CENTRAL FLYING SCHOOL

The CFS was formed at Upavon, Wiltshire, in May 1912 and is acknowledged as the world's oldest military training establishment. Its initial purpose was to train pilots for the naval and military wings of the Royal Flying Corps, but in March 1920 the school began to train instructors for RAF Flying Training Schools on the principles of Smith-Barry's School of Special Flying. The standard trainer operated by the school was the Avro 504K, with Sopwith Snipes for advanced work. In October 1926 the school moved to Wittering but returned to Upavon in August 1935.

On 7 May 1946 the CFS was re-established at Little Rissington and reverted to its function as the sole establishment for the training of flying instructors. The school's principal training aircraft in the early post-war years consisted of Tiger Moths for basic flying instruction and Harvards for advanced training. On 1 May 1952, the CFS (Basic) Squadron opened at South Cerney with Harvard, Prentice and Provost trainers, while the CFS (Advanced) Squadron was formed at Little Rissington with Provosts, Meteors and Vampires.

In early 1955, the CFS was tasked with the evaluation and compilation of a basic training syllabus for the first stage of the official Service trials of the Jet Provost T Mk.1. On 25 June 1955, a team led by Sqn Ldr W. G. 'Bill' Drinkell and comprising Flt Lts Morrice, Walker and Houser were appointed to carry out the initial evaluation of the aircraft, two of which (XD676 and XD679) were delivered to South Cerney on 22 July 1955. The evaluation began five days later and, although originally scheduled to last for twelve weeks, was completed by 25 August and the aircraft were transferred to No.2 FTS, RAF Hullavington, to join three other production aircraft participating in the second phase of the experimental all-through flying training programme.

Air Cdre Christopher Paul CB DFC was the CFS commandant between 1954 and 1956. Towards the end of 1954, he had been informed that one of the school's tasks was to assess the suitability of the Jet Provost for training and the following is an extract from his personal account which was published in *RAF Little Rissington: The Central Flying School Years* by Deacon, Pollock, et al:

> In the summer of 1955 we got our first Jet Provost. In fact the alterations were considerable, for the piston engine, the Alvis Leonides, was removed and a small jet engine, the Armstrong Siddeley Viper, substituted in a central position in the fuselage, much further aft. We did a lot of flying on this first version and, in spite of its appearance, it was well liked. It did, however, seem to me to introduce a number of new problems.
>
> The intention of the Air Ministry was that the Jet Provost, like the Piston Provost before it, should be the RAF's ab initio trainer, and that the pupil pilot should do as much training on this jet as possible; in fact right up to the stage of getting his Wings. But it was very soon apparent that, with a performance approximating to the early marks of Spitfire, the Jet Provost was capable of getting very rapidly into situations which earlier piston-engine trainers could not attain, and that its performance not only enabled it to use much more of the sky including the upper air space, but to exploit to its best advantage, this ability had to be used to the full. My own feeling, after some experience with it, was that the RAF might very well find that the Jet Provost was too much of an aeroplane for a pilot's first flight when beginning to learn. This was the last major task during my two years with

the CFS, and I get some satisfaction that from knowing that the Jet Provost which finally resulted has served the RAF very well.

With the completion of the all-through jet training evaluation at Hullavington in November 1957, seven Jet Provost T Mk.1s, XD675-680 and XD693, were issued to Little Rissington to form an aerobatic flight – The CFS Jet Aerobatic Team. As the RAF's basic flying training schools were scheduled to be equipped with the later Mk.3 version, the AOC-in-C RAF Flying Training Command, Air Mshl Sir Richard Atcherley, requested that the CFS should form a team with the Jet Provost T Mk.1s and appear at the SBAC Display, Farnborough, the following year.

Formation aerobatic displays by CFS instructors had been a traditional item at the Hendon air displays since 1920 and Atcherley had been a member of the school's Genet Moth team, which had thrilled the Hendon crowds during 1927 and 1928 with its innovative routines and demonstrations of inverted flying. He suggested the inclusion of the inverted routine for the 1958 Farnborough show and had the fuel tanks of the Jet Provosts modified accordingly. The Jet Provost T Mk.1, however, was not ideal for display flying, being underpowered for formation aerobatics which resulted in a limitation of the team's routines. In the end the inverted routine was not used as it was considered "too dangerous".

Norman Giffin arrived at Little Rissington in April 1957 and was appointed as leader of the CFS Jet Provost team.

> At the end of 1957, the evaluation of the Jet Provost T Mk.1s at Hullavington was completed and it had been decided to go ahead with all-through jet training using an improved version of the Jet

31. Between July and August 1955, the CFS at Little Rissington carried out the preliminary Service trials with two Jet Provost T Mk.1s to evaluate the aircraft as ab initio trainer and to formulate a training syllabus. (BAe Systems Heritage Warton-Percival/Hunting Collection)

32-33

Provost. This made the long-legged Mk.1s available for instructor training at Little Rissington and my flight was chosen to do this. I cannot remember where the original idea of a Jet Provost aerobatic team came from but I know that the AOC-in-C, 'Batchy' Atcherley was very keen that we should try to introduce some inverted flying into our display routine and he authorised the fitting of special inverted flight fuel systems to the aircraft. Unfortunately, the Jet Provost Mk.1 had about 1,800 lbs of thrust and this severely limited the formations that we could fly and also made any inverted display impractical, much to Batchy's disappointment, I suspect.

The Jet Provosts were painted in a red and white scheme at St Athan [including XD675, XD676, XD678, XD679 and XD680] which I designed to emphasise the differences between the top and bottom surfaces. This was in anticipation of being able to do all or part of the routine, flying inverted; the 1933 CFS Tutor team had a sunburst design on the top wing for a similar purpose. We also had smoke generators fitted to the underside of the wings, which were used to great effect during our final loop.

The team were all volunteers and included Flt Lts Don McClen, Fred Packer and Pete Millington, with Mike Edwards as the reserve. None of us had any previous experience of formation aerobatics. We wanted to call ourselves 'The Red Pelicans' but the Meteor team of previous years had ambitions to continue into 1958 and since they had used the name 'Pelicans', they were unhappy about us using it. In the end we settled for the rather uninspiring name – 'The CFS Jet Aerobatic Team'.

Our first formation practice was on 3 March 1958 and we collected the team aircraft from St Athan on 2 April (I collected XD676 with Ron Wilkinson, the Armstrong Siddeley rep) where they had been resprayed in the new colour scheme. We made our debut at the RAFA display at Hucknall on Whit Monday, 26 May, alongside the Hunter display team of 111 Squadron. The only incident we had was during a display at Little Rissington for a visiting Thai air force delegation in August. Whilst concentrating on his formation during landing, Peter Millington had the misfortune to suffer a wheels-up landing following an undercarriage malfunction; Peter called me on the radio not to brake too hard as he was sliding along on his belly and had no means of slowing down. I must admit I do not remember that. All I remember is seeing Peter running across the grass as we turned off the runway and that was quite a shock. We were not told what the Thai delegation made of his departure from the scheduled programme.

Following repairs to the undersurface of the Jet Provost (XD679), it was returned to service the following February.

The Jet Provost team flew seventeen displays during the 1958 season, including Hucknall (26 May), Plymouth (3 June), Henlow (18 June), Exeter (28 June), Staverton (28 June), Baginton (19 July), Culdrose (21 July), Little Rissington (28 August), Colwyn Bay (30 August), SBAC Farnborough (1-7 September), Jersey (18 September) and Cosford (20 September).

The 1959 display season began with the CFS being in the unusual position of not being able to provide a team of four Jet Provosts for the forthcoming year. A shortage of manpower and a lack of available aircraft to equip a team eventually led to the suggestion that it would be possible to divert three aircraft from the existing fleet of Jet Provost T Mk.1s (XD675 – XD680) and work up a routine of synchronised aerobatics. Flown by Flt Lts Jim Rhind and 'Curly' Hirst, the synchronised pair became known as 'the Redskins'.

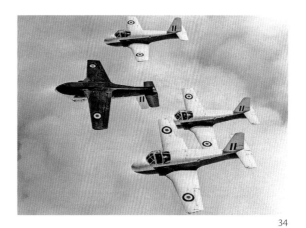

34

'Curly' Hirst had displayed Hunter and Piston Provost aircraft since 1954. He was posted to the CFS staff in June 1958 and recalls the Jet Provost team.

The Jet Provost Mk.1s proved to be a bit of an embarrassment to the CFS. They had a pneumatic system rather than hydraulic and were notoriously difficult to keep serviceable. They really had served their purpose and had validated the new pilot training syllabus of all-jet training at Hullavington. At CFS, they were being used to acquaint QFIs with the type – which well deserved the phrase 'constant thrust variable noise' because they (and the Mk.3) were notoriously underpowered. I think the commandant was rather pleased when Jim Rhind and I found a use for them as a synchronised aerobatic team.

In 1959, the CFS had a problem with providing sufficient aircraft to form an aerobatic team of four aircraft, plus a spare, making an almost daily requirement of five serviceable aircraft. The problem was caused by only having a total of six Jet Provost T Mk.1s, which was reduced to five after an accident. After a great deal of research and hard work the engineers said that they could only guarantee a total of three of the Jet Provost aircraft for the

32. The CFS Jet Aerobatic Team flew seventeen displays during the 1958 season, including a week at the SBAC Show, Farnborough, in September. (Hunting via Norman Giffin)

33. Members of the CFS Jet Aerobatic Team in 1958, including (left to right) Flt Lts Don McClen, Norman Giffin (leader), Fred Packer and Peter Millington. (Norman Giffin via Ray Deacon)

34. Despite being a CFS tradition, the 'inverted leader' formation by the CFS team was soon proved impractical because of the thrust limitations of the Armstrong Siddeley Viper turbo jet. (Norman Giffin)

aerobatic season. So, Jim Rhind and I made a proposal for a CFS pair flying these aircraft in a series of synchronised aerobatics in a show lasting about six minutes.

The aircraft retained the red and white colour scheme and were fitted with a Bristol Siddeley Viper engine, which had been designed to power a guided weapon. It did not give much in the way of thrust but just enough to fly the aircraft safely and to teach the fundamentals of jet-engine handling techniques. However, the handling characteristics were excellent and, in particular, the well balanced ailerons.

Jim Rhind suggested the title of 'the Redskins' for the pair and we started working up a routine which involved various assorted manoeuvres such as the mirror formation and flying towards one another at low level and pulling up to meet each other at the top of the loop. Both aircraft then executed a flick roll and completed the loop near the ground while passing one another. The content of the shows was practised and changed according to the weather conditions, particularly the wind strength and direction which had a significant effect on the displays. The CFS engineers also devised a scheme whereby smoke canisters were fitted under each wing and ignited at a suitable moment by a switch in the cockpit. The smoke lasted three or four minutes and was very effective in tracing the flying contours of each aircraft as they approached one another.

A total of thirty-four displays were flown during the season, with the first public appearance at Hucknall on 18 May 1959. The climax of the season being the SBAC Show at Farnborough in September, where the display gained the approval and admiration of the more-informed spectators. Subsequent displays for the team included Jersey, RAF Tangmere, Biggin Hill, Shawbury, West Malling, Chivenor, Stradishall and finally, RAF Shawbury for HRH the Duchess of Gloucester on 22 October.

The CFS Jet Provost T Mk.1s at Little Rissington were also used for converting staff instructors and for the advanced phase of the student courses, and on 19

April 1958, two students of No.191 Course became the first to complete their conversion training on the type. The following year, **Flg Off Ian Sheppard** of No.196 Course became the first all-through jet-trained pilot to undergo an instructors' course at CFS, having previously received ab initio training on the Jet Provost at Hullavington.

I commenced flying on No.196 Course on 9 December 1958 at RAF Little Rissington on the Provost T Mk.1. I took my final handling test with Sqn Ldr Mock on 15 April 1959, and last flew at CFS on 22 April 1959. I think the published statement that 'Flg Off I. A. L. Sheppard was the first all-through jet-trained pilot to undergo an instructors' course at CFS, (he) having no previous piston-engined flying experience' is probably true. What that statement does not tell you is that in the first stages of the course I did not do very well (though whether that was anything to do with my previous experience or not I cannot say) and had to be put under review. I then had a change of instructor, who had

35-36

a very different approach, and with whom I got on very well – and as a result of his efforts I passed out as a B.1, which was relatively unusual – the expectation was that people would pass out as B.2.

In July 1959 the first batch of Jet Provost T Mk.3s allocated to the CFS (XM360, XM361 and XM365) were collected from Lyneham by Flt Lts Norman Giffin, Fred Packer and Bert Cann. Two months later, one of the original aircraft to be delivered to the CFS (XM360) made the type's public debut at the Battle of Britain shows at Cottesmore and Bassingbourn, flown by Fg Off Bruce McDonald.

The first course to receive instruction with the new Jet Provost T Mk.3s as part of their QFI training – No.199 Course – assembled in June and split up in mid-September,

with thirteen students going to Vampires, six to Jet Provosts and two to the Meteor. The course was completed on 26 November 1959 and the six students who became the first to graduate as Jet Provost QFIs – Flt Lts Chris Wilmot, Andrew Whittaker, and Fg Offs Barry Dale, James Watts-Phillips, Alex Read and Brian Stephens – were posted as instructors to No.2 FTS at Syerston. **Dickie Lees** was a student on No.204 Course.

My first flight on the course was on 19 July 1960 in a Piston Provost. The course was split evenly between Piston Provost and Jet Provost. I did forty-seven hours on the Piston Provost and fifty-one hours on the Jet Provost (includes four hours night flying). The course ended on 16 November 1960. During the Piston Provost stage we were introduced

35. Jet Provost T Mk.1s (including XD679) of the CFS synchronised display pair the Redskins at the Biggin Hill Battle of Britain Day, 19 September 1959. Flown by Flt Lts Jim Rhind and 'Curly' Hirst, the team took part in thirty-four shows between May and October 1959, including a highly commended appearance at Farnborough in September. (Jerry Hughes)

36. Deliveries to the RAF began on 31 July 1959, when a batch of Jet Provost T Mk.3s were delivered to the CFS, Little Rissington, including XM365:R-A, XM360:R-E and XM361:R-F. (Hunting/Giffin/Deacon)

37. Early-production T Mk.3s XM355:RA, XM360:RE and XM361:RF flying in formation over the Cotswold countryside soon after entering service with CFS in July 1959. (Hunting via Norman Giffin).

to side-by-side seating for instructing, flying from both seats either as trainee instructor (in the right-hand seat) or as a student (real or acting) in the left-hand seat. Having learnt the basic 'patter' to instruct we moved on to the Jet Provost to apply it for our future posting as Jet Provost instructors. As the Jet Provost was easy to fly, I cannot say flying the Piston Provost had any bearing on flying the Jet Provost, what it had done was taught us the basic exercises necessary to teach someone to fly, e.g. effect of controls, straight and level flight, turning, stalling and spinning, etc.

By December 1960 the CFS Piston Provosts had been withdrawn and the QFI training syllabus was completed at Little Rissington on the Jet Provost. **Alan Pollock:**

> No.208 Course began on 8 May 1961. The Piston Provosts had now gone and for two-thirds of us we were an early straight-through course on the Jet Provost T Mk.3. Our syllabus was ninety-six hours for the applied stage, the remaining third split between Chipmunk, Vampire (the final CFS Vampire course – No.216 Course – ran from November 1962 to May 1963) or Varsity. We completed the course in September 1961.

On 23 November 1961, deliveries of the Jet Provost T Mk.4 to the CFS began with two aircraft, XP549 and XP550, followed by two more, XP551 and XP553, in December. With the introduction of the Jet Provost Mk.4, with its more powerful Viper 202 engine, the syllabus was changed to introduce students to high altitude flying and the associated differences. This upper air work in the Mk.4 was a replication of what the student carried out at lower altitudes, including general handling, instrument, navigation and formation flying, all done at altitude to demonstrate the effect of changed IAS/TAS relationship in thinner air.

The basic instructor and refresher courses run by the CFS were the responsibility of the school's Flying Wing, which comprised two squadrons, Basic and Advanced. Four main courses of just over thirty students and eight refresher courses were completed each year, with each of the main courses lasting between five and six months. During this time the student was required to complete two weeks of ground school, a further five weeks of ground school with flying on alternate days, and the remainder almost entirely flying. **Richie Profit** was a student on No.217 CFS Course between 18 February and 15 June 1963.

> We had a very interesting selection of experienced pilots on the course, including Ray Hanna (of subsequent Red Arrows and vintage War Birds fame). There were about five first tourists on this course (an unusually high number), all of whom subsequently went on to Hunters and then a variety of fast jets – Harrier and Phantom mainly.
>
> The CFS syllabus had an extensive ground training component – principles of flight, aerodynamics, meteorology etc, etc. The flying syllabus covered everything that ab initio students were going to experience during their training – aircraft handling, aerobatics, instrument flying, formation flying, navigation, night flying etc. The aim was to demonstrate a technique/manoeuvre / whatever while explaining what we were doing (easier said than done initially!), then talking the 'student' through the particular exercise (the 'student' was one's instructor or another member of the course) and then correcting the 'student's' errors (which were made intentionally).
>
> We usually (not always) flew Mk.3s for the initial training exercises and then moved on to the Mk.4 and this was the case with the real students throughout my time as an instructor. Incidentally, this did take more out of the Jet Provost's airframe fatigue life that led to a shortage of Mk.4s later in the aircraft's time in service.

On 3 September 1969, the first Jet Provost T Mk.5, XW287, was delivered to Little Rissington and officially handed over the following day by P. J. 'Pete' Ginger, senior production test pilot of the corporation's Preston Division. A second aircraft (XW288) was delivered to the CFS at the end of the month. **Sqn Ldr John Robinson** was the OC Standards Flight during this period.

38

I was tasked with the introduction of the Jet Provost T Mk.5 to Training Command, together with a pilot from Examining Wing. This included redefining some of the flying training syllabus especially with high level handling as the aircraft was partially pressurised and permitted operations at higher altitudes than the unpressurised JP3s and 4s. Subsequently I had to convert the CFS instructors to the type and assisted with converting pilots at other flying training units.

On 19 September 1969 I carried out the acceptance air test on Jet Provost T Mk.5, XW287, with Flt Lt Alan Elsegood of the Examining Wing. This was the first Jet Provost T Mk.5 to come to us and we used this aircraft to carry out trials on how it would fit into the flying training syllabus by establishing differences in handling techniques and formulating procedures when compared to the Jet Provost T Mk.4. We flew over eighteen hours on this aircraft while carrying out the trials and on 14 October I carried out the acceptance air test on a further aircraft, XW288. From then on other Jet Provost T Mk.5s were added to the fleet and conversion flights were carried out on the Jet Provost instructors. In December 1969 I had a hand in training the Red Pelicans' pilots for the 1970 season, who were to form the team on the Jet Provost T Mk.5. There was no specific date when the Jet Provost Mk.5 was fed into the training of instructors but it gradually replaced the Mk.4.

With the gradual re-equipment of the CFS inventory with Jet Provost T Mk.5s, the withdrawal of the T Mk.4s

began in October 1969 as the aircraft were transferred to No.27 MU for storage; the last (XN467) being flown to Shawbury on 16 June 1970. By way of compensation, between February and July 1974 the school's fleet was augmented with the delivery of upgraded Jet Provost T Mk.3As and T Mk.5As, following the modification programme at Warton.

By the end of 1975 the withdrawal of the Jet Provost Mk.3 establishment was virtually complete with eight aircraft having departed to Kemble and two to BAC Warton for conversion to T Mk.3A. The most significant event of the year, however, was the decision contained within the government's Statement on Defence Estimates which recommended the closure of twelve stations or airfields, including that of RAF Little Rissington. The gradual run down of the station began almost immediately, and in April 1976, the last Jet Provost course (No.276 Course) was completed, bringing eighteen years of flying training on the type at station to an end before the CFS moved to Cranwell and was absorbed into the RAF College. The final fly-past over its 'spiritual home' on 12 April was marked by mixed formations comprising the aircraft types flown by the school, led by the Wg Cdr Flying, 'Cas' Maynard, which included five Jet Provost T Mk.5As, flanked by two box formations of eight Jet Provost T Mk.3As.

Its stay at Cranwell was to prove brief, however; a crowded airspace and a spell of bad weather which resulted in a backlog of flying hours, found the CFS HQ, Jet Provost Squadron and the Examining Wing moving to Leeming to join the Bulldog Squadron in September 1977. One significant aspect of the move was the reorganisation of the Jet Provost and Bulldog Training Flights as a training squadron responsible for all refresher training of former instructors returning to flying duties.

38. In September 1969, XW287 became the first Jet Provost T Mk.5 to enter RAF service when it was handed over to the CFS, RAF Little Rissington, by P. J. 'Peter' Ginger, senior production test pilot of BAC's Preston Division and 'Ricky' Richardson, BAC's RAF liaison officer. It was later sold to a buyer in the USA in 1994 and is currently registered as N287XW. (BAe Systems Heritage Warton-Percival/Hunting Collection)

Dave McIntyre:

When I joined the RAF, I had hoped to fly Hunter FR10s, but after finishing on the Gnat at Valley, I was posted to Canberra PR7s, and subsequently to Vulcans. The safest way to crossover was via CFS, and I managed to get a place on No.290 Course at Leeming in May 1979.

The course began with a couple of months of ground school, followed by a few weeks of half classroom/half flying on the T Mk.3As. The first flights reacquainted us with the Jet Provost, culminating in an instrument rating before starting the course proper. There were several options on the course, depending on the exercise to be learnt. The more challenging lessons involved a trip with your instructor demonstrating the exercise. Two students would then fly together on a 'mutual' where the student instructors gave the lesson to each other, and this was followed by a 'give-back' where one presented the lesson to one of the CFS instructors. Less demanding exercises omitted the mutual, and as one's confidence increased the give-back was occasionally given without a prior demonstration.

Two months and approximately sixty hours flying later, the mid-course intermediate handling check was flown. Those selected to stay on the Jet Provost went on to fly the T Mk.5As, whilst the multi-engine guys went off to the Jetstream at Finningley, and the Hawk guys to Valley.

My final handling test was flown after another thirty-seven hours and the postings were decided once everyone had finished. The multi-engine and Hawk guys returned to Leeming for the graduation photograph taken on 8 November 1979, before being told of their postings on the dining-out night. I was fortunate enough to be the one guy selected to stay at Leeming and move across to the RFS hangar.

So I never got to give the basic flying lessons we had been taught on the course. Learning to adapt one's skills to dealing with experienced pilots was a steep learning curve, as many of the refresher students were better pilots than me. It took a few weeks to settle down, but once I got my confidence, I really began to enjoy the role.

In September 1984 the school moved, once again, to Scampton. **Group Captain Tom Eeles:**

The CFS move to Cranwell in April 1976 was highly unpopular and it just didn't work, so CFS moved again to Leeming which it shared with No.3 FTS. It still wasn't quite right so when it was decided to make Leeming an air defence base in 1981 the CFS moved again, in September 1984, to Scampton, where it had the base to itself. The Red Arrows were also moved there from Kemble, much to their annoyance as it put them under the nose of their senior supervisor, the commandant. Thus Scampton replicated what had been the situation at Little Rissington, all CFS together apart from helicopters (at Shawbury) and the Hawk element (at Valley).

A further programme of defence cuts and planned reduction in the overall size of RAF flying training was announced by the government in July 1994 and eventually resulted in the closure of Scampton. The HQ CFS was also drastically downgraded and returned to Cranwell in May 1995, with the only instructor training at Cranwell being with the Bulldog/Tutor; all other instructor training being conducted at Linton, Valley and Shawbury. In 1989 the Short Tucano T1 turboprop trainer was introduced to replace the Jet Provost at Cranwell and in June 1992 the last T Mk.5As were finally withdrawn.

CFS DISPLAY TEAMS The CFS had developed an enviable reputation for producing fine aerobatic teams, and the success of the previous Jet Provost T Mk.1 display teams was continued with the Central Flying School Aerobatic Team, which was formed at the beginning of 1960 with four Jet Provost Mk.3s. One of the original team members was **Bruce McDonald.**

The four pilots in the team were Flt Lt Roy Langstaff (leader), Flt Lt Dave Brambley (No.2), Fg Off Bruce McDonald (No.3) and Flt Lt Gerry Nicklin (No.4). We started practising in January 1960 and our first

show at the French National Air Day at Bourges/Avord on 14 May, which would be followed by its UK public debut at the RAFA display at North Weald on Whit Monday. A total of thirty-three official displays were flown that season, including an impressive demonstration of synchronised aerobatics at the Paris air show in June and a week at the SBAC Farnborough show in September.

In March 1962, the number of aircraft flown by the CFS Jet Provost team was increased to five. In previous years the four-aircraft formation had performed synchronised aerobatics in two pairs but with the addition of a fifth aircraft the team was able to introduce a number of new formations. The team also became the first to operate with the newly delivered Jet Provost T Mk.4 and was renamed the Red Pelicans, with instructors drawn from 1 Squadron. These included Flt Lt Ian 'Snowy' McKee as leader, with Flt Lts Keith Beck, Ian Bashall, John Rolfe, Dick Fox and Tony Doyle as the reserve pilot. **Flt Lt Ian Bashall** joined the CFS staff in January 1962.

We completed twenty-nine shows that season, six of which were abroad; we opened the season with a show in Cambrai on 13 May, which was followed by trips to Denmark, France and Belgium. We continued to include the traditional mirror routine in the display, which was flown for the first time that year for the Wright Jubilee competition at Little Rissington on 14 May.

The highlight of our year was the Farnborough show, between 3-9 September. At some point the second ejection seat was removed and a drum of hydraulic fluid for the smoke was mounted in its place. This meant that some aircraft were flown from the right and some from the left, depending on the position the pilot flew in the formation. We were always the first item each day and I recall that we upset the commentator when we completed our formation landing with smoke and completely

display was at Thorney Island on 21 May, by which time we had six aircraft (XM411, XM413, XM423, XM425, XM426 and XM428) modified with a smoke generator under each wing. We did some thirty official displays that season, including the National Air Rally at Lorient in France and a week at the Farnborough air show, culminating with the Battle of Britain Days at Biggin Hill and Tangmere.

In October 1960, the team helped celebrate Nigerian independence when it flew to Lagos and carried out a series of displays, culminating in a final show for President Nkrumah at Accra Airport on 6 October. The team returned home on 19 October and completed one more display for HM the Queen Mother, before disbanding.

For the 1961 season, the CFS Jet Provost aerobatic display team was led by Flt Lt Frank Brambley. The manufacturers had fitted the team's six new aircraft (XN512, XN549, XN550, XN554, XN557 and XN573) with a full smoke generator system to provide the team with coloured smoke during its display and were delivered in March. The team quickly began working up for its first

39. The second CFS Jet Provost formation display team was formed in January 1960. The team's Mk.3s are depicted in box four formation over the Gloucestershire countryside the following July. (via Ray Deacon)

fogged the tower. The formation was subsequently banned for the rest of the week. We completed our last show at Shoreham on 22 September.

The 1963 season began in January when CFS instructors were asked to volunteer for the aerobatic team. Although it was first thought that there would be six pilots – five for the team and one reserve, together with nine aircraft modified with smoke installations, it was eventually decided that it would be a six-man team with no reserve. Led by the previous year's deputy, Flt Lt Ian Bashall, the team's nine aircraft – XP549 to XP554 and XP571 to XP573 – were also painted in a new all-over Day-glo orange colour scheme by Hunting Percival and became known as 'The Red Pelicans, 1963'. Thirty-three shows were flown by the team, which included a trip to France on 21 July to take part in a four-hour air display at Lyon/Brice, organised by Meetings Nationaux de l'Air. Described as a "presentation of Service aerobatic teams of the NATO countries", the event was held in front of 50,000 spectators and included contributions by teams from France, Italy and Belgium. The Jet Provost team was later presented with the coveted Coupe Shell Berre trophy for its fine display.

By the end of the 1963 season, the Air Ministry had eventually decided that the English Electric Lightning fighters which formed the current Fighter Command display team were totally unsuitable for the type of aerobatics that an air display demanded. Faced with very little alternative as to a suitable replacement, the Red Pelicans became the RAF's premier aerobatic team for 1964, by default.

The 1964 team was led by Flt Lt Terry Lloyd and training for the season got off to an unfortunate start in March, when two aircraft (XP639 and XR670) collided during a practice session near Moreton-in-Marsh, forcing Flt Lt Dick Cox to eject. Cox was slightly injured as a result of the accident and did not return to the team, his place being taken by Flt Lt Eric Tilsley.

As the RAF's leading aerobatic team, the Red Pelicans' first official display was for the Wright Jubilee Trophy event at Little Rissington on 28 April, followed by its public debut at North Weald on 18 May. Two weeks

later, the team made its first overseas appearance at Stavanger/Sola, Norway, on 31 May, where it shared the display programme with two Lightnings of 111 Squadron, a Canberra from Wildenrath and a Valiant bomber from Wyton. High winds caused the cancellation of many items at the event, organised by the Norwegian Aero Club, but Terry Lloyd was determined to continue with the display and led the team through a series of formation changes, with each aircraft alternating red, white and blue smoke at various stages of the twelve-minute routine. The low run in 'mirror' formation by Flt Lt Herbert Lane, inverted above Flt Lt Brian Nice's aircraft, reportedly drew a collective gasp from the 25,000 crowd.

Further shows included the Royal Netherlands Aero Club show at Groningen/Eelde on 13 June, Exeter on 20 June, the Royal Observer Corps at RAF Ternhill on 21 June, followed by the Belgian Air Force Day at Brussels on 28 June. The French National Air Day at Metz on 5 July was a five-ship formation led, at short notice by Brian Nice as Terry Lloyd was unfit, and on 16 July it laid on a display for the Imperial Defence College at RAF Honington, before returning to the continent for a show at Chaumont at the end of the month.

The climax of the team's season was the SBAC Show at Farnborough in September, when it gave a series of synchronised displays with the RAF's first team of Gnat aircraft – the 'Yellowjacks' from 4 FTS, RAF Valley. **Terry Lloyd:**

> Since the time allotted for the RAF participation at the 1964 SBAC display was severely limited it was decided that the Red Pelicans and the No.4 FTS Gnat Team (the Yellowjacks) should combine to represent the RAF in a display of co-ordinated aerobatics at Farnborough. In preparation for the combined show we went to Valley from 7 to 21 August 1964. The differing performance and manoeuvrability of the two aircraft had to be carefully considered: the Gnat used more height in both looping and rolling manoeuvres than the Jet Provost but with their higher speed the Gnats were able to spend less time in wing-overs and repositioning. Initially the team leaders flew sorties to assess how

to overcome the problems. The work up began and, by trial and error, it became obvious that it was essential that both teams commenced the display from a common datum point. Thus after individual formation take-offs by both teams a combined formation with the Gnats leading the Jet Provosts was decided upon. On arrival the two formations split and commenced the show with both leaders varying the time and distance flown in wing-overs to ensure that their teams were correctly positioned for each manoeuvre. With practice the teams were able to achieve a maximum of seven to ten seconds between consecutive display manoeuvres.

Ideally the most impressive finale to the display would have been a pull-up by the Red Pelicans for a bomb burst, with the Yellowjacks pulling up through the stem of the Red Pelicans' smoke followed by their split. Unfortunately this was not possible, as allowance had to be made for the six Lightnings of

40-41

92 Squadron to fly through just prior to the ending of the co-ordinated display. Both teams therefore carried out their individual finale to the display with the Yellowjacks completing a looping break after the Red Pelicans' bomb-burst. This was followed by a Gnat stream landing and a 'Delta' six-plane formation landing by the Red Pelicans.

40. The routine of the Red Pelicans team at the Farnborough show in 1964 included a synchronised display with the Gnat aircraft of No.4 FTS, the Yellowjacks. (Ray Deacon)

41. Members of the RAF's premier aerobatic team in 1964: Flt Lts Terry Lloyd, Brian Nice, Dennis Southern, Bill Langworthy, Eric Tilsley and Herbert Lane. (via Terry Lloyd)

The success of the Yellowjacks and the subsequent formation of the RAF Aerobatic Team – the Red Arrows – in 1965, found the CFS without an official Jet Provost display team; the Red Pelicans having stepped down as the premier team at the end of the season.

Although the Red Arrows had replaced the Jet Provost team at Little Rissington, it was left to four enthusiastic volunteers, led by Bill Langworthy, to convince the authorities of the need to form a second team. **Roy Booth** recalls the team:

> The 1965 team was a very curious affair, officially approved but disapproved of by some of the 'wheels' at Little Rissington. We were the only team denied the use of the Red Pelicans title and maybe we should have called ourselves 'The Not The Red Pelicans'.
>
> When the Red Pelicans disbanded at the end of the summer of 1964, Bill Langworthy campaigned to form a four-ship team using the red Jet Provost T Mk.4s, now part of the 1 Squadron fleet, for which he met considerable resistance. However, although we could fly the red Jet Provosts, we were forbidden to call ourselves the Red Pelicans. We were never given a reason, so we were called 'The 1965 CFS Jet Provost Aerobatic Team'. The Red Pelicans title was restored for the 1966 and subsequent seasons. So 1965 was the only year that the Red Pelicans did not officially exist. 1 Squadron's generic call sign was 'Tango' so we called ourselves 'Tango Red'.

By early 1966 the Red Pelicans had relinquished its six, older aircraft in favour of a batch of new Jet Provosts (four aircraft drawn from XS212, XS213, XS217, XS222, XS225, XS226, XS229 and XN468) finished in the new, Signal Red colour scheme, the first of which was delivered from re-spray at Kemble in April. Leader of the team was the CFI, Wg Cdr Eddie Edmonds, a former Meteor display pilot, and the season began with a show at Staverton on 23 April 1966; the Red Pelicans gave twenty-five displays that season, including two in Germany.

Sqn Ldr 'Curly' Hirst returned to the CFS in January 1966 and assumed the leadership of the Jet Provost team

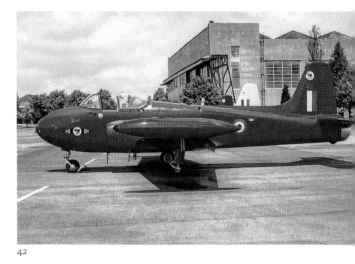

42

the following autumn. The other team members of the 1967 team were Flt Lts Derek Smith, Malcolm Lovett and Captain Jack Snow USAF. A very busy season of twenty-three scheduled shows began on 22 April 1967 with a display at Stradishall for the Cooper Trophy, followed by the Biggin Hill Air Fair and the US Armed Forces Day at Alconbury in May. The team also displayed at Istres and Orléans in France and Koksijde in Belgium before giving its last show at South Cerney on 20 October.

Flt Lt Derek Smith was appointed as team leader for the 1968 season. Flt Lt Malcolm Lovett stayed on as No.3 from the previous year and was joined by Flt Lts John Robinson as No.2 and John Blake as No.4. The team flew the all-red Jet Provost T Mk.4s. During the pre-season work up there was an unfortunate accident on 26 February when two aircraft collided during a practice formation sortie over the Cotswolds. Both Derek Smith and his passenger were able to safely abandon the aircraft (XS229) near Guiting Power, while the other aircraft flown by John Blake (XP675) was fortunate to return to base. The CFS commandant's comments were that "one couldn't make an omelette without breaking some eggs" and the team were cleared to continue practising, albeit without the manoeuvre that had caused the accident. The weather that year was particularly unfavourable and restricted the team to twenty-three displays, beginning with the Skyfame Museum show at Staverton on 31 March.

For the 1969 season the Red Pelicans featured a new line-up, with Sqn Ldr John Robinson taking over the lead, Flt Lts Tony Davies as No.2, Richard Mackenzie-Crooks as No.3 and Rod Clayton as No.4. The red Jet Provost T Mk.4s were retained and the team's first show was for the British Air Ferries air display at Lydd airport in Kent, on 6 April. On 24 May, an estimated crowd of 65,000 people flocked to the USAF Armed Forces open day at Wethersfield, causing a traffic jam of over five miles. Braving the elements, the Jet Provost team was fortunate to lay on its display before a violent afternoon thunderstorm caused the event to be abandoned.

Included in the twenty-three displays laid on during the 1969 season, the team flew five displays for visiting dignitaries; the highlight being the visit of HRH the Queen, HM the Queen Mother who was commandant-in-chief to the CFS, HRH the Duke of Edinburgh and HRH the Prince of Wales to Little Rissington on 26 June for presentation of the Queen's Colours to the CFS. This was celebrated with a range of static exhibitions and aerobatic displays by the Red Arrows, Red Pelicans and the Tomahawks. Operating out of Kemble for the visit, the Jet Provost team narrowly avoided abandoning its show when the programme overran its schedule and the aircraft almost ran out of fuel. **Rod Clayton:**

> We displayed for HM the Queen and the other royals. The weather was poor on the day with a low cloud base and I think that either the Arrows did not display or were curtailed to a 'flat display' whilst we were able, according to my logbook, to do a full display. (I think we may have inched in a bit into our 500-foot base height!) I remember orbiting Stow-on-the-Wold for what seemed hours; apparently, the Duke and Prince of Wales got very interested in the static display and this caused the huge time slippage; I think our display that day was done with virtually no fuel to spare. John Robinson did a great job to carry it off. By the way, in addition to presenting CFS with new colours, the Queen Mother said that the CFS theme tune

43

would be, from then on *Those Magnificent Men in their Flying Machines.*

On 5 October 1969 the team flew to Germany for a show at Jesenwang Airport, near Munich, which would be its last display with the Jet Provost T Mk.4. A month earlier, in September 1969, the first of a new batch of pressurised Jet Provost T Mk.5s had been delivered to the CFS and issued to the Red Pelicans in readiness for the 1970 season. As the aircraft were part of the CFS fleet, they wore the standard training colour scheme of red, white and grey, the team's only concession being the addition of a Pelican motif in red on the fin and its title on the rear fuselage.

Sqn Ldr Eric Evers was appointed to lead the 1970 team. He had previously been a member of the No.3 FTS Jet Provost team at Leeming for two seasons before returning to the CFS as deputy chief instructor.

> The team comprised Terry Francis (No.2), John Davy (No.3), Ken Tait (No.4) and Rod Brown who flew the spare aircraft to overseas shows and also commentated during the displays. We flew twenty-three shows that year, beginning with our first public display at Blackbushe airfield on 25 May 1970. The Jet Provost 5 was not fitted with smoke-making equipment and my own view was that it was certainly

42. Depicted in its new signal red colour scheme soon after its arrival at Little Rissington in May 1966, Jet Provost T Mk.4, XS225, was one of a batch of replacement aircraft for use by the CFS display team, the Red Pelicans. (Ray Deacon)

43. Jet Provost T Mk.5s of the CFS display team, the Red Pelicans, during 1971, led by Flt Lt Terry Francis. The formation pair includes XW287, the first Mk.5 to be delivered to the CFS. (Dave Newham via Ray Deacon)

better for formation aerobatics than the earlier marks. The rest of the team were all new to formation aerobatics so the Mk.5 was all they knew. In selecting the team members you can imagine the excitement I had giving dual instruction to the numerous volunteers for the 1970 team, all of whom had never tried it before. Many were disappointed, including a USAF captain whose wife never forgave me but I believe that we finished up with the right team on merit. The team's routine was the same as that of the 1969 team.

In July 1971, HM the Queen Mother visited Little Rissington once again in her capacity as honorary commandant and was entertained to displays by two of the school's teams – the Red Pelicans and Red Arrows. Formed the previous February, the Jet Provost team was led by Flt Lt Terry Francis and included Flt Lts Bruce Donnelly, Peter Langham and Robert Lewis. In its full display season the team also performed at Upper Heyford, Staverton, Exeter, St Athan, St Mawgan and Little Rissington. Leader of the 1972 team was Flt Lt Clive Mitchell, who had flown with the Cranwell Poachers the previous year. He was joined by Flt Lt Bob Lewis from the 1971 CFS team, Flt Lt Peter Tait and Captain Dick Lord, USAF, all of whom were flying instructors on the Little Rissington 'Waterfront'. **Clive Mitchell:**

> In January 1972 I was selected to lead the team for the forthcoming season. I can't remember why but there was a delay in our being allowed to start to practise as a four-ship until the very end of March. From then on we flew sixteen sorties at 5,000 feet, seven at 1,500 feet before being cleared to 500 feet, our display minimum height ready for our first display on 20 May.
>
> We flew at twenty-nine display venues in the UK, Germany, Belgium and Italy. During the season I was promoted to squadron leader on 1 July and left for the MoD just after Christmas. During the last couple of months at Little Rissington I was involved in the fly-offs for the next year's team that was to be led by Ivor Gibbs.

The 1973 team line-up comprised Sqn Ldr Ivor Gibbs, Captain Dick Lord, USAF, as No.2, Flt Lt Bruce Byron, RAAF (who would later lead the RAAF aerobatic team, the Roulettes, flying MB-326Hs at East Sale, Victoria) as No.3 and Lt Marcus Edwards, RN, as No.4; the manager of the 'international' team was Flt Lt Adrian Wall. Despite the restrictions imposed by the fuel crisis, which made everyone mindful of operating costs, the team carried out a creditable fifty-one displays during the season, including seven on the Continent. With shows at Staverton, Middle Wallop, Silverstone, Greenham Common, Cranfield and Yeovilton, the team's final performance was at Linkenheim near Karlsruhe, Germany, on 23 September 1973, following which the Red Pelicans was disbanded as part of the government's economy measures.

RAF COLLEGE CRANWELL

The Royal Air Force College was established in 1919 to provide basic and flying training for the future leaders of the Royal Air Force and was the entry point for all those who wished to become permanent officers in the RAF. Initially the courses lasted two years, but by the 1950s this had expanded to three. Prior to the introduction of the Jet Provost, all flying training took place at the College: basic training on Percival Provosts and advanced training on either de Havilland Vampires or Gloster Meteors.

The first Jet Provost T Mk.3s arrived at Cranwell in June 1960, with No.81 Entry becoming the first to receive basic training on the aircraft the following September. Coinciding with the arrival of 81 Entry, the academic syllabus was improved to allow cadets to gain degrees in humanities, or AFRAeS. To achieve this within the three-year course, only basic training was carried out at Cranwell on the new Jet Provost Mks.3 and 4. On 31 July 1962, the first batch of Jet Provost-trained cadets graduated with their Wings at Cranwell, progressing to advanced flying courses at either RAF Oakington or RAF Valley.

44

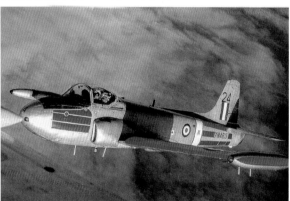

45

46

Rod Brown received his flying training with No.82 Entry.

The first year was taken up by general service training and academics and the occasional flying in the Chipmunk (about five hours). We began basic flying training during the second and third years, which included ground school and flying the Jet Provost 3 and the Jet Provost 4 (about eighty hours), academics and some general service training.

In June 1968, thirty-one instructors flew a formation fly-past over the College in the shape of the royal cipher as part of the celebrations for the RAF's 50th birthday. The following month, twenty of the College's Jet Provost T Mk.4s flew in formation over the Farnborough air show, led by the CFI, Wg Cdr J. M. A. Parker. One of the pilots taking part was **Bob Screen.**

44. Following the delivery of the first Jet Provost T Mk.3s to Cranwell in 1961, the RAF College used them to provide fly-pasts at graduation ceremonies. This image depicts one of a handful of informal College teams produced during this period before the formation of the Cranwell Poachers. The pilots of this particular formation were drawn from Flt Lts J. R. Lees, D. J. Hine, Master Pilot F. Bright and Flt Lt A. R. Pollock (BAe Systems Heritage Warton-Percival/Hunting Collection)

45. Jet Provost T Mk.3, XM463:24, of the RAF College, Cranwell in 1968. It was later modified as a T Mk.3A and presented to the RAF Museum in 1991. (Sqn Ldr Dick Bell)

46. Publicity photograph of Jet Provost T Mk.3s from the RAF College dispersed at Cranwell's satellite airfield, Barkston Heath, ca. 1961. The third aircraft in the line-up was written off in August 1962 when it spun into the ground at Girton, Cambs, during company trials. (Cranwell Archives)

The twenty-ship formation was to commemorate the 50th anniversary of the formation of the RAF. We practised over the RAF College on 3 September and then flew the '50' over Farnborough on 20, 21 and 22 September. I was in XR673 and I think we operated out of Lyneham.

Also in 1968, it was decided that all future permanent commission officers would be university educated and graduates would attend Cranwell after their studies for one year of officer training. Pre-entry training for candidates for the graduate entry scheme (GES) took place in university air squadrons and pilot training was carried out in three stages – primary, basic and advanced. The primary stage, for those who had not served in a UAS, took place at the primary flying school at RAF Church Fenton, and was a short course on the Chipmunk designed to introduce the student to the elementary arts of flying. It also served to eliminate those who, in their early air work, demonstrated that they did not have the aptitude to make the grade as Service pilots. The second, or basic, stage of pilot training was carried out on the Jet Provost at Linton-on-Ouse, Leeming and Cranwell. When they had successfully completed the basic stage of their training the students were awarded their Wings.

No.1 Graduate Entry (GE) arrived on 1 September 1970, and between that date and 16 August 1974, fourteen GE courses were trained at Cranwell. **Nick Rusling** was a member of No.2 GE between March and September 1971.

The graduate entry was very different from the three-year Cranwell cadet entry. The GE lasted about nine months and comprised three months of officer training and six months of flying training leading to Wings. I flew about 200 hours on the Chipmunk, of which one-third was as captain, both out of RAF Ouston when I was on Northumbrian University Air Squadron whilst I was at Durham University and out of White Waltham on London University Air Squadron when I was at King's College, London. I didn't have a PPL, but as a result

of the Chipmunk flying I had a preliminary flying badge (PFB). At Cranwell I flew a total of 125 hours of which forty was as captain, following which I was posted to Valley to fly the Gnat.

John Robinson was promoted to squadron leader and posted to Cranwell in August 1970 as OC Headquarters Squadron. He first had to undertake the Junior Command and Staff Course, eventually arriving at the College in mid-October.

Cranwell was one of the last training units to get the Jet Provost Mk.5 and it fell to me to start collecting them from Warton and then check out the staff. I collected the first aircraft, XW336, from Warton on 17 December 1970.

On one of the delivery flights I did a low-level aerobatic display on arrival at Cranwell for graduating students' parents and friends, and afterwards I learnt from Engineering Wing that my ejection seat would not have worked as someone at Warton had not connected it up properly!

I had no handover for my post as my predecessor and good friend, Sqn Ldr Bill Jago, had already left on his posting. Complications came with the advent of the graduate entry scheme which was being adopted to replace the time-honoured flight cadet system for which the RAF was famous and had provided air ranking officers and commanders for the RAF for many years. The first GE course ran from 8 March to 20 August 1971 and included one eminent student, HRH the Prince of Wales. The GE students were all graduates from a university and had flown with the associated UAS and their flying course was suitably reduced. Their total time at Cranwell was ten months whereas the flight cadets' course was three years with only the last year devoted to the flying. There was an overlap of three years when both flight cadets and graduate entrants were in residence at the College with the last cadet entry, 101, graduating on 16 March 1973.

In April 1976 the CFS was transferred to Cranwell following the closure of Little Rissington and pooled its aircraft with the RAF College. This, however, would prove to be a temporary expedient due to the lack of space at Cranwell and the incompatibility of fitting instructor training with student flying in quite a small circuit, and in September 1977, the CFS echelon moved, once again, to Leeming.

Two months earlier, on 29 July 1977, the College had been privileged to mark HM the Queen's Silver Jubilee celebrations at RAF Finningley when twenty-two Jet Provost T Mk.5As drawn from No.1 FTS, Linton-on-Ouse, and RAF Cranwell staged a combined fly-past over the royal dais. **Flt Lt Art Stacey** was a QFI at Cranwell from February 1976 to June 1981.

I was in the 'Symbolic 25' for the Queen's Silver Jubilee fly-past in July 1977. The overall formation leader was Wg Cdr John Lewis, Cranwell's chief instructor, and consisted of two parts: the '2' (eleven aircraft) was flown by instructors from 1 FTS Linton-on-Ouse and the '5' (also eleven aircraft) by instructors from the RAF College Cranwell. Each aircraft had two pilots to allow for any redundancy making a total of forty-three pilots. The 44th member was the station navigation officer from Cranwell who was responsible for navigating the whole formation and on one occasion he set his watch incorrectly which resulted in the whole formation being one minute late at one of the rehearsals!

The fly-past was a great example of organisation and timing, and the participating formations were brought by various routes until they reached the initial point, near Goole, at the start of the twenty-five-mile long display corridor which ended at Worksop.

We had one rehearsal of the '5' at Cranwell on 9 June then flew up to Linton for full formation practices on 7 July before the fly-past for Her Majesty at RAF Finningley on 29 July and a repeat for the public the following day.

With the departure of the CFS from Cranwell, student flying training at the College underwent further radical changes in December 1978 with the introduction of the direct entry scheme; the first course to begin training under the scheme being initial officer training (IOT) No.34 Course. Subsequent courses included university cadet graduates (UCG), graduate direct entrants (GDE), non-graduate direct entrants (NGDE) and ex-serving airmen; DE courses ran concurrently with the GE courses but flew the Jet Provost T Mk.3A. This increase in the training commitment resulted in an additional twenty-four Jet Provost T Mk.3As and T Mk.5As being delivered to the College during this period. **Michael Napier** joined 34 Basic Flying Training Course at RAF College Cranwell at the beginning of May 1982.

The whole initial officer training (IOT)/basic flying training school (BFTS) system underwent a massive change in January 1978. Prior to that graduates entered the RAF under the graduate entry scheme, which involved a short (but physically tough) IOT course at Cranwell after which those who had achieved Cranwell entry standard (CES) on a university air squadron continued to do a short (nominally 100 hours) BFTS course on the Jet Provost T Mk.5 at Cranwell. Meanwhile, non-graduate direct entrants did a longer IOT course at Henlow and then (along with graduates who had not reached CES) went on to the long BFTS course on the JP3/JP5 at the Vale of York FTSs. In 1980, the IOT courses at Henlow

47. On 29 July 1977, the Silver Jubilee Review of the RAF at Finningley was marked by a mass fly-past of twenty-two Jet Provosts drawn from the RAF College and No.1 FTS. (Steve Carr)

were completed on a common course at Cranwell and the flying training students were then spread across all three of the flying training schools.

After IOT student pilots were either sent directly to the flying training schools (if they had previous flying experience) or to the flying selection squadron at Swinderby if they had not. Theoretically, ex-UAS students who had achieved the Cranwell entry standard were sent to Cranwell, while the rest were divided between 1 FTS at Linton-on-Ouse and 7 FTS at Church Fenton. In practice there was a bit of mixing and there were a number of direct entrants at Cranwell. Cranwell was equipped exclusively with the Jet Provost T Mk.5A (or JP5A as we knew it), whereas the Yorkshire FTSs had the JP Mk.3A for the basic phase and the JP Mk.5A for the advanced phase of the course.

In my time (1982-83) 32 Course (3 Squadron) and 33 Course (1 Squadron) were all ex-UAS graduates who were commissioned from 56 IOT course, while 34 Course (2 Squadron) was made up from a mixture of ex-UAS graduates commissioned on 57 IOT and 58 IOT (the latter, including me, being re-coursees from 56 IOT) and a handful of direct-entry FSS students from 57 IOT.

My first flight at Cranwell was on 17 May 1982 – a 'familiarisation flight', which was really just a 'free' look-see. In comparison to the Bulldog, which I'd flown previously on the UAS, the JP5A was a large and solid machine. We sat in bulky (but not particularly comfortable) ejection seats in a relatively roomy cockpit which afforded a good lookout. The JP5A was fully pressurised, so it boasted an electrically powered canopy (one had to hand-crank the canopy on earlier marks!) which made it seem incredibly modern and sophisticated. That was about the level of sophistication, though, as the black-painted cockpit looked distinctly archaic. The cockpit was divided by a centre console which carried the instructor's throttle (the student, in the left-hand seat had another throttle on the left-hand console) and (if I remember correctly) the flap lever and the HP fuel cock. The flight instruments were

in front of the student, but the standby artificial horizon – actually a FH32 attitude indicator – was more central. Although it was supposedly the 'standby instrument' it was actually very much better than the primary artificial horizon.

The JP5A was relatively well-powered: it climbed reasonably well and seemed to have a comfortable margin of power in the circuit. That was not the case in the JP3: I recall our hilarity when I refreshed at Linton on hearing a tannoy message that JP3 wing-tip tanks were not to be filled because the weather was too hot. In fact the JP3 was known to be a 'variable noise, constant thrust' machine and was somewhat gutless.

The Cranwell course was divided into a basic phase common to all students, followed about two-thirds of the way through by an advanced phase in which fast jet (Group 1), multi-engine (Group 2) or helicopter (Group 3) students flew differing syllabuses tailored for their generic aircraft type.

I completed the basic phase and continued to the Group 1 Phase 1 advanced phase [Group 1 Phase 2 was the Valley AFTS course]. This part of the course covered mixed profile (i.e. hi-lo-hi) navigation, close formation and low-level navigation, culminating in a final navigation test and then a final handling test on 12 May 1983 (which covered everything learnt in the previous year). I finished the course having flown 140 hours, including nearly seven hours at night and thirty-five hours of instrument flying. Of my total, forty hours were flown solo.

The Jet Provost itself handled OK, but it did have quite high control forces and I did not find it a particularly responsive aeroplane. The view was pretty good outside and it gave a solid ride at low level. It was solid in the circuit, with – if I remember correctly – an approach speed somewhere near ninety-five knots. It would aerobat OK and was one of the few jet aircraft that could be stall turned. Most jet engines surge when exposed to large rates of yaw, but the JP's Viper engine did not. The JP was OK in formation, although it didn't have a lot of excess power and looking across the cockpit made flying number three in close formation seem like very hard work.

On 1 February 1989 the College's flying element became No.3 FTS and the delivery of the first Short Tucano T MK.1 to Cranwell in June 1991 heralded the replacement of the Jet Provost as a basic training aircraft. With the graduation of No.88 Course on 11 October 1991 and the imminent withdrawal of the Jet Provost from the College, the occasion was marked with a fly-past of Jet Provosts in a diamond nine formation over Cranwell. The last College Jet Provost was transferred to No.1 FTS, Linton-on-Ouse, in December 1991.

'GOLDEN EAGLE FLIGHT' In March 1971, HRH Charles, Prince of Wales arrived at the College to begin his five-month flying training course, with the rank of flight lieutenant. The Prince of Wales had previously flown Chipmunk and Basset aircraft before arriving at Cranwell and joined the first graduate entry there, consisting entirely of post-graduates who had already received preliminary pilot training and advanced instruction on Jet Provosts. Two Jet Provosts, XW322 and 323 – codenamed 'Golden Eagle Flight' – were allocated for the prince during his four-month course and maintained by a team of fifteen ground crew; both aircraft featuring the royal (Prince of Wales) cipher on the engine intakes. Two experienced flying instructors were also assigned to supervise his training – Sqn Ldrs Dick Johns and John Robinson – during which he flew

just over 92 hours, 23½ of them solo. He passed his final handling test on 8 July 1971 and was awarded his Wings from Air Chf Msl Sir Denis Spotswood, chief of the Air Staff, at the passing out parade from Cranwell. **John Robinson:**

While the new aircraft programme was happening, the Golden Eagle project to train HRH the Prince of Wales was being launched [he joined No.1 GE on 8 March 1971] and I was tasked as the deputy QFI. The primary QFI was Sqn Ldr R. E. 'Dick' Johns, who ultimately became a chief of Air Staff. Both the 'Golden Eagle' Jet Provost Mk.5s, XW322 and 323, arrived at Cranwell on 15 December and 11 December, respectively. They had been specially built at Warton, which each night were locked under guard in a hangar, and our own ground crew. There was no such thing as 'ground tested and found serviceable' as any item that was put unserviceable in the aircraft technical log had to be investigated and cleared. On the acceptance air tests for each aircraft I had to flame-out the engine, allow it to cold soak for a period and then relight it; I chose my days and position carefully for this. The work up on the two aircraft involved some 200 hours flying each. We also had to check out a navigator who would 'ghost' Prince Charles on certain solo flights.

Prince Charles had already some flying experience as he flew Chipmunks while at Cambridge University and then moved on to the Beagle Bassett, a light twin piston-engined communications aircraft. I first flew with Prince Charles on 29 April 1971 and took my turn throughout his training, which covered all aspects from the standard student pilot syllabus. All his training flights were operated in a specific airspace over Lincolnshire and monitored by a radar controller based at

48. On 15 May 1971, Flt Lt HRH the Prince of Wales and his primary QFI, Sqn Ldr R. E. 'Dick' Johns, flew a batch of first day covers to mark the 30th anniversary of the first jet flight at Cranwell. (Author's Collection)

Northern Radar at RAF Lindholme. I flew with him to Little Rissington for the annual CFS Association Reunion on 9 July when he was guest of honour. Prince Charles graduated with 1 GES on 20 August 1971 when he was presented with his Wings.

At the beginning of September 1972 we learnt that Prince Charles was returning to Cranwell for a refresher course. Dick Johns had been posted so it was left to me to get organised. I collected the two Golden Eagle Jet Provost T Mk.5s from the maintenance unit at Kemble (on 25 September and 27 September) and the previous security arrangements were re-established. Prince Charles was also to fly in a Hawker Hunter at RAF Valley and Peter Squire was to be the QFI. Prince Charles had his first refresher flight on 23 October and after three days flying we flew to Valley for his Hunter flight. One of the Golden Eagle Jet Provost T Mk.5s, XW 323, was presented to the RAF Museum at Hendon as a permanent exhibition on 17 December 1992.

RAF COLLEGE DISPLAY TEAMS The arrival of the first Jet Provost T Mk.3s in November 1960 and the reorganisation of the College's flying training programme to accommodate the new, all-through scheme found its Vampire trainers being finally withdrawn by March 1962.

Between 1956 and 1961, the College had produced a number of Vampire display teams and the Jet Provost also proved suitable for formation aerobatics. Although there had been a handful of unofficial Jet Provost 'teams' operating or working up at Cranwell between 1961 and 1962, the first formal College Jet Provost team appeared in the late summer of 1963, led by Sqn Ldr Iain Panton. By November the team had adopted the name – The Poachers – which had been coined from the College's official march, *The Lincolnshire Poacher,* by team member, Flt Lt Hugh Mayes, and gave its first official display for the graduation of No.84 Entry on 17 December 1963. **Iain Panton:**

Over the years, Flying Wing at Cranwell had formed many aerobatic teams to show the flag to visitors and to take part in graduation day flying displays. During the summer term of 1963, 2 Squadron had the privilege of providing the team. The team, which coined its present title and used it as its r/t call sign, comprised one squadron commander, two flight commanders and one QFI, who was also a part-time College flight commander.

The Poachers were limited to four aircraft and the team resisted the temptation to include too many changes in formation in case it bewildered the spectators – quite apart from creating the impression that the leader could not make up his mind!

By late 1965 the original members of the Poachers were posted and the next College team was formed by the CFI, Wg Cdr John Parker, who arrived at Cranwell in August 1967 and selected Flt Lts Bill Jago, Ted Hudson and Pakistani exchange officer, Flt Lt Bahar-ul-haq as fellow members. The team's first display was at Cranwell on 8 June 1968 and its Jet Provosts were finished in the standard red, white and grey colour scheme, with the College light blue bands around the rear fuselage and the stylised name 'Cranwell Poachers' later added in white on the wing-tip tanks.

In October 1968 Wg Cdr John Parker reluctantly gave up the leadership of the team and passed the command to Flt Lt Bill Jago with the suggestion that it assumed a greater display commitment, including appearances at international events. With this in mind, **Bill Jago** carefully selected three members from the available QFIs to make up his team.

I chose Bob Screen, Rod Harrison and Geoff Timms, all ex-fighter pilots who had completed an operational tour on Hunters. We had our final check-out by the commandant in April 1969 and our first display was at Jurby, Isle of Man, on 26 April 1969, followed by two displays at American Armed Forces Days. Our first overseas display was at Balen in Belgium on 8 June, for which we had 'Cranwell Poachers' painted on the wing-tip tanks. Generally we did shows in the UK. We also did shows at Brilon and Werdohl Flying Clubs in Germany, and completed the season with a show at Biggin Hill on 20 September. We always made the effort to try and land at the display airfield to increase the feeling of involvement with the team. Not only did it give a possible recruit a chance to have a closer look at the aircraft he may fly or service, it also did our egos good to sign masses of autographs; at one time, I believe that my going rate was down to fifty Jagos for one Ray Hanna!

One of the many highlights of the 1969 display season was an appearance at the RAFA show at Woodford on 28 June, when the team was brought in as a last-minute replacement for the Red Arrows. The immaculate twenty-five-minute performance by the four Jet Provosts earned the Cranwell team a big round of applause from the crowd of 75,000 spectators attending the event.

Sqn Ldr John Robinson had previously flown as No.2 with the CFS Red Pelicans in 1968 and was appointed as its leader, the following year. He was subsequently posted to the RAF College as OC HQ Sqn, successfully leading the Poachers between 1971 and 1973.

John Robinson's command of the team also coincided with the arrival of the first Jet Provost T Mk.5 at Cranwell in December 1970. He took a close interest in the new colour scheme for the team aircraft, which had been designed by the College's PR department. The aircraft were finished in an attractive paint scheme comprising a white triangle under the nose, upon which were four small red triangles representing aircraft. From these, three pale blue bands extended, one along the centre of the fuselage and the others curving upwards to the fin. Individual letters were applied to the fin and the team's new name, the Poachers (the name 'Cranwell' being dropped) appeared on the sides of the aircraft. Subsequent variations to the scheme would include the curving blue band being extended to the rudder in 1972. Twelve aircraft were eventually painted in this striking colour scheme.

The first show of the season usually began in May but the continuing demand for the Cranwell team to attend air shows often took the display season into October. The 1971 team was made up of Flt Lts Daz James No.2 (ex-Hunters), Ian Macfadyen No.3 and Clive Mitchell No.4 (both ex-Lightnings) and took part in twenty-nine air shows during the season, beginning with a display at Liverpool/Speke airport on 1 May.

A total of thirty-two displays were flown during the 1972 season, which began on 29 April. There followed a very active programme of overseas displays being flown at Wildenrath, Greven, Zwartberg, Dortmund, Auf dem Dümpel, Meschede, Butzweilerhof and Bremgarten all in Germany and spaced from May to October.

The Poachers display team was officially reformed in March 1975 (see p.36) with Flt Lts Eddie Danks, Martin Stoner and Dave Webley joining Sqn Ldr Peter Curtin. The team's Jet Provost T Mk.5As were also repainted with a large red sunburst design on the white wings and tailplanes; the distinctive colour scheme giving an instant indication as to the aircraft's position.

With the posting of Eddie Danks in November 1975, the slightly revised line-up of the Poachers for the 1976 season included Sqn Ldr Peter Curtin, Flt Lts Martin Stoner, Dave Webley and Philip Boreham. In a summer blessed with glorious weather, the season began on 23 May with the Shropshire Aero Club display at Sleap, followed by a further twenty-eight shows which included Blackpool, Woodford, Halton, Exeter, Mildenhall, Bentwaters, Folkestone, Goodwood, and the Battle of Britain celebrations at Finningley and Leuchars.

Above: XM384 was delivered to No.2 FTS, RAF Syerston, in
January 1960. It was written off in a mid-air collision with
another Jet Provost during a formation aerobatic practice in
May 1966. (HAL via Terry Lloyd)

03 FLYING TRAINING SCHOOLS AND THEIR DISPLAY TEAMS

No.1 FLYING TRAINING SCHOOL

No.1 FTS was reformed at RAF Syerston in May 1955, equipped with Percival Provost T Mk.1s and responsible for basic flying training for Royal Navy and Royal Naval Volunteer Reserve pilots before they progressed to RAF Valley for advanced jet training.

In November 1957 the school moved to RAF Linton-on-Ouse and continued to provide initial flying training for all prospective Fleet Air Arm pilots, with the basic squadron flying Piston Provosts and the advanced squadron equipped with Vampire T MK.11s. The students graduated from Linton and transferred to either RNAS Lossiemouth (Sea Hawks) or RNAS Yeovilton (Sea Venoms and Sea Vixens) for operational training.

The school's first Jet Provost T Mk.3 was delivered in August 1960 and training began in October with No.93 Course, a mixed Piston Provost/Jet Provost course. Having reached its full complement of Jet Provosts in February 1961, the school's Piston Provosts were finally withdrawn by the following July. Unfortunately, two of its original Jet Provost aircraft were lost in quick succession during this period because of flying accidents: XM477 in March and XM469 in May 1961; both aircraft being replaced within weeks by new aircraft from No.27 MU, coinciding with the delivery of the first Jet Provost T Mk.4s in April.

Among the naval officers to receive basic flying training on the Jet Provost at Linton was **Bruce Hutton,** a student with 102 Fixed Wing Course between January 1962 and February 1963.

> The Jet Provost Mk.3 was a real workhorse and a great introduction to the world of fast jets. The Jet Provost Mk.4 was just coming into service at this time, and within a few weeks they would eventually replace the Jet Provost Mk.3s. We just flew them a couple of times dual whilst the instructors were evaluating them.
>
> Twenty-two guys started on No.102 and No.103 Courses in January 1962 and these were eventually combined as people were 'washed out'. I think nine of us eventually received our Wings.

The whole fourteen-month course at Linton comprised Jet Provost and Vampire flying up to Wings. I made my first flight in a Jet Provost (XN501) on 24 January 1962 and flew about 120 hours before progressing to the advanced stage of the course in August. We then flew a further 100 hours on the Vampire and graduated from Linton on 23 February 1963.

The fixed-wing pilots were then posted back to the navy at Lossiemouth at the beginning of March to convert on to the Hunter and then, for me, the Scimitar.

On 13 October 1964, the graduation of No.9 (Linton) Course marked the official end of advanced flying training for RAF students on Vampire trainers at Linton-on-Ouse. The previous March, No.8 FTS at Swinderby had been disbanded, leaving No.1 FTS at Linton-on-Ouse as the last Flying Training Command School to operate the type. With all naval fixed-wing training concentrated at Linton, the school ran courses for both the Jet Provost and Vampire; the RAF students having previously been awarded their Wings at the completion of their basic training.

Following his graduation on the Jet Provost at Leeming, **Bob Screen** transferred to No.1 FTS in July 1964 to complete his flying training with No.9 (Linton) Course.

> The Jet Provosts at Linton were used for the basic training for navy pilots whereas the Vampire was for RAF advanced training. There were eight pilots on No.9 (Linton) Advanced Training Course, all from basic training on the Jet Provost at Leeming and were sent to the Vampire because of the backlog on the Gnat at Valley caused by accident(s) and unserviceability. We graduated from Linton in October 1964.

In January 1968, the school once again began to provide basic flying training for RAF students and the first entry graduated the following June. The school also trained small numbers of foreign and commonwealth students and **Mark Fielding** was the only

49

RAAF student pilot on No. 5 Course, which ran from April 1969 to March 1970.

I was in the UK on exchange with the Royal Air Force because the RAAF could not train sufficient pilots quickly enough to meet actual and expected demand for the war in Vietnam, in which I subsequently served. Three more RAAF students served at Linton on No.6 Course.

In late 1969 Chipmunk training was also transferred to RAF Church Fenton as the Royal Navy Elementary Flying Training Squadron and the basic training of naval fixed-wing pilots did not recommence until 1976, when three Royal Navy students completed the Jet Provost course at No.1 FTS and received their Wings later that year. The school also trained a handful of Singapore armed forces and Jordanian pilots during the period that I was there.

On 30 September 1969 a Jet Provost (XN575) of No.3 FTS, based at Leeming, crashed on take-off for reasons we were not told. The only person on board the Jet Provost was a student pilot with No.36 Course, Plt Off Chris Woolmer, who died as a result of ejecting outside the capabilities of the seat. Chris was the RAF student who met me at York railway station on my arrival from Australia.

On 14 June 1968, more than fifty different types of RAF aircraft were on show at Abingdon as part of the RAF's 50th anniversary celebrations. In one of its most comprehensive exhibitions before HM the Queen, the event also included thirty-one Jet Provosts drawn from Linton-on-Ouse, Syerston, Leeming and Acklington, which flew the Queen's cipher in formation over the Oxfordshire base. Leader of the Linton formation, Sqn Ldr Sidney Edwards, and thirteen of his QFIs had earlier flown to RAF Gaydon to rehearse for the event. The first practice formation was carried out on 10 June,

49. 'Sid's Mob'. Pilots from No.1 FTS, Linton-on-Ouse, which took part in the Royal Review fly-past at Abingdon, led by Sqn Ldr Sid Edwards, in June 1968. (via Steve Waddington)

followed by the complete formation the next day; No.1 FTS forming the 'E', Nos. 2 FTS and 3 FTS forming the 'II' and No.6 FTS forming the 'R'. The official formation fly-past was flown twice on 14 June; once for HM the Queen, followed by another for the general public.

Following the cancellation of the replacement fixed-wing aircraft carriers for the Royal Navy, the ab initio training of naval fixed-wing pilots came to an end at Linton on 31 July 1969 with the graduation of the last entry, comprising seven naval officers of No.142 Course; the event being marked with a fly-past of various formations of naval aircraft and a display by the Red Arrows aerobatic team. Their place at Linton was taken by RAF students and a small number of foreign and commonwealth students, while the training of naval helicopter pilots was transferred to Church Fenton.

The following December, No.1 FTS became the first to receive the Jet Provost T Mk.5 with the arrival of XW298 and XW299; the new aircraft completely replacing the school's Jet Provost T Mk.4s by July 1970. From that date, the Mk.3 and Mk.5 operated in conjunction at Linton, with the Mk.3 being used for the basic stage of the students' training and the Mk.5 for Group 1, Phase 1: 'Fast Jet Lead In', training students to progress to fly either the Gnat or Hawk.

On 18 March 1970, **Fg Off Steve Carr** became the first student to receive instruction on the Jet Provost Mk.5.

I was on No.8 Course, from September 1969 until September 1970. My first jet flight was in Jet Provost Mk 3, XM472, on 13 October 1969 with Flt Lt Marchant. My first jet solo was in Jet Provost Mk.3, XN508, at Elvington airfield near York on 30 October, launched off by Flt Lt Alick Nicholson, who, as was the norm then, remained my main instructor throughout the whole year of the basic flying training course. The next six months consisted of re-enforcing all the special handling techniques required when things go wrong. Sorties would include a normal departure, perhaps a navex and/or aerobatics but invariably conclude with a simulated engine failure or fire, a hydraulic/electrical/undercarriage/

flap/throttle failure. The emphasis was on knowing the published drills by heart, but at the same time recognising the specific unique aspects of each event and managing intelligently.

Then, on 18 March 1970, I became the first student to fly the new Jet Provost Mk.5 (XW297) with my instructor, Flt Lt Tim Allen. The experience was a quantum leap from what had gone before. Now we were capable of much faster speeds, more rapid control responses (aileron roll in the climb), and high altitudes where handling was quite different. Bubble canopy, shiny new interior with canted throttle, quiet and pressurised, we had now joined the 'big boys'.

The emphasis thereafter was on applied flying, making use of this enhanced performance to fly longer at low and high level, fly and navigate at night, and how to fly in formation. Flying solo for the first time in close formation in a smooth new jet banking over the Yorkshire countryside was a wonderful surreal experience never to be forgotten.

In November 1970 I flew in the Gnat T1 for the first time, starting the advanced course at RAF Valley. On completion, front-line postings were extremely limited, and I was among those sent to Canberra 'holding' tours. I actually loved flying the Canberra which is often rightly described as a 'Jet Provost on steroids'. Frustrated by the delays, I volunteered to become a QFI and in April 1975 I found myself back full circle as a Jet Provost instructor at Linton-on-Ouse.

To develop and maintain the highest possible standards of flying instruction, re-categorisation and upgrading of QFIs, a Standards squadron was an important element of each flying training school. **Flt Lt Tim Allen** was a QFI at Linton-on-Ouse between September 1968 and June 1970.

All the flying training schools had a Standards squadron which did more or less as its name implied. A brand new B2 QFI would be posted in from CFS and go to Standards, which would enable the local 'wheels' to assess their new man and to teach him local idiosyncrasies and procedures. Then the QFI would be sent to one of the 'waterfront' squadrons to start training students. Periodically (at least annually) the QFI would fly a standards check with one of the guys on the Standards squadron to iron out any odd habits he had developed and to check his competence. They also did upgrades from B2 to B1, but not to A2 or the god-like A1, which was reserved for CFS. Standards would examine the students e.g., final handling check, his graduation exercise. A Standards QFI would often be involved in the decision to 'chop' someone. Anything unusual would usually go to Standards squadron, so the first place a new aircraft like the Jet Provost 5 would go would be Standards, who would have at least one man already checked out on it by CFS. He would then check out the other Standards pilots and they would between them come up with the local procedures for the aircraft before converting 'waterfront' pilots. Standards staff was a squadron leader (OC Standards) and around four experienced A2 or A1 QFIs.

In March 1971, the school suffered an unfortunate, tragic accident when a Jet Provost T Mk.5 (XW300) was involved in a mid-air collision with a Sea Prince of the Linton-on-Ouse Station Flight. The Jet Provost had been engaged on a navex at 4,000 ft in cloudless sky conditions at the time of the incident and crashed near Selby, North Yorkshire. Sadly, all three crew members were killed and the subsequent Board of Inquiry concluded that the crews had failed to see each other in time to take avoiding action.

Although basic flying training for naval pilots at Linton had finished in July 1969, students still received elementary flying training with the Royal Navy Elementary Flying Training Squadron at Leeming. The majority of its graduates were subsequently posted to RNAS Culdrose to fly helicopters but those selected for the prospective Sea Harrier squadrons were transferred to Linton for a basic training course on the Jet Provost. In July 1976, the first three naval fixed-wing students – Lts Bill Covington, Greig Browne and Hugh Slade – joined the Jet Provost course and graduated with their Wings

in January 1977; the reviewing officer at the parade being Rear Admiral John Roberts, Flag Officer Naval Air Command. Slade and Covington later flew Sea Harriers with 809 Squadron during the Falklands War.

The highlight of 1977 was the Silver Jubilee Review of the RAF at Finningley on 29/30 July, where aircraft of every single type currently in service were selected to represent seventy operational RAF squadrons and training units before HM the Queen. Following an inspection of the ground exhibitions, the Queen was entertained with a mass fly-past over the royal dais of fifteen formations, comprising 137 aircraft and led by twenty-two Jet Provosts from No.1 FTS and the RAF College in a '25' formation (see also p.57).

The project officer for the Royal Review fly-past was **Sqn Ldr Eddie Danks.** He had been appointed to form 4 Squadron, No.1 FTS, in November 1975, and later during his tour he became DCFI to Wg Cdr Mike Hayden.

> The overall formation leader for the Jubilee fly-past was Wg Cdr John Lewis, the chief instructor from the RAF College, Cranwell. Cranwell provided the digit '5' for the fly-past, while Linton provided the number '2', led by Wg Cdr Hayden, the deputy leader for the whole '25' formation.
>
> The whole exercise was mounted and flown from Linton-on Ouse, which was quite an engineering and logistics feat. The Cranwell aircraft were flown up each day, as required, or pre-positioned the day before. Each 'digit' comprised of eleven Jet Provost Mk.5A aircraft, dual-manned, plus Flt Lt Garth Bennett from the Standards squadron at Linton as 'whip'. Station navigation officers (both pilots) were aboard each of the two lead Jet Provosts. We held ground spare aircraft, but no airborne spares.
>
> The formation training progressed very well and I do not recall any airborne technical issues within either digit, nor a single flight safety issue throughout the whole event. Each digit worked up initially at its own base, and this project took total priority over any flying training. At Linton, Wg Cdr Hayden and I started dedicated training on 4 July, with the

50-51

first full '25' formation flown three days later. We positioned all twenty-three aircraft (including the whip) on the duty runway at Linton, taking off in threes and twos at rolling intervals. The formation's route was a long one, heading eastwards initially from Linton out to the coast, before turning south and positioning for a final direct westerly run towards the centre point of the show, which was situated on the west mid-side of Finningley's runway.

The actual Royal Review '25' formation was flown on 29 July in front of Her Majesty the Queen (and defence secretary Fred Mulley who fell asleep next to her!). The weather was good and our '25' formation was a great success, arriving smack on time at the VIP datum. We transited in threes and then all formed up like one of Mallory's 'Big Wings' (quite an achievement?) before arriving majestically overhead the dais at RAF Finningley exactly on time.

We repeated the whole process the following day for the general public attending RAF Finningley's Open Day, again very successfully. A huge effort was put in by so many personnel at both Linton-on-Ouse and Cranwell to achieve this fly-past and we enjoyed it immensely. It was a privilege to be involved in the occasion.

In April 1992, the first replacement Short Tucano T Mk.1 turboprop basic trainer was delivered to the school and the initial course began its flying phase in January 1993; the Jet Provost instructors being converted to the new aircraft with the conclusion of each course. With the gradual withdrawal of the Jet Provost from Linton, the official farewell fly-past ceremony took place on 20 May 1993, when fifteen Jet Provosts formed the initials 'JP'. With the graduation of the last Jet Provost course (No.125 Course) on 4 June 1993, the final student to receive BFT on the Jet Provost was Flt Lt Nigel Curtis, who transferred to RAF Valley for advanced training on the Hawk. **Gp Capt Tom Eeles** was the station commander at Linton-on-Ouse from 1992 to 1994:

Linton-on-Ouse was the last FTS to receive the Tucano to replace the Jet Provost. I delivered the first Tucano (ZF209) to Linton on 3 April 1992, simply because I was the only one there that had flown it before. We did retain the Jet Provost alongside the Tucano for much longer than originally planned

as there was a big backlog of students who had been trained on the Jet Provost waiting to move on to the next stage and it was not considered cost effective to refresh them on a new aircraft.

Course length was about 120 hours, slightly shorter for ex-UAS students who might have had as much as 200 hours Bulldog flying during their time at university. There were usually four courses running concurrently, along with a steady trickle of refresher students, spread amongst three 'waterfront' squadrons. There was also a smaller Standards squadron which looked after QFI currency checks, QFI category upgrades and annual categorisation.

In addition to this I also had the Royal Navy Elementary Flying Training School, located at our relief landing ground at Topcliffe and flying Bulldogs. All RN pilots went through this course of around 100 hours; those selected for fast jet remained at Linton for the Jet Provost course then went to Valley. Thus I had a large student population, so much so that we had to build a new accommodation wing on the officers' mess in 1993.

Course content was broken down into general handling, formation, night flying, navigation and instrument flying. There were also a number of test sorties and of course a final handling test. There

50. On 20 May 1993, a first day cover was issued to mark the official withdrawal of the Jet Provost from No.1 FTS, RAF Linton-on-Ouse, featuring the pilots taking part in the event. (Gp Capt Paul McDonald)

51. Jet Provost T Mk.3A, XN495, of No.1 FTS overhead the flight line at Linton-on-Ouse. It was badly damaged in a flying accident in August 1983 and relegated as an instructional airframe

at RAF Halton. The nose section is preserved at Redhill. (BAe Systems Heritage Warton-Percival/Hunting Collection)

52. Gp Capt Tom Eeles, station commander and CO of No.1 FTS, Linton on Ouse, with T Mk.3A XN589/9143M, an aircraft in which he first flew solo as a cadet at Cranwell in 1963. It was positioned as a gate guard in March 1992. (Gp Capt Tom Eeles)

was an allowance for sorties curtailed by poor weather or aircraft unserviceability, and an allowance for sorties that failed due to student performance which now needed extra teaching.

On 22 July 1993, Tom Eeles led the school's final formation of five Jet Provost T Mk.3As to Shawbury for disposal, routing via local stations which had an association with the aircraft: Scampton (CFS), Cranwell and Brampton (HQ RAFSC).

NO.1 FTS DISPLAY TEAMS   In February 1961, the school's aerobatic team was reformed with a mix of RAF and navy instructors. Flt Lt Ron Corck was appointed as leader of the team, with members including Lt Carl Davis RN, Flt Lts Hugh Rigg and Dick Fox. However, following a mid-air collision at Syerston in February 1961, HQ Flying Training Command decided that a four-ship formation was too dangerous and reduced the team to three aircraft. As a result, Flt Lt Dick Fox was dropped from the team and it became known as 'Gin Section', making its debut performance at RAF Dishforth on 10 June 1961. This was followed by the Navy Days at Arbroath (24 June), Abbotsinch (8 July), Culdrose (15 July) and Lossiemouth (22 July). **Hugh Rigg** explains the origins of the team name.

When I arrived at Linton in June 1960 the station aerobatic team comprised four Vampire T 11s called 'Linton Blacks'. The Vampires were withdrawn and it was during 1961 that the first Jet Provost team was formed, led by Ron Corck. It was called 'Gin Section' because Ron and I had both been on 60 Squadron in the Far East, in which the formations were not called the usual red, blue, green colours, but gin, whiskey, brandy and vodka. We took over as the official station team and displayed at FAA Air Days and the RAF's Battle of Britain Days, together with the occasional ROC days.

We were fairly restricted, of course, in what we could do with three aircraft, but we looped and rolled in various formations and always ended in a bomb burst over the centre of the airfield. It was not easy rolling three or four Jet Provost 3s because of the lack of thrust, and one's timing on the throttle was critical to stay in position. It all changed for the better with the extra thrust from the Jet Provost 4 and life became much easier.

Each year the line-up of the school's display team was changed through postings, and the 1962 'Gin' team saw Lt Carl Davis, RN, being appointed as leader, with Flt Lts Duncan Robinson as No.2 and Hugh Rigg as No.3. The team also re-equipped with the newly-delivered Jet Provost T Mk.4s and, with a slightly reduced display commitment, began its season on 1 May 1962 with a display for the AOC's parade at Linton-on-Ouse.

Leader of the 1965 and 1966 teams was Flt Lt Norrie Grove, an experienced QFI and display pilot. The team – now renamed as 'Gin Formation' – not only included a solo display pilot in the line-up, but also incorporated a new and original manoeuvre in its seven-minute routine – the 'Gin Sling'. Team member, **Lt (now Lt Cdr) Pierre Cadoret RN,** elaborates.

> In the spring of 1965, Norrie Grove, Doug Smith and I got together and worked up for that year's summer season. Pete Jarvis was the solo display pilot, bringing a touch of class to the show. He was arguably the best solo aerobatic pilot in the RAF at the time, having won the Wright Jubilee Trophy on two occasions and was the station solo display pilot between 1963 and 1966. We regularly performed at such venues as Brawdy, Lossiemouth, Arbroath, Church Fenton, St Mawgan, St Athan, and at local displays and graduation parades.
>
> As a mark of respect to our naval colleagues, Norrie introduced a manoeuvre called 'Gin Sling' which entailed changing the lead position during a line-astern loop. It was during this manoeuvre that I lost a bit of my paintwork on Norrie's aircraft, it was only the slightest of touches and after a small paint job the aircraft was flying again the next day.

By 1967 the 'Gin' formation aerobatic team had increased its number to four aircraft and had become firmly established on the air show circuit, flying sixteen shows around the country between April and October. The final 'Linton Gin' display team was formed in January 1969 and consisted of Sqn Ldr Sid Edwards, Flt Lt Dave Waddington, Fg Offs Al Colesky and Joe Whitfield.

The team's early-morning practice sessions were carried out to avoid disrupting the school's flying training programme and soon attracted the attention of the local newspaper, which wrote:

> "The team have to practise at dawn when most of the station personnel are asleep. So it is hardly surprising that they have chosen that other early-morning riser, a cockerel, as a mascot and earned them the nickname 'the Wakey Wakey team'."

Joe Whitfield recalls that, with the benefit of hindsight, it was not one of his better ideas!

The team made its debut at RAF Shawbury on 3 May and twenty-five shows were given that year, both in the UK and Germany. Among its many memorable highlights was an eleven-aircraft formation loop with the Fouga Magisters of the Belgian air force aerobatic team, 'Les Diables Rouges', during an after-show event at RAF Gaydon on 21 September. The team's last display was for the USAF personnel at RAF Menwith Hall, Harrogate on 27 September 1969.

Formed in January 1970, the Linton Blades became the school's first display team to be equipped with Jet Provost T Mk.5s; the original members being Flt Lt Dave Waddington (leader), Flt Lts Dave Coldicutt, Graham Wright and Fg Off Dudley Carvell. Former Hunter pilot, **Joe Whitfield** flew with both the Linton Gin and Blades teams.

> I flew with the Gin team in the 1969 season and stepped into the newly named team in March 1970 after one of the team members had dropped out. It would appear that HQ, No.23 Group was not happy with the alcoholic link to 'Gin' and decided to change the name to 'Linton Blades', which was derived from the school's crest. We were not amused with this as 'gay' as in 'gay blades' was starting to come into common use and the military was homophobic in those days. Understandably, we took some stick!

The Blades display sequence was cleared by the AOC, No.23 Group, AVM Bird-Wilson at the end of April and

53. Almost certainly belonging to the aerobatic display team of No.1 FTS, Gin Formation, XP637 was noted at RAF Odiham in July 1963. (Tony Breese Collection)

its first public display was at RAF Church Fenton on 2 May 1970. This was followed by the team's first overseas show at Wiesbaden on 10 May and further shows in Germany at Horcht (11 July), Gelnhausen (12 July) and Ailertchen (13 July), followed by Lossiemouth, Leconfield and Newcastle. A total of eighteen shows were completed and the team's last show of the season was at RAF Leuchars on 19 September.

With thirty-four shows during the 1971 season, which included five overseas trips to France, Germany and Italy, the team continued into the 1972 season with a further twenty-five shows, led by Sqn Ldr Duncan Robinson, a former member of the Linton Gin teams in 1962 and 1963. The Linton Blades gave its last display at Toulouse/Francazal air show on 22 June 1973, following which it came to a sudden and abrupt end when Don Oakden was posted at rather short notice to Saudi Arabia. Without a leader, and with little consideration to finding a new one, the team was immediately disbanded.

No.2 FLYING TRAINING SCHOOL

Following an increase in the demand for pilots as a result of the Korean War, No.2 FTS was reformed at RAF Cluntoe in Northern Ireland on 1 March 1953, equipped with Prentice and Harvard trainers. The following year, the school moved to RAF Hullavington, now equipped with Piston Provosts and a few Chipmunks.

In 1955, No.2 FTS was selected to implement the second phase of the Service evaluation of the proposed all-through jet-training syllabus. On 25 August 1955 the first two Jet Provost T Mk.1s (XD676 and XD677) arrived from South Cerney and the initial 'experimental' ab initio course – No.113 (Jet) Course – comprising eighteen students, twelve of whom had no previous flying experience, got under way. By the end of September flying training had started, with the first student, Plt Off R. T. 'Dick' Foster, going solo on 17 October 1955 after eight hours and twenty minutes of dual instruction; by the time the eighth and final Jet Provost had been delivered

to the school in December, the remaining students on the course had also successfully soloed, with average time of ten hours and thirty-five minutes. **Ian Sheppard** was one of the members of the first course.

On 2 September 1955 we transferred from Kirton in Lindsey as newly-commissioned acting pilot officers. I began flying training at Hullavington on 26 September and went solo on 20 October after five hours and forty-five minutes of training.

However, on 26 March 1956 a small group of us were sent up to RAF Swinderby and our brief was that we were to be taught to fly the Vampire trainer up to the point where we would normally be sent solo, no further. I see that I flew a Jet Provost, XD693, at Hullavington on 24 March and the next entry is for 26 March 1956: 'Vampire T MK.11, Flt Lt Pete Poppe, Self, Famil. 40 mins.' We flew on 26-28 March and 3 April, and I amassed a total of four hours and fifty-five minutes.

On 6 April 1956 we were back at Hullavington flying the Jet Provost and completed the course on 25 April 1956, having flown a total of forty-six hours dual, and thirty-eight hours and fifteen minutes solo flying. On 7 May 1956 we commenced our advanced flying training at No.8 FTS, RAF Swinderby – but this time 'we' consisted of about half the course and appear to have become No.113a Course – so presumably those left behind at Hullavington became No.113b Course. We were eventually all reunited again at Swinderby and duly graduated on 23 January 1957. I was then posted to No.233 OCU, RAF Pembrey.

The second course – No.120 (Jet) Course – assembled and commenced flying on 18 July 1956. This particular course received the prototype Jet Provost T Mk.2, XD694, in September for a comparative evaluation. **Anthony Haig-Thomas** arrived from Kirton in Lindsey on 10 July 1956 to join the second course.

We started the course with eighteen students of which eleven eventually went on to join No.116 Course at Swinderby to fly Vampires. I had my first flight

(XD676) at Hullavington on 19 July 1956 followed by thirteen dual trips before going solo on 31 July after nine hours and thirty minutes. This was about normal. The first all-through jet courses were coded 'White Mouse' – as in the blind leading the blind!

On 27 July, I was detailed to fly circuits in Jet Provost (XD677) at our reserve strip at Keevil with an instructor, Flt Sgt Jock Naismith. During one landing, the starboard undercarriage leg fractured; the aircraft lurched off to starboard, but before it cartwheeled Jock Naismith took over and we landed back at Hullavington with two wheels up and one hanging down and swinging free. The cockpit filled with smoke from hot oil and by the very short time it took me to undo my harness my instructor was a small dot on the horizon. The fracture was caused by a fatigue crack and occurred because they had been landing the aircraft on grass at Keevil, which was then banned.

We had one Jet Provost Mk.2 (XD694) which the first course did not have, which arrived in September 1956. I think only four of us flew it and we switched easily between the long and short-legged versions with no trouble.

We were actually on mid-course leave in January, having done about seventy hours, when we received urgent telegrams to return to Hullavington as soon as possible. The Air Ministry had decided to see if we could cope with roughly half the normal basic training hours. There was then a mad rush to get final tests done and I only flew eighty hours on the Jet Provost, but the time to first solo was much less on the Jet Provost rather than the Piston Provost. I had ninety hours when I did my first solo on a Vampire.

It would seem to have been a successful experiment in that, as far as I can remember, those of us who made it onto the Vampire all graduated in December 1957. I had 221 hours when I got my Wings.

A third and final course – No.125 (Jet) Course – began in March 1957 and was completed the following November. The 'Hullavington Experiment' had been considered a success and subsequently showed a saving of twenty-five hours during the advanced stage on the Vampire, and an overall saving of twenty hours on the complete Wings course. Official figures also showed that during the eighteen-month evaluation at Hullavington, the Jet Provosts had flown 4,000 hours and made over 11,000 landings. Various teething problems had been encountered, and despite occasional engine and undercarriage failures, the flight safety record remained high and only one aircraft (XD692) had been written off as the result of a flying accident.

The completion of the Jet Provost evaluation at RAF Hullavington resulted in an official announcement that RAF Flying Training Command was to standardise on the improved Jet Provost T Mk.3 basic trainer, and in November 1957 No.2 FTS transferred to Syerston with its Piston Provosts; the Jet Provost aircraft being passed to CFS Little Rissington for instructor training and to form an 'aerobatic flight'.

On 20 August 1959, No.2 FTS became the first RAF flying training school to receive the Jet Provost T Mk.3. A further four aircraft were delivered direct from the manufacturer at the end of the month. By the time the first course began in October the unit's establishment had increased to twelve aircraft.

With most of the school's Piston Provost instructors having already received brief familiarisation training with the Jet Provost, the first all-through jet training course – No.143 Course – began on 7 October 1959. As the pace of the training increased, a further six QFIs (Flt Lts Barry Dale, Brian Stephens, Andrew Whitaker, Chris Wilmot and two 'creamed off' graduates, James Watts-Phillips and Alex Reid) arrived from CFS in December 1959. **James Watts-Phillips:**

> We were all posted to Syerston on 'A' Flight, where the existing instructors were converting to Jet Provosts. The first ab initio course was in October 1959 and began flying training on 29 December. The course length at Syerston was nine months for standard courses and six months for ex-university air squadron courses. Students flew 110 hours of which about sixty were dual and fifty were solo.

54

The course finished in September 1960 and all the students were posted to Swinderby for advanced training on Vampires. The rest of the flights converted to Jet Provosts as they finished their Piston Provost courses and I think that would have been complete by June/July 1960.

The only foreign students during my time there were the Sudanese, eight of them, and I believe they had done the basic Piston Provost course twice at Ternhill. They came to our flight for 'jet conversion' – a twenty-hour course with no solo flying and thirty minutes night flying. They were not very good but completed the course. We were led to believe that when they went back to the Sudan they were celebrated and Colonel Nasser of Egypt gave them six MiG-15 aircraft!

In the spring of 1960 we had several flame-outs as a result of a brown woolly caterpillar (seriously) crawling up the engine's P2 air sensor. This caused a vast reduction in power and/or a flame-out with no ability to relight. The aircraft was easy to land following a flame-out and this failure seemed to

happen to instructors. I only remember one student, Terry Peate, having a flame-out and he landed successfully. I also recall one student ejected in a spin he could not recover and I had an incident where the in-spin behaviour was bad and recovery slow. The rigging was checked and no problem was found. But when I flew the aircraft after the check it was different. I was a lowly flight lieutenant and the pilots of Huntings were sceptical. Other than that the aircraft was fairly serviceable but we had a few radio and instrument failures in the early days. We, jokingly, thought that the aircraft was given to No.2 FTS to sort out the problems before the aircraft was allowed to be used by Cranwell.

John Lloyd was a student on No.151 Course.

Our course would have been one of the earlier all-through jet courses on the Jet Provost Mk.3. My logbook shows that we started flying at Syerston on 1 May 1961 and the course was completed on 23 March 1962. It was referred to as an all-through jet

55

training course, i.e. starting on the Jet Provost and then Wings qualification on the Gnat (or Vampire). It was a 240-hour course over eighteen months.

After Syerston we were originally scheduled to fly the Gnat at Valley, but due to late delivery and serviceability problems with the Gnat, Flying Training Command had to re-open Swinderby which had been closed down as an advanced flying school and soldier on with the venerable old Vampire T11 to complete several of the courses. In the event, our course was split fifty/fifty at very short notice halfway through the training and we were given the choice of continuing on the Vampire or going to Oakington on the Varsity. I elected to go on the Varsity and after graduation four of us were sent off to Tern Hill to learn to fly on helicopters. So what started out as an all-through jet training course for us four was anything but!

In March 1961, eight Kuwaiti students also arrived at Syerston and completed the first half of their jet familiarisation course by July. The Kuwait government had previously placed an order with Hunting Aircraft for six armed Jet Provost T Mk.52s and the students at Linton were especially provided with two aircraft by the manufacturer for the weapons' phase of their training syllabus. **Terry Lloyd** was involved in the training of the Kuwaiti students at Syerston.

I arrived directly from CFS on 18 July 1960 and was in C Flight; Flt Lt Norman Clayton was the flight commander and Sqn Ldr Ray Downes was the squadron commander, commanding both C and D Flights.

I flew with my first Kuwaiti student (Lt Safar) on 10 April 1961 and subsequently flew with Lts Hamza, Samdan Ajeel, Sumait and Ateeji. My last Kuwaiti trip was with Lt Hamza on 20 July 1961. Incidentally, all the Kuwaitis were already qualified pilots with a mixed experience of types. During that period they advanced from basic familiarisation to navigation and formation flying, including a limited amount of battle formation training.

Bob Osborne was a member of No.152 Course between June 1961 and April 1962.

I remember some Kuwaiti pilots being trained at Syerston on Jet Provosts that were armed for the combat bit. The RAF instructors used to make the Kuwait guys sit there with their arms folded for the taxiing part of the sortie in case they hit the wrong switch! The students bought new white Jaguar Mk.2s with consecutive number plate registrations. They would come down from the rooms, start the engines and leave them running while they had breakfast so that the short run of around half a mile to the flights could be in a car with the heaters working.

In May 1962, the school took delivery of its first Jet Provost T Mk.4s, which were used by No.155 Course as the first to implement the all-through Wings course on the type. The course began the previous March and the seventeen students flew a total of 160 hours before graduating and receiving their Wings on 18 January 1963.

Nick Tillotson had joined the RAF in May 1962 and began his flying training with No.158 Course in November of that year. The following year he ejected from a Jet Provost after encountering difficulties during a spinning exercise, the impact of which would cause major changes to be made to the subsequent ab initio training syllabus.

54. Jet Provost T Mk.3s of No.2 FTS, Syerston, 22 March 1960. No.2 FTS became the first basic flying training school to receive this version in August 1959. (HAL via Terry Lloyd)

55. A busy flight-line at RAF Syerston during 1960. A scene which was repeated at many flying training stations. (BAe Systems Heritage Warton-Percival/Hunting Collection)

On 19 April 1963, he had been scheduled to fly two solo general handling exercises, which were to include spinning. On the first flight, in Jet Provost Mk.4, XP623, he decided to initially spin to the left. During recovery, the aircraft entered a steep, high rotational spin from which it was slow to recover. He then carried out a spin to the right from which the aircraft recovered more quickly than was normal, i.e., as soon as he started to move the stick forward from fully aft.

Following this trip, he was debriefed by his instructor, during which spin recovery and his previous experience was discussed. He was briefed to fly a second GH exercise, as programmed, and the aircraft allocated to him was again, XP623.

At the appropriate time in the flight, a spin to the left was entered. This time, on recovery, the aircraft entered a steep high rotational spin from which no sign of the spin stopping was observed and at the abandon aircraft height of 5,000 feet, with the aircraft still spinning, the pilot ejected. The aircraft crashed just east of the A46 near the village of Thrussington, Leics. The subsequent Board of Inquiry decided that the accident was caused by 'pilot error', but Nick was allowed to continue pilot training and awarded his Wings on 11 October 1963.

Solo spinning for ab initio students was banned after this accident and remained in force for the remainder of the service life of the aircraft. Available records show that there were a series of Jet Provost spinning incidents and other successful ejections at about this time; Nick Tillotson's was the only spinning accident which involved a solo student.

By co-incidence, when Nick later got into a conversation with a RAF SNCO airframe fitter, the subject turned to the Jet Provost. Nick said he had abandoned one and related the circumstances, to which the SNCO responded that he had been a member of an investigation team, examining the problems of Jet Provost spinning. He remarked that rudder travel was not at that time subject to routine examination and after a few months in service, rudder travel was found on some aircraft, to be not as set by the manufacturer. It was then included in the scheduled service and that was one of the reasons spinning accidents stopped.

Nick Tillotson went on to fly the Jet Provost Mk.3A and Mk.5A for the last seven years of his service, both as a unit test pilot at Cranwell and as a QFI at Linton-on-Ouse, and never encountered any further spin problems.

By early 1969, a reorganisation of the RAF Command structure and a reduction in the requirement for pilots began to impact on the flying training programme and No.2 FTS was informed that it would disband as a basic flying training school in the near future. **Dick Allen** was a student on the penultimate course.

We started in December 1968 and I first flew the Jet Provost on 8 January 1969. We were No.182 Course and the seventeen 'survivors' received our Wings on 28 August 1969 (no-one was killed on the course, but a number got chopped).

We were a strange course, a mixture of ex-UAS cadets and an 'experimental' group (myself included) who had done a longer Chipmunk course – with the navy! The theory was that having sixty hours on the Chippie against the normal thirty, we could manage with the fewer Jet Provost hours that the ex-UAS guys got. To make life even more interesting, the 'experimental' half only flew the Jet Provost 4, which was a bit sporty directly after the Chipmunk.

We were also the last proper course graduation from Syerston. Normally the junior courses made up supporting flights and sections on the formal, final parade, but the last course had no-one junior and so – while 'par for the course' for the reviewing officer normally being a one star or even a mere group captain – we got a ACM, no less than the famous Gus Walker. He had only one arm, having lost the other in the war and, as a course project and for our final graduation dinner, we put together a sort of *This is Your Life* for him, reuniting him with some local acquaintances he hadn't seen since the war.

The last basic flying training course at Syerston – No.183 Course – began in February 1969 with eighteen students and, despite the gradual withdrawal of the school's fleet of Jet Provosts, was completed on 19 December 1969.

56

On 16 January 1970 No.2 FTS was disbanded and reformed the same day at Church Fenton, comprising the RAF's primary flying squadron and the Royal Navy elementary flying training squadron. Both units being equipped with Chipmunk T MK.10 aircraft.

NO.2 FTS DISPLAY TEAMS In May 1960, No.2 FTS formed its first aerobatic display team to fly the Jet Provost T Mk.3, comprising Flt Lts Dai Jones, David Rowe, Reg Stock and Master Pilot Jock McTavish. Known shows carried out by the team that year included a display for the visit of the Duchess of Kent to Syerston on 27 July and the Battle of Britain celebrations at Norton and Valley on 17 September 1960.

For the 1961 season, a more permanent display team was formed with Flt Lt John Speadbury as leader and members including Flt Lts James Watts-Phillips, Willy Wilmott and Barry Dale. Training began with an unfortunate mid-air collision during a practice sortie over Syerston in February, and while there were no injuries,

the aircraft were slightly damaged and was considered enough for the AOC Flying Training Command to order the reduction of formation aerobatic teams to three aircraft. The team from Syerston laid on at least one show later in the year with an appearance at the RAF Leuchars Battle of Britain celebrations in September.

By the beginning of the 1962 season, the school's display team had adopted the name 'Viper Red', which had been derived from the Jet Provost's Bristol Siddeley Viper engine. With three instructors, Flt Lts Wally Elsegood, Pete Jennings and Bill Dodds, the team laid on displays for the local graduation parades and re-equipped with Jet Provost T Mk.4s in May 1962. The final displays of the year included the Battle of Britain shows at Coltishall and Wyton in September.

56. In May 1960, No.2 FTS formed its first aerobatic display team to fly the Jet Provost T Mk.3. Team members comprised Flt Lts Dai Jones, David Rowe, Reg Stock and Master Pilot Jock McTavish. (via Reg Stock)

By September 1965, two of the school's current display team members had been posted and replaced by Flt Lt Bill Surtees and Fg Off Bill Aspinall. Training began again the following spring, and during an early practice formation sortie over Woodborough, Notts, on 26 May 1966, two of the Jet Provosts flown by Don Henderson (in XP631) and Flt Lt Tim Thorn and student pilot, Plt Off Sedman (in XM384), were involved in a mid-air collision. All three pilots ejected safely and landed close to the wreckage, while Flt Lts Bill Aspinall and Bill Surtees were able to return to Syerston with their damaged aircraft. As a result of the accident, all team activities were cancelled for the rest of the year.

The following year, the restrictions placed on formation aerobatic flying in the aftermath of the mid-air collision had been partially lifted with a resumption of display flying by two instructors, Sqn Ldr 'Cas' Maynard and Flt Lt George Lee. Named 'Viper Red 1967', and flying a routine of synchronised and formation aerobatics with two Jet Provosts (XP677 and XS176) the pair completed fifteen shows during the season.

As a result of restored confidence in display flying following the completion of the successful and demanding season by the previous team, Sqn Ldr Cas Maynard was asked to form a new four-ship team in February 1968. Named the Vipers, the team obtained official approval from the AOC, No.23 Group in May and opened its display season with a show at the Edinburgh Air Day on 22 June 1968. It went on to complete twenty-three shows before being disbanded in early October.

The final station display team formed for the 1969 season included Sqn Ldr John Merry, Flt Lts John Abell and John Haddock, Fg Offs Terry Hall and 'Mitch' Mitchell. While the previous teams had shown some reluctance to adopt a colour scheme for its aircraft, the 1969 team painted the fin, rudder and wing-tip tanks of its Jet Provosts in white, and proudly displayed its name 'The Vipers' in black on the rudder. In addition, the rudder also carried a green outlined triangle enclosing a red snake forming the figure '2' – a Viper. Known examples in this scheme included XP617:49, XP630:50, XP641:34, XR644:36 and XR707:45. **John Merry** recalls the team's final season.

The team from Linton called Gin was renamed at about this time and became known as the Swords (from the station crest), so our deputy chief instructor, Sqn Ldr Mick Haydon suggested that we call ourselves 'VAT 69 – Viper Aerobatic Team, 1969'. Alas, it was not to be!

Our first show was at Leicester on 25 May, with another four shows at Digby, Cranfield, Leeming and Halton. Our last display was a NATO event at Bierset/Liège in Belgium on 22 June 1969 in the presence of King Baudouin. The reason why we disbanded so early was that one of our members injured himself and, as the station was closing down at the end of the year and was running down flight by flight as the students graduated, we hadn't enough resources to spare to train a replacement.

No.3 FLYING TRAINING SCHOOL

No.3 FTS reformed at Leeming on 15 September 1961, with its first three Jet Provost T Mk.3s (XN574, XN606 and XN629) being delivered direct from Luton. The first course of fifteen students arrived in October and flying training began later in the month.

By the end of December 1961, the unit had finally achieved an establishment of twenty-four aircraft, coinciding with the start of a second course which comprised a number of former university air squadron students. The following month a second training squadron was formed to cope with the increase in the number of aircraft and in August 1962, No.6 Course became the first to include foreign students when five members of the Royal Jordanian Air Force joined the twenty-one RAF students undergoing training at Leeming. The course was eventually completed in July 1963.

The ab initio courses were initially designed to last thirty-six weeks (120 hours) before the students proceeded to AFTS. However, by the time the fourth course began on 7 March 1962 the structure had been amended. Under the revised scheme the student was required to

57-58

complete a 160-hour course lasting forty-eight weeks, covering basic training on the Jet Provost 3 and advanced flying on the more powerful Jet Provost 4, the first of which had been delivered on 21 March 1962. On completion of the course the students received their Wings before progressing to their advanced training.

Rod Dean was a member of No.8 Course, which ran from 7 January 1963 to 10 January 1964.

The course started on the Jet Provost 3 and I went solo in XM459 on 19 March 1963 after nine hours and thirty-five minutes dual. At about mid-course (June 24 for me) we swapped to the Jet Provost 4 for all the advanced formation, low level, aeros etc. This explains why there are so few JP4s around these days as we got through the fatigue life much quicker doing the advanced stuff than the work on the Jet Provost 3. For normal day-to-day operations the Mk.3 normally only had half-full wing-tip tanks because of the performance. The total course length was, I think, 160 hours and I did a total of 167 (sixty-four on the Mk.3 and 103 on the Mk.4) over the year.

No.3 FTS took delivery of its first T Mk.5 (XW315), on 17 July 1970, followed by a second aircraft (XW314) at the end of August. By the end of the year the school had an establishment of seventeen Mk.5s on strength and began to gradually phase out its Mk.4s, the last of which left in February 1971.

The school maintained a healthy flight safety record during its time as a basic training unit, the most serious accident being a mid-air collision near Northallerton in April 1965. However, bird strikes were a constant threat, especially during low flying and on airfield boundaries, where circuits and landings were regularly carried out and the risk to aircraft and their crews were considerable. One such example was on 29 June 1971 when a Jet Provost Mk.3, XN558, crashed at Dishforth, North Yorkshire, after suffering a multiple bird strike at 350 feet. The aircraft had flown into a flock of racing pigeons just after take-off, which had been released just outside of the airfield boundary by an individual who was not aware the airfield was operational. The student, Flt Lt C. S. Hall, and his instructor, Flt Lt 'Bob' Thompson, safely ejected at 300 feet. The aircraft was a complete write-off.

By 1974 the reduction in the requirement for pilot training in the RAF saw the graduation of the final training course on 11 October, which also marked the disbandment of No.3 FTS as a basic flying training school; the unit having trained 930 students on the Jet Provost since its formation in September 1961.

NO.3 FTS DISPLAY TEAMS Formed in January 1962, the unit display team of four Jet Provost T Mk.3s led by Sqn Ldr R. W. 'Paddy' Glover, with Flt Lts G. J. 'Bill'

57. The markings on the tip tank of this Mk.4, XR648, at Wattisham in August 1967, confirm that it was part of the No. 2 FTS synchronised pair, Viper Red 1967. The team restored much of the confidence in display flying following a suspension in formation aerobatics. (Roger Lindsay).

58. The Vipers team from No.2 FTS at Syerston in 1969: Flt Lts John Abell, John Haddock, Sqn Ldr John Merry (leader), Flt Lt Terry Hall and Flt Lt Mitch Mitchell (commentator). (John Merry)

59

Bailey, W. H. W. Norton and K. Marshall began training immediately. **Bill Bailey:**

> In 1962, we did our display flying with Jet Provost Mk.3s and flew to Jersey via Lyneham on 12 September to give a display for RAFA. The last show I did was on 5 October 1962 for the Sudanese CAS at Hullavington.

In March 1963, the unit began to receive Jet Provost Mk.4s which, for the next two years, formed the basis of the school's display team, led by Sqn Ldr Dave Tanner DFC. Appearances at shows were limited and, with the posting of its leader in July 1964, the team's brief existence came to an end.

The Gemini Pair was formed in March 1968 (see also p.31) and the synchronised pair's routine – which included a roulette manoeuvre and a formation 'Noddy' stall turn – was officially approved in May. The team made its first public appearance at Bentwaters on 25 May and was ably supported throughout the season by the station's solo aerobatic display pilots, Flt Lt Roger Pyrah and his deputy, Flt Lt Jerry Pook.

In July 1970, the first Jet Provosts were delivered to the unit, two of which were operated by the Gemini Pair. **Ron Pattinson** was a member of the team in 1970 and 1971.

> I arrived as QFI at Leeming in March 1969. During that summer, Gemini pilots were Pete Rayner and Jerry Pook. Both these chaps were posted so two new team members were required. That was myself and Gordon Revell, a first tourist, who was later killed in a rather bizarre accident while flying a Harrier.
>
> I guess our signature manoeuvre was the 'mirror' formation, which at that time was not flown by any other formation team. The manoeuvre was flown with the leader inverted and the No.2 maintaining formation. The change from the Jet Provost 4 to the Jet Provost 5 was made between the 1970 and 1971 seasons. With the change, the envelope around the aircraft was very different, especially around the cockpit with the larger, more bulbous, pressurised cockpit.
>
> During the work up to the 1971 season, the Red Arrows had suffered a mid-air collision while performing a 'roulette' manoeuvre. We started the season with the 'roulette' manoeuvre as part of our display sequence, as it had been throughout 1970. The MoD twigged halfway through the season and banned it immediately, leaving us to revamp the whole display at no notice. In addition, our shiny new brochures also had a picture of the roulette cross and we were forced to doctor all the brochures by removing the offending picture.

In 1973, Flt Clive 'Bob' Thompson and Fg Off Graham 'Dusty' Miller became the last two pilots to fly as Leeming's synchronised display team and between May and October they appeared at forty-three air shows in the UK and Europe in front of an estimated audience of

60

61

more than one million people. The Gemini Pair made its last appearance at Duxford on 14 October 1973. The following year the team was expanded to four aircraft and renamed as the 'Swords'. **Air Mshl Sir Graham 'Dusty' Miller:**

> 1973 was the final year for the vast majority of RAF flying school aerobatic teams, primarily due to the then modern phenomena of a fuel crisis and the 'winter of discontent' when the nation was looking at a three-day working week. The MoD took the view that squandering jet fuel would not look good so decided to reduce its offering to the 1974 display season to the Red Arrows plus one surviving four-ship Jet Provost team. RAF Leeming (No.3 FTS) got the job to provide the Jet Provost team so had to increase Gemini to a four-ship, thus making the name (and the team) redundant at a stroke.

Formed in 1974 following the disbandment of the Gemini Pair, the school's display team, the Swords, was equipped with four Jet Provost T Mk.5s led by Flt Lt Clive 'Bob' Thompson. The name of the team was taken from the sword emblem on the unit crest and it also received some limited sponsorship for publicity material from the Wilkinson Sword Company.

59. Bird strikes were a constant threat to aircraft while flying at low level. This aircraft, XN558 of No.3 FTS, suffered a multiple bird strike just after take-off from Dishforth and crashed after the crew ejected, 29 June 1971. (via Clive 'Bob' Thompson)

60. Jet Provost T Mk.5A, XW406, of the Gemini Pair synchronised display team from No.3 FTS, Leeming, flown by Flt Lt John Galyer in 1972. (Dave Trusler)

61. Two Jet Provost T Mk.5As of the Gemini Pair, escort Ray Hanna in a Spitfire IXB belonging to Sir Adrian Swire, the chairman of Cathay Pacific Airlines, to Leeming on 4 July 1972. The Jet Provosts were flown by former Canberra strike pilots, John Galyer and David Trusler. (Dave Trusler)

The team was cleared for display on 24 June 1974 and made their debut at a press day held at RAF Leeming on 1 July 1974. The first public display was at RAF Finningley on 3 July 1974 and the team eventually flew some forty-one displays during its existence, including one at Auf dem Dümple, near Cologne. On 11 October 1974 the Swords gave their last shows at the Rolls-Royce Open Day at Filton and the graduation of No.65 Course on return to Leeming.

62

SCHOOL OF REFRESHER FLYING/ REFRESHER FLYING SQUADRON

The Refresher Flight was originally formed within the HQ Squadron, No.3 FTS, at Leeming on 1 December 1964. Commanded by Flt Lt C. H. C. Hardie, the unit's task was to provide refresher training for pilots from the School of Refresher Flying (SoRF) at Manby, which had been unable to cope with the large number of aircrew returning to flying posts. The first students arrived on 2 December and began flying the following day.

The flight continued to operate in this role until the SoRF at Manby was transferred to Leeming on 3 December 1973 and absorbed into No.3 FTS as No.1 Squadron/No.3 FTS. By this time the role of the SoRF had been expanded to restore the flying skills of pilots who had been on a ground tour, students who had been 'chopped' from AFT at RAF Valley, or pilots who were cross-rolling to fast jets. With the delivery of the first Jet Provost T Mk.5As in January 1976, the unit was renamed as the Refresher Flying Squadron (of 3 FTS).

Between June 1979 and February 1982, **Gp Capt Paul McDonald** held various posts with the RFS, including as QFI, IRE and flight commander:

No.3 FTS was a traditional BFTS with the Jet Provost Mks.3 and 5. On 11 October 1974, the role of No.3 FTS changed and it stopped undertaking ab

initio training when the final training course graduated. Instead three new units arrived. The multi-engine training squadron (METS) with its Jetstreams joined No.3 FTS, as did the Bulldogs of the newly formed Royal Navy elementary flying training squadron (RNEFTS) in December 1974. The third unit was the School of Refresher Flying which operated out of Manby/Strubby with its Meteors and later, Jet Provosts. With the closure of those airfields the Jet Provosts came to Leeming but you couldn't have another school, or a school within a school so it became a squadron – the Refresher Flying Squadron – in October 1976.

I joined the RFS in June 1979 and immediately went into Standards squadron for two weeks to learn how to adapt the basic teaching learnt on my CFS instructor's course to meet the needs of a very different type of student: refresher students were all qualified students. The squadron ran the short jet refresher course lasting eight weeks, with two weeks of ground school and six weeks of flying, during which the students completed thirty-five flying hours at quite an extensive rate. Our students came from the widest range of backgrounds and had either been filling staff appointments and were going back to a flying job, or were cross-rolling, changing perhaps from a heavy aircraft or helicopters, to fast jets.

When I joined the RFS, the unit flew only the Jet Provost T Mk.5As from within the centralised pool of aircraft at Leeming. From September 1981 we began to use the Mk.3A. This was because some of our task, predominantly the refreshing of former fast-jet pilots returning to the front line, was transferred to Brawdy where a small flight of Jet Provost T Mk.4s was included within 79 Squadron, a Hawk squadron. Two RFS instructors were also posted there.

With the reduction of our task during the beginning of 1982, we continued to fly the Jet Provost Mk.5s for currency; most of our instructional sorties were now conducted in the slower and much older Jet Provost Mk.3A. My final sortie was on 23 February 1982 before I was transferred to No.4 FTS at RAF Valley to undergo advanced flying training on the Hawk and my eventual posting to a Tornado squadron.

In August 1982, confirmation was received that RAF Leeming was being officially considered for the planned establishment of the RAF's Tornado ADV squadrons, which would include its based units being either disbanded or transferred to other locations. As a consequence of this decision, on 29 March 1984, the RFS moved to Church Fenton and, with the reduction in the demand for pilots under current RAF budget cutbacks, No.3 FTS was disbanded on 26 April 1984.

On 1 February 1989, No.3 FTS was reformed again from the flying element of the RAF College, equipped with the Jet Provost T Mk.5A. With the delivery of the first Short Tucano in August 1991, the official withdrawal of the unit's Jet Provosts was marked with the graduation of No.88 Course and a fly-past of Jet Provosts in a diamond nine formation over Cranwell on 11 October 1991. The last Jet Provost Mk.5A left the unit on 29 October 1991.

No.6 FLYING TRAINING SCHOOL

By the end of the war, No.6 FTS was based at RAF Ternhill and equipped with a succession of piston-engine training aircraft, including Harvards, Tiger Moths and Percival Prentices. In July 1953, it became the first flying training school to be equipped with the Percival Provost T1.

To avoid the increase of civilian airways routes in the area, No.6 FTS moved from Ternhill to Acklington in August 1961 and replaced its Percival Provosts with Jet Provost T Mk.3s, the first of which was delivered direct from Luton, the same month. Training began with the first jet ab initio course (No.162 Course) on 13 September 1961 with twenty-four students, followed by the second course (No.163 Course) in December. **Richie Profit:**

I returned to No.6 FTS as a 'creamed off' QFI in June 1963, having previously been a student with No.161 Course at Acklington on the Piston Provost from September 1961 to April 1962. In my opinion, the Piston Provost was the perfect basic flying training aircraft: good performance, fully aerobatic and sufficiently difficult to fly to weed out early in the course those more suited to an alternative career. The Jet Provost was a satisfactory aircraft for basic flying training but it was too easy to fly, which meant that student weaknesses did not become apparent until much later in the course. Secondly, the Mk.3 was underpowered which limited its aerobatic capability, Furthermore, a student could not be left too long to sort out a problem he was having before it was necessary for the instructor to take control (particularly on landing). These problems were resolved by the Mk.4 (the first of which was delivered in June 1962) and had significantly more engine thrust.

In 1962 the unit was also involved in the implementation of the RAF's revised flying training programme, the '160 hours to Wings' course. **George Kirk** was one of the students on the first course.

I trained at RAF Acklington on the Jet Provost Mks.3 and 4 and graduated on 15 March 1963. Up to this time in RAF pilot training, Wings were

62. Depicted getting airborne from RAF Leeming in 1980, Jet Provost Mk.5A, XW433, of No.3 FTS. Following extensive service use, it was registered as G-JPRO in November 1999 and is operated by Classic Air Force at Coventry. (Dave McIntyre)

63

awarded at the end of advanced flying training. Our course at Acklington (No.165 Course) was the first to be awarded Wings at the end of BFTS, along with a concurrent course at, I think, Church Fenton. Half of the Acklington graduates went to Oakington to train on the Varsity and the other half, including myself, went onto the Vampire T11 at Swinderby, where we were joined by some guys from Church Fenton.

The school had been traditionally associated with the flying training of foreign and commonwealth pilots, including those from the Sudan, Iraq and Kuwait. **Mike Butt** qualified as flying instructor at CFS, Little Rissington, in June 1962, following which he was posted to 6 FTS, Acklington, where he was appointed as a flight commander and then Standards officer until September 1967.

We had eight Sudanese students at Acklington, who arrived in July 1962. Two were very good and gained their Wings with No.166 Course. The rest were re-coursed to No.167 and they graduated as officer cadets in August 1963 along with 168 Course. Those getting their Wings were El Kareem, El Daw and Dafalla. By that time we had lost Officer Cadets Eisa and Kalifa, as well as El Hassan and Hag Ali. I seem to have arrived at nine students. They were late going solo in the Jet Provost, in excess of fifteen hours, as I remember that they had problems coping with the circuit and R/T. Air Mshl Gus Walker paid us a visit and suggested they rode bicycles around a marked circuit on the dispersal making the appropriate R/T instructions. Kalifa (translated into 'headman's son') asked if he could

make a comment. He said the bicycles were a good idea but there was another problem in that none of them could ride a bike. Kalifa could not go solo in the Jet Provost so he was destined to be sent home. The rest of the course then said, "If he goes we all go". (headman's son and loss of face?) To overcome this he was sent to RAF Ouston where the CFI, Sqn Ldr Barwell I think, eventually sent him solo in a Chipmunk. This satisfied the rest of the course and after Kalifa left the rest stayed.

On 14 July 1967, the school jointly celebrated its Golden Jubilee and the graduation of No.182 Course. Following the salute and presentation, guests were entertained with a flying display by the Red Arrows, fly-pasts by current RAF aircraft and performances by the station's formation aerobatic team and solo display pilot.

One of the last ab initio courses to graduate from No.6 FTS was No.184 Course, which was completed on 16 February 1968. The event was of special significance to the school as it also marked the graduation of the 1,000th student to be trained at the FTS. **Guy Gibbons** was one of the students on No.184 Course. He had joined the RAF in September 1966 and, after a short period with the Aircrew Holding Unit at Topcliffe, he joined the course on 10 April 1967.

Our course was fairly normal for the time – approx. thirty-eight members including three Australians, a doctor who was going to be an AvMed specialist, and an engineer who would be involved in test flying. As far as I remember a few of us had flown before (mainly civilian – I had a flying scholarship as had some others) so effectively we were all ab initios. Not everyone graduated – I remember three guys being chopped and at least one withdrawing voluntarily, whilst another was re-coursed (unusual) but went on to become a test pilot so couldn't have been that bad.

These were the days of the all-through jet training – we did 145 hours on the Jet Provost 3 and 4 before receiving our Wings and going on to AFTS – RAF Valley for Gnats, RAF Ternhill for rotary and RAF Oakington for Varsity/multi-engine.

Our first three weeks were all ground school and covered virtually every subject associated with aviation – aerodynamics, engine theory (both piston and jet), airmanship, Morse code (up to six words per minute to get a pass), met theory and so on. Eventually we started learning more about the Jet Provost and its workings just before we were allowed to join the flying side of the course. For the next six months or so (until we became senior course) we alternated between flying and ground school, normally day on day off, but if any exams were coming up (either flying or ground) we would spend more time at the appropriate bit of the school.

So to start with was the run up to first solo; normally about eight hours from first flight – if you took longer than ten hours it was straight onto review! I went solo at Ouston just on eight hours, and after a bit of circuit consolidation it was back to Acklington for upper air work and general handling both dual and solo, all on the Jet Provost 3. My impressions of the aircraft were quite favourable (I knew no better) – it seemed to have plenty of power, was relatively easy to fly (although not to my instructor's satisfaction) and fulfilled all you wanted of a basic trainer; we also started on instrument flying (IF) which was later to give me quite a scare. After some forty hours we started on navexes; again medium level to start with, before descending into the weeds (or so it seemed) for low-level work.

Minimum heights were 250 ft dual and 500 ft solo – seemed really low until I started flying Shackletons at 100 ft and helicopters even lower. After that there was formation (much more than today), tail chases, aerobatics (I enjoyed but probably wasn't very good), night flying, and more consolidation – and plenty of solo flying. At the end of the course forty-five of my total of 145 flying hours was solo. Compare that with today, when a pilot finishing (say) the rotary course of approx 145 hours will probably do no more than ten or fifteen.

My basic handling check occurred in August after some fifty-odd hours or so; the next day I had one dual sortie in a Jet Provost 4 before being sent

solo for another hour; after this nearly all my sorties were in the Mk.4 except for a couple of landaways. The Jet Provost 4 was a totally different beast power wise; I can't remember the actual figures, but the acceleration was much more noticeable (think difference between Ford Focus ST and base model). The actual check list was the same (hence minimal conversion) – I seem to remember 135 checks from cockpit entry to taxi. Acklington had three runways – the long (main) one, a shorter one and one very short pointing at Acklington Church; this last one was only for staff or senior student take-offs in Jet Provost 4s – even so there were a few near misses. You should also remember these were the original unmodified Mk.4s – same weight as the Mk.3 with no extra navigation kit or pressurisation and they were quite 'hot ships', even with the wing-tip tanks full.

About the first week we were there we were hauled out of ground school to go help look for an Arab student. Sitting in the middle of the runway was a Jet Provost sans wheels and an open cockpit; apparently he had forgotten to lower the wheels, ignored the red Very light from the runway caravan and done an immaculate landing but couldn't get it to taxi, realised his error, and had done a runner into the gorse and heath land beyond the runway (it was said by the other students on his course he would have been shot for damaging a jet in his country). Anyway his escape and evasion skills were quite good and it was the following day before he was found.

Shortly after we started the course we were told the '10,000th student' would graduate on our course, but no one would know who it was until the day. In the end I think it went to a student called Alasdair Beaton (he later went on to fly Buccaneers). Needless to say a lot of effort went into the day – as usual a big Wings parade with all three flights but this time an RAF band as well, and an open day for all

63. Jet Provost Mk.3, XN551, visiting RAF Little Rissington soon after its delivery to No.6 FTS in October 1961. (Ray Deacon)

the guests which included a selection of the aircraft used by 6 FTS, from an Avro 504 to Jet Provost.

With the graduation of No.184 Course, No.6 FTS was disbanded as a pilot training unit on 30 June 1968. Two years later, on 1 May 1970, the school was reformed at Finningley within No.23 Group as an air navigation school from the amalgamation of 1 ANS (Varsity T1) and No.2 ANS (Varsity T1). In August 1970 they were joined by twelve HS Dominie T Mk.1s and the unit's first three Jet Provost T Mk.3s, XM419, XN506 and XN509, which were used in the training of student navigators on the basic course, the following month. By the end of year the unit's Flying Wing comprised twenty Varsities, thirteen Dominies and seven Jet Provosts.

At the beginning of 1971, a short 'low and fast' phase was introduced to the courses using Jet Provost T Mk.4s, the first of which were delivered in March 1971. Three years later, the Varsity had been withdrawn from service, and since its planned replacement, the Argosy, had failed to materialise, No.6 FTS was left to continue with its remaining Jet Provosts and Dominies.

In November 1975, a batch of T Mk.5s modified for use as long-range, low-level navigational trainers were delivered to No.6 FTS. The modifications included removing the nose strakes and fitting 48-gallon tanks to the wing tips to increase the range and endurance. The modified aircraft – unofficially referred to as the T Mk.5B – included XW287:P, XW291:N, XW293:Z, XW296:Q, XW298:0, XW302:T, XW304:X, XW306:Y, XW307:S, XW309:V, XW311:W, XW324:U and XW352:R and were first used on No.6 Air Defence lead-in course between November/December 1975.

64

By 1976, courses at Finningley had been extensively revised to meet the changing demands of the front line, especially with the steady decline in the need for navigators. The planned entry of the Tornado into RAF service, complete with digital computer systems, also found a requirement for 'streaming', where navigators completed a longer, thirty-nine-week basic course on the Dominie (forty-four hours) before being role-streamed to either Group 1 'fast jet' or Group 2 'multi-engine'. Those streamed as 'fast jet' went on to a specific course on the Jet Provost (twenty hours), roughly equivalent to the pilot's Jet Provost/Hawk syllabus. With the replacement of the single-seat Hunter by the Hawk in 1978, student navigators were then able to proceed to the TWU at either Chivenor or Brawdy for a further thirty hours of crew co-ordination training in the back seat of Hawk aircraft to obtain fast-jet experience before progressing to an OCU.

Steve Wilson was a member of No. 272 Course at Finningley from January 1981 to April 1982.

No. 6 Flying Training School comprised the air navigation school (ANS) and while I was there also the multi-engine training school (METS), which trained pilots on Jetstreams. I presume the air engineers school and air electronics operators school were also units of No.6 FTS.

The air navigation school then had units of its own. The nav specialists ran the ground school and were possibly involved with teaching the aero-systems course, they certainly would have been graduates of that course. On the flying side there was basics although I can't remember what the official title was. Once the navigators were streamed Group 1 or Group 2 they would go to advanced training. I don't know what the high-level guys were called. For the fast-jet lot we had the low-level training squadron (LLTS) – colloquially known as 'Louts'.

The LLTS trained at low level and used Jet Provosts and Dominies, these were clearly the same airframes that had been used in the basic phase and the same pilots although the LLTS instructor/navigators probably did mostly low level and the guys

65

I can call to mind had fast-jet/Vulcan backgrounds. I presume that the Jet Provosts were part of LLTS administratively despite being involved in basic and advanced training, air defence as well as ground attack.

I was the first real first tourist navigator posted to the Tornado GR.1 and I flew twenty-two hours and fifty minutes on the basic course and fifteen hours and forty minutes on the advanced course at Finningley. Courses started at monthly intervals and I was on the first of the new syllabus, we were not taught astro-navigation unless posted Group 2 and low-level radar use was a key element.

We had done low level and targets in the Jet Provost at 240 kts and then 300 kts before being streamed as 'fast jet'. Next was low-level Dominie which was systems management and terrain-avoiding radar techniques from the back and visual navigation from the right-hand seat. I'm sure they had Tornado training in mind at this stage but they had no idea how to prepare me. Next it was back to the Jet Provost where I was paired with a guy posted to Buccaneers and we took it in turns to lead the low-level pairs. We were due to graduate in March 1982 but they held us to combine the ceremony with No.273 Course in April.

Changes within the school during 1988 resulted in the Jet Provost squadron being re-labelled as the low-level and air defence training squadron on 21 March. Also

64. Jet Provost Mk.4s were operated by No.6 FTS at Finningley for training student navigators during the short 'low and fast' phase of their course. XP560 was delivered to the unit in March 1971 and ended its days on the fire dump, four years later. (via Wg Cdr Jeff Jefford)

65. In 1975, thirteen T Mk.5s were modified for use as long-range, low-level navigational trainers with No.6 FTS at Finningley and unofficially designated as T Mk.5Bs. (via Steve Wilson)

66

in 1988, the wings of some of the Jet Provost fleet began to fail the routine structural fatigue tests and five 'low fatigue' T Mk.5s (XW322:D, XW325:E, XW429:C, XW431:A and XW438:B) were issued as replacements; work on these particular aircraft included the fitting of wing-tip tanks by a working party at Scampton during November 1988.

As a result of the major cutback in the RAF's flying training programme under the government's Defence Costs Study in 1994, it was decided that all navigator training would be transferred to No.3 FTS at Cranwell and that Finningley would close in 1996. As a consequence, the Jet Provost was withdrawn from its navigation training role and on 14 August 1993, four aircraft of the No.6 FTS/LLADTS made a final farewell fly-past in a 'dying swan' formation over the airfield; the school's last five Jet Provosts being flown to Shawbury for disposal, the following month. No.6 FTS was disbanded on 31 March 1996.

NO.6 FTS DISPLAY TEAMS In September 1962, the school's aerobatic display team, 'Suntan/Cock's o' The North', made its debut at the Acklington and Leuchars Open Days. Originally formed by OC No.1 Squadron, Sqn Ldr Tony Winship, the team flew a mix of Jet Provost T Mk.3s and T Mk.4s and confined its demonstrations to local events, including course graduations, village fetes and Battle of Britain shows. In 1964 Flt Lt Johnny Walker took over as leader, and he led the team again during 1965 when it temporarily became a four-ship team, fully equipped with Jet Provost T Mk.4s.

Following a decision to restrict the number of station teams, the 'Cock's o' The North' was disbanded following its final display at RAF Stradishall on 3 October 1965.

Flt Lt Horace Farquhar-Smith was a member of the team in 1964/1965.

Unlike the Syerston team we normally flew the Jet Provost 4, which was considerably more powerful than the Jet Provost 3, but still not powerful enough to be flown normally on a line-astern loop – full power had to come on at a very early stage, despite the fact that one was catching up the aircraft in front. On a number of occasions we tried to fly the leader on a Jet Provost 3 and, although it was not too bad, for a whole variety of reasons we remained with the Jet Provost 4.

No.7 FLYING TRAINING SCHOOL

No.7 FTS was reformed at Church Fenton in No.23 Group on 13 March 1962 and equipped with Jet Provost T Mk.3s and T Mk.4s. The first ab initio course began on 24 April 1962, with the twenty-six students commencing their flying training on 9 May 1962. **Dougie Marr:**

I did my Wings course on the Jet Provost in 1963/1964 at Church Fenton and remember that bitter winter, students clearing the runway of snow with shovels so that we could fly, the new experience of sitting beside one's instructor (a change from the Chipmunk with its tandem cockpit), and flying unpressurised at 35,000 feet. We were on No.8 UAS Course (December 1963-July 1964), all of us having learned to fly at university on the Chipmunk, so we had a 160-hour course reduced to a notional 120 hours.

The Jet Provost 4 was more powerful than the Jet Provost 3 and so to be looked forward to. Our instructors were a mix of wartime experienced 'hairies', front-line pilots and the odd 'creamie'. We learned airmanship the hard way as weather, icing, rudimentary navigational aids and early radar

67

equipment all posed challenges. Accidents happened and the then AOC pronounced that "there were no bad students only bad instructors". Great morale booster for our QFIs! I can't say that the early Jet Provosts were popular but they served a purpose and were a step forward from the Piston Provost which they replaced. Moving on to the Gnat was a huge step forward in performance and avionics and was a delight to fly by comparison.

Flt Lt John Robinson completed his QFI course at Little Rissington and was posted to No.7 FTS as an instructor in June 1964.

I settled in to B Flight with Sqn Ldr Bill Waite as the squadron commander and Flt Lt Cyril Peters as the flight commander. We had a complement of eighteen instructors on the squadron as did 2 Squadron, the other unit on the FTS.

After initial familiarisation with the local area and procedures it was into instructing with 'real' students; in the first month I logged almost fifty hours flying. This then settled down to between thirty to forty hours per month. We were allocated three to four students to each instructor and one of the first I had was Mike Schofield who became the CO of the Queen's Flight. In early 1965 I had a Jordanian student, one of four on the course.

During my time at Church Fenton two courses were devoted to university air squadron students who had gained a degree at university and had flown with the attached UAS; this entitled them to a slightly shorter course on the Jet Provost as they had gained their flying badge.

In the main the students responded well to the way of life at 7 FTS. When they graduated they were posted to advanced training schools at RAF Valley on fast jets to fly Gnats, to RAF Oakington to fly multi-engined piston Varsity aircraft or to RAF Ternhill to fly helicopters. Valley always welcomed the products at Church Fenton as they knew that we turned out a good, reliable pilot.

Every three months there was a course graduation with Wings presentation ceremony and it was a great time for the instructors to mount a fly-past of FTS aircraft usually about twelve in different formations for each course.

Early in 1966 we learnt that 7 FTS was to close at the end of the year. This was unexpected but nevertheless we continued with the courses we had but as each one passed out so the flight that had been responsible for its students disbanded until at the end I was the last flight commander with the last course to graduate from No.7 FTS. There were final formation fly-pasts to all the Yorkshire RAF stations and the one final one for the graduation when I led a diamond formation of nine Jet Provosts. All that remained was to ferry the aircraft to various units and sort out postings for all the staff. The last aircraft departed in mid-December 1966, coinciding with my posting to the CFS.

On 17 November 1965, No.17 Course, comprising seventeen students, including three from the Royal Jordanian Air Force, became the last to graduate from the school. The unit continued to provide advanced training for foreign national students on Vampire T Mk.11s until it was disbanded on 30 November 1966.

66. In 1975, thirteen Jet Provosts were modified for use as long-range, low-level navigational trainers with No.6 FTS and unofficially referred to as the 'T Mk.5B'. One such aircraft was XW429 depicted at Chivenor on 28 July 1993, which was withdrawn from service the following September. (Author's Collection)

67. Jet Provost T Mk.4, XP678, of No.7 FTS at the USAF Armed Forces Day at Alconbury in May 1964. (Roger Lindsay)

In April 1979, the school was reformed at Church Fenton to resolve the RAF's pilot shortage pending the introduction of the Panavia Tornado into operational service. The first four Jet Provost T Mk.3As (XM376, XM475, XN473 and XN640) had arrived from Cranwell the previous month and on 2 April 1979, Church Fenton was officially opened with a fly-past of eight aircraft led by the station commander, Gp Capt J. A. Bell. Later in the month, the aircraft fleet was augmented with the arrival of the first Jet Provost T Mk.5As (XW371, XW372, XW417 and XW419).

Student training had previously been carried out at Linton-on-Ouse and the school 'inherited' two courses – No.32 Course (five students; graduating 2 August 1979) and No.35 Course (seventeen students; graduating 16 November 1979), which were trained with 1 Squadron. On 11 June 1979, the school's first 'home-grown' course, No.39 Course (seventeen students) began flying with 2 Squadron and graduated in February 1980.

Soon after reforming, the school suffered its first fatality on 3 July 1979 when a Jet Provost T Mk.5A (XW371) crashed near Lancaster during a low-level navigation exercise in bad weather; the student from No.32 Course being killed.

Tim Simpson was a student pilot on No.22 Course at Church Fenton from February 1985-April 1986. He returned to Church Fenton as a first-tour QFI in July 1987, serving until September 1989 when he went through the system again and ended up flying Tornado GR1s for nine years in Germany.

No.22 Course started with eleven student pilots. We lost one during circuit consolidation and another on the run up to 'spin aeros check'. The remaining nine finished the basic phase and were then streamed; we had five go on to Group 1, Phase 1, (fast-jet lead-in), one went Group 2, Phase 1, (multi-engine lead-in) and three going Group 3, Phase 1, (helicopter lead-in). These courses were also completed at Church Fenton, with only the Group 1 Phase 1 guys converting to the Jet Provost Mk.5A. At the end of these courses, we had lost another from the fast-jet stream who went multi-engine.

68

I went to Valley and was 'creamed off' and went to the Central Flying School at RAF Scampton, returning to Church Fenton as a QFI in July 1987. My time at Church Fenton was very enjoyable both as a student and as an instructor. I was only twenty-two years old when I went back as a QFI and that occasionally created difficulties gaining respect from some of the older students, but it did allow me to understand the plight of the student pilot better having just done the course that they were doing.

I remember the Jet Provost most fondly: the Mk.5A was a real sports car! I thought that every 'creamie' QFI should have been issued with their own as they were super fun to fly, their Achilles heel being their very low fuel storage (2,150 lbs), which you could get through in thirty-five minutes on a low-level nav exercise. Indeed, looking through my logbook, most Mk.5 flights were less than an hour in duration. The Mk.3A had the same amount of fuel, but having no pressurization system and a smaller engine, seemed to give it a marginally better endurance, at the expensive of performance. Both were great training aircraft which benefited tremendously from side-by-side seating.

In 1989, the first replacement Short Tucano T Mk.1 was delivered to the unit and course flying began in December. With the completion of the Jet Provost courses, the aircraft were dispersed to other units, the last T Mk.5A being withdrawn in September 1991. The school was disbanded again on 31 March 1992.

NO.7 FTS DISPLAY TEAMS In April 1965, **Flt Lt Duncan Robinson** was asked to form a three-ship aerobatic team to take part in the local SSAFA air display. He recalls its brief existence:

> I returned to No.7 FTS at Church Fenton in September 1964 and started doing formation aerobatics there in April 1965 with what was to become known as the 'Pudding Formation', named after the Yorkshire pudding. I was leader, Flt Lt Colin Thomas was No.2 and Flt Lt 'Ben' Gunn flew as No.3. We did three displays, including the SSAFA Display at Church Fenton on 7 June and the Battle of Britain shows at Colerne and Abingdon on 18 September 1965.

COLLEGE OF AIR WARFARE / SCHOOL OF REFRESHER FLYING

Formed on 1 July 1962 by the renaming of the RAF Flying College at Manby, the College of Air Warfare was responsible for many post-graduate courses for RAF officers and aircrew. All jet flying was carried out at nearby Strubby, with No.3 All Weather Jet Refresher Squadron (AWJRS) being tasked with restoring pilot handling skills; the AWJRS being an element of the College and equipped with Meteor T Mk.7s and F Mk.8s.

In July 1962, the AWJRS became the School of Refresher Flying (SoRF) as part of a reorganisation of training units, and in February 1964 its Meteors were gradually replaced following the delivery of the first Jet Provost T Mk.4s, XS186, XS209 and XS210.

Brian Hoskins joined the School of Refresher Flying, RAF Manby, in June 1969.

> I believe that the RAF had always given pilots returning from ground tours some refresher flying. In the early 1970s the SoRF was extremely busy with a large number returning to flying posts (flight lieutenants, squadron leaders, wing commanders and group captains). At the same time there was a big backlog in all stages of pilot training whilst the Harriers, Jaguars and Phantoms settled into service. Most of the pilots in the backlog required a refresher after months of holding.
>
> The SoRF ran about twenty-five courses a year and the length of the courses for those returning to flying posts depended on how long they had been on the ground and how long they had available – but basically they were long or short courses, comprising a basic thirty-hour course and a forty-five-hour course, respectively. We followed the basic CFS syllabus – pure flying, circuits, PFLs, aerobatics, IF, formation and navigation including low flying. The pace was basically set by how quickly the skills returned and our main aim was to restore the confidence they had before being posted to ground tours. If they made good progress their later sorties could be planned to reflect their next aircraft and role. Often though we only had time for the pure flying and IF and had to leave the advanced flying to the OCUs.
>
> We had a set course for the holding pilots but, again, much depended on how much time they had before their next course. Some, with very long holding time, returned to us at every stage of flying training. Our main aim was to restore their pure flying skills and to give them confidence for the next stage of training.
>
> The SoRF was quite large with the basic structure of a wing commander OC Flying, two squadron leaders, squadron commanders and a Standards Flight. Airwork did all the engineering tasks.
>
> I spent three-and-a-half years there, until September 1972, and flew 1,400 hours – 700 instructing and 700 other flying – mainly with the college aerobatic team, which I led between 1971 and 1972.

68. A fine airborne image of Jet Provost T Mk.5A, XW360, of No.7 FTS Church Fenton. It served with the school between July 1980 and August 1990. (Tim Simpson)

69-70

On 3 December 1973, the School of Refresher Flying was transferred to Leeming (see p.82) and its aircraft were pooled with No.3 FTS to become 1 Squadron / No.3 FTS; the CAW having disposed of its last Jet Provost the previous month and amalgamated with the RAF College, Cranwell to become the Department of Air Warfare.

COLLEGE OF AIR WARFARE DISPLAY TEAMS

Between 1955 and 1964, the RAFFC/CAW had operated a number of successful Meteor display teams and was keen to continue this tradition following its re-equipment with Jet Provosts. The original CAW Jet Provost team made its public debut at Elstree on Whit Sunday,

5 June 1965, and comprised Flt Lt Bill Shrubsole as leader, with Flt Lts Jack Bancroft, Terry Bliss, Alan Sheppard and Flt Sgt Don Soames-Waring as the solo aerobatic pilot.

Former Shackleton pilot, **Alan Sheppard** joined the School of Refresher Flying in December 1964 and flew with the team between 1965 and 1967.

> The team started off as the 'RAF College of Air Warfare Formation Aerobatic Team' and had this title for at least the first three years. Various team names were mooted in 1965 or 1966, including 'Astrals' and 'Magistrates', which were coined by Terry Bliss; it was only crew room banter and they were never used. We only did seven displays the first year, but things later picked up as Bill Shrubsole's strategy paid off and our reputation grew.

Under Bill Shrubsole's leadership, the team continued to develop and in March 1968, permission was granted for the formation of a new, totally re-vamped College Jet Provost team – the Macaws, the name being suggested by Bill Shrubsole and derived from the title

Manby College of Air Warfare. Painted in an attractive overall light grey, the team became one of only two to have its own special colour scheme when it featured a red fin and rudder, wing-tip tanks and stylised bird motif on the nose, together with the team name on the fin in white. Training for the new season had begun in January, with the first show at Waddington's 'Neighbours Day' on 3 May. Of the eighteen displays carried out that season, two were in Belgium (Brustem and Charleroi) and one in Holland (Leeuwarden).

A further change in colour scheme for the team aircraft in 1969 saw the Jet Provosts repainted in the new red/white/light aircraft grey scheme of Flying Training Command, with a stylised white band on the wing-tip tanks and a smaller representation of the 'perched parrot' emblem painted on the nose; in successive years, this design would be modified to incorporate a flying Macaw emblem. This would also be Bill Shrubsole's last season as leader of the team. A founder member and leader of the Macaws since 1965, Bill Shrubsole was subsequently promoted to squadron leader and awarded the AFC.

By 1971 the Macaws became the last formation display team in the RAF to fly the Jet Provost T Mk.4; the remaining teams having re-equipped with Jet Provost T Mk.5s. A feature of the team's display was the close box formation inverted fly-past, which had been originally introduced into the display routine by Bill Shrubsole. The Macaws also became the only British jet aerobatic team to fly a complete formation of four aircraft inverted – the others being the French national team, 'La Patrouille de France' and 'Les Diables Rouge' from Belgium.

The 1973 Manby team – Flt Lts Pete Diggance, John Aldington, Mike Fox and Mick Marriott – opened its season on 28 April with shows at Thorney Island and Hamble. On 2 June the team suffered a slight set-back when John Aldington was seriously injured after falling off the wing of an aircraft. To fulfil its display commitment, the team decided to continue with three aircraft and a modified display sequence, beginning on 19 June with a show at Manby for the Royal College of Defence Studies.

In September 1974, No.229 OCU at Chivenor was disbanded and its task transferred to the newly-formed Tactical Weapons Unit at Brawdy. The move to Brawdy coincided with the delivery of two Jet Provost T Mk.3s, XN579 and XN584, which were initially used by the Standards Flight to assist in the training of RAF and army forward air controllers with the Joint Forward Air Control Training and Standards Unit (JFACTSU). By February 1976 the Jet Provost T Mk.3s had been replaced by Jet Provost T Mk.4s and the unit was renamed as 1 TWU in July 1978.

Rod Dean commanded the JFACTSU at Brawdy between 1979 and 1981.

> The Forward Air Control training with Jet Provosts was not just for the controllers to get air experience. The majority of the flying was for the Jet Provosts to act as fighters for the trainee FACs to control onto targets for practice.
>
> Each FAC had to control a minimum number of target attacks before he could be qualified and the Jet Provost was a lot cheaper to operate than either the Hawk or the Hunter. At Chivenor we had used the Chipmunk for the same role which was hilarious at times given the slow speed of the Chippy. I can't remember how long the FAC course lasted but it was certainly only weeks and not months.

In August 1981, C Flight of No.79 (R) Squadron was formed at Brawdy with the additional tasks of refreshing pilots returning from ground tours and UK

NO.1 TACTICAL WEAPONS UNIT / 'C' FLIGHT No.79 (R) SQUADRON, BRAWDY

69. Four Jet Provost T Mk.4s operated by C Flight, 79 (R) Squadron, for FAC training at Brawdy in 1985. (via Dave McIntyre)

70. Jet Provost T Mk.4, XP690, of the College of Air Warfare was part of a mixed formation flown on 20 July 1972, comprising Varsities, Dominies and sixteen Jet Provosts, to mark the forthcoming closure of RAF Strubby. The formation was re-flown on 8 September, the official close-down date of Strubby. (Laurie Bean)

orientation courses for foreign exchange students. **Dave McIntyre** was posted from the Refresher Flying Squadron at No.3 Flying Training School, RAF Leeming, in August 1981 to form C Flight, No 79 (R) Squadron.

At the time, all pilots out of recent practice were given a short refresher course to re-familiarise them with the environment, but in order to cut costs it had been decided to send returning fast-jet pilots direct to the tactical weapons units. The trouble was that a few were so out of practice that they were struggling on their initial Hunter and Hawk flights, and the Jet Provosts at Brawdy were being under-utilised.

At that time, there were three Jet Provost Mk.4s at Brawdy; the main user being the Joint Forward Air Control Training and Standards Unit (JFACTSU). Two of the aircraft were camouflaged (03/XP547 and 04/XP564) and painted in 79 Squadron markings. The third, 05/XS178, was still in her red and white Support Command (training) colours.

Foreign national pilots, although current, often needed an introduction to RAF procedures, and although the JFACTSU pilots had prepared a brief course, they weren't qualified instructors, and it occasionally conflicted with their primary task of training FACs.

As OC of the newly formed C Flight on 79 Squadron, my brief was to prepare a formal syllabus offering a series of lectures and ten hours of flying to prepare the students for their TWU course. Since the requirements were broadly similar, it became known as the UK orientation course (UKOC), and after a few trips to complete my check-out on Jet Provost T Mk.4s, my work began in earnest on 22 September 1981. In the following six months I flew over 150 hours with over a dozen students, mostly senior RAF officers, and two USAF and one German pilot, as well as helping out JFACTSU with their FAC training sorties.

On 22 April 1982, I was flying in the 'old' 04/ XP564, on a low-level navigation exercise over the

Welsh hills near Aberystwyth with Commander Arun Prakash, who was destined to command the Indian navy's first Sea Harrier squadron, and later became the First Sea Lord. As he increased power to climb over a mountain, the engine failed to respond, and during the course of investigating the problem, the power reduced to idle, and we were forced to eject, landing in the Nant-y-Moch reservoir near Machynlleth.

Otherwise uninjured, I had sustained compression fractures to four of my vertebrae which required me to lie in a bed in the RAF Hospital at Wroughton near Swindon for three weeks. The Falklands War was getting serious, and I managed to bag a private room with a TV, so I was able to keep up with the events as they unfolded, and brief the doctors at the end of the day. I was banned from flying for three months while the fractures stabilised during which time one of my former colleagues at RFS – Flt Lt Herbie Sutcliffe – was sent to replace me as we had a growing commitment to provide courses for senior officers returning to flying duties and foreign national pilots on exchange assignments. The new '04' – XR679 – arrived on 26 April and was already camouflaged by the time I flew with Herbie on an engine air test on 20 July.

As the numbers of refresher and UKOC students increased, it became apparent that borrowing a Mk.4 from Shawbury to cover peak periods was not enough, so we had acquired XS219 (06) on 19 March 1982 – just before I dumped the original 04 in the Nant-y-Moch reservoir. XP564 was replaced by XR679 in April 1982 and I first flew her on 25 July 1982 after I was declared fit to fly again.

We continued to borrow Mk.4s from Shawbury from time to time – e.g. XP638 from December 1981 to March 1982 and again in May 1983. We also borrowed XS181(F) in March/April 1983.

We had also acquired a fourth Jet Provost – 06/XS219 – and so, with two staff pilots, we were able to introduce formation flying to the syllabus. Before

long, Herbie was offered a fast-jet course and in January 1983 he was replaced by Flt Lt Mike Williamson, and together with the JFACTSU pilots we were able to launch our first four-ship formation on January 22. It was quite an achievement as one or other of the jets was usually in the hangar being serviced.

My last Jet Provost flight was in 05/XS178 on 25 September 1986, which turned out to be quite eventful as we were asked to act as SAR top cover for a Hawk student who had ejected into the sea off the Pembrokeshire coast.

On 31 March 1989 the unit's last four Jet Provosts (XP547, XR679, XS178 and XS219) were officially withdrawn and issued to No.2 SoTT, Cosford, as ground instructional airframes.

71. Jet Provost T Mk.4, XR679, was issued to the TWU at Brawdy in April 1982. The attractive markings on this aircraft were an unofficial, one-off paint scheme to mark the official withdrawal of the Jet Provost from the unit in March 1989. (Ray Deacon)

Above: Strikemaster Mk.80As in close formation near Faisal's Finger in the Saudi Arabian desert. The nearest aircraft, '1130' was returned to the UK in 2000 and is still airworthy on the airshow display circuit. (BAe Systems Heritage Warton-Percival/Hunting Collection)

04 BAC 167 STRIKEMASTER AND FOREIGN SALES

72

73

The BAC 167 was a development of the Jet Provost T Mk.5 and produced in response to a requirement from overseas air forces for a light-attack aircraft, designed for counter-insurgency operations (COIN).

The major internal feature of the BAC 167 was the installation of a Viper 535 (20F20) engine of 3,410 lbs thrust, which was considered an improvement over the 2,500-lb Viper 11 of the Jet Provost T Mk.4 and T Mk.5; this increase in power was also considered as advantageous to overseas customers where a weapons-carrying ability for a dual trainer/COIN aircraft was required and where a hot/high environment reduced engine performance.

The BAC 167's stressed wing provided the ability to carry a variety of underwing loads of up to 3,100 lbs on four pylons per wing. The options typically included four 75-gallon fuel tanks, four 500-lb bombs, 24 SURA R80 rockets, eight 25-lb practice bombs or 20-lb frag-mentation bombs, four eighteen-tube SNEB 68-mm rockets or two 0.5-inch mini-gun pods. In addition, two 7.62-mm Fraser-Nash machine guns, with 600 rounds of ammunition, were fitted in the lower intake lips. An optional G90 camera gun could also be installed in the nose cone with LFS 5, GM 2 or SFOM gun sights being provided for either or both seats.

A revised fuel system also included conformal fuel tanks on the wing tips, each containing 48 imperial gallons. The internal fuel carried in the outer wings and three self-sealing bag tanks in each inner wing, provided total capacity of 270 imperial gallons. With a 3,100-lb weapon load, plus internal armament, the aircraft had a maximum ferry range of 1,450 nautical miles and an endurance of four hours.

Continued flight evaluation and rig testing failed to indicate any problems caused by the additional loads carried by the BAC 167. It was, therefore, decided to retain the undercarriage units of the previous produc-tion Jet Provost aircraft as the increase of the all-up weight of the airframe failed to justify any major struc-tural change.

In October 1968 the BAC 167 was finally renamed as the Strikemaster and two prototype aircraft were allocated for company trials, G27-8 and G27-9, the first of which had been flown on 26 October 1967 by com-pany test pilot, Reg Stock.

The first customer for the Strikemaster was Saudi Arabia, which placed an order for twenty-five aircraft in December 1965 as part of a complete air-defence system package worth more than £100 million. This

74

75

would prove to be the biggest single order for the Strikemaster, the first of which was delivered to the King Faisal Academy in Riyadh in September 1968 to serve in the training and light-attack role.

Over the next ten years, a total of 151 Strikemasters were built for overseas customers: 141 being produced at Warton, with deliveries finally completed when a replacement aircraft (1135) was officially handed over to Saudi Arabia in May 1978.

With the increased production of the Jaguar tactical strike fighters at Warton, it was decided to assemble a further ten Strikemasters at Hurn against future sales. Hurn had already manufactured the wings for the Jet Provost since 1966 and was short of work following the completion of the contract to build the BAC 1-11 short-range jet airliner. Therefore, in November 1979 the first Strikemaster fuselage for the newly established Hurn final assembly line was transferred from Warton and made its initial flight on 7 August 1980 as G16-26. The following month it was registered as G-BIDB for use as a company demonstration aircraft. It was joined by Hurn's second Strikemaster, G16-27/G-BIHZ, which made its first production test flight on 23 October 1980.

Among the many sales demonstrations carried out by the two aircraft included the Farnborough and Paris air shows, together with displays and evaluations for various visiting foreign ministers and defence attachés. In May 1981, G-BIDB and G-BIHZ were flown to Khartoum to

72. Cockpit layout of a Strikemaster. (BAe Systems Heritage Warton-Percival/ Hunting Collection)

73. Typical weapons load capable of being carried on the wing strong points of the Strikemaster, including fuel tanks, bombs, rocket pods and 7.62-mm gun pods. Additional practice bombs and flares could also be carried in the ML 100 Carriers. (BAC)

74. Two company demonstration Strikemaster Mk.89s, G-BIDB and G-BIHZ, at Bournemouth in May 1981. Flown by Reg Stock and Don Thomas, the two aircraft were flown to Khartoum to celebrate Sudan Armed Forces Day. The aircraft had been temporarily diverted from the Ecuadorian order for various evaluations and displays, including the SBAC and Paris air shows. (BAC via Reg Stock)

75. In November 1979, ten Strikemaster airframes were transferred from Warton to Hurn for completion. These included the one in the foreground, which was sold to Ecuador as Mk.89, FAE260, in November 1987. (BAe Systems Heritage Warton-Percival/Hunting Collection)

76-77

being subjected to an arm's embargo following a renewed outbreak of fighting in the country. The next three Strikemasters made their maiden flight from Hurn, but with the closure of the site in May 1984 the four uncompleted aircraft were returned to Warton by road. Of the seven remaining Strikemasters, one was delivered to Oman (425) in September 1986 and the remaining six were sold to Ecuador, including the last four to be delivered from Warton (FAE261-264) on 21 October 1988.

celebrate Sudan Armed Forces Day in the presence of Presidents Nimeiri of Sudan and Sadat of Egypt. The pilots who flew them were Reg Stock and Don Thomas. The aircraft were then returned from Khartoum to Hurn.

Sales of the Strikemasters assembled at Hurn were slow to materialise until 1983, when the Sudan government offered to purchase the complete batch. The first three aircraft (141, 142 and 144) were delivered from Hurn in November 1983, with the remaining airframes

BAC STRIKEMASTER VARIANTS
Saudi Arabia (1968-1978)
▸ Strikemaster Mk.80 F/f 26 Oct 1967: twenty-five aircraft.
▸ Strikemaster Mk.80A: twenty-two upgraded aircraft as part of a follow-up order.
South Yemen (1969)
▸ Strikemaster Mk.81 F/f 15 Feb 1969: four aircraft.

Oman (1969-1986)
- Strikemaster Mk.82 F/f 29 Nov 1968: twelve aircraft.
- Strikemaster Mk.82A: twelve aircraft as part of a follow-up order.

Singapore (1969-1970)
- Strikemaster Mk.84 F/f 2 Aug 1969: sixteen aircraft.

Kuwait (1970-1971)
- Strikemaster Mk.83 F/f 17 Dec 1969: twelve aircraft.

Kenya (1971)
- Strikemaster Mk.87 F/f 19 Aug 1970: six aircraft.

New Zealand (1972-1975)
- Strikemaster Mk.88 F/f 15 Feb 1972: sixteen aircraft.

Ecuador (1972-1988)
- Strikemaster Mk.89 F/f 29 June 1972: twenty-two aircraft.

Sudan (1983)
- Strikemaster Mk.90 F/f Aug 1980: three aircraft.

FOREIGN SALES OF STRIKEMASTER AND JET PROVOST

BOTSWANA As a result of increasing tension and border incursions in Southern Africa, the Botswana Defence Force (BDF) was formed during the latter part of 1977, initially equipped with a variety of multi-role transport and training aircraft. To enhance its strike capability, the BDF acquired nine Strikemasters from BAC; the aircraft having previously been operated by Kuwait and Kenya and placed into store at Warton. The first three aircraft were delivered to Francistown in April 1988.

Derick Bridge was appointed by BAC to run the Botswana operation.

I started at Warton in January 1988 and began the conversion training for two BDF instructors, the following month. We flew OJ1 initially until OJ2 was rebuilt, then used them until 18 March. By then OJ3 was completed and we set off for the ferry to Botswana on 22 March, being led by an HS 125. I flew OJ2 with Capt Chris Lempoletse; OJ1 was flown by Chris Yeo, director Flight Ops at Warton with Capt Peter Molatedi, while OJ3 was flown by Phil Dye. The route was Warton, Bordeaux, Tangiers, a diversion to Casablanca, Agadir, Las Palmas. After that it was Nouakchott, Freetown, Kinshasa, Mbuji-Mayi, Lusaka and then Francistown on 3 April. It took thirteen days because of technical issues in Morocco.

Francistown was the main operating base for the aircraft, being a joint civil/military airfield with a single runway, no taxiways and basic facilities. The Strikemasters also used Notwane when operating in the south of the country, with Selebi Phikwe as the nearest diversion airfield and Maun in the north for its refuelling facilities. BDF Air Wing squadrons were assigned with a 'Z2', which was used as a designation for 'squadron'.

Flying training began immediately following the delivery of the first three aircraft, continuing with the two BDF instructors until September when the first six students arrived following their initial training on the SAL Bulldog. In July, a second batch of Strikemaster aircraft was delivered to Francistown (OJ5, OJ6 and OJ7), followed by the last three in September (OJ4, OJ8 and OJ9).

The second intake of students arrived in August 1989, by which time the flying training syllabus had been modified to include battle formation, weapons, combat and practice interceptions. As the Strikemaster

76. The newly established Strikemaster assembly line at Hurn in September 1980, with the first company demonstration aircraft, G-BIDB, in the foreground. Ten Strikemaster airframes were assembled at Hurn and deliveries of the first three to Sudan began in November 1983. (Author's Collection)

77. Jet Provost T Mk.55, '167', was one of three aircraft delivered to Sudan from Hurn in March 1969. It was written off in a flying accident, two months later. (BAe Systems Heritage Warton-Percival/Hunting Collection)

79-80

was also an 'operational' aircraft, a rudimentary firing range was established where the students carried out weapons training with cannon and rockets.

Unfortunately, the BDF lost three aircraft in flying accidents during this period. **Derick Bridge** again:

> OJ5 – 29 April 1989: We flew a six aircraft formation for a small display at Gaborone stadium for Armed Forces Day and, at the insistence of the BDF, we had to include three students. After initial flyover as a Vic formation of five aircraft, plus one more in the box, a break-away of the three students followed with 'OJ4' and 'OJ5' doing a 60-degree bank, left and right, and box pulling up to 45 degrees and rolling, then going left. After the break the right-hand

aircraft continued pulling and rolling until it crashed. The student was Lt Lekhutile, who didn't survive.

> OJ9 – 21 November 1989: A student, Lt Chalegbwa hit a Kudu, which was one of a herd of seven antelope which crossed the runway ahead of him as he was doing a 'roller' landing at Francistown. His evasion attempt caused him to leave the runway and the aircraft crossed the grass before hitting a rocky mound which removed the nosewheel and damaged the nose before pitching the aircraft into the air again for a short distance. The second impact collapsed the main undercarriage, creased the fuselage, broke both rear spar attachments and the port upper mainspar attachment. Also damaged were the wings, flaps, tip tanks and starboard tailplane.

OJ4 – 12 December 1989: Failed to recover from a deliberate spin and crashed about twelve miles to the west of Francistown. Major Chris Lempaletse QFI and student Lt Chalegbwa both ejected safely, although Lempaletse suffered a crushed fracture of the spine.

NOTE: It was common practice for the BDF to issue the same serial number to more than one aircraft. Hence there were two Strikemasters with the serial OJ4. The first (ex-ZG813 then KAF121) was written off in November 1989 and replaced by another Strikemaster (ex-Kenya AF 601). The latter was registered as G-AYHR in April 1997, and later as G-UNNY.

In 1996, thirteen ex-Canadian CF-116s (ten single-seater CF-5As and three trainer CF-5Bs) were ordered to replace the Strikemasters, and in April 1997, with the exception of OJ3 which became a 'gate guard' at Base Thebephatswa, the surviving aircraft were sold to Global Aviation at Binbrook, where they were refurbished for re-sale to the civil market. In February 2003, two of these aircraft, OJ4/G-UNNY and OJ5/G-BXFP, were sold to 'Strikemaster Films' and acquired by the Force Aérienne de la Côte d'Ivoire for 'reconnaissance flights and pilot training' with the registrations TU-VRA and TU-VRB, respectively. TU-VRA was known to have arrived in Malta on 15 February 2003 and immediately impounded, only to continue its ferry flight to Algiers on 22 March 2003 because of a legal loophole. A French newspaper reported that the aircraft was subsequently flown by mercenary pilots during the bloody civil war and was thought to have been damaged during an attack on Yamoussoukro airport by French forces on 6 November 2003. The second aircraft, allegedly purchased for spare parts and still in RNZAF markings, arrived in Malta during February 2003 and

was shipped out on 21 May 2004. Both aircraft were noted at BA Abidjan in May 2015, however, and reportedly awaiting scrapping by UNO.

CEYLON In 1958, Ceylon became the first country to place an order for the armed export version of the Jet Provost. The twelve Jet Provost T Mk.51s, CJ701-CJ712, were delivered between December 1959 and December 1960, with the first six aircraft being officially handed over to the jet training squadron at Negombo/Katunayake on 10 December 1959.

On 1 February 1960, the training squadron suffered its first loss when Plt Off N. Lokuge was forced to abandon his aircraft after an engine failure during a rehearsal for the Independence Day fly-past. The pilot ejected safely at 350 feet and made history as the first RCyAF pilot to eject from an aircraft. The Jet Provost (CJ704) crashed in the Negombo Lagoon, Western Province. A further aircraft was lost on 17 January 1966 when it crashed at Katunayake, killing the pilot, Flt Sgt S. Sally.

During 1970, eight aircraft were withdrawn to help reduce defence expenditure and placed into store. The following year, the RCyAF was caught by surprise when the Marxist JVP launched an island-wide insurrection on 5 April 1971; police stations and the RCyAF base at Ekala being attacked in the initial wave. Responding rapidly the RCyAF deployed its limited amount of available aircraft, initially to resupply besieged police stations and military outposts and patrol major cities. To support the beleaguered government forces, the Jet Provosts were taken out of storage and returned to service within three days, carrying out attacks on rebel locations while operating with No.6 Squadron. One aircraft is known to have been lost during this period when it crashed in Trincomalee on 13 April 1971, killing the pilot, Fg Off M. D. S. R. Wijetunga.

78. The first three Strikemaster Mk. 83s were delivered to the Botswana Defence Force on 22 March 1988. (BAC via Derick Bridge)

79. Noted at Luqa in March 2003, Strikemaster Mk.87, TU-VRA (ex-OJ4/

G-UNNY), en route to Algiers. The aircraft was one of two sold to Strikemaster Films and acquired by the Force Aérienne de la Côte d'Ivoire. (Roberto Bennetti)

80. Strikemaster Mk.87 TU-VRB

(ex-OJ5/G-BXFP) of the Force Aérienne de la Côte d'Ivoire, BA Abidjan, 2 May 2015. This was the second Strikemaster to be obtained from Strikemaster Films in May 2004. (Jacques Guillem)

Preserved airframes: Sri Lanka Museum, Ratamala: CJ701 (actually CJ711) and CJ704; SLAF's Eagles' Lakeside Banquet & Convention Hall, Attidiya: 'CJ712'; Anuradhapura AB CJ710 main gate; Batticaloa AB CJ706; Colombo AF HQ CJ712; Jaffna CJ709; Trincomalee AB CJ707; Wirawila AB CJ701.

ECUADOR In December 1972, eight Strikemaster Mk.89s (FAE243-FAE250) were delivered to the Ecuadorian air force. These aircraft were initially operated by the Escuela Superior Militar de Aviación (military aviation school) at BA Ulpiano Paez, Salinas, replacing the North American T-6 Texan as an advanced training aircraft.

In 1974, the aircraft were transferred to BA Taura, Guayaquil, where they were formed into the Escuadron de Combate 2113, with the dual role of jet conversion and close air support under the command of Capt Francisco San Pedro. For advanced training duties, a flight from the unit was maintained on permanent detachment with the military aviation school.

As a result of the number of original aircraft written off due to flying accidents, a further eight Strikemaster Mk.89As (FAE251-FAE258) were acquired in May 1976 to maintain the squadron's operational role. With the delivery of the first batch of BAe Jaguar ES and EB aircraft in January 1977, the squadron was transferred again to the newly built Eloy Alfaro AB, Manta, on 18 October 1978 to form Escuadron de Combate 2313 'Halcones'.

By November 1978, the FAE had lost seven of its sixteen Strikemasters and **Wg Cdr Mick Ryan** was attached to the unit at Quito to ascertain the probable cause of the accidents.

The Ecuadorians were saying that the crashes were due to the layout of the instruments in the Strikemaster and the Jaguar, which was the standard RAF layout. They panicked BAC when they said they would not buy another squadron of Jaguars because of this. So BAC paid for me, as OC CFS Examining Wing, and one of their own engineers to do an audit of the accidents and the Ecuadorian air force. We

were flown out to Quito in November 1968 and were there for one month. I was given complete access to the seven fatal Strikemaster accidents at that time. One was a student doing low-level aerobatics over the sea in front of his parent's house and he misjudged it and flew into the sea. The other six were all loss of control in cloud. One came out of the bottom of cloud at about 2,000 feet going vertical and plunged straight into the river. It was some time before they found the wreckage.

I then spent a month flying with all levels of pilots from basic training students through to front-line pilots. They had very bad weather on the coastal plains where they did most of their flying. It was rather like the UK with a base at 2,000 feet and solid up to 20,000 feet. I found, for example, one student on his first solo formation flight was taken up through solid cloud to 20,000 feet where they practised formation flying in bright sunlight above cloud. He managed this as it was a straight climb to height when in cloud. On the standard recovery, over-head-outbound descent-inbound descending turn at half the height plus 1,000 feet – final descent to below cloud on the way back in to the airfield – they had led this poor student through extremely thick cloud where it was said that it was difficult to see much beyond the wing tip. Inevitably with such an inexperienced pilot, when they turned inbound he lost contact with his leader and had to roll out wings level for thirty seconds then resume the inbound turn as an individual aircraft. This is an awful manoeuvre even for an experienced pilot good at

instrument flying. The student came out of cloud at very high speed going vertical having lost control.

I also found that the Ecuadorians had chosen to be trained all over the world: Russia, USA, UK and other air forces. They had no formal instrument training system and no need to re-qualify once you passed your initial instrument rating test whereas the RAF require re-qualification every six months and a minimum amount of practice and real instrument flying. The Ecuadorians had picked those bits from each of the foreign air force schemes that they liked – usually because they were fairly easy – and did not require re-qualification. This poor instrument training along with exposing students to difficult situations was the theme and cause of the other six accidents. I explained that the standard instrument layout in all RAF aircraft was a safety factor, not the cause of the loss of control.

In my final report I spelt all this out and recommended that they adopted the RAF instrument training and re-qualification system. I laid out a detailed training and testing programme for all levels of their aircrew. As an example of their attitude to flight safety and experience I was rather disturbed to find that the staff officer from their air ministry who had been allocated to look after us, was also in the habit – along with many others – of deciding that he was bored with his desk job and ground tour in the ministry and would, on a whim, act as co-pilot on the scheduled internal airline flights from Quito to the coastal airports. There was no qualification control or checking and they considered this quite normal.

81. The first six Jet Provost T Mk.51s for the Royal Ceylon Air Force were officially handed over to the jet training squadron at Negombo/Katunayake on 10 December 1959. (BAe Systems Heritage Warton-Percival/Hunting Collection)

82. As a result of the number of original aircraft written off due to flying accidents, a further eight Strikemaster Mk.89As (FAE251-FAE258) were acquired by Ecuador in May 1976 to maintain the operational role of Escuadron de Combate 2113. (BAe Systems Heritage Warton-Percival/Hunting Collection)

83

On 27 January 1979, a further Strikemaster (FAE255) crashed after an engine fire. This was followed by a series of similar unexplained engine failures, which resulted in the FAE grounding the aircraft and temporarily disbanding the squadron until a full investigation had been carried out. Suggestions that the aircraft had arrived in the country with inherent technical problems, especially the Viper engines, were not accepted by BAe as no apparent faults were discovered in either of the two engines returned to Rolls-Royce for examination.

In April 1981, BAe test pilot **Reg Stock** and an engineer returned to Ecuador, determined to restore confidence in the operation of the aircraft and its engine. During the visit, considerable advice was offered on how to improve matters and during which it was accepted by them that pilot error could have been partly responsible for many of the accidents.

The first two Ecuadorian Strikemaster aircraft were tested by me at Salinas in January 1973. The next one, '245' was originally tested by the training squadron commander from Taura (eventually a BAe Jaguar base) who apparently started the test by beating up the airfield. The initial pilots' conversions were done by me training five pilots and encompassing general handling (especially spinning), instrument flying, formation, night flying, firing guns, rockets and dropping bombs, all in less than two months. I returned to the UK in March 1973.

It was pointed out to them that their aircraft attrition rate was far in excess of any other operator of the Strikemaster and both BAe and the CFS made subsequent visits to the FAE to suggest operating improvements but, as ever, it was up to the Ecuadorians to implement them. This could have been due to a number of factors including inexperience and insufficient training by properly qualified personnel. I can only state that no defect was found in one of the failed engines which were returned to Rolls-Royce for examination.

The company was asked by the FAE to offer advice on how best to operate their remaining aircraft and the company wished to reassure them of the basic reliability of the aircraft and its engine. The investigative trip to Ecuador was between 7-20 April 1981. I have a telex dated 16 September 1981 requesting a pilot and technician for a year's duty in order to assist in the operation of the Strikemaster as recommended by BAe. The pilot was, I believe, Bob Blagborough.

With the renewed outbreak of fighting over the disputed area on the border with Peru between January and February 1981, the squadron was reactivated under the command of Lt Rodrigo Bohorquez and deployed to Guayaquil International Airport to take part in the brief military clash – the Paquisha war. The squadron returned to the area again in January 1985 when another localised conflict – the Cenepa war – broke out.

During 1985, Ecuador expressed an interest in acquiring six more Strikemasters by negotiating a deal with BAe to acquire further aircraft from an embargoed order originally destined for Sudan. Some of the aircraft had been held in storage at Samlesbury in expectation of an eventual order and were released for sale in mid-1987. The first two (FAE259 and FAE260) were delivered to Ecuador in November 1987, followed by the last airframes to be assembled at Hurn (FAE261-264) on 21 October 1988.

Following the FAE's re-equipment with Mirage jet fighters in late 2009 and the delivery of the first Embraer A-29B Super Tucanos at BA Manta, the Strikemasters were officially retired on 10 February 2010. Following their withdrawal from service, ten aircraft were placed in open store at AB Manta. In addition, FAE246 is preserved at the Museo Aéreo de la Fuerza Aérea Ecuatoriana, Quito, FAE252 is with Escuela Superior Militar de Aviación Salinas/BA Ulpiano Paez and FAE262 is at Bahia.

83. Strikemaster Mk.89s belonging to Escuadron de Combate 2313 'Halcones' of the Ecuadorian air force. This particular section includes the last Strikemaster airframes to be assembled at Hurn (FAE261-264) which were delivered to Ecuador in October

84

IRAQ On 1 January 1964, the Iraqi air force became the fifth country to place an order for the Jet Provost, worth £1.5 million for twenty Jet Provost Mk.52s (600-619). The order followed several years of operations with piston-engined Provosts, a number of which had been exported to Iraq in 1955.

The first three Mk.52s (600, 601 and 602) departed from Luton for Rashid air base on 31 August 1964, flown by Reg Stock and two Iraqi pilots, Capt Hakam and Lt Mohammed. The Iraqi order was eventually completed on 28 April 1965 when '618' and '619' were delivered by Eric Bucklow and Vyrell Mitchell, respectively.

In service, the Jet Provost was used for basic and advanced training at the Air Force College, Basra, and for weapons training at the Fighter Leaders School, Al Rasheed/Alwihda/Tikrit air bases. The Iraqi flying training programme comprised primary training on the Percival Provost, basic training on the Jet Provost and MiG-15 UTI, followed by advanced training on the Jet Provost and MiG-21 UTI.

By 1974, the Jet Provost had been replaced by the L-29 Delfin jet trainer and a small number of the survivors were thought to have been used as instructional airframes at Tikrit Air Academy, Al Sahra, at which '610' and '612' were noted in a derelict condition in 2003.

1988. (Jacques Guillem)

84. Jet Provost T Mk.52, 600, at Luton in August 1964, awaiting delivery to the Royal Iraqi air force. (BAe Systems Heritage Warton-Percival/Hunting Collection)

KENYA The Kenya air force (KAF) was formed in June 1964. To maintain a responsive and effective air force in the face of political and military unrest in the region, six Strikemaster Mk.87s (601-606) were ordered in 1969 to equip its first strike squadron.

The first two aircraft left Warton on 5 February 1970 and arrived at Eastleigh Airport, Nairobi, eight days later. **Terry Lloyd** was the pilot of the first aircraft to be delivered.

> The two Strikemasters (601 and 602) were flown by myself and David Curry, accompanied by Paul Lewis, the British Aerospace engineer who would be based at Eastleigh in support of the aircraft. Prior to the ferry flight, David and I had both converted to the Strikemaster at Warton by the senior production test pilot, Pete Ginger.
>
> The Strikemaster squadron was to have six aircraft and these would be ferried from Warton to Eastleigh in three batches; the route for the ferry being determined by diplomatic clearances so was not as direct as one might have expected. Two RAF flying instructors, Flt Lts David Curry and Joe Whitfield, were posted to train the Kenyan pilots on the Strikemaster and a Kenyan pilot, Major Larry Mwanzia, had been earmarked as the squadron commander who, together with Lt Joshi, were at RAF Leeming in 1970 where they converted to the Jet Provost Mk.4.

Terry Lloyd assumed the post of OC Flying at KAF Eastleigh on 4 July 1970. The job specification was to command the Flying Wing, which comprised a transport wing equipped with four DHC Caribou, and three Beaver and six Chipmunk aircraft for training purposes. His remit also specified the introduction of the Strikemaster to the KAF and in the longer term acting as air adviser with a handover of the OC Flying appointment to a Kenyan officer.

Joe Whitfield was one of the RAF flying instructors.

> In mid-1970 I was selected to be part of a team of two to train the Kenya air force pilots on the Strikemaster. The other pilot was Flt Lt Dave Curry, ex-Canberras and also one of the pilots who flew Spitfires during the making of the film, *The Battle of Britain*. We both arrived in October 1970 to await the completion of the Strikemasters at Warton.
>
> I was due to collect and deliver one of the first two aircraft, 601 and 602, but dental problems caused me to miss out. I did, however, take part in the ferrying of one of the second two aircraft, 603 and 604. After post-production air tests at Warton we set off for Kenya on 9 February 1971. Even though we had drop and tip tanks the legs were fairly short. The routing took us via Thorney Island, Nice, Brindisi, Athens, Akrotiri, Diyarbakir (Iran), Tehran, Kuwait, Bahrain, Riyadh and Jeddah, where we were arrested because the Kenyans had not applied for the overflight of Saudi Arabia and the landing rights. Fortunately, the RAF air attaché happened to be there and after pulling some strings we were allowed out. Onwards via Asmara, Hara Meda and the Eastleigh base.
>
> The third pair of aircraft, 605 and 606, departed Warton on 19 March. I was leading with the squadron commander, Major Larry Mwanzia in the right-hand seat. Sqn Ldr Bill Jago, the air ops man from the KAF headquarters was my number two. Same routing, but when we got to Bahrain the Saudis would not let us into their airspace because the Kenyans had again cocked up the diplomatic clearance. We spent a week in Bahrain while that was sorted out.
>
> The first batch of six Kenyans were all very experienced pilots, having done the full Wings course on the Jet Provost. Dave Curry and I trained the pilots using a modified Hunter OCU syllabus. It included low-level navigation, close and battle formation, air-to-air combat, night flying, air-to-ground weaponry (bombs, SNEB rockets, .303 machine gunnery) at a range the squadron constructed north of Mount Kenya. The engineering was carried out by RAF personnel on loan, who also carried out on-the-job training of the Kenyan engineers.

In February 1974 the Kenya air force underwent a major expansion programme with the opening of the Nanyuki air base as the main fighter base while KAF Eastleigh remained the main transport base. The Strikemasters were subsequently relocated to Nanyuki in June the same year and were joined by three Hunter FGA Mk.80s and two Hunter trainers, which were acquired from ex-RAF stocks.

To supplement and eventually replace the Strikemasters, the KAF ordered twelve BAC Hawk Mk.52s in 1969 for both training and light-strike duties, the first of which were delivered the following year. The Strikemasters were subsequently returned to BAC under the terms of the Hawk contract agreement and eventually re-sold to the newly formed Botswana Defence Force in 1988. One aircraft (603) had earlier been written off

85-86

in a tragic accident when it crashed into the jungle near Meru, Mount Kenya, on 22 July 1974.

KUWAIT In August 1961, the Kuwait government placed a contract with Hunting Aircraft, worth over £500,000, for six Jet Provost T Mk.51s (101-106) plus

85. The first two Strikemaster Mk.87s for the Kenyan air force (KAF) were delivered by Terry Lloyd, Paul Lewis (BAe engineer) and David Curry. The aircraft left Warton on 5 February 1970 and arrived at Eastleigh Airport, Nairobi, eight days later. (Terry Lloyd)

86. Strikemaster Mk 87, '604' was delivered to the Kenyan air force in February 1971. It was later operated by the Botswana Defence Force and sold to a buyer in the USA in 1999. (Jacques Guillem)

87-88

November 1969 and deliveries began on 19 March 1970. The serials of the Kuwaiti order were 110 to 121; the last two aircraft being allocated the temporary civilian registrations, G-AYVK and G-AYVL, respectively, for an appearance at the Paris air show. The order was completed on 2 July 1971.

In September/October 1986, nine of the surviving aircraft (110-115, and 119-121) were sold back to BAC and placed into store, pending their eventual re-sale to Botswana Defence Force three years later.

NEW ZEALAND In November 1970, New Zealand placed a £3.5 million order for ten Strikemaster Mk.88s (NZ6361-NZ6370) to replace its ageing de Havilland Vampires in the pilot training and strike conversion roles; the order also included spares, equipment, training conversion and freight charges. The first aircraft, NZ6361/G27-197 was rolled out from the Warton production line on 9 February 1972 and made its maiden flight on 15 May. Ten days later, the aircraft was handed over to the NZ high commissioner in a ceremony at Warton, following which BAC project pilot, Reg Stock, flew it as part of a brief demonstration to the gathered crowd.

The first three aircraft were shipped to New Zealand in October 1972 and transported to Wellington for assembly by the aircraft servicing section. The following month, the minister of defence, Mr A. McCready, officially handed over the first aircraft to the CO, Sqn Ldr John Hosie, who received it on behalf of No.14(F) Squadron at Ohakea. On 28 October 1972, NZ6361 became the first Strikemaster to operate in New Zealand, being flown by Sqn Ldr Hosie and Flt Lt Graham Lloyd.

Initial flying training for the RNZAF student pilots was completed on the Harvard at Wigram and No.14(F) Squadron's role was to provide fighter lead-in training for those destined to fly the McDonnell Douglas A-4K Skyhawks. The first Strikemaster course (No.32 Jet Conversion Course) began at Ohakea in December 1972.

In January 1973, the last three of the original order for the Strikemaster were delivered to the squadron, coinciding with the planned introduction of an advanced training and strike conversion phase into the

spares and initial technical assistance. This assistance included the training of the first eight pilots at RAF Syerston during 1961, where they were provided with a Mk.51 from Hunting for the armament phase of their course.

On 25 January 1962, the aircraft were delivered to No.27 MU at Shawbury for onward delivery to Kuwait to form the first squadron of jet aircraft, based at Rumaithiya Airport. Very little is known of their subsequent careers except that they were withdrawn from service in 1971, and that at least four were believed to have been involved in serious flying accidents. Of the survivors, 101, 104 and 105 were preserved with the Kuwait Air Force Collection located at Kuwait International Airport, while 103 was at the Museum of Science & Industry, Kuwait City.

In 1969, the Kuwait air force placed a further order for twelve Strikemaster Mk.83s as part of its modernisation programme to replace the existing fleet of Jet Provost T Mk.51s. The first aircraft was flown in

flying training programme. To facilitate a streamed system which provided for the basic training on the Aerospace CT-4B Airtrainer at Ohakea, then completion of the fighter lead-in phase before reaching Wings standard, the NZ government approved the purchase of an additional six Strikemasters (NZ6371-NZ6376), which were delivered between April-June 1975. These additional aircraft provided for an operations flight within 14(F) Squadron, where those awaiting conversion to Skyhawks could carry out 110 hours of tactical flying and limited weapons training.

Sqn Ldr Larry Olsen was the CO of No.14(F) Squadron from February 1975 to June 1978.

During 1975 six new Strikemasters were delivered to bring the total up to sixteen. The four Skyhawk aircraft utilised for conversion training were transferred to 75 Squadron and the last two months of 1975 concentrated on instruction training in readiness for the first pilot training course due at Ohakea in January 1976. This first course had

completed a little over 100 hours on Harvards at Wigram before completing the advanced phase of approximately 110 hours on Strikemasters with 14(F) Squadron. The syllabus included dual and solo basic weapons training in air-to-ground: 2.75" rockets, 45-degree dive bombing, and 50' AGL level skip bombing. The first course graduated on 28 May 1976. From then on, two advanced stage courses of four to five months duration were conducted

87. Jet Provost T Mk.51, '103', was delivered to Kuwait in January 1962. It was last reported to be with the Museum of Science & Industry, Kuwait City. (HAL via Terry Lloyd)

88. Noted at Muharraq during January 1964, this Jet Provost T Mk.51, '101', of the Kuwait air force is fitted with rocket rails. (Gordon Macadie)

89. Strikemaster Mk.88s were delivered to No.14 (F) Squadron, RNZAF, in 1972. The fleet was grounded on several occasions during the early 1980s when fatigue cracks were discovered in the tail fins and main wing structures, resulting in their eventual replacement by the Aermacchi MB339CB. (Author's Collection)

each year. When the Harvards were retired (mid-1977) the basic phase at Wigram moved to the CT-4 Airtrainers. As well as its pilot training role, 14(F) Squadron continued with operational training for pilots destined for the Skyhawk. The squadron's operations flight shared the pool of Strikemasters with the pilot training flight. Most strike role pilots spent approximately three to six months in the operations flight.

By the early 1980s concerns were being expressed about fatigue cracks that were discovered in the Strikemasters' tail fins and main wing structures due to the amount of low-level operational flying being carried out by the squadron. In August 1985, further structural defects were discovered and the aircraft were temporarily grounded. Although a permanent repair was not considered to be practical, six sets of replacement wings were acquired from BAe and fitted the following year to extend the service lives of the aircraft; the 're-winged' aircraft included NZ6361, 62, 64, 69, 71 and 72.

Further temporary groundings and subsequent revised course intakes resulted in a search for a replacement aircraft for the Strikemaster and, under the title, 'Project Falcon', the eventual acquisition of the Aermacchi MB339CB was agreed in March 1990. The first three aircraft were handed over to the RNZAF in April 1991.

With the completion of the Strikemaster's last squadron exercise, 'Falcons Roost 31', at Gisborne in November 1992, three aircraft, NZ6361 (Sqn Ldr M. Longstaff/Wg Cdr Wood), NZ6363 (Flt Lt G. Dobson/Flt Lt Wilton) and NZ6370 (Sqn Ldr B. Keightly, Sqn

CO) made a final fly-past over the Manawatu region on 17 December 1992, following which the type was officially withdrawn from service.

Of the sixteen Strikemasters originally delivered, three aircraft were written off. On 3 July 1985 – NZ6367 crashed at Kiakoura, South Island during a low-level exercise after hitting a wire (pilot ejected); 20 November 1991 – NZ6369 crashed into dense forest, 15m north-east of Taupo during low-level navigational training flight as part of exercise 'Falcons Roost' during a detachment to Tauranga (pilot killed); 27 October 1992 – NZ6368, uncontrollable spin and crashed Pahiatua (pilot ejected). Two of the surviving aircraft, NZ6373 and NZ6374 were donated to the RNZAF Museum at Wigram and Ohakea, respectively, where they are preserved in their original squadron markings. A further five aircraft were allocated for the engineering school at Woodbourne (NZ63, 65, 66, 75 and 76) and the remaining six (NZ6361, NZ6362, NZ6364, NZ6370, NZ6371 and NZ6372) were sold to Aermacchi as part of the purchase deal for replacement aircraft in April 1993.

Between 1973 and 1981, 14(F) Squadron was known to have operated at least three Strikemaster display teams. The first team of four aircraft was led by the CO, Sqn Ldr John Hosie, and appeared at a number of venues from March 1973, including Palmerston North, Whenuapai, Kaitaia and Hokitika. The team's final appearance was at the prestigious RNZAF 50th anniversary display at Wigram in June 1973. Four years later, a further squadron four-ship team led by Sqn Ldr Peter Curtin was formed to take part in the 50th anniversary of the first crossing of the Tasman Sea by Kingsford Smith's Fokker Trimotor, the 'Southern Cross', at Auckland on 10 September 1978. The final Strikemaster display was an appearance at Ohakea's Air Force Day on 28 February 1981 by Sqn Ldr Peter Faulkner and Flt Lt Lockie Milne, who provided a synchronised routine for the event.

In June 1993, seven former RNZAF Strikemaster Mk.88s (NZ6361 to NZ6364, and NZ6370 to NZ6372) were imported by International Air Parts and stored at Sydney/Bankstown airport, Australia, for refurbishment and re-sale. Of these, one aircraft, NZ6364, was imported to the USA in September 1993, where it was subsequently registered as N6364Z and operated by Dragon Aviation Inc, at Wilmington, Delaware. It was joined in the USA in 2013 by NZ6361, which had been operated by various companies in Australia as VH-ZEP, until being sold to the Attack Aviation Foundation in Las Vegas as N309JP, the following year.

In October 2006, NZ6363/VH-JFZ was bought by Michael Costin at Tocumwal, NSW, and was restored to airworthiness in a camouflaged Zimbabwe air force paint scheme. Michael Costin also purchased NZ6371, which had been restored at Bankstown and registered as VH-ONP in December 1995. NZ6372 was registered as VH-LLD in November 1994 and flew in its original colour scheme with various owners until it was sold to RNZAF Strikemaster Ltd at Lower Hutt, New Zealand, in March 2014 and re-registered as ZK-BAC.

A further aircraft, NZ6370, became VH-RBA on 22 December 1995 for Michael Broadbent of Southport, Queensland, and was also restored to an airworthy condition in its original RNZAF markings. In January 2011, it was sold to a buyer in New Zealand and re-registered to Strikemaster Ltd, Auckland, as ZK-STR, the following year. Two further Strikemasters, NZ6372/ZK-BAC and NZ6362/ZK-NTY, were purchased in March and September 2014, respectively, and all regularly appeared at air shows in New Zealand, representing classic aircraft operated by the RNZAF.

In January 2017, display flying with Strikemaster Ltd came to an end when NZ6362 and NZ6370 made their final appearance at the Tauranga air show. Maintenance costs and the reduction in the availability of spare parts resulted in the decision to sell both aircraft to Blue Air Training in Las Vegas, USA. The two Strikemasters joined a further six operated by the

90. Following its withdrawal from service, Strikemaster Mk.88, NZ6370, spent the following seven years in Australia before being purchased by Brett Nicholls in 2010. It became the first privately-owned Strikemaster to be returned to New Zealand and is registered as ZK-STR with Strikemaster Ltd, Auckland. (Brett Nicholls)

company in Nevada, which is contracted to provide close air support training to the US military.

NIGERIA During the 1967-1970 Biafran war, Airwork Services assisted the Nigerian government in procuring two Jet Provost T Mk.51s (143 and 157) from the Sudan air force. The aircraft were flown from Khartoum to their operating base at Makundi in August 1967 and given the Nigerian air force serials NAF701 and NAF702. Although very little is known of their subsequent careers, one aircraft is reported to have been badly damaged during ground-attack operations.

OMAN During the early 1950s, the long-running dispute over the border between Saudi Arabia and Oman resulted in an armed rebellion by Imam Ghalib bin Ali's brother, Talib, who occupied many villages in Central Oman. The beleaguered ruler, Sultan Said bin Taimur, sought British support and between July 1957 and February 1959, detachments of rocket-armed RAF Venom aircraft carried out a series of air strikes against forts occupied by the rebel Omani Liberation Army.

Following the insurgency in Central Oman, the Sultanate of Muscat and Oman established a small air arm under RAF supervision. Known as the Sultan of Oman's Air Force (SOAF) it became operational at Bayt al Falaj, Muscat, in March 1959 and was initially equipped with two SAL Pioneer CC.1s provided by 78 Squadron in Aden. Shortly after the arrival of the SAL Pioneers, the SOAF took delivery of three of an eventual nine Hunting Provost T Mk.1 aircraft for use in the close-support role; the aircraft being supplied from ex-RAF stocks and converted to armed T Mk.52s by Hunting Aircraft. In 1962 the Pioneer aircraft were replaced by DHC Beaver AL.1s, both of which proved invaluable with their STOL capabilities in the rugged, hostile environment of Oman. The SOAF was manned by seconded RAF personnel and Airwork technicians on a two-year contract.

Under an agreement signed in 1958 the Royal Air Force leased part of Masirah Island, off Oman's southern coast, as a staging post. It also operated from the air base at Salalah, the capital of Dhofar province in

91

the south-west, which was heavily defended and became the main operational base for SOAF action against the communist-backed guerrillas.

The Dhofar rebellion had been initially supported by Saudi Arabia in 1962, and was intensified in 1967 with the establishment of the People's Democratic Republic of Yemen (PDRY). The campaign quickly moved from a tribal revolt into a major communist rural insurgency backed by the USSR and the People's Republic of China. This support gave the separatist rebels an important source of arms and supplies, including assault rifles, heavy machine guns, mortars and RCLs (a portable, recoilless missile launcher), which stiffened the resolve of the 'adoo' (enemy) forces, whose aims went to greater autonomy for their region and an improvement in living standards, to an overthrow of the Sultanate.

In May 1967, the SOAF suggested to the Sultan that it would be advisable to equip a strike squadron with Strikemaster close-support aircraft and an initial order was placed for twelve Strikemaster Mk.82s (401-412) the following month. The aircraft were delivered by Airwork pilots between March and August 1969, forming the primary establishment of 1 (Strike) Squadron at Salalah.

On 14 March 1969, one of the first Strikemaster aircraft (402) was transferred from Salalah to the SOAF headquarters at Bayt al Falaj, and despite early teething problems with engine overheating and cracked canopies, the aircraft were soon declared as operational. **Paul Lewis** was the resident BAC engineer.

Soon after the arrival of the first two aircraft, the cracking of the Perspex canopies manifested itself. We had no spares available and there was an urgent need to get pilots converted in order to provide much needed air support to forces on the ground in Dhofar. It turned out that BAC were already aware of the problem, since it had occurred on Saudi Arabian Strikemasters. From my recollection, the cause was put down to the drilling of fastener holes in the Perspex, through which the Perspex to canopy metal frame bolts passed. The holes were rough internally and ridges caused stress concentrations which led to cracking. I suspect that the high temperature differentials between ground and higher altitudes, experienced in Saudi and Oman, exposed the problem and this is why it did not occur in the UK. The problem was eventually resolved but the canopies were not fully interchangeable, so a lot of work had to be done in order to make them fit the aircraft and the problem, thankfully, never re-occurred.

By the time that the last of the Strikemasters had been delivered the situation in Oman had become critical, and in July 1970 the autocratic Said bin Taimur was overthrown by his son, Qaboos bin Said, in a bloodless coup. He immediately instigated positive steps to remove the source of the rebellion. This included confronting the growing number of incursions into Omani territory from South Yemen and it was decided to attack guerilla bases there with all available SOAF strike aircraft; one of the earliest actions being on 12 September 1970 when an attack on the fort at Taqa in south-western Oman was repulsed by Strikemaster aircraft.

Typical Strikemaster operations against known enemy locations in the wild, mountainous region of Dhofar, were often made as the result of intelligence information and the normal sortie length was about one hour. Typical weapon loads carried included 32 Sura rockets, two 7.62-mm machine guns or sixteen Sura rockets and two 540-lb HE bombs; the rockets being fired singly or in pairs and fitted with either a high-explosive warhead of about 2 kg or an incendiary charge. The Strikemaster's two built-in FN 7.62-mm machine guns were used for harassing operations, carrying a thousand rounds of ammunition which provided thirty seconds firing time if both guns were used simultaneously; aiming was achieved by a simple fixed sight. To reduce the all-up weight, the aircraft were frequently flown on operations without the right-hand seat installed.

The Bayt al Falaj airstrip consisted of a fairly narrow concrete runway of about 2,300 yards, laid towards the seaward end of a valley (wadi). The headquarters comprised a few corrugated metal buildings alongside the dispersal, which itself was situated alongside the runway. At the side of the dispersal was a small hangar, large enough to hold the equivalent of about six or seven Strikemaster aircraft, which were serviced by engineers provided by Airwork Services Ltd.

In August 1970, **Wg Cdr P. J. 'Curly' Hirst** was appointed as the commander SOAF, replacing Sqn Ldr Alan Bridges.

The Sultan of Oman's Air Force was an integral part of the Sultan's Armed Forces (SAF). The SOAF unit at RAF Salalah was designated 'SOAF(TAC)', and as such was to earn itself a first-class reputation as an operational unit. Under my command I had just one squadron which contained a variety of different aircraft types: twelve Strikemasters, four Beavers, three Dakotas, two AB206 and two AB205 helicopters, one Caribou and one Skyvan. All the pilots were British and about one-third were on secondment from the Royal Air Force. On my arrival the sum total of pilots amounted to about twenty-five. At this point I should perhaps mention and describe the other two-thirds of the pilot force. They were known as 'contract pilots'. That they were mercenaries in the true sense of the word cannot be denied but they would not fit the generally held

91. On 12 January 1969, Strikemaster Mk.82, '401' became the first of an initial batch to be delivered to the Sultan of Oman's Air Force. It was involved in a fatal accident near Mudhayy in Dhofar in July 1971. (BAe Systems Heritage Warton-Percival/Hunting Collection)

perception with which most people hold regarding a typical mercenary. These men were, almost without exception, superb and professional pilots, and also they were extremely pleasant, courteous, brave and good ambassadors for the UK.

In 1970 the SOAF(TAC) pilots were detached to Salalah on rotation from Muscat. The detachment consisted of three Strikemaster aircraft and one Beaver, with about five pilots accommodated in the officers' mess at RAF Salalah. The pilots flew both types of aircraft. The Beaver operated routine passenger services around the small airstrips in Dhofar, and occasionally acted as a spotter aircraft for Strikemaster operations. The Strikemaster's Sura rockets, a Swiss armament built under license in the UK and sold at enormous profit by British entrepreneurs, was the main attack weapon used by the Strikemasters. The rockets were extremely accurate and each contained a lethal punch when used against the small groups of enemy personnel. The target would often be a small cave or opening in a cliff wall that had been previously identified, and in which the rocket would be expected to kill all the occupants. However, the rockets were so expensive, and the budget funds so critical, that every rocket was fired only after the pilot was certain that its use was fully justified. Every firing was investigated and the over enthusiasm of the younger pilots had to be curbed otherwise we would have exhausted our stocks of rockets before they could be replaced. The other main offensive weapon was the 500-lb general-purpose bomb which could be fused for either an air or a ground burst. Again, this weapon was extremely expensive and effective, but it was even more costly than the rockets so it had to be used with even greater caution. To conserve weapon stocks, bombing attacks were made dropping one bomb at a time and, unless there was a good reason for dropping the second bomb, the aircraft would return to base and land with a bomb still carried underneath one wing.

On 12 April 1972, we lost a Strikemaster (405) when the pilot raised the aircraft's nose too high and too early during one of his first conversion sorties, and ran off the end of the Bayt al Falaj runway at high speed; the aircraft was damaged beyond repair and subsequently used as spares. I sent the pilot back to the UK straight away.

The aircraft frequently returned to Salalah after receiving a remarkable amount of damage from small-arms fire during a sortie. Unfortunately, this was not always the case and in mid-1971 two aircraft were written off within a month of each other: on 18 July 1971 Fg Off Del Moore was involved in a fatal accident when his Strikemaster (401) clipped a rock while flying at low level near Mudhayy in Dhofar; despite attempting to eject from his stricken aircraft, it proved too late and he was killed when it struck the ground.

Two months later, on 15 September, two Strikemasters were tasked with the routine patrol of the surrounding plains and the jebel overlooking the base searching for adoo activity. The pilots were in luck and a group of rebels were spotted inside the Wadi Jarsis, armed with a RCL and preparing to fire on Salalah. The two aircraft immediately turned into the attack and flew into the mouth of the wadi, opening fire on the retreating guerrillas. Low on fuel, the second aircraft decided to return to base, leaving Barrie Williams (in 410) to make a second attack on the adoo position. This would prove a fateful decision as a stray bullet severed the low-pressure fuel line of the Strikemaster's engine and, as he climbed away from the attack, Williams' only option was to abandon the aircraft. At one hundred feet and a mile-and-a-half from the runway, he ejected using the secondary emergency handle of his seat. The parachute had barely time to deploy when the pilot hit the ground and he was killed.

Bombing and rocket attacks made against the PDRY fort across the border at Habrut, similar targets in the north-east of PDRY and some of the buildings and military facilities in and around the town of Hauf, just over the border, were achieved with great effect. Hauf was known to contain the headquarters and supply buildings for the enemy forces and this was chosen as the main target for the SOAF raids. On one such raid in

May 1972, the buildings were attacked in the morning but photographs showed that the main building had escaped unscathed. A repeat attack was made during the afternoon, by which time the PDRY had organised a better defence and the Strikemasters met with heavy small-arms fire. Several of the aircraft suffered damage, including the Strikemaster flown by Peter Hulme which was hit during the second attack on the target. With the electrics out and the radio dead, the greatest problem for Hulme was fuel being sprayed into the cockpit from the engine and the imminent possibility of an explosion. With great skill, Hulme glided back to Salalah and executed a dead-stick landing. He was subsequently awarded Oman's highest military honour, the Sultan's Gallantry Medal.

The turning point of the Dhofar campaign occurred on 19 July 1972, when a force of some 300 adoo guerillas carried out a concerted and well-planned attack on the coastal town of Mirbat. Although taken by surprise, the garrison of nine SAS soldiers and thirty Omani troops bravely fought back and suffered heavy casualties. After three hours of intense fighting, a call for air support by the SAS commander was answered by two Strikemasters, which carried out a low-level strafing attack. Many of the enemy were killed on the protective barbed wire fence around the town, with the remainder put to rout during gun and rocket attacks by the Strikemaster aircraft. A second pair of Strikemaster aircraft was rapidly made available to take over from the original pair, thus maintaining air cover during the vital part of the operation. At the same time, helicopters flew in reinforcements and the battle was over, resulting in a momentous victory for the SAF and a great blow to the prestige and morale of the enemy. This was the one and only time the enemy made a frontal attack with large forces; thereafter, contacts reverted to the former style of guerilla operations.

In early 1973, with the intention to strengthen and develop the air force, the SOAF headquarters moved out of their old premises at the Bayt al Falaj airstrip near Muscat into new accommodation at the newly completed Seeb International Airport. Seeb had been built as both a civil airport and a military airbase, each element sharing the flying facilities of the airfield and with separate operating and support areas.

The more secure situation of northern Oman made Seeb an ideal location for training. Newly arrived pilots destined for the squadrons in Dhofar all went through a programme of conversion-to-type and operational training before proceeding to Salalah. For the Strikemaster pilots, live weapons training took place on the Hajar range, close to Muscat

Gp Capt (later AVM) Les Phipps was the CSOAF between 1973 and 1974.

> Seeb was formally opened as an international airport by Sultan Qaboos on 23 December 1973. It was a grand occasion when everybody who was anybody was there. But I was not there on the ground all of the time for as a concluding item in a fly-past of SOAF aircraft there was a formation aerobatic display by a pair of Strikemasters. I led Flight Lieutenant Nick Rusling in an eight-minute routine which we were later told had caused the crowds to cheer. It had been nothing special – the usual loops, rolls, pull ups, low-level orbits and head-on passes. The Omanis had not seen this sort of thing before in their country!

92. Strikemaster Mk.82, '407', of No.1 (Strike) Squadron, SOAF, at Salalah in April 1972. It was sold to the Republic of Singapore Air Force in May 1977 and is currently with Vintage Aviation Inc, in South Carolina, USA. (Jacques Guillem)

The Salalah area also became a focus of operations against the rebels. The base had been previously attacked from the plain, but by March 1973 the adoo had obtained weapons with sufficient range to hit Salalah from the escarpment itself. On 8 March 1973, one surprise attack caused extensive damage to several aircraft on the airfield when, with incredible accuracy, at least six mortar rounds landed on the aircraft servicing pan and one Strikemaster and three helicopters were damaged by shrapnel. When the excitement finally abated, Gp Capt Les Phipps was in one of four Strikemasters scrambled to attack the escarpment positions from which the adoo had launched such an effective attack on the Salalah airfield. By the time the aircraft had been scrambled and reached the likely positions, however, the adoo had gone, leaving the pilots to put down fire on the whole area to show where they had been – and to deter them from coming back. Two Strikemasters returned with damage from ground fire during the action. Four more Strikemasters were later scrambled to attack likely lines of the enemy's withdrawal. A total of nine bombs, forty-one rockets and 1,000 rounds of ammunition were fired during the whole operation.

To replace those aircraft written off or damaged by enemy action a second batch of eight Strikemasters Mk.82As (413-420) was delivered between March and July 1973 and the strength and typical deployment of No.1 (Strike) Squadron stood at sixteen aircraft: twelve at Salalah and four at Seeb.

Strikemaster pilot, **Nick Rusling,** compiled a personal log during his time in Oman.

For the first two weeks after my arrival in January 1973 the squadron was concerned in the main with routine top cover for the helicopter and transport resupply to the contested area in the west (Mainbrace), centre (Hornbeam) and east (Hawk and White City). Occasionally targets of opportunity

would be engaged and mainly harassing or suppression fire was put down in a likely wadi area.

The squadron working day was obviously flexible but usually from first to last light. Although the afternoons were normally quiet the squadron retained a commitment for two aircraft on standby each morning and afternoon, seven days a week. The squadron and brigade were agreed of a readiness state of green (thirty minutes), amber (ten minutes) and red (four minutes) from request received at SOAF Ops to wheels up.

For the first time in several months RAF Salalah came under a RCL attack from the mouth of the Wadi Jarsis at lunchtime on 30 January 1973. This first attack was unsuccessful and all the rounds dropped short of the camp fencing; the enemy position was engaged by airfield defensive armament and jet strikes. A second, unexpected attack the following evening was more successful, with one round landing near the control building and another damaging an Iranian chopper. As a result of these two attacks, inadequacies in operating procedures were reviewed with regard to the future dispersal of the jets. Thereafter aircraft were also, to some extent, protected by an enclosure of burmails [sand-filled oil drums].

By 1973-74, the focus of operational attention was the border with South Yemen, where the adoo had set up a camel train arms supply route running eastwards along the Omani coast and into the interior. The Omani forces had countered this by occupying the jebel near the border overlooking the route but their position at the Sarfait Jebel was isolated and under constant mortar attack.

All movement into and out of Sarfait, including resupply, had to be by air. Landing on the rough landing strip had become very risky for fixed-wing aircraft who were easy targets for small-arms fire (and eventually surface-to-air missiles) whilst airborne, and whose arrival usually prompted intense mortar attack directed at the strip. Most resupply missions were therefore by AB205 helicopters, spiralling down from 10,000 feet to avoid the small-arms fire and spending minimum time on the ground. Only when there was an operationally essential load would a Skyvan fly in, usually at dawn and with Strikemaster diversionary air cover.

To the east of Sarfait the rugged jebel also saw much action as camel trains or other adoo activity had been located by the ground forces, while the Shershitti Caves complex, a notorious adoo stronghold with arms dumps, became familiar Strikemaster territory and both areas were subjected to frequent attacks.

By 1975 the war gradually swung in favour of the SOAF forces and the final battle of the Dhofar war was a helicopter assault across a deep gorge to capture the Darra Ridge. This was a highly risky operation because it was known that the adoo had SAM-7 heat-seeking missiles and diversionary strikes on the jebel were carried out to confuse the enemy as to the identity of the main attack.

During one such diversionary operation in support of Operation Badree on 19 August 1975, the commander of the SOAF Dhofar Brigade was visiting a SAF position near the border when ten Katyusha rockets struck the position in quick succession. In response, a pair of Strikemasters was called in and attacked the enemy positions to the north of Shershitti.

As the Strikemasters turned for home, a Soviet SAM-7 missile was fired from the enemy position and struck the tail of one of the aircraft (406); the pilot, Flt Lt Roger Furlong, ejected into the Wadi Jawt. Fortunately, a helicopter was in the vicinity on a resupply mission and began a search for the downed pilot. Despite intense ground fire and at least one more SAM-7 being launched, which missed its target, the helicopter was able to winch the pilot to safety. In all, twenty-three SAM-7s were fired during the operation, accounting for the Strikemaster and a helicopter.

The following month, on 29 September, a second Strikemaster (419) was hit by a SAM during a further

93. As a protection against enemy mortar attacks at RAF Salalah, the SOAF Strikemasters were enclosed in the dispersals with burmails (sand-filled oil drums). (Les Phipps)

94-95

pre-selected strike, but the pilot was able to get the badly damaged aircraft back to Salalah, despite numerous holes in the jet pipe and elevator controls.

By January 1976, with the gradual decline in support for the rebellion and the increased pace of SOAF counter-insurgency operations, Sultan Qaboos declared that the war was officially over. Despite this announcement, ground-attack operations against the adoo continued on 14 September 1976, when three waves of Strikemasters attacked enemy fighters in an area to the west of Salalah, near the PDRY boundary, with eleven 500-lb bombs and sixty-eight Sura rockets.

This would prove to be the last ground-support operation to be carried out by the Strike squadron, although top cover for the ground forces and vulnerable re-supply helicopters was maintained by the Strikemasters until December 1976. Fighting by the Sultan's forces in the central and eastern areas would continue for a number of years, however, until the adoo's hold in the Dhofar was finally crushed.

At least ten Strikemaster aircraft had been either shot down or badly damaged during the eight years of ground-support operations in Oman, and in July 1976 the SOAF took the opportunity to obtain a further five Strikemaster Mk.82As (421-424) which had been held in storage at Hawarden. This brought the establishment of No.1 Squadron to seventeen aircraft, of which eight

were operational and four held in reserve/store, including 403, 411, 412, 414, 415, 417, 418, 420, 421, 422, 423 and 424; another five aircraft being allocated for eventual sale to Singapore: 402, 404, 407, 408 and 409.

The Strikemasters continued to be a popular training aircraft and a royal command was issued to form a flying training school at RAF Masirah in January 1977, and that the first course would begin training when the Omani students returned from elementary flying training in the UK.

Outstanding problems regarding the purchase of the new base and the necessary instructional equipment were resolved, and the squadron's Strikemasters began their transfer from Salalah to Masirah in January 1977, with the move being finally completed on 21 March 1977. The RAF finally departed Masirah on 31 March 1977 and it became SOAF Masirah, the following day; the occasion

being celebrated with Hunter firepower and helicopter SAR demonstrations, a formation fly-past by eight Strikemasters depicting the figure '1', and an aerobatic display by the CO of No.1 Squadron, Frank Milligan.

Flying training for No. 1 Course began in April 1978, following a syllabus formulated by **Frank Milligan,** as amended and agreed by SOAF HQ staff officers, and ultimately CSOAF.

The flying syllabus was based on the RAF's Jet Provost syllabus but with substantial differences to allow for the local conditions (e.g. aircraft and instructor availability, lack of radio/navigation aids, desert/sea/remoteness, weather, Ramadan and fasting, other holidays, the requirement to introduce elementary weaponry at an early stage). Prior to commencing the course students had completed elementary flying training in the UK. The Strikemaster course was basic flying training but with an advanced phase tacked on for those students destined for fast jets; students destined for transport aircraft did their advanced phase on Defender aircraft. Wings were presented on completion of the second phase of basic training. The thorough ground school training programme was devised and masterminded by the chief ground instructor, Colin Richardson. It commenced before any flying was done and continued, integrated and keyed with flying throughout the course. Students already had an excellent command of the English language and had also successfully completed a maths/science course before starting the FTS ground school.

At the beginning there were a lot of unknowns; consequently the flying syllabus evolved with experience. Initially it was to be about 152 hours for the basic phase and sixty hours for the advanced phase on the Strikemaster but by early 1978 the basic phase had already increased slightly. It was envisaged that it would be roughly a year before Wings were awarded. The standard achieved was

94. A line-up of No.1 Squadron's Strikemasters at Thumrait in November 1977. Later that day the unit flew a diamond nine formation fly-past to mark the Oman National Day celebrations. (Frank Milligan)

95. On 29 September 1975, Strikemaster Mk.82A, '419' was hit by a SAM-7 heat-seeking missile during a pre-selected strike. The pilot was able to get the badly damaged aircraft back to Salalah, but it was not repaired and the nose section was converted to a procedures trainer when the squadron moved to Masirah. (via John Merry)

96. Four Strikemasters of No.1 Squadron, RAFO, including '412' and '414' shown here, were re-painted in national colours to provide the escort for the visit of HM Sultan Qaboos to Masirah in 1992. The flight was appropriately named the 'Red Barons'. (BAe Systems Heritage Warton-Percival/Hunting Collection)

97. The flight line of the Flying Training School at Masirah in 1992. The Strikemaster aircraft featured a variety of colour schemes which included the disruptive extra dark sea grey and dark sea grey camouflage of the nearest aircraft (418) and a glimpse of a further two belonging to the 'Red Barons'. (BAe Systems Heritage Warton-Percival/Hunting Collection)

comparable to RAF students, with some students achieving high to above average assessments and graduating to Hunters and Jaguars.

On 15 July 1984, the squadron suffered its first training accident while operating from Masirah when Strikemaster 411 force-landed near Ghaba, Oman, during a simulated engine failure exercise. The aircraft was completely wrecked when it hit a large mound of sand, with both pilots suffering minor injuries; a replacement aircraft, 425, was acquired from BAC in September 1986.

On 1 August 1990, the Sultan of Oman's Air Force was formally renamed the Royal Air Force of Oman, marking a continued step in its modernisation and re-equipment programme. This programme also saw the withdrawal of the last operational Strikemasters in November 1999 following their replacement with Swiss-built Pilatus PC-9M turboprop training aircraft.

A number of aircraft are preserved or relegated for use as ground instructional airframes at Al Ansab, Masirah, Salalah, Thumrait and Seeb; the most prominent of these is Mk.82A, 423, which is preserved at the Sultan's Armed Forces Museum, Muscat. A further three airframes, Jet Provost T Mk.3As, XM403, XM471, and T Mk.5A, XW438, were also known to have been obtained from ex-RAF sources and used by the RAFO Technical College at Seeb as training airframes.

SAUDI ARABIA On 21 December 1965, Mr John Stonehouse, parliamentary secretary to the MoA, announced in the House of Commons that a consortium of British firms had been awarded a contract to supply Saudi Arabia with a complete air-defence system. The contract, worth more than £100 million, comprised forty BAC Lightning single-seat fighters and twin-seat trainers, an air defence and surveillance radar system, and a quantity of Raytheon Hawk surface-to-air missiles. Deliveries of the BAC Lightnings began in July 1968.

The Saudi flying training programme was also revived and the order included twenty-five BAC Strikemasters for use in the basic training and light-attack role. This would be BAC's biggest export order for the Strikemaster, which were built in two batches: an initial order of twelve Strikemaster Mk.80s (901-912) and a second batch (1101-1113).

The first aircraft, 901 (G27-8), took to the air on 26 October 1967 with BAC project pilot, Reg Stock, at the controls, and which, together with 902 (G27-9), were retained until September 1969 for development work. Deliveries began on 26 August 1968 with three aircraft (903, 904 and 905) ferried from Warton flown by Reg Stock and two Airwork pilots, Bernard Saxby and Reg Allum. The aircraft arrived at Riyadh, five days later. The original Strikemaster order was completed in July 1969.

The RSAF Strikemasters equipped Nos. 9 and 11 Squadrons of the newly opened King Faisal Air Academy (KFAA) at Riyadh; 9 Squadron being a basic jet training unit, while 11 Squadron provided weapons training. Saudi students completed the first twelve months on academic training and seven months primary training on the Cessna 172, comprising some twenty hours of flying. The students then graduated to the Strikemasters for a further 160 hours of training and were awarded their Wings before moving on to helicopters, transport or fighters. The majority of flying instructors were ex-RAF, none of which were allowed to fly operationally with the RSAF and the original requirement called for sixty-five per cent of the Strikemasters to be fully available for flying duties at the start of each working day.

Following a long and varied career, **Sqn Ldr Bob Pugh AFC** resigned from the RAF in 1968 and joined Airwork Ltd on contract to the RSAF. He was appointed

99

as the squadron commander of the first jet training course, flying Strikemasters at the KFAA, Riyadh. Following a familiarisation course at Warton, he flew one of the first Strikemasters (907) out to Saudi Arabia in October 1968.

I resigned from the RAF so that I could join Airwork to go to Saudi Arabia as a QFI on the reformation of the RSAF. This was a very large contract for the UK with Airwork supplying the personnel (pilots, ground crew and support staff) and BAC the aircraft. Some QFIs like me were sent to Warton to get some time on the aircraft and to help with the delivery flights to Saudi. There was no formal training given, one merely flew with the test pilot doing acceptance tests from the factory and helped with the testing. An Airwork pilot had to complete one solo flight of ten minutes for insurance purposes.

My delivery flight on 23 October was the second to be made – three aircraft had gone a few weeks before. We were two aircraft, test pilot and

navigator in the lead and me solo as No.2. My aircraft had a specially constructed container in the right-hand seat for personal luggage.

On arrival I found that the Saudi students had completed the stage of the ab initio training on the Cessna 172Gs and were ready to move on to the next stage of their training. I trained the first Saudi student to fly solo in a Strikemaster at Riyadh before moving on to Dhahran after a year to fly T-33s with the OCU.

98. Saudi Arabia became BAC's biggest customer for the Strikemaster with an order for twenty-five aircraft to be used in the basic training and light-attack role. The first aircraft ('901' G27-8) flew in October 1967 and deliveries to the King Faisal Air Academy at Riyadh began in August 1968. (BAC via Reg Stock)

99. A formation of Strikemaster Mk.80s of the Royal Saudi Air Force. The nearest aircraft was presented to the Imperial War Museum at Duxford in April 2002. (BAe Systems Heritage Warton-Percival/Hunting Collection)

In 1972, a further order was received from the RSAF for ten Strikemaster Mk.80As (1114-1123), which featured a number of improvements, including an upgraded avionics fit; deliveries began in November 1973. This order was followed by a final batch of twelve Mk.80As (1124-1135) between September 1976 and May 1978 to provide for the expansion of the Royal Saudi Air Force and compensate for a number of Strikemasters lost in accidents. Two Mk.80As from the final order for Saudi Arabia, 1133/G27-299 and 1134/G27-300, were allocated the temporary civilian registrations, G-BESY and G-BESZ, respectively, for an appearance at the Paris air show in June 1977. Both aircraft were delivered to Riyadh from Warton the

following month by Reg Stock and Bob Pengelly. The Saudi order was completed on 10 May 1978, with the delivery of a replacement aircraft, 1135.

Rod Brown was a member of the KFAA from March 1979 until April 1982.

No.9 Squadron of the King Faisal Air Academy was responsible for primary or elementary flying training instruction for the KFAA cadets at Riyadh Airport. The students followed the RAF training programme which lasted about six months and the number per course varied. We also flew the Strikemaster in the basic flying training role with No.9 Squadron of KFAA. Up to about two years before I started at Riyadh, basic weaponry was taught on our Strikemasters but this was discontinued and, as far as I know, the Saudi Strikemasters were never used in the light-attack role.

Following the introduction of turboprop Pilatus PC-9s to No.9 Squadron in 1987, some of the '9xx' Strikemasters were transferred to No.11 Squadron and renumbered to fill the gaps caused by losses in the '11xx' range. The last Strikemaster sortie was flown on 4 January

1997 and at least twelve aircraft were believed to have been written off in flying accidents between October 1969 and September 1986. Four of the survivors were preserved in the RSAF Museum at Riyadh (911, 1123, 1124 and 1127) and another four were passed to the technical college at Dhahran. Twelve aircraft were also sold to Global Aviation, Humberside, during 2000 for resale to the civil market, including: 1102, 1104, 1105, 1108, 1112, 1114, 1115, 1120, 1121, 1125, 1129 and 1130. On 13 April 2000, one aircraft (1133) was presented to the IWM collection at Duxford as a reflection of the ties between the British and Saudi Arabian governments.

SINGAPORE In July 1968, Singapore placed an order for sixteen Strikemaster Mk.84s (300-315) for use as advanced trainers for its fledging air arm, the Singapore Air Defence Command (SADC). Deliveries from Hurn began on 6 October 1969 with 301, 302 and 303 flown by Airwork pilots, Messrs. Williams, De Souza and Kelly, the aircraft arriving at RAF Tengah on 17 October and officially handed over to the minister for defence, the following day. The Strikemasters were issued to No.130 (Eagle) Squadron, which was formed at RAF Tengah in June 1970 as one of two component squadrons of the flying training school; the other squadron being No.150 (Falcon) Squadron, operating Cessna 172Ks.

To welcome the arrival of the first three Strikemasters at RAF Tengah, a simple ceremony was held on 18 October 1969, graced by the defence minister, Mr Lim Kim San and representatives from Hawker de Havilland Ltd, which was contracted by the Singapore government to assist SADC ground crew in the maintenance of its new fleet. In the ceremony, Mr Lim announced that the SADC would conduct its own jet training from December onwards. Pilot recruits going through four months of basic military training followed by sixteen months in

102-103

FTS on the Cessna 172K followed by advanced flying training on the Strikemaster. He also proudly announced that coincidentally, on that same day in the UK, a Wings presentation ceremony was being held for the first four SADC pilots to be trained by the RAF. These four pilots would go on to advanced training on the Hunters with the RAF in the UK and return to Singapore to form the nucleus of SADC's first Hunter squadron.

With further deliveries to the squadron, the first local FTS course began in January 1970 with a mixture of loan service and contract instructors, thereby enabling the SADC to train its students up to Wings standard at Tengah, rather than overseas. Four Singaporean pilots initially received flying training in the UK, including John Norfor, Timothy de Souza and Hoe Kim Bock, who returned immediately to join 130 Squadron at

100. Resplendent in its Air Defence grey colour scheme, Strikemaster Mk.80 '908' was delivered to the Royal Saudi Air Force in October 1968. (Jacques Guillem)

101. Former Saudi Arabian Strikemaster Mk.80A, '1128' on the dump at Dhahran following an accident in September 1986. (BAe Systems Heritage Warton-Percival/Hunting Collection)

102. The first three Strikemaster Mk.84s for the Republic of Singapore Air Force were delivered by Airwork ferry pilots from Hurn on 6 October 1969. (Jacques Guillem)

103. Strikemaster Mk.84, '300/A' of No.130 Squadron, Republic of Singapore Air Force, Tengah. (BAe Systems Heritage Warton-Percival/Hunting Collection)

Tengah; whereas Capt Gary Yeo proceeded to the CFS, Little Rissington, for training as an instructor and returned in April 1971 to join 130 Squadron as the first Singaporean QFI. The first FTS course was completed in October 1970.

On 15 September 1971, the RAF handed over Tengah to the SADC, which became Tengah air base (TAB). The following year, the flying training school and its two squadrons were relocated to Changi air base in February 1972 as a result of increased fighter operations at Tengah.

To augment the Strikemaster fleet, two further purchases were made, including four Strikemaster Mk.81s and seven Jet Provost T Mk.52s from South Yemen. The Strikemasters were ferried to Changi air base in pairs by contract pilots in March and June 1974, respectively. The four Strikemaster aircraft being: 320:W (ex-501), 321:X (ex-502), 322:Y (ex-503) and 323:Z (ex-504). The seven Jet Provost T Mk.52s, 350 (ex-101), 351 (ex-102), 352 (ex-104), 353 (ex-105), 354 (ex-106), 355 (ex-107) and 356 (ex-108) were shipped to Singapore by RSS *Endurance*, a LST of the Republic of Singapore Navy, arriving in Singapore in October 1974. The aircraft were refurbished and the first one took to the air in December 1975. Due to the significant differences between the Strikemasters and the Jet Provosts, the latter was not used to support the cadet courses but instead primarily for the flight instructor courses. The Jet Provosts were withdrawn in 1981 when it became increasingly difficult to continue operating the aircraft due to the lack of spares and high maintenance costs.

On 1 April 1975, the SADC was renamed the Republic of Singapore Air Force (RSAF) and due to its rapid expansion programme, five additional Strikemaster

104

Mk.82s (327 ex-402, 328 ex-404, 329 ex-407, 330 ex-408 and 331 ex-409) were purchased from Oman to cope with the heavy demands being placed on the FTS training programme. The five aircraft were ferried to Singapore from Seeb Airport by a team of five pilots and a technician, led by Capt Patrick Foo, CO of 130 Squadron, arriving at Changi air base in May 1977.

With the development of Changi as Singapore's new international airport, the FTS and its units moved again, in July 1981, to Paya Lebar Airport, where 130 Squadron continued to operate the Strikemasters until 1986, when they were finally withdrawn and replaced by the Siai-Marchetti S211 advanced jet trainer.

One airframe, 301, is preserved at the RSAF Museum, Paya Lebar, while the remaining thirteen airworthy airframes were sold to an Australian aircraft broker.

NOTE: The Mk.84s were given letter codes, painted in white on the fin and nose shortly upon their arrival. These were: 300:A, 301:B, 302:C, 303:D, 304:E, 305:F, 306:G, 307:H, 308:J, 309:K, 310:L, 311:M, 312:N, 313:O, 314:P and 315:R. The ex-Yemeni Mk.81s were also given letter codes: 320:W, 321:X, 322:Y, 323:Z. No letter codes were given to the ex-Yemeni Jet Provosts or the ex-Omani Mk.82s.

As a means to improve visibility, three Strikemasters and two Jet Provosts were painted in a red/white paint scheme similar to that used by the RAF Training Command. These were 301:B, 321:X, 323:Z, 354 and 356. The new scheme may not have fully met its objectives as no other aircraft were similarly painted and the aircraft retained the red/white scheme until their withdrawal.

SOUTH YEMEN Prior to the withdrawal of British forces from the Aden Protectorate in November 1967, the British government set about creating the South Arabian Air Force, with its headquarters at Khormaksar. Together with Douglas DC-3 transport aircraft, Augusta-Bell Sioux helicopters and DHC Beaver communication aircraft ordered on behalf of what was then known as the South Arabian Federation government, were eight ex-RAF Jet Provost T Mk.4s. The airframes had been previously converted by Marshall of Cambridge

to T Mk.52 standard and the first two, 101/XS223 and 102/XS224, were delivered from Brize Norton on 12 August 1967. The order was completed on 31 January 1968 and the aircraft included 101/XS223, 102/XS224, 103/ XS227, 104/XS228, 105/XP666, 106/XP684, 107/ XR652 and 108/XR661.

The following year, a further four Strikemaster Mk.81s (501-504) were delivered from Hurn on 6/7 August 1969. By the time the aircraft had arrived, however, a new government had taken over control in the country, which was renamed the People's Democratic Republic of Yemen in December 1970; the air arm became the People's Democratic Republic of Yemen Air Force and was re-equipped with Soviet-built aircraft. The maintenance contract for the aircraft had previously been awarded to Airwork Ltd, but the company was not invited

105-106

to apply for the contract again and all British aircraft were subsequently sold, including four Strikemaster Mk.81s and seven Jet Provost 52s, which were supplied to Singapore in March and October 1974, respectively.

SUDAN Following the country's independence, the newly-formed Sudan air force (SAF) obtained its first armed Provost T Mk.53 training aircraft in July 1957. In early 1961, it became the second overseas air arm to

104. Former Jet Provost T Mk.4, XP684, was converted to T Mk.52 standard and operated by the Singapore Air Defence Command, Changi. It had been acquired from South Yemen in October 1974 and was a small number of aircraft painted in a red/white paint scheme similar to that used by the RAF Training Command. (Y. K. Goh)

105. The first Jet Provost T Mk.52 was delivered to the South Arabian air force in August 1967. (AVM Sir John Severne)

106. Four Strikemaster Mk.81s were delivered to the renamed Peoples' Democratic Republic of Yemen Air Force in August 1969. Following the country's re-equipment with Soviet-built aircraft, they were sold to Singapore in March 1974. (BAe Systems Heritage Warton-Percival/Hunting Collection)

107-108

109

acquire the Jet Provost when four aircraft were funded as a gift by the British government, together with the facilities to provide the jet conversion training of twelve officers at RAF Acklington and Syerston.

The four Jet Provost T Mk.51 aircraft (124, 139, 143 and 157) were delivered to the Sudan air force, leaving Luton on 17 October 1961 and flown by RAF pilots under the leadership of Flt Lt David McCann; the 3,500-mile ferry flight to Khartoum being completed in a week, supported by a Valetta transport aircraft from RAF Manby.

In early 1962, a further order for Jet Provost T Mk.52s (162, 173, 175, 180, 185, 190 and 195) was placed by the Sudan government, with deliveries between November 1962 and January 1964 to equip No. 2 Fighter-Attack Squadron. The Jet Provosts had an unfortunate start with their combat training when four pilots were reportedly killed in flying accidents; the first of which, 139, crashed on take-off from Wadi Sayyidna air base, near Omdurman, on 26 May 1962. This aircraft had been one of the first Jet Provosts to have been

delivered to Sudan and a replacement, 181, which was originally allocated for Venezuela and temporarily registered as G-ASEZ, suffered a similar fate when it crashed at Idilidje Canton de Mangobo, Chad, on 7 April 1963 and was never taken on charge by the SAF. A further crash on 13 June 1962 (124) brought the number of lost aircraft to three in less than two months. The four airmen involved in the accidents were among the first twelve Sudanese pilots to have been trained in the UK.

By August 1969, the establishment of the SAF included ten Jet Provost T Mk.51/T Mk.52 aircraft, together with five, newly-acquired T Mk.55s (167, 177, 187, 192 and 197). Sudan became the only country to be equipped with the armed, export version of the Jet Provost T Mk.5, which had been delivered from Hurn between March and June 1969.

In 1983, Sudan approached BAC with an offer to buy the remaining ten Strikemaster aircraft being held at Hurn against possible sales. Three of the aircraft, designated as Mk.90s (141, 142 and 144) were delivered in November 1983 before the British government imposed an arms embargo because of the country's continuing, bloody civil war.

The fates of the Sudanese Jet Provosts and Strikemasters are unknown, although two Jet Provost T Mk.51s, 143 and 157, were transferred to Nigeria in August 1967 and Strikemaster Mk.90, 142, was noted with the military museum, Khartoum, in 2015.

VENEZUELA On 5 September 1962 an order from the Venezuelan air force (FAV) for fifteen Hunting Jet

Provost T Mk.52s (E-040 to E-054), plus spares and ground equipment, was announced at the Farnborough air show, with delivery beginning later the same year.

The first aircraft, E-040, completed its maiden flight on 29 November 1962 and was officially handed over during a ceremony at Luton attended by Mr Ian Brown, test pilot 'Mutt' Summers, Mr Ron Brown of Hunting Aircraft, and the Venezuelan air attaché, Lt-Col Suarez. The event was also attended by Lts Dorta, Miliani and Sequias of the Venezuelan air force, all of whom had recently completed a CFS instructors' course at Little Rissington.

All fifteen aircraft were test flown at Luton before being shipped to Venezuela and re-assembled at Boca de Rio air base, Maracay, where they were test flown again by company pilot, Reg Stock, with Lts Sequias and Dorta as observers; the first aircraft (E-040) was flown and handed over on 27 March 1963. The last aircraft (E-054) had its initial flight check on 18 November 1963; Reg Stock then left the country five days later.

During 1964, the FAV formed an aerobatic display team, 'Los Aguiluchos', comprising four Jet Provost aircraft led by Captain Luis Viana. Based at the military aviation school's air training group headquarters at Mariscal Sucre AB, the team's role was to demonstrate the capabilities of the FAV and promote patriotism during public and international events. Although succeeded by a team of four de Havilland Vampire aircraft in 1965, a further display team of three Jet Provosts from the air training group, 'Los Jaguares', appeared at the 50th anniversary celebrations of Venezuelan aviation at La Carlota AB in July 1970.

The Jet Provosts were finally replaced by North American T-2D Buckeyes in 1978. During fifteen years of

110

operational service with its Jet Provosts, it was the FAV's proud claim that, despite losing one aircraft in July 1965 when a cockpit fire forced the two pilots to eject over Lake Valencia, it had not suffered a fatal accident.

It is known that the Jet Provosts were renumbered at a later stage of their service with the FAV and it has proved difficult to determine the serial tie-ups with any accuracy. In 1990 several airframes were noted in a derelict condition at El Libertador, Palo Negro, and were thought to have been subsequently scrapped; these included 3309 (ex-E-050), 4704 (ex-E-043), 5354 (ex-E-048?), 5634 (ex-E-042) and 6750. Further airframes, 5324 and 9415, were noted at Maracay/Mariscal Sucre, while 6780 and E-040 are with the Museo de la FAV, Aragua, Maracay.

107. Jet Provost T Mk.51 of Sudan air force, prior to delivery in October 1961. (HAL via David McCann)

108. Jet Provost T Mk.52, G-ASEZ, was originally intended for the Venezuelan air force. In March 1963 it was diverted for delivery to Sudan and crashed in a forced landing whilst on the ferry flight from Fort Lamy to Sudan, the

following month. It was returned to Luton and scrapped in January 1964. (BAe Systems Heritage Warton-Percival/Hunting Collection)

109. Strikemaster Mk.90 '142' was one of three aircraft delivered to Sudan in November 1983 before the British government's arms embargo, having been previously held in store at Hurn against

possible sale. It was noted at the Sudan Military Museum, Khartoum in April 2015. (via Ian Carroll)

110. The first Jet Provost T Mk.52 for Venezuela on an air test in November 1962. It was officially handed over the following March and last noted in a derelict condition at El Libertador during 1990 as '9385'. (BAC via Reg Stock)

Above: Cockpit layout of the Jet Provost Mk.51, which included an armament selector panel and two reflector sights.
(HAL via Terry Lloyd)

111

112

Former wartime fighter pilot, **Sqn Ldr Allan Corkett,** was an instructor with No.2 FTS at RAF Cluntoe, NI, in April 1953, transferring to Hullavington the following year and was an instructor on the 'Jet Provost Flight' from September 1955 until November 1957.

The world's first ab initio jet training experiment was carried out at No.2 FTS, RAF Hullavington, Wilts, which became the only flying training school to operate both the Piston Provost and Jet Provost at the same time.

Early in 1955 two Jet Provosts had been used at the CFS during the preparation of a provisional training syllabus. However, the fact that the training of the first pupil pilots had commenced as soon as the flying instructors had been completed, meant that the service trials of the aircraft were being undertaken at the same time. It would, therefore, have been quite remarkable if teething troubles had been absent during the most intensive flying, often undertaken (as usual during flying training) by very inexperienced and quite often by ham-fisted pilots.

The first course of pupil pilots to fly the Jet Provost commenced their training in September 1955, and there would be a further two courses completed before the end of the flying training experiment in November 1957. This unique trial, to evaluate the concept of pupil-pilots' flying training being carried out on only jet aircraft, was completed by eight flying instructors and eight aircraft. I was fortunate to be instructing on the aircraft throughout the two years.

The Jet Provost was a most pleasant aircraft to fly, with no handling problems. The very small Armstrong Siddeley Viper engine was first rate, with a very unusual characteristic for a jet engine at the time, in that (if need be) the throttle could be operated – in like manner to a piston-engine throttle – without the slightest tendency to flame out.

Nevertheless, I recall that there were the usual minor problems, which were soon dealt with, and three even more serious snags (which were design problems) resulted in only minor damage to particular aircraft, and were sorted out without any serious disruption to the flying programme.

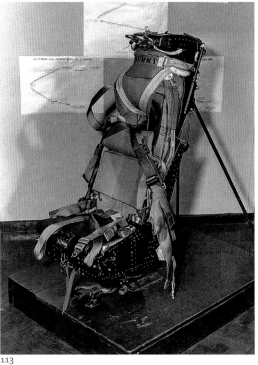

113

114

Mike Edwards was the reserve pilot for the CFS Jet Aerobatic team in 1958, flying the Jet Provost T Mk.1.

I see that I did my share in converting staff instructors to the Jet Provost Mk.1 but I took no part in the student courses. I always understood that the Jet Provost was regarded as the easy option for ab initio pilot training, and that the piston version was more difficult. Reasons given included the much better forward view from the cockpit, the lack of propeller slipstream over the fin and rudder causing swing on take-off, the centre of gravity being forward of the mainwheels instead of aft giving nose-down pitch on premature touchdown instead of bouncing back into the air and the superbly easy

engine handling. Plus no run up before take-off, no need to clear the engine in a glide, no idle period before shut-down, etc.

I was the team's reserve pilot during the 1958 display season. I would start up the reserve aircraft behind the hangar somewhere, take their place if any of the four went u/s, and if all four got airborne I would scramble through the crowd up to the tower to do the commentary. Lovely for the blood pressure!

I did do a few of the displays. The funniest was on a really evil day with a low cloud base in September 1958 when I foolishly tried to do my 'singleton' performance at Odiham. After a long stand-off I ran in to start with a simple loop, but looking

111. Side-by-side seating arrangement for the pupil and instructor in the cockpit of the Jet Provost, which was totally enclosed by a sliding hood. (BAe Systems Heritage Warton-Percival/Hunting Collection)

112. The Viper engine was mounted in the centre fuselage and was accessed by two maintenance access panels. (BAe Systems Heritage Warton-Percival/Hunting Collection)

113. Martin-Baker Mk.4 lightweight

ejection seat. (BAe Systems Heritage Warton-Percival/Hunting Collection)

114. The hinged nose cap provided access to the radio and electrical control equipment, batteries and oxygen charging plant. (Hunting via Norman Giffin)

down as I went over the top I realised it wasn't Odiham – it was Farnborough all set up for the SBAC show. So I managed to roll out and stay in cloud getting a quick QDM from Odiham and making an impressive arrival there directly out of cloud. Nobody had noticed this slight error so please don't tell Norman Giffin – he still thinks I was a competent performer.

In August 1958 we decided to fit some RAF Regiment battlefield smoke generators under the wings, operated by the landing light switch, and I was sent to air test them. They gave off a gratifying amount of smoke but on landing we found the wings under the fuel tanks were badly scorched and I can't recall the system being used in anger. We also had a go at tying the wings together but we kept breaking the string and anyway we were afraid it might get into the intake so we threw that idea away too.

In March 1959 they were planning to move all the fast jets away whilst they resurfaced the runway at Little Rissington and they presumed the slower Jet Provost 1 could join the piston brigade using the grass. The grass was very soggy and the poor old Jet Provost with its 1,200-lb of static thrust could barely achieve 30 knots.

David McCann was a CFS instructor and involved in the delivery of the first Jet Provosts to Sudan in 1961.

I seem to recall that it was someone at Flying Training Command who decided CFS should provide the leader for the Sudanese delivery flight as we had some experience of flying Jet Provost T Mk. 3s to Africa with the trip to Nigeria the previous year. I was spare at the time so I got the job but, to share the excitement, the other pilots came from training schools within No.23 Group. I think that all the ground crew came from RAF Syerston to where Hunting delivered for a brief work-up period. The Jet Provost T Mk.51 aircraft which we were delivering to Sudan were, like the Mk.3, short of oomph and lacking in range; it was, of course, unpressurised so flying at height was uncomfortable.

The other pilots were Flt Lts Ian Hamilton, Hugh Rigg, Kit Thorman, Flg Off Roger Austin and Master Pilot 'Shep' Sheppard – six pilots for four aircraft so we were covered in case of sickness or any other problems. Ian flew with me, Hugh and Roger flew together and Kit and Shep went solo. We were supported by a Valetta from RAF Manby to carry the ground crews and spares and bring us back from Khartoum.

We gathered at Syerston on 5 October 1961 and spent a couple of weeks putting about ten hours on each aircraft, ironing out any snags and planning our route; most of the flying was devoted to cross-countries at 25,000 ft to check fuel consumption. After several delays we eventually got away from Syerston on 18 October (I was flying 124) and flew down to Thorney Island where we spent the night. The weather over France was rather poor the following day so we only got as far as Villacoublay, near Paris. The following day was better and we staged through Orange to Nice, where we night-stopped. RAF Luqa, Malta, was the next target, via Decimomannu, Sardinia, before we moved on to Africa, landing first at Bengazi.

On 22 October we spent the night at RAF El Adem. Everybody was a little apprehensive about the legs next day – Alexandria, Cairo West, Luxor – as the RAF didn't stage through Egypt at that time, being only five years since the Suez campaign; we were, however, flying aircraft with Sudanese markings, with no RAF insignia on our flying suits but the Valetta was plainly an RAF aircraft. In the event the Egyptians were very courteous if not that efficient: at Cairo West they were able to top up our oxygen so we flew at 10,000 ft down to Luxor where we were housed in a splendid hotel.

24 October should have been the 'big day' – our arrival at Khartoum. After take-off from Luxor, we flew low down the Valley of the Kings before climbing to height and heading for a refuelling stop at Wadi Halfa. However, as we prepared for the big moment, our first and only snag occurred when Hugh's aircraft would not start. As the ground crew

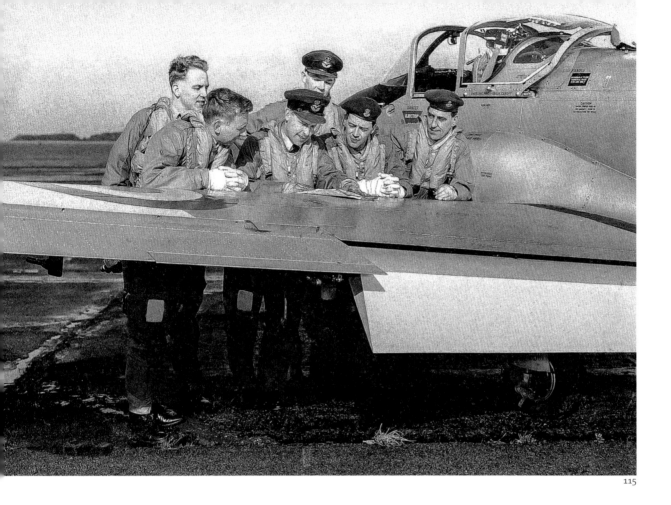

115

decided what was wrong, I decided that we should stay the night as it was important all the aircraft should arrive together, if at all possible. That night we were accommodated on a very rusty paddle steamer that had, I suspected, been moored on the bank of the Nile for many years.

The ground crew pulled out all the stops and got the aircraft serviceable so the next day we flew down to Khartoum, the longest leg of the trip. We did a few passes over the airfield and went out on a broad sweep over Khartoum and Omdurman. I decided not to push my luck any further and brought the flight in for a break and landing but the Sudanese officers were delighted with our show of bravado and were sorry I had not prolonged the display. It was a great moment for them, the arrival of their first jet aircraft, and they wanted maximum publicity for their tiny air force.

The trip made a refreshing change from routine flying training in the UK. I am left with pleasant memories plus a model of the aircraft I flew, which

was presented to us by Huntings. Mine has survived fifty-three years – better than the aircraft itself, which was written off a few months after I delivered it to Khartoum!

Colin Wilcock completed his basic flying training with No.6 FTS.

Having completed my initial training at RAF South Cerney, Glos, in July 1963, I was posted to No.6 Flying Training School (FTS) at RAF Acklington, Northumberland, on No.171 Course. The course started with the usual intensive ground school for the first few weeks and then we flew either morning

115. In October 1961 four T Mk.51 aircraft were delivered to the Sudan air force, leaving Luton on the 17th and flown by pilots under leadership of Flt Lt David McCann of CFS; the other pilots were Flt Lt Hugh Rigg and Fg Off Roger Austin from No.1 FTS, and Flt Lts Christopher Thorman, Ian Hamilton and Master Pilot Hedley Shepherd from No.2 FTS. (HAL via David McCann)

or afternoon and had ground school lessons during the other part of the day. Along with all the students on my course, I was an acting pilot officer (APO), having been commissioned on graduation at South Cerney. There were twenty-nine of us on 171 Course including twelve students from Iraq, and the next course included two students from Kuwait. The Iraq government had just fallen out with Russia and so the guys joined us from Russia where they had only been allowed to taxi clipped-wing Yaks. The course in front of us was made up of ex-university air squadron students, and as such they had completed a fair bit of the course at university before coming to Acklington. My only memory of my first sortie in the Jet Provost was of discomfort as I had overtightened the top straps and was crunched up in the seat. The usual exercises were flown and I went solo on 10 October 1963 with 11½ hours. Although I can't remember exact numbers, some of the course were chopped before solo – indeed we lost members all along the way (right up to my time on the Lightning OCU – Lightnings were my first operational tour) – even though rumour had it that a very senior officer had stated that there were no bad students – only bad instructors. From my logbook the various phases of the course included pre-solo handling and circuits.

To keep us out of the way of all the experienced students we were sent off to the relief landing ground at RAF Ouston to carry out our pre-solo and early post-solo flying. Once solo, consolidation was carried out in the circuit followed by aircraft handling exercises such as steep turns, practice engine failures, aerobatics and stall/spin training. The most contentious of these exercises was the turn-back. If the engine were to fail on take-off there was the bang seat to save oneself. However, Her Majesty's Government liked us to try and preserve the aircraft so above about 500 feet we were expected to carry out a turn-back. This involved turning just off the stall speed into wind and trying to land on one of Acklington's three runways. This manoeuvre was often not successful, and, following

an actual failure, could place the crew in a much more dangerous situation as they would now be very low and slow yet still have to eject. Nevertheless the RAF persevered with this manoeuvre and, although not many engines failed on take-off, I believe the odd accident occurred during the training. Instrument flying was introduced quite early in the course and we sat a series of progress tests starting with an elementary instrument grading test and finishing, at the end of the course, with a white instrument rating (the lowest rating awarded to pilots in the RAF). Navigation was carried out throughout the course, and this culminated in two land-away sorties. My dual sortie was to RAF Syerston, and my solo sortie was to RAF Leeming. I think that we all felt a great sense of achievement when we had successfully taken a Jet Provost away on our own and returned it safely.

Formation flying was introduced towards the end of the course, and this started out with simple echelon sorties finally winding up to tail chases to prepare us for future postings to fighters. The only unusual event during our night-flying phase was that we carried it out at the relief landing ground at RAF Ouston because the lights at Acklington were being replaced. This gave us a chance to do extra formation as we would leave Acklington at the end of the day's flying for the other courses (about 1800hrs) and return at daybreak for the aircraft to be ready for the first wave at 0830hrs. About a month before the end of the course came the dreaded final exams set by the Command Exam Board. I think we all passed these although many hours of midnight oil were spent in revising.

One of the students on the course in front of me had to carry out a forced landing at RAF Boulmer when the engine failed. Boulmer was a disused airfield and on touchdown he saw a fence which he could not avoid but he still managed to stop safely. I do not know what happened to the aircraft, but believe that the engine failure was caused by the previous student who had dropped a used sick back over the side which was then sucked into the engine. He probably did this because airsickness was a cause of suspension from training, and he was hoping not to be found out.

The RAF insisted on starting us all from scratch even though a few of us had had some civil flying experience. To show the value placed on civil qualifications early on an instructor popped his head round the door of the students' crew room to ask if anyone had a private pilot's licence. A friend, who was very proud of his private licence, and told us all about it, answered, expecting a good deal, and was told to go and make the tea.

Morse was a required skill and many days were spent listening to dots and dashes. There was a test at the end and I think we all just scraped through. In fact it was not till I was required to get an airline licence when I retired from the RAF that I really learnt Morse.

Prior to getting to Acklington we had been issued with our flying kit at South Cerney and told to wear the helmet so that we could become accustomed to it before we flew. Evenings were then spent swatting for final exams wearing cloth helmet, bone dome and oxygen mask – not necessarily the most comfortable of outfits. One other thing that we did at Cerney was to carry out a practice ejection. A contraption consisting of a long ladder and a bang seat were mounted on the back of a large truck which went round the UK visiting stations. When it arrived at Cerney we were all kitted out and strapped into the seat. Everyone else then stood clear and in our own time we pulled the handle. The charge in the seat was far less than that in an operational seat to avoid injuring us this early in our careers. I remember that there seemed be an age after pulling the handle before the seat gun fired, during which I could hear the timers running. I then got a hefty kick in the back and was shot up the ladder about twenty feet. After swaying there for a few seconds the seat was lowered to the ground, I unstrapped and the next victim took my place. I have no idea how long this introduction to ejecting continued, but don't think it is still in vogue.

We started flying the Jet Provost Mk.3 which during my time was de-rated to 98% to conserve the engines. This made the Mk.3 even more underpowered and definitely earned the nickname 'constant thrust variable noise machine'. Nevertheless, the Jet Provost Mk.3 was for all of us a handful in the early days. Once comfortable in the cockpit after my initial flight I quickly felt at home. The aircraft was easy to manoeuvre on the ground as it had a wide undercarriage track. Steering was by pressing on the toe brake on the side to which you wanted to turn, and once moving the aircraft would trundle along on idle power. We were expected to learn all the checks quite early on – no check lists were allowed by the RAF in jet trainers or single-seat aircraft. As the thrust was not excessive, the initial take-off acceleration was a bit pedestrian, but the aircraft was soon up and away. In flight it was pleasant to fly although the stick forces were quite heavy – indeed on a later solo sortie I took the Jet Provost Mk.4 up to its limiting speed of 400 knots and the controls felt almost solid. The aircraft required concentration on trimming to get the accurate flying demanded by our instructors, but once mastered was relatively easy to fly accurately. The stall was docile, with buffet occurring a few knots before the stall. There was no artificial stall warning system, but the aircraft recovered readily when the control column was moved forward till the buffet stopped and full power was selected.

Aerobatics were fun and the Jet Provost was capable of most, although the RAF would not allow any flick manoeuvres. Throughout the course our aerobatic repertoire was gradually expanded as the RAF felt aerobatics were a great way of providing confidence and situation awareness. Indeed there is talk of all pilots, including airline pilots, being exposed to some vigorous manoeuvring to prepare them for any upsets that might occur in their normal jobs. Spinning was introduced early on as solo aerobatics was not allowed until one was proficient in spin recovery. The spin was conventional with an entry from about ninety-five knots. The aircraft

would perform a level roll through 180° before set-
tling down to a nose-low spin with each turn taking
around three seconds. Recovery was full opposite
rudder then stick forward till the rotation stopped.
I remember during a spin check the instructor
emphasising that I must check for direction of turn
by looking at the turn and slip before applying
rudder. To make this clear he tapped the instrument and broke the glass – so ended the sortie.
Navigation was conducted at 180 (three miles per
minute) to make calculations in the air easy. The
Jet Provost was stable enough to be able to monitor
the height and speed without having to give this
too much attention so allowing time for all the
other tasks involved in navigating around the UK.

After a couple of months we were converted to
the Jet Provost Mk.4 – a slightly more powerful
aircraft. I remember during the first take-off being
caught out by the much better acceleration and
nearly failing to get the gear and flap up by the
limiting speeds. The Jet Provost was easy to fly in
formation, but echelon port was more difficult as
we had to look across the cockpit – made even
worse when dual. The aircraft was not too difficult
to fly in the circuit, and landings did not seem to
take too long to learn. Circuits consisted of flying
downwind and preparing to land by selecting gear
down and take-off flap. The turn from downwind
to final was a continuous 180° turn, selecting full
flap about halfway round. The aim was to roll out
at around 300 feet and reduce to the threshold
speed (from memory 105 knots) just over the runway. As the aircraft was levelled a few inches above
the runway the throttle was closed and the aircraft
allowed to land gently on the runway – at least
that's the theory, but it took a bit longer to become
proficient and before being sent solo three good
circuits and landings were needed.

I got my Wings on 7 August 1964. I was due to
go to Valley on the Gnat and actually got there after
my holiday at home in Nairobi. However, the Gnat
was going through a bad patch and I was initially
sent to the RAF College of Air Warfare at RAF Manby

where I was a co-pilot on Varsities till late November when I went to RAF Strubby and did AFTS on
the Meteor. I finished the course in March 1965
and I was posted to 85 Squadron on Meteors till
July and then to Chivenor on Hunters in August.
I went to Coltishall on the Lightning in December
and was posted to 5 Squadron at Binbrook in April
1966 – almost exactly three years from joining the
RAF in Nairobi.

Dave McIntyre was a member of No.12 Course, No.1
FTS at Linton-on-Ouse:

The course began on 11 May 1970 and involved about
145 flying hours (about fifty-five on Mk.3s and ninety
on Mk.5s) before our graduation on 7 April 1971. At
the time, the Gnat was still the advanced trainer, and
all BFTS students flew both 3s and 5s – the streaming
came at the end of the course. The fast-jet Hawk
lead-in syllabus was introduced some time after
we had left.

I'm pretty sure we started with fifteen RAF
guys, plus four Jordanians. Of the original fifteen,
five (myself included) went on to Valley, five to
Oakington, and one to Shawbury. Three failed;
one was re-coursed and one was killed in a mid-air
collision with a Royal Navy Sea Prince over Church
Fenton in March 1971. Two of the Jordanians also
failed. As was often the case, we picked up a couple
of guys who had been re-coursed, but I don't remember how many.

I also remember the first loss of a Jet Provost
Mk.5 (XW297) during a tail-chase incident on 17
September 1970. The pilot's name was Chris Wilkins
and he lost control after entering a high-rotational
spin, a characteristic that caught a few people out
if they didn't use the approved spin recovery tech-
nique. I am sure that he was on the senior course
on our squadron.

Sean Chiddention was an instructor at the RAF College, Cranwell, and successfully competed in the Wright
Jubilee Aerobatic Competition at RAF Valley on 15 May
1987. He was not only the youngest pilot to win the

competition but also achieved the distinction of winning the trophy two years in succession.

The competition was for all Jet Provost instructors from RAF Cranwell, Scampton, Finningley, Church Fenton and Linton-on-Ouse, with each station holding its own selection competition before the main event. The winner from each station went forward to compete in the Wright Jubilee competition, which was held at either Scampton or Valley, depending upon the weather on the day. The winner of the overall competition then went on to be the Jet Provost display pilot for the season.

The 1987 event was held at Valley and I competed in XW335. I was fortunate to win and went on to become the youngest-ever display pilot as a flying officer, aged twenty-two. As a Cranwell instructor I was aware of the Poachers aerobatic team and elected to have my aircraft (XW323 and XW374) painted in their colour scheme. The two aircraft were selected based on their low fatigue lives, both having been in storage early in their careers. One of these aircraft (XW323) had been flown by Prince Charles during his time at Cranwell in 1971.

The first public display was just two weeks later at Prestwick. Through the season I flew forty-three displays, mostly in XW374 with XW323 as the spare. Most weekends consisted of taking both aircraft, as a pair, using the call sign 'Poacher Formation', the second aircraft being flown by one of the other Cranwell instructors and each carrying a volunteer and hard-working engineer. The final display of the season was flown at Tours in France on 4 October, in XW323.

In 1988, and still with sufficient time remaining of my 'creamie' tour, I managed to successfully defend my title and went on to display again for the 1988 season. The competition was again held at Valley on 10 May and I flew XW428, with a normal paint scheme in order not to pre-empt the outcome. The format in 1988 was similar, with XW323 taking the lead role.

The first display, of the thirty-seven that season, was flown at Bournemouth on 4 June in XW323 and the last time was at RAF Newton on 18 September, again in XW323. There was supposed to have been a further display weekend to include St Athan and Abingdon on 25 September but the fatal crash of the RAF Phantom at Abingdon, two days previously, brought a premature end to the season and the sad loss of Chris Lackman and Jack Thompson. The end of the season marked the end of my instructional tour and I returned to Valley for a Hawk refresher course and on to Brawdy to complete my TWU course, before going to the Jaguar on 6 Squadron at Coltishall.

Following a tour at Coltishall, completing two Maple Flag exercises, deployment to the Gulf ahead of Gulf War 1 and three operational deployments to patrol the Northern Iraq no-fly zone, I was selected to join the Red Arrows. I joined at the end of 1992, to fly the 1993, 1994 and 1995 seasons, as Red 2, 7 and 6. In my final year, I was the leader of the 'synchro pair', completing a world tour through the winter of 1995/96 and a total of 135 public displays, a record total. I left the team on promotion to squadron leader to return to the Jaguar as a flight commander on the Jaguar OCU (16 [R] Squadron) at Lossiemouth in March 1996.

Gp Capt Tom Eeles was the station commander at Linton-on-Ouse during the withdrawal of the Jet Provost from service. His appointment also included the title of OC No.1 FTS.

Going right back to the 1960s, I was trained on the Jet Provost Mk.3 and Mk.4 at Cranwell where I was a flight cadet from 1960-1963. We started on the Jet Provost 3 but moved on to the Mk.4 fairly quickly after early first solos. The Mk.4 had the more powerful Viper and had a brisk performance compared to the Mk.3. We used to do high-level formation sorties around 30,000 ft, in an unpressurised cockpit with only a simple WW2-style economiser oxygen system. Unsurprisingly the medics didn't approve of this, which led to the Mk.5, which had the same engine as the Mk.4 but with a completely new pressurised cockpit and a more modern oxygen system capable of providing pressure breathing, if needed. Because of the loss of thrust created by having a pressurised cockpit the Mk.5 was not as brisk as the Mk.4, but it was better than the Mk.3. The Mk.4 was very popular for aerobatics and so got worn out really quite quickly, ending up at Shawbury where the remnants were flown to provide aircraft for the u/t air traffic controllers to play with.

However, the Jet Provost Mk.3 soldiered on right up to the end, again being used for the early sorties. The Mk.3A and Mk.5A were the final versions in service, having had an avionic upgrade to replace the old DME system with VOR/DME/ILS and a VHF/UHF radio. The Mk.5 had rather unpleasant spinning characteristics so sprouted very rough leading edges and strakes on the forward fuselage. Additionally, at the flying training schools they did not fly with tip tanks fitted, as it was possible to get into a spin which could not be recovered from if flown solo. At Finningley, the navigator training school, they all had tip tanks fitted as they were virtually never flown solo.

In the early 1980s there was a move to replace the Jet Provost with a more economic aircraft, as fuel prices were going up fast. CFS favoured a turbo prop, as it believed the Jet Provost's handling was too docile by way of introduction to jet flying; students got through only to fail when introduced to the front-line fast jets, at the most expensive stage of training. Their argument was that a trainer with high torque from the engine would be a more challenging aircraft whilst also being more economic than a pure jet. Their argument won the day, and after a prolonged competition the Short Tucano was selected to replace the Jet Provost and first came into service in 1988 at CFS, where I was OC Examining Wing. However, in an attempt to make its handling 'jet-like', it wasn't any more difficult than a Jet Provost, it went much slower – 300kts in a terminal velocity dive – it was unpressurised

so limited in max altitude permitted and was tandem rather than side by side to mimic the Hawk. Personally I far preferred the Jet Provost Mk.5.

Linton-on-Ouse was the last FTS to receive the Tucano to replace the Jet Provost. I delivered the first Tucano to Linton in April 1992, simply because I was the only one there that had flown it before. We did retain the Jet Provost alongside the Tucano for much longer than originally planned as there was a big backlog of students who had been trained on the Jet Provost waiting to move on to the next stage and it was not considered cost effective to refresh them on a new aircraft, the Tucano. We flew the last Jet Provost Mk.3As to Shawbury for disposal on 22 July 1993, a formation of five aircraft, routing via Scampton (CFS), Cranwell and Brampton (HQ RAF). I led the final formation in XM424.

Nigel Courtis became the last student to complete his BFT on the Jet Provost when he graduated from No.1 FTS at Linton-on-Ouse in June 1993.

I was originally on No.117 Course at Linton between July 1991 and May 1992. After this course had finished I was held for some time at Brize Norton expecting to return to Linton for a multi-engine lead-in course. I returned to Linton in March 1993, was loosely appended to 125 Course, and managed to turn my refresher into a (longer) Group 1 lead-in, which I think is why the rest of 125 had finished ahead of me. I thoroughly enjoyed that time on the Jet Provost, and looking back there was some great flying. There was certainly an atmosphere that this was the end of an era amongst the instructors who had more freedom than usual with the syllabus. I remember the final sortie quite clearly as it was my check ride with the then Wg Cdr McDonald. The Jet Provost was limited by lack of fuel, but he had devised a final check to get the most out of the aircraft. This included a low-level navigational exercise to the north-west of Linton, then meeting up with another Jet Provost which happened to be in the area for formation and tail chasing. We finished

116

by doing circuits at Topcliffe and I recall the wing commander trying to run me out of fuel by asking to see more and more circuits. After I had made the (correct) return to base decision, he asked for another circuit anyway and said he would take responsibility for the fuel after that. He flew us back to Linton, which gave me an unusual chance to relax. I passed! But I don't think there were too many other options.

I didn't begin my AFT at Valley until 24 October 1994 and eventually became combat ready on the Tornado F3 on 22 October 1998, and had a fantastic time on Nos.5 and 29 Squadrons. Later, I returned to Linton to instruct, and finished my time in the RAF as a squadron leader before leaving to start a second career in British Airways as a senior first officer, flying the Airbus A380.

WRIGHT JUBILEE TROPHY

The Central Flying School is acknowledged as the centre for the promotion and development of the highest standards of flying proficiency and, in common with other squadron and training establishments, regularly awards trophies to its most successful students at the end of each training course. These awards included the Brabyn Trophy for the best individual aerobatic display on the advanced part of the course, the Clarkson Trophy for the best individual aerobatic display by a student on the applied basic part of the course, and the CFS Trophy for the best all round student. In addition, the CFS hosted the annual Wright Jubilee Trophy competition for solo aerobatic flying between selected flying instructors from RAF jet flying training schools, the RAF College, Cranwell and the RAFFC, Manby. This section records the eighteen Jet Provost instructors who achieved success in the competition between 1956 and 1990.

The Wright Jubilee Trophy was originally presented by the RAFA to the Air Council in December 1953 to commemorate the 50th anniversary of powered flight. The set routine by competitors comprised a compulsory aerobatic sequence of a loop, slow roll, roll off the top of a loop, eight-point hesitation roll and vertical roll, which was followed by an individual continuous sequence lasting two minutes. The competition was judged by the commandant of the CFS and staff members, with the winner subsequently demonstrating his routine at air displays throughout the season.

The first competition was held at Little Rissington on 21 September 1954 in front of a panel of judges drawn from the CFS supervisory staff, including the chief instructor, Wg Cdr F. L. Dodd DSO DFC AFC. Aircraft taking part in the event included Meteors and Vampires and was won by Fg Off R. P. V. Woodward in a Meteor trainer from No.209 AFS, Weston Zoyland. The following year was a unique occasion when the competition was jointly won by two instructors: Plt Off Dennis Lowery from No.8 FTS Swinderby and Flt Lt Ron Dick from No.5 FTS Oakington. Both pilots flew Vampire trainers.

Although the event had been dominated for the first two years by Meteor and Vampire instructors, a Jet Provost T Mk.1 from No.2 FTS, Hullavington, first competed in the 1956 event and was successfully flown by Fg Off R. N. 'Dicky' Rumbelow. Rumbelow

116. On 4 June 1993, Flt Lt Nigel Courtis of No.1 FTS became the last RAF student to receive training on the Jet Provost. He is seen at Linton-on-Ouse with the OC Flying Wing/CI, Wg Cdr Paul McDonald. The Jet Provost is XW319. (Capt Nigel Courtis)

had previously been a member of 208 (Meteor) Squadron and qualified as a QFI in 1956, winning the course aerobatic trophy. He later became a flying instructor with No.2 FTS at Hullavington and Syerston. Following his success at the competition, Rumbelow undertook a number of solo engagements and was forced to make an emergency landing while en route to a display at Little Rissington in August 1956 when the engine of his Jet Provost (XD692) failed; there had been several, similar incidents involving the aircraft's Armstrong Siddeley Viper engine flaming out under negative 'G' and all subsequent aerobatic flying in Jet Provost T Mk.1s was banned until the following February. In April 1957, Rumbelow left the RAF to join Hunting Aircraft as a test pilot.

With the gradual withdrawal of the Vampire and Meteor from RAF Flying Training Command, 1962 became the first year that the Jet Provost regularly took part in the competition. Although won by a Vampire trainer from No.4 FTS, Worksop, the runner-up was

Brian Shadbolt in a Jet Provost from RAF Acklington.

In early 1962, Sqn Ldr Tony Winship decided that a No.6 FTS formation display team was needed to liven up graduation parades for our student courses and AOC's inspections. He asked me if I liked to do the solo spot and go on to do the Wright Jubilee Trophy competition at Little Rissington. The team's first display was for the AOC's parade on 15 May 1962, which unfortunately clashed with my participation in the Wright Jubilee Trophy – I came second while flying Jet Provost T Mk.3 XM474. After this I did North Weald, Swansea and the Battle of Britain show at Acklington on 15 September. It all went a bit quiet until March 1963, when I started to practise for the Wright Trophy again, which I unfortunately missed because of a flying accident in April. My next show was in August 1963 for a passing out parade, following which I flew the height and speed flyby and later the solo slot at the

Battle of Britain show in September. By January 1964 I was planning to leave the RAF to join Qantas, so Geoff Gough was set up to take over the solo spot. Looking for a bit of variety I suggested that we tried working up as a synchronised pair. We started in early January and did our first show for a visit of the secretary of state for air on 13 February 1964. My subsequent solo displays included Jubilee Trophy (28 April 1964 – I came second again, in Jet Provost Mk.4 XR675), AOC's (8 May), a graduation parade (18 May), North Weald (18 May) and Wolverhampton (19 June). This was my last display as I left the RAF in July 1964.

Winner of the 1963 competition, which was held at Little Rissington on 15 May, was Fg Off Terry Nash from No.6 FTS, Acklington, in a Jet Provost. The 1961 and 1962 winner, Flt Lt David Proctor (No.4 FTS), flying a Vampire trainer came second, while Flt Lt Timothy Riddihough (No.1 FTS), also in a Vampire, was third. **Terry Nash:**

Throughout my time at No.6 FTS between February 1960 and June 1963, I was one of the school's solo aerobatic display pilots, initially on the Piston Provost at RAF Tern Hill, then at RAF Acklington, and finally on detachment at RAF Ouston. In October 1962, I converted to the Jet Provost at Acklington and began low-level aerobatic practices and displays, the following April.

Every flying training school was invited to field a competitor for the Wright Jubilee Trophy competition at Little Rissington and I became the school's nominated Jet Provost display pilot for the 1963 competition when Brian Shadbolt was hospitalised following a flying accident. I flew down from Acklington in a Jet Provost T Mk.4, XP674, on 13 May but, because of bad weather, the competition was temporarily postponed until the following day.

The routines of the two aircraft had some similarities, but the Jet Provost Mk.4 (more so than the Mk.3 which had marginally less power) offered scope for some new manoeuvres such as an outside turn (turning the aircraft inverted by pushing 'G', rather than the usual upright/pulling version), a slow speed loop (demonstrated by entering with the undercarriage down, the limiting speed for which was below that at which a loop could usually successfully be performed), and more prolonged periods of inverted flying (both aircraft engines would run for a similar time when inverted, but the Piston Provost would rapidly lose flying speed in straight and level inverted flight).

My competition routine was an inverted fly-past along the display line, usually the main runway; bank to the left into a bunted outside (upside-down) turn through ninety degrees; roll ninety degrees to the left to put the aircraft the right way up, but banking forty-five degrees to the right; high 'G' turn to the right through 270 degrees to line up with the display line; slow speed loop ('trademark TJN'), entered with the undercarriage down (limiting speed 120kts?); recover to the vertical, then stall-turn towards the spectators; recover to level flight for an ultra-slow roll along the display line; recover to vertical for a stall-turn towards the spectators; recover to level flight for an ultra-slow eight-point hesitation roll; recover to the vertical for a hammer-head stall followed by 180-degree roll to line-up with the display line; Porteous loop (which involved entering into, and recovering from, a spin when inverted at the top of the loop); recover to level flight, invert and depart.

I returned to Acklington on 16 May and took part in a number of displays, including Speke Airport on 1 June 1963, the RAFA show at North Weald on 3 June 1963, and Chivenor and Plymouth on 15 June 1963. These were the last shows as I was posted to the Hunter OCU at Chivenor in June 1963, and subsequently to 54 Squadron at West Raynham.

117. Jet Provost T Mk.4, XR697, of No.3 FTS, at Little Rissington for the Wright Jubilee Trophy competition on 10 May 1966. (Author)

118-119

Subsequent Jet Provost pilots to be awarded the trophy included Pete Jarvis of No.1 FTS, who had the distinction of winning the competition on two occasions (28 April 1964 and 11 May 1965) (see p.71).

In August 1966, Flt Lt Roger Pyrah from No.3 FTS had successfully competed for the Clarkson Trophy and followed this achievement by winning the Wright Jubilee Trophy at Little Rissington on 18 May 1967.

Following a number of solo aerobatic shows during the season he returned the following year in an attempt to retain his title but was forced to withdraw from the competition when the elevator of his Jet Provost jammed and he had to make an emergency landing.

The following year, on 22 May 1968, **Flt Lt Dick Bell** from the RAF College, Cranwell, suitably impressed the judges with his unique display repertoire, which included an inverted entry over the crowd line to open his display and a succession of slow loops and rolls with the under-carriage down.

> I realised that if I kept the wings or aircraft moving all the time, the crowd would not have any idea what I was going to do next, and would stop and look. My aim was to try to stop them eating their sandwiches while I performed in front of them. So, close to the ground, always rolling or moving and doing stuff that no one else had ever done before. It took a lot of practice to perfect each manoeuvre, and to see that it was safe close to the ground. I did over 100 hours practice during the season, and always the week before a display.

His subsequent displays during the 1968 season included: Church Fenton (3 June); Cranwell (8 June); Cranwell (27 June); Exeter (29 June); RNAS Lossiemouth (13 July); RNAS Arbroath (20 July); Teesside (3 August); Valley (10 August); Biggin Hill (14 September) and Cranwell (10 October).

The RAF College continued its run of success when former Lightning pilot, Flt Lt Dennis Willison, won the trophy in 1969. He also became the first winner of the trophy to have the tail surfaces of his Jet Provost (XR643) painted in the College colours and feature his initials, 'DJW', on the fin.

On 3 June 1970, Fg Off Paul Dandeker reclaimed the Wright Jubilee Trophy for No.3 FTS and went on to complete a full season of shows between June and September. In August 1970, he accompanied the school's Gemini Pair display team to Chambéry in France, performing to a capacity crowd at Thonon-les-Bains on Lake Leman.

Following his win at Little Rissington in May 1971, Flt Lt Peter Norris brought the trophy back to Cranwell;

120

his Jet Provost, XP586, featuring an attractive colour scheme similar to that of the 1969 winner. He used the same display routine for the competition and his displays throughout the season, which included RAFC Cranwell (22 May); Mildenhall (31 May); RAF Church Fenton (11, 12, 13 June); RAF Biggin Hill (12 June); RAF Cranwell Civic Day (24 June); RAF Binbrook for visiting headmasters/university professors at their conference (26 June); Woodford (4 July); Lords' Taverners at Cranwell (9 July); RNAS Lossiemouth (14 July); BAe Warton and RAF Stafford (31 July).

The RAF College again produced a winner for the 1973 event, Flt Lt Bill Tyndall, being the first successful competitor to fly the new Jet Provost T Mk.5. As with the previous display seasons, the College's aerobatic team, The Poachers, would be joined by the solo pilot for most of the overseas shows; in 1971 it was Flt Lt Peter Norris followed by Flt Lt Bill Tyndall in 1972 and 1973.

Bill Tyndall was followed by Flt Lt Rome Ryott of No.6 FTS in 1974. Two years later, former Lightning pilot, Flt Lt David 'Duck' Webb, of No.1 FTS demonstrated his remarkable aerobatic skills by winning the

118. On 22 May 1968, Flt Lt Dick Bell from the RAF College, Cranwell, suitably impressed the judges with his unique repertoire, which included an inverted arrival over the crowd line to open his display. (Sqn Ldr Dick Bell)

119. Based on the colour scheme of a previous RAF College winner of the Wright Jubilee Trophy, Flt Lt Peter Norris included

his initials on Jet Provost Mk.4, XP586, as seen at Biggin Hill, 11 June 1971. (David Howley)

120. On 3 June 1970, Flying Officer Paul Dandeker reclaimed the Wright Jubilee Trophy for No.3 FTS and went on to complete a full season of displays between June and September. (Paul Dandeker)

121-122

123

RAF Linton-on-Ouse station competition – the Jarvis Trophy – before his success at the Wright Jubilee Trophy event at Cranwell in May 1976. Against stiff competition from Austria, Denmark, France, Germany, the Netherlands, Norway and the USA, he also became the first ever winner of the Embassy International solo jet aerobatics competition at Greenham Common on 2 August and subsequently formed the Wright Jubilee Pair display team with Flt Lt Eddie Danks.

The 1977 Silver Jubilee year competition at Cranwell was won by Flt Lt Martyn Ashton of No.6 FTS, RAF Finningley, who featured a stylised RAFA emblem on the fin of his Jet Provost Mk.5A, XW306. Later that year, the CFS left Cranwell and the Wright Jubilee Trophy was held for the first time at RAF Leeming on 18 May 1978; the competition being won by Fg Off Ray Coates of No.1 FTS in a Jet Provost T Mk.5A.

The 1979 winner was a former member of the CAW display team, The Macaws, Flt Lt Mick Marriott of No.6 FTS, while Flt Lt Les Hatcher of No.7 FTS claimed the trophy at the 1981 event.

At the end of 1981, **Flt Lt Rob Chambers** was posted to Cranwell as an instructor. The following year he was selected to represent the College in the competition, having previously won the squadron and Wing nomination:

The competition was held at Leeming on 24 May 1982. It was my first year as a QFI at Cranwell and I won flying Jet Provost Mk.5A, XW336. I subsequently flew displays at Prestwick (4-5 June), RAF Brize Norton & RAF Halton (12 June), Duxford (13 June), RAF Swinderby (20 June), Woodford (26 June), RNAS Lee-on-Solent (17 July), Weston Park (18 July), RAF Brawdy (22 July), Old Warden (25 July), Hertford (Scout camp) (28 July), Newport (7 August), RAF St Mawgan (11 August), Coventry (15 August), Blackpool (21 August), RAF Binbrook (28 August), Crich (29-30 August), Nottingham (29 August), St Albans (30 August), RAF Leuchars (4 September), RAF Finningley (4 September), RAF Abingdon (18 September) and RAF St Athan (18 September).

124

Subsequent winners of the trophy included Flt Lt Chris Topham of No.7 FTS in 1983 and Flt Lt Dave Whittingham of No.1 FTS in 1985. In May 1987, Fg Off Sean Chiddention from the RAF College became the first contestant in twenty-two years to win the trophy on two consecutive occasions (see p.139). The 1989 competition was won by another future member of the Red Arrows, Flt Lt Andy Offer of No.1 FTS, Linton-on-Ouse.

From 1990 the Wright Jubilee Trophy was awarded to the best overall display from a Support Command flying instructor and the Jet Provost competed against Tucano, Hawk and Bulldog pilots. The event also marked the introduction of a new award – the Spitfire Trophy – for the best Jet Provost/Tucano display pilot, both of which were presented to Flt Lt Andy Legg of No.6 FTS. Although the 1991 contest would be awarded to a UAS pilot, Andy Legg would retain the Spitfire Trophy and achieve the distinction of being the last Jet Provost pilot to win the Wright Jubilee Trophy.

121. Former Lightning pilot, Flt Lt David 'Duck' Webb, of No.1 FTS demonstrated his aerobatic skills by winning the RAF Linton-on-Ouse station competition, the Jarvis Trophy, prior to his success at the Wright Jubilee Trophy event at Cranwell in May 1976. He also became the first ever winner of the Embassy International solo jet aerobatics competition at Greenham Common in August and subsequently formed the Wright Jubilee Pair display team with the deputy CFI, Sqn Ldr Eddie Danks. He is seen following his return from Greenham Common. (Eddie Danks)

122. The Wright Jubilee Trophy was held for the first time at RAF Leeming on 18 May 1978 and was won by Fg Off Ray Coates of No.1 FTS in a Jet Provost T Mk.5A. (via Eddie Danks)

123. During his first year as a QFI at Cranwell, Flt Lt Rob Chambers successfully competed in the Wright Jubilee contest at RAF Leeming on 24 May 1982. (Rob Chambers)

124. The RAF Linton-on-Ouse solo display pilot, Flt Lt Steve Howard, formates with the reserve aircraft in 1992. The specially designed colour scheme was applied to two Jet Provost T Mk.3As of No.1 FTS, XM424 and XM466. (via Tom Eeles)

125

CIVILIAN DISPLAY TEAMS

NWMAS STRIKEMASTER TRIO The North Wales Military Aviation Services Ltd (NWMAS Ltd) was formed at Hawarden in September 2001 to maintain a variety of military aircraft types, including the Strikemaster, Jet Provost and Hunter.

In February 2005, Strikemaster Mk.82A, G-SOAF, a former Royal Air Force of Oman aircraft, was jointly acquired by the directors of NWMAS Ltd, Mark Petrie and John Rowley. Retaining its SOAF colour scheme, the Strikemaster was displayed for a number of years at shows in the UK and Republic of Ireland.

For the Kemble Air Day in June 2007, three Strikemaster aircraft made a debut appearance as a display team in a tight formation non-aerobatics sequence flown by Mark Petrie in Mk.82A, G-SOAF, John Rowley in Mk.80A G-FLYY (ex-Saudi air force), and George Begg in his personal Mk.87 G-UVNR (ex-Kenyan and Botswana air forces).

TRANSAIR JET PROVOST/STRIKEMASTER DUO In November 1994, the prototype Jet Provost T Mk.5, XS230, was purchased by Tom Moloney of the Transair Pilot Shop and registered as G-BVWF. The aircraft was completely refurbished, retaining its 'Raspberry Ripple' paint scheme from its time with the A&AEE, Boscombe Down and re-registered as G-VIVM in March 1996. The previous January, Bob Thompson had also purchased Jet Provost T Mk.5A G-BWEB/XW422, and after rebuild had it painted in the same 'Raspberry Ripple' paint scheme. Both aircraft had the Transair logos applied and named as the 'Transair Jet Provost Duo'; the team's display routines being inspired by Bob Thompson's former leadership of the Gemini Pair and Swords RAF aerobatic teams during 1973 and 1974.

As Tom Moloney had by now gained a large amount of solo display experience but very little formation aerobatic experience, it was agreed that Tom should lead and Bob would undertake the formation flying parts of the display. On 15 April 1996 the first Transair team display practice was carried out and on 11/12 May 1996 the team completed its first two displays at the North Weald air show; a further fifteen displays were given that season, including the RIAT at Fairford. In 1997, the team began their second display season at the North Weald show in May and went on to complete a total of eight shows, including RAF Waddington in June.

At the end of the 1997 display season, Bob Thompson decided to upgrade to a Strikemaster Mk.87, OJ5/G-BXFP (ex-Botswana Defence Force), which was repainted as RNZAF NZ6361. By July 1998 the aircraft was fitted with a more powerful Viper 535 engine to make formation flying much easier and featured purpose-built, black underwing simulated bombs which housed diesel oil for the smoke system. Tom Moloney also decided to upgrade at the same time and purchased OJ4/G-UNNY (ex-Kenyan air force and Botswana Defence Force). The team was now renamed as the Strikemaster Duo and was in existence for only the 1998 display season, with nineteen appearances which included Londonderry, NI, and Kemble, both on 31 May, Biggin Hill on 6 June and Sunderland on 2/3 August.

At the end of the season it was mutually agreed to stop the formation team displays because of escalating costs, although both pilots continued with solo Strikemaster display work. In August 2000, the Strikemaster Duo briefly reformed for a one-off appearance at the Kemble Open Day.

In 2003, both aircraft were sold to a company called Strikemaster Films Ltd, and later became involved in a dubious sale to the Force Aérienne de la Côte d'Ivoire.

TEAM VIPER In 2008, experienced display pilot, Gerald Williams, began to assemble a display team of four Strikemaster aircraft and pilots. He had previously

126-127

demonstrated ex-Saudi Strikemaster Mk.80, ZU-JAK, in South Africa and Swaziland, two years earlier. In October 2006, the aircraft was slightly damaged in a landing accident at Durban and returned to the UK for repairs, where it was registered as G-UPPI in December 2008.

The original members of the team included Chris Heames, Gerald Williams, Justin Hughes and Mark Petrie, with Mark Southern and Matt Masters joining later. The team aircraft were Strikemaster Mk.84 G-MXPH '311' ex-Royal Singapore Air Force; Mk.87 G-UVNR 'OJ10'; Mk.80A G-VPER '1130' ex-Royal Saudi Air Force and Mk.82A, G-SOAF.

On 26 April 2009 Gerald Williams' aircraft, G-UPPI, suffered an engine failure during a training flight and force-landed in a field near Tiverton, Devon. The aircraft

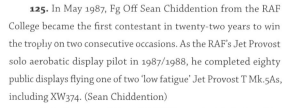

125. In May 1987, Fg Off Sean Chiddention from the RAF College became the first contestant in twenty-two years to win the trophy on two consecutive occasions. As the RAF's Jet Provost solo aerobatic display pilot in 1987/1988, he completed eighty public displays flying one of two 'low fatigue' Jet Provost T Mk.5As, including XW374. (Sean Chiddention)

126. Strikemaster Mk.84 G-MXPH served with the Republic

of Singapore AF between 1970 and 1988, and was eventually returned to the UK in 1995. It is currently owned by Richard S. Partridge-Hicks at North Weald and flies with its original colour scheme and serial. (Ray Deacon)

127. Sqn Ldr Dan Arlett in Strikemaster Mk.80A, G-VPER, during the last appearance of the Viper Jet Formation Team, Kemble, 20 June 2010. (Ray Deacon)

was written off, which unfortunately deprived the team of a spare airframe.

Named 'Team Viper' after the Strikemaster's Rolls-Royce Viper engine, the team's debut appearance was at the Connemara air show in May 2009, following which they demonstrated at the Biggin Hill International Air Fair and the RNLAF Open Day at Volkel in June, the Royal International Air Tattoo, Fairford, and RAF Waddington in July, and RAF Leuchars in September.

The 2010 display season began with a three-week tour of the Middle East, including displays at Bahrain on 21-23 January, Al Ain on 28-30 January, and the world famous Red Bull Air Races in Abu Dhabi. 2010 also saw the team gradually replace the Strikemasters with Hawker Hunters, initially presenting a mixed four-ship of two Hunters joined by two Strikemasters before progressing to a full four-ship of Hunters at the RAF Leuchars and Sanicole International Air Show in September that year. The last appearance of the four-ship Strikemaster display was at the Kemble air show in June 2010.

SWORDS AVIATION Although not a display team per se, Swords Aviation is a syndicate based at North Weald, Essex, that owns and operates two Jet Provost aircraft, providing its members with all aspects of basic and advanced jet pilot training. The aircraft include the only airworthy Jet Provost T. Mk.52, G-PROV, which was originally built as a T Mk.4, XS228, and later saw service with the South Arabian Federation Air Force and the Republic of Singapore Air Force, before being sold to Mike Carlton's Hunter One Collection in November 1983. It was acquired by its present owner in June 2001 and is painted in its original South Yemen colour scheme and coded '104'.

The second aircraft is the former T Mk.5 prototype, XS230, which was involved in test and development work with BAC, A&AEE and the ETPS, and became the last Jet Provost to be flown in RAF service on 14 July 1993. Sold at auction in November 1994, it was originally placed on the civilian register as G-BVWF. The Jet Provost later joined the Transair display team and re-registered as G-VIVM in March 1996, before being transferred to the International Test Pilot School at Cranwell in 1998. It was acquired by its present owner in November 2001.

JET AEROBATICS In 2016, Dan Arlett and Ollie Suckling combined their respective skills as part of Jet Aerobatics to offer two options for flying displays in the UK: a proven solo aerobatic display or a pair's display

with either Jet Provost Mk.5 or the Jet Provost Mk.5/Mk.3 in a series of close formation manoeuvres and solo aerobatic manoeuvres. Both aircraft being based at North Weald.

Former Team Viper pilot, Dan Arlett, flew Jet Provost T Mk.5A, XW324/G-BWSG, which retained the colour scheme of its previous service with No.6 FTS at RAF Finningley. Dan Arlett was joined by Ollie Suckling, who flew the Jet Provost display team's T Mk.3, XN637/G-BKOU. Both pilots had previously rehearsed the pair's routine in 2015, and appeared at twelve shows between June and September 2016.

NEW ZEALAND WARBIRDS ASSOCIATION Strikemaster aircraft were highly regarded in New Zealand due to their long association with the RNZAF, three of which, together with a further ex-Saudi example were operated in an airworthy condition. These include Brett Nicholls' NZ6370/ZK-STR, which was obtained by Strikemaster Ltd in April 2012; NZ6362/ZK-NTY, formerly VH-AGI and acquired in September 2014; while Christchurch-based business man, Brian Hall purchased the ex-Saudi airframe, ZK-VPR/1130, in May 2011.

All Strikemasters in New Zealand were privately owned and none were syndicated because of the difficulty of gaining insurance for ex-military jets. Brett Nicholls' two Strikemasters were operated under NZ CAA Adventure Aviation rules for commercial joy flights from Ardmore. **Brett Nicholls:**

> The maintenance provider for the Strikemasters was Pioneer Aero Ltd, Ardmore Airfield, Papakura, Auckland. I purchased the first Strikemaster (NZ6370) to come back to New Zealand and shipped it back from Australia in 2010. It was the first privately-owned Strikemaster to fly in New Zealand and the first ex-RNZAF to return to NZ skies after the RNZAF sold them in 1994 to Aermacchi (as part of the sale and purchase agreement of the RNZAF buying the Aermacchi as the government wanted the Strikemasters to be removed from NZ). It was a monster effort to get it on the NZ CAA register as it was 'first of type' on the civilian register –

previously it was only on the military register i.e. an RNZAF asset. Then came the Saudi Strikemaster, first flying in 2013 (from the UK, ex-G-VPER), then NZ6372 first flying in 2014 and finally my other one NZ6362, which first flew in 2015.

Following its official retirement from the RNZAF, the first public appearance by a Strikemaster (NZ6370) in New Zealand was at the Classic Flight's air show in April 2011. This was followed by the first two-ship Strikemaster display (NZ6370 and NZ6372) at the biennial Wings over Wairarapa air show at Hood aerodrome in January 2015. The appearance at subsequent events by a mixed formation display team was typified at the Warbirds over Wanaka show on Easter 2016 when the two Strikemasters were joined by two Vampire trainers for a thrilling display of aerobatics, including a formation loop by all four aircraft (see also pp.113-114).

128. Featuring the logo of the International Test Pilots School on the fin, former Jet Provost Mk.5 prototype, XS230/G-VIVM, with Swords Aviation at North Weald, October 2014. (Ray Deacon)

Above: Jet Provost Mk.5s on the final assembly line at Warton.
(BAe Systems Heritage Warton-Percival/Hunting Collection)

APPENDICES

APPENDIX 1
RAF JET PROVOST DISPLAY FLYING TEAMS 1958–1976

1958

Four Jet Provost T Mk.1s of the CFS
Little Rissington
The Central Flying School Jet Aerobatic Team
Flt Lts N. H. Giffin, D. McClen, F. W. J. Packer and
D. Millington. Reserve: Flt Lt M. Edwards
XD675, XD676, XD677, XD678, XD679, XD680, XD693

1959

Two Jet Provost T Mk.1s of CFS
Little Rissington
The Redskins
Flt Lts P. J. Hirst and J. R. Rhind (synchronised
display team)
XD675, XD676, XD677, XD678, XD679, XD680

1960

Four Jet Provost T Mk.3s of CFS
Little Rissington
The Central Flying School Aerobatic Team
Flt Lts R. Langstaff and F. R. Brambley, Plt Off B. A.
D. McK McDonald and Flt Lt J. G. Nicklin
XM411:R-G, XM413:R-H, XM423:R-K, XM425:R-L,
XM426:R-N, XM428:R-M

Four Jet Provost T Mk.3s of No.2 FTS
Syerston
Flt Lts W. D. P. Jones, D. J. Rowe and R. T. Stock, M
Pilot J. McTavish
XM370:9, XM383:27, XM405:34, XM409:39

1961

Four Jet Provost T Mk.3s of the CFS
Little Rissington
The Central Flying School Aerobatic Team
Flt Lts F. R. Brambley and D. T. McCann,
Plt Off B. A. D. McK McDonald and Flt Lt I. K. McKee.
Reserves: Flt Lts T. H. Whittingham and W. W. Elsegood
XN511:R-W, XN512:R-X, XN549:R-W, XN550:S-A,
XN554:S-E, XN557:S-F, XN573:S-G

129

Four Jet Provost T Mk.3s of RAF College
Cranwell
Flt Lts J. R. Lees, D. J. Hine, Master Pilot F. Bright
and Flt Lt A. R. Pollock
(The above being just one example of the handful of
informal College Jet Provost teams produced during
this period at Cranwell and Barkston Heath)

Four Jet Provost T Mk.3s of No.1 FTS
Linton-on-Ouse
Gin Section
Flt Lt R. G. Corck, Lt C. C. N. Davis, RN, Flt Lts H. W.
J. Rigg and A. P. Fox (Team reduced to three aircraft
in early 1961, resulting in Flt Lt Fox being removed)
XM465:16, XM467:15, XN461:22, XN469:25, XN502:29,
XN504:34, XN506:31, XN507:33, XN509:35, XN556:18

130-131

132-133

129. The CFS Jet Provost Aerobactic Team at the Biggin Hill Press Day in September 1961 From left to right: Wally Elsegood (reserve pilot), Bruce McDonald (No.3), Frank Brambley (leader), Dick Whittingham (reserve pilot), and David McCann (No.2). Absent is 'Snowy' McKee (No.4) who had ejected from a Jet Provost (XM423) the previous month. (Dave McCann)

130. Jet Provost T Mk.1s of the CFS Jet Aerobatic Team in a formation climb during early 1958. The team was led by Flt Lt Norman Giffin. (Don McClen)

131. A shortage of manpower and lack of available aircraft led to the formation of the CFS synchronised pair, the Redskins, in 1959 with two Jet Provost T Mk.1s flown by Flt Lts Jim Rhind and 'Curly' Hirst. (Norman Giffin via Ray Deacon)

132. The CFS Jet Provost team, the Red Pelicans rehearsing over south Gloucestershire for the 1962 SBAC show at Farnborough. (via Ray Deacon)

133. Recovering from a formation loop, the No.2 FTS Jet Provost team on 19 July 1960 – Flt Lts Jones, Rowe, Stock and Master Pilot McTavish. (via Reg Stock)

Four/three Jet Provost T Mk.3s of No.2 FTS
Syerston
Flt Lt J. A. Spreadbury, Fg Off B. J. Stephens, Flt Lts J. E. Watts-Phillips and C. J. Wilmot (Flt Lt C. J. Wilmot dropped from team following a mid-air-collision in Feb 1961)
XM371:12, XM402:31, XM408:38, XM409:39, XM410:41

1962

Five Jet Provost T Mk.4s of CFS
Little Rissington
The Red Pelicans
Flt Lts I. K. McKee, K. F. Beck, I. Bashall, J. E. S. Rolfe and R. G. Fox. Reserve: Flt Lt A. J. R. Doyle
XP550:41, XP551:42, XP552:43, XP553:44, XP554:45, XP572:48, XP573:49

Three Jet Provost T Mk.4s of RAF College
Cranwell
Flt Lts J. Gale, J. F. Farley and S. Cutbill

Three Jet Provost T Mk.4s of No.1 FTS
Linton-on-Ouse
Gin Section
Lt C. C. N. Davis RN, Flt Lts D. M. Robinson and H. W. J. Rigg
XP589:36, XP621:38, XP626:39, XP627:40, XP637:42

Three Jet Provost T Mk.3s of No.2 FTS
Syerston
Flt Lts W. W. Elsegood, P. D. Jennings and W. Dodds. Reserve: Flt Lt D. A. Bell
XM374:11, XM412:40, XM414:45

Four Jet Provost T Mk.3s of No.3 FTS
Leeming
Sqn Ldr R. W. Glover, Flt Lts G. J. Bailey, W. H. W. Norton and K. Marshall.

Three Jet Provost T Mk.3/Mk.4s of No.6 FTS
Acklington
Cock's o' The North/Suntan
Flt Lt J. S. Laing, Fg Offs R. A. C. Wakely and R. I. Morris. Reserve: Flt Lt M. R. D. Butt. Solo display pilot: Flt Lt B. M. Shadbolt
XN603:7, XP638:42, XP662:45

1963

Six Jet Provost T Mk.4s of CFS
Little Rissington
The Red Pelicans
Flt Lts I. Bashall, K. F. Beck, A. J. Hawkes, N. T. Raffin, RAAF, B. A. Nice and T. E. L. Lloyd.
XP549:40, XP550:41, XP551:42, XP552:43, XP553:44, XP554:45, XP571:47, XP572:48, XP573:49

134

Four Jet Provost T Mk.4s of RAF College
Cranwell
The Poachers
Sqn Ldr I. H. Panton, Flt Lt H. E. B. Mayes, Flt Lt J. L. Blackford and Flt Lt G. E. Ord.
XP547:82, XP560:75, XP566:81

Three Jet Provost T Mk.4s of No.1 FTS
Linton-on-Ouse
Gin Formation
Flt Lts D. M. Robinson, R. Holliday and H. W. J. Rigg. (In July 1963 the team line-up was changed to Flt Lts R. Holliday, H. W. J. Rigg and T. G. Thornton)
XP616:37, XP633:41, XP626:39, XP637:42, XR665:38, XR668:45, XR672:43, XR674:44, XR700:46

Three Jet Provost T Mk.4s of No.2 FTS
Syerston
Flt Lts W. W. Elsegood, P. D. Jennings and W. Dodds. Reserve: Flt Lt D. A. Bell
XP614:41, XP625:49, XP641:34, XR648:33

Three Jet Provost T Mk.4s of No.3 FTS
Leeming
No.3 FTS Aerobatic Team

Sqn Ldr D. W. Tanner DFC, Flt Lts E. D. Evers
and A. W. Parr
XP686:35, XR697:33, XR677:34

Three Jet Provost T Mk.3 / T Mk.4s of No.6 FTS
Acklington
Cock's o' The North/Suntan
Flt Lt J. S. Laing, Fg Offs R. A. C. Wakely and R. I. Morris.
Reserve: Flt Lt M. R. D. Butt
Solo display pilot: Flt Lt B. M. Shadbolt
XR664:41, XR654:44, XR656:54

1964

Six Jet Provost T Mk.4s of CFS
Little Rissington
The Red Pelicans
Flt Lts T. E. L. Lloyd, B. A. Nice, W. A. Langworthy,
D. F. Southern, H. R. Lane and R. S. S. Cox (Flt Lt Cox
replaced by Flt Lt E. C. F. Tilsley in March 1964)
XP549:40, XP550:41, XP551:42, XP552:43, XP553:44,
XP554:45, XP571:47, XP572:48, XP573:49

135

Four Jet Provost T Mk.4s of RAF College
Cranwell
The Poachers
Sqn Ldr I. H. Panton, Flt Lts H. E. B. Mayes,
J. L. Blackford and G. E. Ord
XP557:72, XP558:73, XP560:74, XR681:94

Three Jet Provost T Mk.4s of No.1 FTS
Linton-on-Ouse
Gin Formation
Flt Lt T. G. Thornton, Lts S. Thomas RN,
and J. Carver RN
XP615:35, XP665:38, XP668:45, XP674:44

Three Jet Provost T Mk.4s of No.2 FTS
Syerston
Viper Red
Sqn Ldr J. M. A. Parker and members drawn from Flt Lts
D. Henderson, J. T. Kingsley and Capt E. R. Harris USAF
XR648:33, XR707:45, XR673:30

Three Jet Provost T Mk.4s of No.3 FTS
Leeming
No.3 FTS Aerobatic Team
Sqn Ldr D. W. Tanner DFC, Flt Lts E. D. Evers and A. W. Parr
XP618:50, XP667: 38, XP675:37, XP686:35, XR697:33,
XR703:30, XS181:32, XS184:53

Three/four Jet Provost T Mk.4s of No.6 FTS
Acklington
Cock's o' The North/Suntan
Flt Lts J. J. Walker and R. D. G. Gunning,
Fg Offs R. I. Morris and H. W. Farquhar-Smith
Solo display pilot: Flt Lt B. M. Shadbolt
XR649:53, XR652:52, XR659:55

1965

Four Jet Provost T Mk.4s of CFS
Little Rissington
The 1965 CFS Jet Provost Aerobatic Team
Flt Lts W. A. Langworthy, D. A. Bell, R. Booth
and J. J. Maynard. Reserves: Sqn Ldr D. McClen and
Flt Lt M. Baston RAAF
XP549:40, XP550:41, XP551:42, XP552:43, XP553:44,
XP554:45, XP571:47, XP572:48, XP573:49

134. The official team line-up of the Red Pelicans in 1963,
including back row: Flt Lt Benny Raffin (RAAF), Flt Lt Terry Lloyd
and Flt Lt Brian Nice. Centre row: Flt Lt Keith Beck and Flt Lt
Tony Hawkes. Front: Flt Lt Ian Bashall (leader). (via Ian Bashall)

135. As the RAF's premier aerobatic team, the Jet Provost T Mk.4s
of the CFS Red Pelicans were presented to the media in August 1964,
prior to their appearance at the Farnborough air show, the following
month. (BAe Systems Heritage Warton-Percival/Hunting Collection)

Four Jet Provost T Mk.4s of RAF College

Cranwell

The Poachers

Sqn Ldr I. H. Panton, Flt Lts J. L. Blackford, P. D. Jennings and G. E. Ord. Reserve: Flt Lt A. L. Thomas
XP558:73, XP559:74, XP560:75, XP561:76, XP565:80, XP566:81, XP548:83, XP584:88, XP575:92, XS181:96, XP667:98

Four Jet Provost T Mk.4s of RAF College of Air Warfare, Manby

The RAF College of Air Warfare Formation Aerobatic Team

Flt Lts W. R. Shrubsole, J. K. Bancroft (replaced by P. R. Evans from July), T. H. Bliss and A. J. Sheppard
XP560:34, XR679:21, XR704: 28, XR705:29

Three Jet Provost T Mk.4s of No.1 FTS

Linton-on-Ouse

Gin Formation

Flt Lt N. Grove DFM, Flt Lt D. A. Smith, Lt P. H. Cadoret RN. Solo aerobatic pilot: Flt Lt P. D. Jarvis
XP662:48, XP668:50, XR665:38, XR699:34

Four Jet Provost T Mk.4s of No.2 FTS

Syerston

Viper Red

Flt Lt D. Henderson and with team members drawn from Flt Lts F. J. Hoare, G. Hall, T. Kingsley and Fg Off G. Lee
XP614:41, XP630:50, XP665:38, XP669:37, XR647:32, XR667:44, XS176:36, XS183:46

136

Three Jet Provost T Mk.4s of No.6 FTS

Acklington

Cock's o' The North/Suntan

Flt Lts J. J. Walker, R. D. G. Gunning and H. W. Farquhar-Smith. Reserve: Flt Lt J. R. Lobley
XR675:59, XS180:61, XR706:62

Three Jet Provost T Mk.4s of No.7 FTS

Church Fenton

The Pudding Formation

Flt Lts D. M. Robinson, A. Gunn and C. J. Thomas
XP617:H, XP670:B, XR655:V

1966

Four Jet Provost T Mk.4s of CFS

Little Rissington

The Red Pelicans

Wg Cdr D. L. Edmonds AFC, Sqn Ldr D. McClen, Flt Lts C. J. Thomas and J. J. Maynard (replaced by C. J. Sturt)
XN468:41, XS212:40, XS213:46, XS217:50, XS222:43, XS225:47, XS226:42, XS229:49

Four Jet Provost T Mk.4s of RAF College of Air Warfare, Manby

The RAF College of Air Warfare Formation Aerobatic Team

Flt Lts W. R. Shrubsole, A. J. Sheppard, T. H. Bliss and A. W. Vine AFM
XP632:30, XR705:29, XS186:10, XS209:11, XS210:12, XS219:35

Three Jet Provost T Mk.4s of No.1 FTS

Linton-on-Ouse

Gin Section

Flt Lt N. Grove DFM, Lt M. E. Todd RN and Flt Lt D. A. Smith
XP615:35, XP616:37, XP662:48, XP668:50, XR665:38, XR699:34, XR700:46

Four Jet Provost T MK.4s of No.2 FTS

Syerston

Viper Red

Flt Lt D. Henderson, Fg Off W. A. Aspinall, Flt Lt W. Surtees and Fg Off G. Lee (Synchronised display team)

137

138-139

1967

Four Jet Provost T Mk.4s of CFS
Little Rissington
The Red Pelicans
Sqn Ldr P. J. Hirst, Capt J. K. Snow USAF, Flt Lts J. D.
Smith and M. S. Lovett. Reserve: Flt Lt K. A. Clark
XN468:41, XS212:40, XS213:46, XS225:47, XS226;42,
XS229: 49

**Four Jet Provost T Mk.4s of RAF College of
Air Warfare,** Manby
The RAF College of Air Warfare Formation Aerobatic Team
Flt Lts W. R. Shrubsole, A. J. Sheppard, P. G. Cowen
and Sqn Ldr A. W. Vine
XP575:33, XR704:28, XS179:20, XS210:12, XS211:14,
XS214:17, XS216:19

136. The little-known Cock's O' The
North display team from No.6 FTS, Ack-
lington, 1965, with Flt Lts Bob Gunning,
Johnny Walker, and Horace Farquhar-Smith.
The team made its debut in September 1962
and was in existence until October 1965.
(Johnny Walker)

137. The Red Pelicans about to join
the circuit at Little Rissington on 18 August
1966: Wg Cdr Eddie Edmonds, Sqn Ldr Don
McClen, Flt Lts Colin Thomas and Chas
Sturt. (Author)

138. Jet Provost T Mk.4s of the College of Air Warfare Formation Aerobatic

Team at Bentwaters in May 1967. (Roger
Lindsay)

139. By 1967, the Jet Provost team
from No.1 FTS, Linton Gin had returned
to performing with four aircraft and
appeared at the RAF Middleton St George
air show in August. (Roger Lindsay)

Four Jet Provost T Mk.4s of No.1 FTS
Linton-on-Ouse
The Linton Gin
Flt Lt T. J. Burns, Lt K. A. Harris RN, Fg Offs B. Todd
and E. A. Hemson
XP561:51, XP615:35, XP627:40, XP637:42, XP668:50,
XP678:45, XR655:52, XR657:37, XR665:38, XR672:43,
XR699:34, XP700:46, XP701:47

Two Jet Provost T Mk.4s of No.2 FTS
Syerston
Viper Red 1967
Sqn Ldr J. J. Maynard and Flt Lt G. Lee
(Synchronised display team)
XP677:35, XS175:36

1968

Four Jet Provost T Mk.4s of CFS
Little Rissington
The Red Pelicans
Flt Lts J. D. Smith, J. B. Robinson, M. S. Lovett
and J. D. Blake
XN468:41, XS213:46, XS217:50, XS222:43, XS225:47

Four Jet Provost T Mk.4s of RAF College
Cranwell
The Poachers
Wg Cdr J. M. A. Parker, Sqn Ldr W. P. Jago,
Flt Lts E. G. Hudson and Bahar-ul-haq PAF
XP555:70, XP556:71, XP558:73, XP584:68, XP671:91, XS181:96

**Four Jet Provost T Mk.4s of RAF College of Air
Warfare Formation Aerobatic Team**
Manby
The Macaws
Flt Lts W. R. Shrubsole, P. G. Cowen,
J. D. T. Wingfield and J. H. Adams
XP629:26, XP640:27, XP672:25, XP686:32, XR704:28,
XS179:20, XS210:12, XS215:18

Four Jet Provost T Mk.4s of No.1 FTS
Linton-on-Ouse
The Linton Gin
Flt Lts M. A. B. Collin and R. B. Mackenzie-Crooks,
Lt D. R. G. Brittain RN and Fg Off P. S. Kiggel.
Reserve: Fg Off B. Todd
XP615:35, XP627:40, XP633:41, XP662:48, XP668:50,
XP678:45, XR655:52, XR666:47, XR672:43, XR699:34,
XR700:46

Four Jet Provost T Mk.4s of No.2 FTS
Syerston
The Vipers
Sqn Ldr J. J. Maynard, Flt Lt P. G. H. Perry, Capt K.
Redding USAF and Flt Lt G. W. Broadbent
XP624:48, XP664:38, XP665:42, XP669:37.

Two Jet Provost T Mk.4s of No.3 FTS
Leeming
The Gemini Pair
Flt Lts E. R. Perreaux and M. R. French
(Synchronised display team)
XM379:10, XP562:49, XP579:44, XS184:62

140

141

142

143-144

1969

Four Jet Provost T Mk.4s of CFS
Little Rissington
The Red Pelicans
Flt Lts J. B. Robinson, A. J. Davies, R. B. Mackenzie-Crooks
and R. M. Clayton. Reserve: Flt Lt J. W. Davy
XS212:40, XN468:41, XS226:42, XS213:46, XS225:47, XS217:50

Four Jet Provost T Mk.4s of RAF College
Cranwell
The Cranwell Poachers
Sqn Ldr W. P. Jago, Flt Lts R. H. Screen, R. F. J. Harrison
and G. W. Timms. Reserve: Flt Lt M. B. Langham
XP583:87, XP584:88, XP555:70, XP556:71, XP671:91,
XS179, XS181:96

**Four Jet Provost T Mk.4s of RAF College of Air
Warfare Formation Aerobatic Team**
Manby
The Macaws
Flt Lts W. R. Shrubsole, J. D. T. Wingfield,
R. H. Stalker and J. H. Adams
XP556:71, XP558:20, XP583:87, XP584: 88, XP672:25,
XP686:32, XR647:15, XR654:34, XR660:17, XR701:26,
XS211:14, XS215:18

Four Jet Provost T Mk.4s of No.1 FTS
Linton-on-Ouse
The Linton Gin
Sqn Ldr S. A. Edwards, Fg Offs A. D. Colesky,
J. J. Whitfield and Flt Lt W. D. S. Waddington.
Reserves: Flt Lt D. C. Coldicutt and Fg Off J. L. Bishop
XP633:41, XP634:49, XP679:36, XP681:53, XP683:51,
XR666:47, XR670:54, XR672:43, XR700:46, XR707:45

Four Jet Provost T Mk.4s of No.2 FTS
Syerston
The Vipers
Sqn Ldr J. F. Merry and Flt Lts J. Abell, J. Haddock
and T. Hall
XP617:49, XP630:50, XP641:34, XR644:36, XR707:45

140. The Macaws display team members in 1968. L-R: Flt Lts Bill Shrubsole, John Wingfield, Jim Adams and Peter Cowen. (via Jim Adams)

141. For its final display season, the Vipers display team from No.2 FTS repainted its Jet Provost Mk.4s in an attractive colour scheme of a white fin, rudder and tip tanks, as seen on XP617 in June 1968. (John Merry)

142. In March 1968, a new, totally re-vamped College of Air Warfare Jet Provost aerobatic team was approved, which featured an attractive colour scheme and named the Macaws. (Bill Shrubsole)

143. Four Jet Provost T Mk.4s of the RAF College display team, the Cranwell Poachers, in 1969. Led by Sqn Ldr Bill Jago, it became the first College team to appear at international events. (Bob Screen)

144. Jet Provost T Mk.4, XP634, No.1 FTS Linton Gin at Leuchars in September 1969. This would be the last Gin team to perform with the Mk.4. (Roger Lindsay)

146-147

FROM JET PROVOST TO STRIKEMASTER

145. Climbing in tee formation, Sqn Ldr Eric Evers led the CFS Jet Provost Mk.5 team while it performed at twenty-three shows during the 1970 display season. (Eric Evers)

146. Depicted during its trademark mirror formation manoeuvre in July 1970, two Jet Provost Mk.4s of the Gemini Pair formate with a Harrier from RAF Wittering. The photograph was taken close to the Eggborough power station, near Selby, with Flt Lt Gordon Revell formating with Fg Off Ron Pattinson. (Ron Pattinson)

147. Jet Provost T Mk.5s of the RAF College Cranwell aerobatic team, the Poachers led by Sqn Ldr John Robinson in 1971. The aircraft feature the original colour scheme devised for the team. (via Roger Lindsay)

148. The Linton Blades team from No.1 FTS in 1970. L-R: Joe Whitfield, Dudley Carvell, Dave Waddington and Dave Coldicutt. (via Steve Waddington)

149. The Macaws in 1971 showing the team emblem on the nose of the aircraft. The team members were all QFIs at the School of Refresher Flying at Manby and included Flt Lts Brian Hoskins, Dave Brooke, Martin Engwell and Pete Diggance. (Pete Diggance)

Two Jet Provost T Mk.4s of No.3 FTS
Leeming
The Gemini Pair
Flt Lts P. R. Rayner and J. J. Pook
(Synchronised display team) XS177:43, XP676:64

1970

Four Jet Provost T Mk.5s of CFS
Little Rissington
The Red Pelicans
Sqn Ldr E. D. Evers, Flt Lts T. R. Francis, J. W. Davy and
K. J. Tait. Reserve: Flt Lt R. D. Brown
XW287:80, XW288:81, XW289:82, XW290:83, XW291:84,
XW292:85, XW293:86, XW294:87 and XW295:88

Four Jet Provost T Mk.4s of RAF College
Cranwell
The Cranwell Poachers
Sqn Ldr W. P. Jago, Flt Lts J. B. Hill, P. J. Day and G. W.
Timms
XP557:72, XP560:75, XP563:78, XP583:87, XP586:90,
XR673:97, XS178:99, XR662:90

**Four Jet Provost T Mk.4s of RAF College of Air
Warfare Formation Aerobatic Team**
Manby
The Macaws
Flt Lts J. D. T. Wingfield, M. Engwell, B. R. Hoskins
and R. Stalker
XP680:23, XP688:22, XR654:34, XS180:10, XS210:12,
XS211:14, XS216:19

Four Jet Provost T Mk.5s of No.1 FTS
Linton-on-Ouse
The Linton Blades
Flt Lts W. D. S. Waddington, J. J. Whitfield,
D. C. Coldicutt and Fg Off D. R. Carvell

XW296:57, XW297:59, XW298:55, XW299:56,
XW300:58, XW301:60, XW302:61, XW303:64,
XW304:62, XW305:63, XW306:65, XW308:67,
XW309:68, XW310:70, XW312:71

Two Jet Provost T Mk.4s of No.3 FTS
Leeming
The Gemini Pair
Fg Off R. W. B. Pattinson and Flt Lt G. Revell
(Synchronised display team)
XR670:63, XS182:55, XP564:61

1971

Four Jet Provost T Mk.5s of CFS
Little Rissington
The Red Pelicans
Flt Lts T. R. Francis, B. Donnelly, M. B. Langham
and R. Lewis
XW287:80, XW288:81, XW289:82, XW290:83, XW291:84,
XW292:85, XW293:86, XW294:87, XW295:88

Four Jet Provost T Mk.5s of RAF College
Cranwell
The Poachers
Sqn Ldr J. B. Robinson AFC, Flt Lts D. A. Z. James, I. D.
Macfadyen and C. Mitchell. Reserve: Flt Lt M. G. Christy
XW360:69, XW363:79, XW352:62, XW359:74, XW357:68,
XW336:60, XW354:65, XW420:91, XW369:81, XW375:90,
XW373:80, XW353:64, XW356.

**Four Jet Provost T Mk.4s of RAF College
of Air Warfare Formation Aerobatic Team**
Manby
The Macaws
Flt Lts B. R. Hoskins, D. Brooke, M. Engwell
and P. J. Diggance
XP680:23, XP688:22, XS180:10, XS215:18, XS216:19

Four Jet Provost T Mk.5s of No.1 FTS

Linton-on-Ouse

The Linton Blades

Sqn Ldr R. M. Turner, Flt Lts D. R. Carvell, D. M. Grey
and A. Nicholson. Reserve: Flt Lt O. M. Hammond
XW296:57, XW298:55, XW301:60, XW302:61,
XW303:64, XW304:62, XW305:63, XW306:65,
XW307:66, XW308:67, XW309:68, XW310:70,
XW312:71

Two Jet Provost T Mk.5s of No.3 FTS

Leeming

The Gemini Pair

Fg Offs R. W. B. Pattinson and R. A. Sergeant
(Synchronised display team)
XW370:49, XW406:48, XW407:50, XW410:51

1972

Four Jet Provost T Mk.5s of CFS

Little Rissington

The Red Pelicans

Sqn Ldr C. Mitchell, Flt Lt R. Lewis,
Capt R. Lord USAF and Flt Lt P. Tait
XW287:80, XW288:81, XW289:82, XW290:83,
XW291:84, XW292:85, XW293:86, XW294:87,
XW295:88

Four Jet Provost T Mk.5s of RAF College

Cranwell

The Poachers

Sqn Ldr J. B. Robinson AFC, Flt Lts C. Woods,
I. D. Macfadyen and Fg Off G. S. Roberts.
Reserve: Fg Off M. A. Micallef-Eynaud
XW360:1, XW363:2, XW352:3, XW359:4, XW357:5, XW336:6,
XW354:7, XW420:8, XW369:9, XW375:10, XW373:11, XW353:12

**Four Jet Provost T Mk.4s of RAF College of Air
Warfare Formation Aerobatic Team**

Manby

The Macaws

Flt Lts B. R. Hoskins, A. J. G. Blyth, K. Walters
and P. J. Diggance
XP640:27, XP688:22, XR701:26, XR704:28, XS177:17,
XS180:10, XS216:19, XS219:35

Four Jet Provost T Mk.5s of No.1 FTS

Linton-on-Ouse

The Linton Blades

Sqn Ldr D. G. Robinson, Flt Lts M. Hall, P. Hood
and J. L. Buckler
XW299:56, XW301:60, XW302:61, XW304:62, XW307:66,
XW311:69, XW312:71, XW334:73, XW364:74, XW374:75,
XW409:78

Two Jet Provost T Mk.5s of No.3 FTS

Leeming

The Gemini Pair

Flt Lts J. T. Galyer and D. G. Trusler
(Synchronised display team)
XW370:49, XW407:50

1973

Four Jet Provost T Mk.5s of CFS

Little Rissington

The Red Pelicans

Sqn Ldr I. C. Gibbs, Capt R. Lord USAF,
Flt Lt B. Byron RAAF, Lt M. Edwards RN
XW287:80, XW288:81, XW289:82, XW290:83,
XW291:84, XW292:85, XW293:86, XW294:87,
XW295:88

Four Jet Provost T Mk.5s of RAF College

Cranwell

The Poachers

Sqn Ldr J. B. Robinson AFC, Flt Lts C. Woods,
B. A. S. Lawrence and E. T. M. Danks.
Reserve: Flt Lt J. Barnett.
XW360:1, XW363:2, XW352:3, XW359:4, XW357:5,
XW336:6, XW354:7, XW420:8, XW369:9, XW375:10,
XW373:11, XW353:12

**Four Jet Provost T Mk.4s of RAF College of Air
Warfare Formation Aerobatic Team**

Manby

The Macaws

Flt Lts P. J. Diggance, J. D. Aldington, M. A. Fox
and M. B. R. Marriott
XP558:20, XP672:25, XR654:34, XR701:26, XR704:28,
XP672:25 XS210:12

150

151

Four Jet Provost T Mk.5s of No.1 FTS
Linton-on-Ouse
The Linton Blades
Sqn Ldr R. I. Oakden, Flt Lts M. Fowler, J. Anders and
J. L. Buckler. Reserve/Manager: Flt Lt D. N. Carnegie
XW304:62, XW306:65, XW310:70, XW311:69, XW312:71,
XW364:74, XW374:75, XW404:77, XW409:78

Two Jet Provost T Mk.5s of No.3 FTS
Leeming
The Gemini Pair
Flt Lt C. R. Thompson and Fg Off G. R. Miller
(Synchronised display team)
XW406:48, XW407:50, XW410:51

150. Jet Provost T Mk.5s of the Linton Blades over a snow-covered Linton-on-Ouse in February 1973. (Author's Collection)

151. The CAW jet formation aerobatic team – the Macaws – in August 1973. The team made its last appearance at Luxeuil in France the following month. (Author's Collection)

152

1974

Four Jet Provost T Mk.5s of No.3 FTS
Leeming
The Swords
Flt Lts C. R. Thompson, J. D. Aldington,
M. A. Fox and R. D. Thomas
XW370:49, XW407:50, XW424:52, XW426:53, XW428:54

1975

Four Jet Provost T Mk.5As of RAF College
Cranwell
The Poachers
Sqn Ldr P. B. Curtin, Flt Lts E. T. M. Danks,
M. B. Stoner and D. L. Webley
XW360:1, XW363:2, XW352:3, XW359:4, XW357:5,
XW336:6, XW354:7, XW420:8, XW369:9, XW375:10,
XW373:11, XW353:12

1976

Four Jet Provost T Mk.5As of RAF College
Cranwell
The Poachers
Sqn Ldr P. B. Curtin, Flt Lts P. M. Boreham,
M. B. Stoner and D. L. Webley
XW360:1, XW363:2, XW352:3, XW359:4, XW357:5,
XW336:6, XW354:7, XW420:8, XW369:9, XW375:10,
XW373:11, XW353:12

152. An 'inverted leader' manoeuvre by the Jet Provost T
Mk.5s of the Swords, No.3 FTS, Leeming. Led by Flt Lt Bob Thompson, the team was formed in April 1974 and took its name from
the sword emblem on the unit crest. (Mike Fox)

APPENDIX 2
TECHNICAL DATA AND HISTORIES

JET PROVOST T MK.1

Engine: 1,640-lb AS Viper ASV5 102 turbo jet
Wing Span: 35 ft 5 in
Length: 31 ft 11 in
Height: 12 ft 8 in
Max Speed: 330 mph
Max AUW: 6,750-lb
Range: 492 miles
Ceiling: 31,000 ft
Time to 30,000 ft: 24.4 minutes

JET PROVOST T MK.2

Engine: 1,750-lb AS Viper ASV8 102 turbo jet
Wing Span: 35 ft 2 in
Length: 31 ft 10 in
Height: 10 ft 2 in
Max Speed: 330 mph
Max AUW: 6,830-lb
Range: 680 miles
Ceiling: 31,000 ft
Time to 30,000 ft: 21 minutes

JET PROVOST T MK.3

Engine: 1,750-lb BS Viper ASV 8 102 turbo jet
Wing Span: 36 ft 11 in (over tip tanks)
Length: 32 ft 5 in
Height: 10 ft 2 in
Max Speed: 326 mph
Max AUW: 7,092-lb
Range: 565 miles
Ceiling: 33,000 ft
Time to 30,000 ft: 21 minutes

JET PROVOST T MK.4

Engine: 2,500-lb BS Viper ASV 11 202 turbo jet
Wing Span: 36 ft 11 in (over tip tanks)
Length: 32 ft 5 in
Height: 10 ft 2 in
Max Speed: 410 mph
Max AUW: 7,400-lb
Range: 600 miles
Ceiling: 31,000 ft
Time to 30,000 ft: 15 minutes

JET PROVOST T MK.5

Engine: 2,500-lb BS Viper ASV 11 turbo jet
Wing Span: 35 ft 4 in
Length: 33 ft 7½ in
Height: 10 ft 2 in
Max Speed: 409 mph
Max AUW: 9,200-lb
Range: 900 miles
Ceiling: 36,700 ft

STRIKEMASTER

Engine: 3,410-lb RR Viper 535 (20F-20) turbo jet
Wing Span: 36 ft 11 in (over tip tanks)
Length: 33 ft 7½ in
Height: 10 ft 2 in
Max Speed: 450 mph
Max AUW: 11,500-lb
Range: 1,450 miles
Ceiling: 31,000 ft

JET PROVOST AND STRIKEMASTER PRODUCTION
AN OVERVIEW OF CONTRACTS

XD674 TO XD680 / XD692 TO XD694 Ten prototype/pre-production Jet Provost T Mk.1 basic training aircraft built at Hunting Percival Aircraft Ltd, Luton, for the RAF under contract 6/Aircraft/9265/CB5(a), dated 24 March 1953. Deliveries between May and December 1955. XD694 converted to prototype T Mk.2.

XM129 Sixth production Mk.1, **G-AOBU,** built under contract 6/Aircraft/14260, dated 11 October 1956, retained by Hunting Percival Ltd for use as a development aircraft and company demonstrator. Registered G-AOBU, loaned to the Controller of Aircraft as XM129 after which it returned to the British Civil Aircraft Register as G-AOBU. Its Permit to Fly expired 13 March 2007 and is currently stored at North Weald as 'XD693/Q-Z'.

G-AOHD, G-23-1 / G-AOUS Pre-production and company demonstration Jet Provost T Mk.2, built by Hunting Percival Aircraft Ltd, Luton, and jointly funded by Hunting and Armstrong Siddeley for development and demonstration work. G-23-1 converted by the Hunting Aircraft Company, Luton, as the T Mk.3 prototype and registered as **XN117** to Contract O.A.2, dated 29 May 1958, for live weapons firing in Khormaksar, 1959.

XM346 TO XM387 / XM401 TO XM428 / XM451 TO XM480 100 Jet Provost T Mk.3 basic training aircraft for the RAF built by Hunting Aircraft Ltd, Luton, under contract 6/Aircraft/14157, dated 9 August 1957. Deliveries between June 1958 and July 1960. XM484 and XM485 diverted to Contract 6/Aircraft/15226, 4 September 1957, for loan to Hunting Aircraft but not built. From June 1973 most surviving aircraft were updated to T Mk.3As by BAC Warton against Contract KA5(c)/466/CBA.5(c), the last being completed in 1976.

XM349,350, 352, 357, 358, 365, 366, 370, 371, 372, 374, 376, 378, 385, 387, 401, 403, 405, 412, 414, 419, 424, 425, 453, 455, 458, 459, 461, 463, 464, 465, 466, 470, 471, 472, 473, 475, 478, 479. One Jet Provost T Mk.3 basic training aircraft for the RAF built by Hunting Aircraft Ltd, Luton, under contract 6/Aircraft/14157/CB5(a), dated 25 September 1958 and delivered in August 1960 as a replacement for XM348 which crashed prior to delivery.

XN137 / XN458 TO XN473 / XN492 TO XN512 / XN547 TO XN559 / XN573 TO XN603 / XN629 TO XN643 / XN467 / 468 TO PROTOTYPE T MK.4 Second production order for 100 Jet Provost T Mk.3 basic training aircraft for the RAF built by Hunting Aircraft Ltd, Luton, under contract KC/E/031. Deliveries between August 1960 and February 1962 (XN458 - XN559 allocated 13 May 1959; XN573 - XN643 allocated 29 May 1959). From 1973 most surviving aircraft were converted to T Mk.3A standard by BAC against Contract KA5(c)/466/CB.5(c). XN459, 461, 462, 466, 470, 471, 472, 473, 494, 495, 497, 498, 499, 500, 501, 502, 505, 506, 508, 509, 510, 547, 548, 551, 552, 553, 574, 577, 579, 581, 582, 584, 585, 586, 589, 590, 593, 595, 598, 605, 606, 629, 634, 636, 640, 641, 643.

XP547 TO XP589 / XP614 TO XP642 / XP661 TO XP688 / XP666 TO G27-92/S YEMEN AS 105 XP684 TO G27-93/S YEMEN AS 106 First production order for 100 Jet Provost T Mk.4 basic training aircraft for the RAF built by Hunting Aircraft Ltd, Luton, (renamed British Aircraft Corporation during 11/1961) under contract KC/E/041, dated 1 June 1960. Deliveries between October 1961 and December 1962.

XR643 TO XR681 / XR697 TO XR707 / XR652 TO G27-94/S YEMEN AS 107 XR661 TO G27-95/S YEMEN AS 108 Second production order for fifty Jet Provost T Mk.4 basic training aircraft for the RAF built by the British Aircraft Corporation, Luton, under contract KC/E/057, dated 2 August 1961. Deliveries between January and October 1963.

153

XS175 TO XS186 / XS209 TO XS231 XS230 / XS231 SUBSEQUENTLY CONVERTED TO PROTOTYPE T MK.5 STANDARD Third production order for thirty-five Jet Provost T Mk.4 basic training aircraft for the RAF built by the British Aircraft Corporation, Luton, under contract KC/E/70/CB5(a), dated 11 April 1962. Deliveries between October 1963 and January 1965.

167 / 177 / 187 / 192 / 197 Jet Provost T Mk.55. Five lightly-armed versions of the T Mk.5 delivered to Sudan between March and June 1969.

XW287 TO XW336 / XW351 TO XW375 / XW404 TO XW438 Sole order for 110 Jet Provost T Mk.5 basic training aircraft for the RAF built by the British Aircraft Corporation, Warton, under contract KC/E/124/CB5(b), dated 29 July 1968. Deliveries between September 1969 and October 1972.

Ninety-three aircraft returned to Warton between October 1973 and January 1976 for up-grading to Jet Provost Mk.5A standard with additional avionics - XW288, 289, 290, 292, 294, 295, 299, 301,303, 305, 308, 310, 312, 313, 314, 315, 316, 317, 318, 319, 320, 321, 322, 323, 325, 326, 327, 328, 329, 330, 332, 333, 334, 335, 336, 351, 353, 354, 355, 357, 358, 359, 360, 361, 362, 363, 364, 365, 366,367, 368, 369, 370, 371, 372, 373, 374, 375, 404, 405, 406, 407, 408, 409, 410, 411, 412, 413, 414, 415, 416, 417, 418, 419, 420, 421, 422, 423, 424, 425, 426, 427, 428, 429, 430, 431, 432, 433, 434, 435, 436, 437, 438. Thirteen Mk. 5s fitted with tip tanks for use as navigational trainers.

Twenty-two Jet Provost T Mk.51. An armed version of the Jet Provost T Mk.3:

Ceylon	12 aircraft	**CJ701 to CJ712**
Sudan	4 aircraft	**124, 139, 143, 157**
Kuwait	6 aircraft	**101 to 106**

Forty-three Jet Provost T Mk.52: An armed version of the Jet Provost T Mk.4:

Iraq	20 aircraft	**600 to 619**
Venezuela	15 aircraft	**E-040 to E-054**
Sudan	8 aircraft	**162,173,175, 180, 181, 185, 190, 195**

STRIKEMASTER PRODUCTION AT WARTON

PS.101-112	Mk.80	**901-912**	Saudi Arabia
PS.113-125	Mk.80	**1101-1113**	" "
PS.126-129	Mk.81	**501-504**	South Yemen
PS.130-136	Mk.82	**401-407**	Oman
PS.137-152	Mk.84	**300-315**	Singapore
PS.153-157	Mk.82	**408-412**	Oman
PS.158-163	Mk.83	**110-115**	Kuwait
PS.164-169	Mk.87	**601-606**	Kenya
PS.170-175	Mk.83	**116-121**	Kuwait
PS.301-310	Mk.88	**NZ6361-6370**	New Zealand
PS.311-318	Mk.89	**243-250**	Ecuador
PS.319-326	Mk.82A	**413-420**	Oman
PS.327-336	Mk.80A	**1114-1123**	Saudi Arabia
PS.337-340	Mk.89	**251-254**	Ecuador
PS.341-346	Mk.88	**NZ6371-6376**	New Zealand
PS.347-350	Mk.82A	**421-424**	Oman
PS.351-354	Mk.89	**255-258**	Ecuador
PS.355-366	Mk.80A	**1124-1135**	Saudi Arabia

Ten Strikemaster airframes transferred from Warton to Hurn for final assembly:

PS.367-368	Mk.89	**259-260**	Ecuador
PS.369-372	Mk.90	**141/42/44**	Sudan
PS.373-375	Mk.89	**261-264**	Ecuador
PS.376	Mk.80A	**425**	Oman

153. Jet Provost T Mk.51, 124, on an early test flight in 1961. It was delivered to the Sudan air force by RAF pilot, Flt Lt David McCann in October 1961. (BAe Systems Heritage Warton-Percival/ Hunting Collection)

JET PROVOST AND STRIKEMASTER PRODUCTION

JET PROVOST T MK.1/T MK.2

XD674 F/f 26-6-54 and slightly damaged in belly landing 18-7-54; CA loan 17-5-55 and to Armstrong Siddeley, Baginton, 26-5-55 for AS Viper engine trials; Hunting Percival 13-1-56 for fuel tests and returned Armstrong Siddeley 21-2-56 for engine development flight trials; AS 4-4-56, A&AEE for Blower Tunnel tests; HP 4-6-57 as test-bed for boundary layer control mods for proposed Handley Page 103 – the project failed to materialise and passed to 71 MU 23-4-58 as GI 7570M; Finningley 1965; Swinderby 2-77 for store and transferred to St Athan 5-79 for regional historic aircraft collection; RAF Museum, Cosford, 11-85

XD675 F/f 3-3-55 and to CA loan 16-5-55; AwCn 23-5-55; A&AEE 7-7-55; returning HP 23-9-55; CA loan 1-11-55; 2FTS/Q-Y 17-11-55; GA Cat 3 11-2-56; brake failure and struck XD680; RoS and returned 2FTS; HP loan 2–7-8-56; RTU as 'Q-Y'; CFS 22-11-57; 27 MU as NES 10-11-59 and sfs Enfield Rolling Mills 9-5-60

XD676 F/f 20-3-55 and to CA loan at HP 11-5-55; AwCn 12-5-55 for A&AEE; to HP 8-7-55; CFS(B) 22-7-55; 2 FTS/Q-U 24-8-55; CFS 19-11-57; 27MU as NES and sfs 9-5-60

154

XD677 F/f 24-4-55; AwCn 10-5-55; Handling Sqn, Manby 10-5-55; HP 21-7-56; CFS(B) 6-8-55; 2 FTS/Q-M 24-8-55; CA loan HP 21-2-56; 2FTS/Q-M 14-3-56; FA Cat 3 27-7-56 swung on landing and stb uc collapsed, Hullavington; RoS & RTU 30-9-56; CFS 19-11-57; 27MU as NES 10-11-59; sfs 9-5-60

XD678 F/f 31-5-55; CA loan HP 30-6-55; AwCn 30-6-55; 2FTS-/Q-N 22-9-55; CA loan 4-10-56; 2FTS 11-12-54; CFS 19-11-57; 27MU 10-11-59 as NES; sfs 9-5-60

G-AOBU Probably originally XD679 but reg to HP as company demonstrator; f/f 5-55; w/up landing at Luton 13-6-55; repair and fitted with wing tanks 1956; AS Bitteswell as flying test bed for Viper 8 and 11 engines, reg G-42-1; **XM129** allocated but not worn; HP Luton (store) 1957; re-reg HP 1-8-58 - 9-58; Shuttleworth Trust Old Warden 28-2-61; Loughborough University as GI 27-4-61; Shuttleworth Trust 1-91; Tim Manna/Kennet Avn 9-91 & reg G-AOBU 17-6-92; repainted as 'XD693/Q-Z' 1998; Permit to Fly expired 3-07; North Weald (store)

155

XD679 AwCn 22-7-55; CFS(B) 22-7-55; arr 27-7-55; FA Cat 3 9-8-55 swung on landing and o/shot; RoS 18-8-55 – 9-9-55; 2FTS 12-9-55/Q-X; FA Cat 3 29-5-56 misjudged take-off; force-landed; RoS 30-5-56 – 5-7-56; 2FTS; FA Cat 4 7-9-56 engine failed during aeros and force-landed, Long Newnton; 8m WNW Hullavington; RIW HP 17-9-56 – 10-12-56; 2FTS 3-1-57; CFS 28-8-58; FA Cat 3 28-8-58 wheels-up landing; RoS HP; CFS 27-2-59; 27MU 10-11-59 as NES; sfs 9-5-60

XD680 F/f 20-8-55; AwCn 31-8-55; 2FTS 1-9-55 FA Cat 3R 1-9-55; RoS HP 2-9-55 – 23-9-55; 2FTS/Q-T 26-9-55; FA Cat 3R 24-10-55 pt u/c collapsed on landing; RoS HP 27-10-55; 2FTS 18-11-56; GA Cat 3R 11-2-56 struck by XD675 while parked; RoS HP 13-2-56 – 29-2-56 2FTS; HP loan 17-8-56 – 20-8-56; 10MU 30-8-57; CFS 19-11-57; HP loan 11-12-57 – 24-3-58; 27 MU & sfs 9-5-60

XD692 AwCn 12-10-55; 2FTS/Q-W 12-10-55; FA Cat 4R 30-8-56 engine failed during aeros and hit stone wall during forced landing, Long Newnton, 8m WNW Hullavington; 7396M ntu 22-10-56; scrapped Hullavington

XD693 F/f 23-11-55; AwCn 6-12-55; 2FTS/Q-Z 6-12-55; HP as laminar flow test prototype HP 103; conv cnx 1956; CFS 19-11-57; 27 MU 19-11-59 as NES; sfs 9-5-60

XD694 Conv to T Mk.2 F/f 1-9-55; A&AEE 5-12-55; damaged 1-5-56 and HP for RiW; A&AEE 9-8-56; Handling Sqn 28-8-56; FA Cat 3R 7-9-56 stb u/c collapsed; 2FTS 2W2-9-56; CA/AS loan 7 6-57 for engine devt trials; 27MU 30-12-59 and NES 29-4-60; sfs 13-10-60

JET PROVOST T MK.2 PRIVATE VENTURE

G-AOHD F/f 3-56 and registered 26-3-56; placed fourth in the British Lockheed International Aerobatic Competition, sponsored by the Royal Aero Club at Baginton, July 1956 and flown by Dick Wheldon; demonstration tour of Scandinavia, February 1957; sales tour of Latin America, April 1958 – August 1958; fitted with new wings; to Australia in March 1959 and re-assembled at Bankstown; to No.1 FTS RAAF Point Cook 22-04-59 (evaluation) as **A99-001;** damage to port undercarriage in ground accident, Point Cook; DH Aircraft Pty Bankstown 30-11-59; charter terminated 7-12-59; reg G-AOHD cnx 11-8-61; sold RAAF and allocated as GI at Sydney Tech College 5-61; Richard E. Hourigan, Melbourne, Vic, 1983; RAAF Museum, Point Cook, Vic 1985 (dismantled; store)

G-23-1 F/f 6-56. Originally built at T Mk.2 for Hunting Aircraft, Luton and registered G-APVF, ntu and issued B Class serial **G-23-1;** A&AEE 4-58; HAL & converted to T Mk.3 prototype and f/f 22-6-58; reg as **XN117** for live weapons firing at Khormaksar, 5-7-58; demo tour of India and Pakistan 8-58 – 10-58; HAL; conv to T Mk.51 and del R Ceylon AF as 'CJ701' 12-59

G-AOUS F/f 8-56, demonstration tour of Canada and USA, Sept-Oct 1956; RAE fatigue tests 23-10-57; F/f as BS test bed of Viper 11 engine as Jet Provost T Mk.2B 23-8-58; Portugal as sales demo and w/up landing at Sintra 30-10-59, iss Portuguese serial 5803 for evaluation against Cessna T-37; crashed after disintegrating in mid-air over Langford Common nr Biggleswade, 16-11-60, killing test pilot, Jack Overbury

JET PROVOST T MK.3 / T MK.3A

XM346 F/f 22-6-58; AwCn 28-6-58; MoS Air Fleet and Hunting 28-6-58; Hunting 8-8-58 for installation and calibration of instrumentation, and handling trials; A&AEE for handling acceptance checks 15-8-58; (Cat.2 4-9-58 u/c collapsed); Hunting (mods) 13-3-59; A&AEE 20-4-59 for completion of handling trials; Hunting for stalling tests 12-5-59; A&AEE for handling trials 25-5-59; Hunting 5-6-59 for repairs and mods; A&AEE 10-6-59, released by RAF 19-6-59; Hunting 6-7-59 for trials and CA mods. trials at high Mach number, investigation of wing and tail mods to improve stalling and spinning 4-9-59; A&AEE check of stalling and spinning and performance evaluation 18-9-59; released by RAF 16-11-59 Hunting for CA mods 7-12-59; 27MU 22-6-60; CFS/R-R 31-8-60; Hunting (mods) 21-7-61 – 22-2-62; 6FTS/26

154. Jet Provost T Mk.1, XD676, of the CFS Jet Aerobatic Team awaiting collection at St Athan in April 1958 following its respray in the attractive red and white colour scheme devised by its leader, Flt Lt Norman Giffin. (Ray Deacon Collection)

155. Jet Provost T Mk.1, G-AOBU, at Luton in 1957. The aircraft was registered to Hunting Percival as a company

demonstrator and featured an attractive silver and white colour scheme with blue markings. It was acquired by Kennet Aviation at North Weald in 1991 and repainted as XD693/Q-Z. The original positioning of the underwing fuel tanks is of interest. (BAe Systems Heritage Warton-Percival/ Hunting Collection)

156. Jet Provost G-AOUS was the last

of the four pre-production T Mk.2s to be produced at Luton. The aircraft was fitted with the more powerful Viper ASV 11 engine in August 1958 and was unofficially referred to as 'Jet Provost T Mk.2B'. The following year it took part in the Daily Mail London-Paris air race and was photographed at Biggin Hill on 12 July 1959. (Jerry Hughes)

13-3-62; RAFC/25 6-5-63; 27MU 19-7-63; NES 28-3-69; SOC 4-6-69 Fire Section, Thorney Island

XM347 F/f 24-7-58; AwCn 25-7-58; CA Hunting (performance trials) 25-7-58; MOS Air Fleet (official acceptance trials) 28-7-58; Hunting (mods) 19-9-58; A&AEE 19-12-58; Hunting for CA mods and prep 10-6-59; 27MU 29-10-59; 2FTS/13 4-12-59, e/f; crashed nr Wragby, Lincs 23-3-61; SOC 27-3-61

XM348 Hunting; engine fire returning from SBAC Show and crashed nr Twyford, Bucks (1) 4-9-58. One Jet Provost T Mk.3 basic training aircraft for the RAF built by Hunting Aircraft Ltd, Luton under contract 6/Aircraft/14157/CB5(a) and delivered in August 1960 as a replacement for XM348 which crashed prior to delivery

XM349 AwCn 24-10-58; MoS Air Fleet for radio trials 24-10-58; Hunting for UHF trials 29-10-58; A&AEE for engine and UHF trials 31-10-58; Hunting for CA mods 6-7-59; 27MU 3-11-59; 2FTS/20 10-12-59; Hunting mods 15-9-60; 2FTS/2 9-11-60; CFS/68 30-9-69; **BAC for T Mk.3A** 19-2-74 – 12-8-74; CFS/68 12-8-74; RAFC/CFS/68 12-4-76; RAFC/CFS/51; 3FTS/ CFS/H 13-9-77; 1FTS 7-8-84; CFS/H 6-9-84 – 11-89; GI 11-6-90 **9046M**; Cosford; Global Avn Binbrook 19-11-93; sold USA & B. Todd, Latrobe, Pennsylvania (store); Air Heritage Museum, Beaver Falls, PA 8-08

157

XM350 AwCn 12-12-58; MoS Air Fleet 12-12-58; Hunting 19-12-58; A&AEE 19-1-59 for intensive flying, nav and engine trials, VHF trials, CA trials, Hunting 15-5-59 (CA mods) Hunting 19-5-59 TI and fuel consumption tests; Free Loan C(A) 31-7-59; BS Eng 17-8-61 for Viper 11 trials; Hunting 22-6-62 to service standard / 23-10-62 CA mods retained at Hunting; RAFC/44 1-7-65; **BAC for T Mk.3A** 5-11-74 – 7-2-75; RAFC 7-2-75; 1 FTS/49 18-2-75; 7FTS/89 27-3-79; 5 MU Kemble 17-6-82; 7 FTS

22-7-82; GI **9036M** 8-3-90; Catterick by 5-90; SYAM Doncaster / AeroVenture 9-6-91

XM351 AwCn 12-2-59; A&AEE 18-2-59; Hunting 30-6-59; 27MU 5-11-59; 2FTS/18 4-12-59; Hunting 9-8-61 for mods to 25-4-62; 7FTS/40 27-4-62; 1FTS/12 22-4-66; 3FTS/12 21-5-67; 27MU 30-7-68; NES 28-3-69; **8070M** 18-12-69; 1 SoTT Halton 28-8-70; 2 SoTT Cosford 2-5-84; NES 6-93; RAF Museum Cosford 01-09

XM352 AwCn 12-1-59; transfer against quota C(A) 12-1-59; CSA Hunting 3-2-59 for TIs and air intake ice detect system; to RAF stock to replace XM456 (crashed) 16-4-64 and loaned to MoA until 31-8-67; CS(A) and A&AEE 5-1-65 for Lightning T Mk.5 ejection seat oxygen system proving trials, oxygen regulator and LOX converter system trials from 23-2-66; 27MU 13-3-68; 5MU 4-8-72; **BAC for T Mk.3A** 18-3-76 – 7-6-76; 3FTS (stored Leeming) 7-6-76; 1FTS/33 2-2-77; 7FTS/92 22-3-79; 1FTS/21 26-5-87; Linton (store) 18-7-88; 27 MU 11-93; Global Avn Binbrook 19-11-93; Sold to USA as **N35378** Lance Toland Assoc, Griffin, GA and reg to W. A. McClure Cooksville, TN 12-7-94

XM353 AwCn and CS(A) 18-2-59; Free Loan BS Eng 12-2-59 for Viper 102 assessment; Filton 21-9-59; to Viper 11 installation for JP 4 24-5-61; Pegasus chase a/c from 27-3-63; Cat 4R 31-10-67 and Recat 5C 8-12-67; by road to 27MU 1-2-68; arrived and NES 6-2-68; Sfs Bushell 3-9-68

XM354 AwCn 12-3-59; C(A) MoS Air Fleet and Hunting 12-3-59 for TIs; A&AEE 16-3-59 for handling; Hunting 25-3-59 for CA mods; 27MU 21-12-59; 2FTS/17 9-2-60; Hunting 24-5-62 – 27-11-62 for mods; 1FTS/21 27-11-62; 27MU 12-10-66; 5MU 8-72; NES 14-2-73; Sfs 8-8-74 Kemble

XM355 AwCn 30-6-59; 5MU 1-7-59; CFS/R-A 31-7-59; Hunting 25-10-60 (mods); CFS/R-A 3-1-61; Cat.3R w/up landing Kemble 3-3-61; RoS 71MU; CFS/R-A 27-7-61 recoded /74; 7FTS/21 22-3-62; Cat 3R 20-2-63 RoS; 7FTS/21 13-3-63; 1FTS/31 26-4-66; 27MU 31-8-66; 5MU 4-8-72; NES 14-2-73; GI **8229M** 17-10-73; 1 SoTT Halton/210/G 17-10-73; Phoenix Avn Bruntingthorpe 8-98; Caernarfon /00; Newcastle College as GI 20-6-06

XM356 AwCn 29-6-59; 27MU 30-6-59; CFS/R-B 31-7-59; Hunting (mods) 4-1-61; CFS/R-B 14-3-61 recoded 70; Cat 3R Aston Down heavy ldg 19-4-61; CFS/70 14-6-61; Cat 3R 2-11-61; CFS/70 4-12-61; 7FTS/22 22-3-62; 27MU 16-5-63; NES 28-3-69; GI **8076M** 18-12-69; Fire Section Linton 3-12-69; derelict St Athan by 9-93

XM357 AwCn 30-6-59; 27MU 30-6-59; CFS/R-C 31-7-59; Cat 3R landing accident, Little Rissington 21-9-60; Hunting (mods) 21-7-61; 3FTS/24 23-2-62; Cat 3R 4-1-72; RoS 71MU; 3FTS/16 6-6-72; **BAC for T Mk.3A** 14-6-73 to 21-12-73; 3FTS/16 9-1-74; CFS/16 4-2-74; 3FTS/16 31-7-74; 1FTS/12 6-9-74; 5MU 10-2-76; St Athan hack 25-6-81; 1FTS/45 17-7-84; Linton (store) 28-7-88; 27 MU 11-93; Global Avn Binbrook 19-11-93; sold USA **N27357** 12-7-94 & reserved W. McClure Cookville; Robert L. Donkel, Portland, Or: reg. 23-7-02; Premier Jets Inc, Portland, Or 22-6-04 (Classic Aircraft Aviation Museum, Hillsboro, Or)

XM358 AwCn 31-8-59; 5MU 4-9-59; 2FTS/7 5-10-59; Hunting (mods) 16-9-60; 2FTS/50 18-11-60, recoded 5; 7FTS/36 26-6-62; CFS/70 30-6-66; **BAC for T3A** 17-4-74 to 10-9-74; CFS/70 10-9-74; CFS/52 12-4-76; CFS/J 5-9-77; 1FTS/53 30-3-84; GI 8987M/53 1SoTT Halton 10-3-89; Colesworth Lincs 8-89; sold 6-93; North Scarle Twyford, Llanwrtyd Wells Powys (private) 02-00; Quackers Indoor Play Centre, Newbridge-on-Wye 7-11

XM359 AwCn 30-6-59; 27MU 30-6-59; CFS/R-D 31-7-59; SRIM embodied 23-5-60 to 4-7-60; ret CFS; SRIM removed 9-11-60 to 5-12-60; to Hunting for mods 4-1-61; CFS/76 ex mods 21-7-61; 7FTS/23 22-3-62; 2FTS/ 2-8-66; 6FTS/23 15-9-66; 2FTS/23 29-12-67; 27MU 6-10-69; 5MU 14-3-72; NES 19-1-75; Sennybridge 28-5-76

XM360 AwCn 30-6-59; 5MU 1-7-59; CFS/R-E 31-7-59; Hunting (mods) 3-11-60; CFS/R-E 4-1-61 recoded 71; crashed Brown Clee Hill, Abdon, Salop (2) 24-1-69; SOC 27-1-69

XM361 AwCn 30-6-59; 5MU 1-7-59; CFS/R-F 31-7-59; Hunting (mods) 18-5-61; CFS 10-7-61 recoded 82; 7FTS/24 14-3-62; RAFC/47 5-4-66; 27MU 26-6-69; 5MU 5-1-73; NES 14-2-73; SOC 8-8-74 and Kemble dump

XM362 AwCn 21-8-59; 27MU 20-8-59; 2FTS/4 30-9-59; Hunting (mods) 15-11-60 – 20-2-61; 2FTS/4 2-3-61; 3FTS/18 1-12-61; Cat 3R u/shot landing Leeming 16-3-64; Recat 4R DA 19-3-64; Hunting 6-4-64; 3FTS/ 24-6-65; Cat4R 6-7-66, BAC Preston 23-8-66; 27MU 16-2-68; 5MU 14-3-72; NES 14-2-73; GI **8230M** 21-3-73; 1 So TT Halton 17-10-73; DSAE Cosford as GI 1985

XM363 AwCn 20-8-59; 27MU 20-8-59; 2FTS/1; Hunting (mods) 24-2-61 to 16-6-61; 2FTS/1; 27MU 12-1-63; NES 28-3-69; SOC 6-8-69 Fire Sect Leeming

XM364 AwCn 21-8-59; 27MU 21-8-59; 2FTS/5 30-9-59; Cat 3R u/c up landing 1-12-60 and Recat 4R 41Gp DA 1-12-60; 60 MU RoS 1-12-60; Hunting 23-1-61; AwCn 14-3-63; CFS/68 18-3-63; 27MU 26-8-69; 5MU 26-1-73; NES 19-1-76; SOC 28-5-76 to Army Apprentices College Arborfield

XM365 AwCn 8-9-59; Free Loan C(A) 8-9-59; Hunting 7-9-59 for aileron stall and spin trials; C(A) 10-9-59; A&AEE 11-9-59 for electrical earth trial; Hunting 7-10-59 (CA mods); 27MU 15-11-59; 2FTS/23 31-12-59; Hunting (mods) 31-7-62; 27MU 21-2-63; 5MU 19-1-73; **BAC for T Mk.3A** 21-4-76 to 31-7-76; 3FTS/J 4-8-76; 1FTS/37 27-1-77; Linton (store) 8-9-88; 27MU 11-93; Global Aviation Ltd, Binbrook 19-11-93; reg **G-BXBH** Lorch Schilling UK Ltd, Norwich 24-2-97/Lorch Airways UK Ltd, Norwich 16-10-97; G-BXBH Provost Ltd, Douglas, Isle of Man 20-5-98; CofA expired 31-8-01: reg cnx 10-10-02; Nth Weald 3-8-06; Bruntingthorpe 05-10

XM366 AwCn 14-8-59; 27MU 20-8-59; 2FTS/2 18-9-59; Cat 3R underwing skin cracking; Hunting (mods) 3-11-60; 2FTS/14 8-2-61; CFS/61 14-7-69; **BAC for T Mk.3A** 18-9-73; CFS/61 7-5-74; 5MU 29-12-75; RAFC/61 4-7-78; 7FTS/87 4-6-79; E/f, cr nr Holme-on-Spalding-Moor 22-10-81; SOC 1-11-81

XM367 AwCn 8-9-59; 27MU 9-9-59; 2FTS/6 1-10-59; Hunting (mods) 16-6-61; 2FTS/6 28-11-61; 3FTS/25 7-3-62 recoded 9; 27MU 31-7-68; NES 28-3-69; GI **8083M** 18-12-69; 1 SoTT Halton/04 2-2-70; 2 SoTT/Z 2-5-84; scrapped at Bruntingthorpe 4-95

157. Originally delivered in October 1958 and operated as a company trials aircraft, XM349 was converted to T Mk.3A standard in 1974. It is depicted with the CFS in June 1980 before being sold to the Air Heritage Museum, Pennsylvania, in 2008. (Roger Lindsay)

158. The sectioned airframe of Jet Provost T Mk.3, XM362, was used to train aircraft engineers at RAF Halton in May 1985. (Gordon Macadie)

158

XM368 AwCn 31-8-59; 27MU 7-9-59; 2FTS/3 28-9-59; Hunting (mods) 24-5-61; 2FTS/3 3-8-61; 3FTS/30 16-3-62, recoded 15; failed to recover from spin and crashed 2m SW Pateley Bridge, Yorks 29-4-63; Cat 5S 29-4-63 & scrapped by 71MU

XM369 AwCn 3-9-59; 5MU 7-9-59; 2FTS/8 8-10-59; Hunting (mods) 24-2-61 – 17-5-61; 2FTS/8; 27MU 18-7-68; NES 28-3-69; 1 SoTT Halton for GI 18-12-69 as **8084M**/69/07/C 19-3-70; Halton (store) 7-12-88; New Blyth (1993); Thorpe Camp East Wretham 12-94; Harry Pound Scrapyard Portsmouth (4-97); Paul Spann Lumb Rossendale Lancs for restoration 2005; sold to private collector at Roelofarendsveen, Netherlands 2011

XM370 AwCn 18-9-59; 27MU 24-9-59; 2FTS/9 16-10-59; 27MU 31-1-63; 5MU 19-1-73; 60MU 7-10-74; 5MU 28-1-75; BAC for **T Mk. 3A** 09-4-76 to 14-7-76; 3FTS Leeming (store) 14-7-76; 1FTS/32 4-2-77; 7FTS/93 22-3-79; 1FTS/10 26-5-87; Global Aviation Ltd, Binbrook 11-93; reg Thomas Haysleden, Rothesham 31-8-94 as G-BVSP; Global Avn 9-94; Special Scope JP Group, Sandtoft 1-9-95; Global Aviation Ltd, Binbrook 19-7-96 (black with yellow trim); Lorch Airways UK Ltd/Shoal Ltd, Norwich 24-10-96; H. G. Hodges & Son Ltd, Long Marston 6-1-00; reg cnx 22-5-14; re-reg Aviation Heritage, Coventry 18-5-15; Weald Aviation (store) 2016

XM371 AwCn 30-9-59; 5MU 1-10-59; 2FTS/12 26-10-59, m/a/c XM402 during aeros; RoS/60MU 9-2-61 – 7-4-61; 3FTS/19 1-12-61, Cat 3R 25-4-62 – 6-6-62; Cat 3R 2-1-63 – 21-2-63; Cat 3R 17-9-70 – 3-12-70; Cat 3R 2-7-73 – 22-8-73; ret 3FTS/S; **BAC for T Mk.3A** 10-6-75 – 24-9-75; CFS/66 2-12-75; RAFC/CFS/53 by 12-4-76; CFS/K 17-8-77; 1 SoTT Halton as GI **8962M**/31 27-4-88; sale by tender 3-92 and exported to El Paso, Colorado, USA as **N4427Q;** Barry Simpson Aircraft Sales, Fountain, CO 23-10-92; Charles B. Simpson, Colorado Springs, CO 8-4-93; Richard D. Janitell, Colorado Springs, CO 5-12-05

XM372 AwCn 18-9-59; 27MU 25-9-59; 2FTS/10 22-10-59; 27MU 30-7-69; 5MU 14-1-72; **BAC for T Mk.3A** 11-2-76 – 20-5-76; 1FTS/55 20-5-76; Cat 3R Dishforth 6-12-85 (u/c up landing); Recat scrap 25-9-86; **8917M** 10-10-86 Linton (crash recovery trg); scrapped 1995

XM373 AwCn 30-9-59; 5MU 1-10-59; 2FTS/11 22-10-59; Cat 4 41Gp DA 29-6-61 Syerston (stalled on t/o, u/c collapsed); recat 5C 3-7-61 and SOC 3-7-61; GI Cranwell **7726M** 26-7-61; fire rescue trg by 4-73; Yorks Air Museum, Elvington

XM374 AwCn 30-10-59; 27MU 3-11-59; 2FTS/16 20-11-59; CFS/71 21-7-69; 27MU 22-1-70; 5MU 25-4-72; **BAC for T Mk.3A** 1-3-76; 3FTS/L (store) 20-6-76; 1FTS/56 5-1-77; RAFC Cranwell/56 17-1-78; 7FTS/83 12-7-79; 1FTS/18 14-5-87; 27MU Shawbury by 2-93; NES and sold USA; reg **N374XM** to Fred Flaquer Rifle CO 11-4-95; Edward L. Cagen, Miami, FL13-4-98; Sam D. Kennedy, Eureka, CA 20-9-00 (flies as RAF "XM374")

XM375 AwCn 31-10-59; 27MU 3-11-59; 2FTS/14 19-11-59, FA Cat 4R nosewheel collapsed, Syerston 27-9-60; Hunting RIW 7-11-60 – 16-6-61; CFS/S-J 19-6-61; 3FTS/11 5-10-61; RAFC/23 11-3-65; 27MU 26-9-66; 5MU 29-9-72; NES 14-2-73; GI **8231M** 21-3-73; 1 SoTT Halton/212/B 4-12-73; Cottesmore crash rescue trg by 7-90

XM376 AwCn 30-10-59; 27MU 3-11-59; 2FTS/15 19-11-59, Cat 4R o/shot landing Leeming 19-4-63; Hunting RIW 29-4-63; 27MU 11-3-64; RAFC/46 22-9-65; 27MU 29-9-66; 5MU 18-8-72; **BAC for T Mk.3A** 23-3-76 – 14-7-76; 3FTS Leeming store/M 14-7-76; 1FTS/57 5-1-77; RAFC Cranwell/57 27-1-78; 7FTS/97 21-3-79; 1FTS/27 2-6-87; Shawbury 22-7-93; Global Avn Binbrook 19-11-93 and reg **G-BWDR** 6-6-95; Wael O. Bayazid. Humberside 14-5-99; (Permit to Fly expired 2002); Global Aviation Ltd, Humberside 14-12-05; reg cnx 8-12-2010 and exported to the Rahmi M. Koç Museum, Istanbul, Turkey, 4-09

XM377 AwCn 31-10-59; 27MU 5-11-59; 2FTS/17 20-11-59; crashed Syerston (u/c up landing) 4-2-60; SOC 4-2-60

XM378 AwCn 16-11-59; 27MU 20-11-59; 2FTS/21 21-12-59; CFS/60 9-5-69; **BAC for T Mk.3A** 3-4-74 – 13-9-74; CFS/60 13-9-74; 5MU 30-10-75; 1FTS/38 29-7-87; 1FTS/34 by 9-88; CFS/F 10-2-89; 7FTS/81 10-7-89; 1FTS/34 12-89; 1FTS/32 5-92; 1FTS/34 11-92; Shawbury (store) 22-7-93; Global Aviation Ltd, Binbrook 24-8-94 and reg **G-BWZE** 29-11-96; Frank Heneghan/Lorch Schilling UK Ltd/Lorch Airways UK Ltd/Shoal Ltd, Norwich 24-2-97; L/A Engineering (2000) Ltd, Norwich 17-1-00; crashed short of runway during emergency landing, Lelystad, Netherlands 14-10-00

XM379 AwCn 5-11-59; 27MU 10-11-59; 2FTS/19 4-12-59; 6FTS/8 18-5-62; 3FTS/10 3-5-63; 27MU 29-10-69; 5MU 10-5-72; NES 19-1-76; SOC 28-5-76; Princess Marina College, Arborfield

XM380 AwCn 30-11-59; 27MU 21-12 59; 2FTS/29 2-2-60, recoded 9; e/f; crashed 1m S Seagrave, Leics 29-7-63

XM381 AwCn 30-11-59; 27MU 9-12-59; 2FTS/25 1-1-60, recoded 5; RAFC/43 30-6-65; 27MU 21-9-66; 5MU 31-5-72; NES 14-2-73; GI **8232M** 1 SoTT Halton/D 21-3-73; burnt by 1996

XM382 AwCn 30-11-59; 27MU 17-12-59; 2FTS/28 21-1-60; failed to recover from spin and crashed 3m NE Melton Mowbray 17-6-60; Cat 5S 20-7-60

XM383 AwCn 30-11-59; 27MU 4-12-59; 2FTS/27 11-1-60; A&AEE 1-11-60 for spinning trials with 200 hour airframe until allocated to Linton-on-Ouse ex-loan 9-1-61; 2FTS/27 16-1-61, recoded 1; BS Engines Filton 26-9-69 for engine relight system trial (transferred to MoD 23-12-69); 27MU 12-12-69; St Athan 26-6-70; 6FTS/S 21-12-70; RAFC Cranwell/48 26-3-71; **BAC for T Mk.3A** 18-9-74 – 18-12-74; RAFC Cranwell 18-12-74, 1FTS/45 16-1-75; 7FTS/90 27-3-79; Scampton 1990; NES 3-92 and sold private owner nr Crowland; Newark Air Museum by 2-00

XM384 AwCn 30-11-59; 27MU 10-12-59; 2FTS/26 1-1-60, recoded 4; m/a/c XP631 over Woodborough, Notts, during aerobatics 26-5-66; SOC 10-6-66

XM385 AwCn 30-11-59; 27MU 4-12-59; 2FTS/24 1-1-60, e/f and u/shot landing Syerston 8-3-60; SOC 11-3-60

XM386 AwCn 30-11-59; 27MU 4-12-59; 2FTS/22 21-12-59; GA Cat 4R 17-8-64, DA 20-8-64; BAC Luton (repair) 27-8-64; CFS/69 13-9-65; 27MU 17-7-68; NES 18-4-69; GI **8076M** 18-12-69; 1SoTT Halton/3 2-2-70; 4SoTT St Athan/8 8-9-93; Stamford PTA, East Wretham 1994

XM387 AwCn 22-12-59; 27MU 11-1-60; 2FTS/35 8-2-60; 3FTS/25 12-11-63, recoded T; **BAC for T Mk.3A** 11-6-75 – 30-9-75; 3 FTS 6-10-75; 5MU 23-10-75; CFS/I 5-5-81; 27MU Shawbury 4-3-92; Global Aviation Ltd, Binbrook 19-11-93; sold to USA and reg **N387TW** 19-7-95; Iowa Lake Birds of Prey Inc, Armstrong, IA

XM401 AwCn 22-12-59; 27MU 31-12-59; 2FTS/30 2-2-60; CFS 18-3-63; 3FTS/23 10-9-63, recoded L; 1FTS loan 30-7-74; 3FTS/L 3-9-74; **BAC for T Mk.3A** 11-12-74 to 21-3-75; 3 FTS Leeming store/L 1-4-75; 1FTS/17 8-1-76; FA Cat 3 10-4-80; sold and stored North Humberside

XM402 AwCn 24-12-59; 27MU 1-1-60; 2FTS/31 3-2-60; Cat 3P and 4R 9-2-61; Hunting 3-3-61; 27MU 10-10-61; 6FTS/23 18-1-62; Cat3R heavy landing, Acklington RoS 60MU 8-11-63 - 19-12-63

recoded 18; 27MU 15-3-68; NES 28-3-69; GI **8055M** 19-9-69; 9 SoTT Newton 21-11-69 as **8055A (MC8055A/M)**; 1 SoTT Halton/23 22-2-74; Shawbury BDR; West Raynham CRT 1-5-90; Fenland & West Norfolk Avn Museum (later as Bambers Garden Centre, Wisbech, Norfolk) 10-9-95

XM403 AwCn 22-12-59; 27MU 5-1-60; 2FTS/32 3-2-60; 1FTS/22 15-1-63; **BAC for T Mk.3A** 7-1-75 – 1-5-75; 1FTS/22 1-5-75; 3FTS/CFS/M 7-9-77; CFS/A 4-84 – 11-89; 27MU 1989; GI **9048M** 9-84, 2 SoTT Cosford/V by 1990; RAF Explosives Ordnance Disposal Unit, North Luffenham 1999; SOAF Tech College, Muscat-Seeb, Oman as GI 102

XM404 AwCn 31-12-59; 27MU 1-1-60; 2FTS/33 4-2-60; 3FTS/17 1-12-61; 27MU 25-7-68; NES 28-3-69; **8055MB (MC8055B/M)** 9 SoTT Newton 21-11-69; 1 SoTT Halton/2/250 25-2-74; Fire and Emergency Training College, Moreton-in-Marsh 4-93; Bruntingthorpe 9-14 (cockpit section); South Yorkshire Aircraft Museum, Doncaster (cockpit section; loan) 10-15

XM405 AwCn 31-12-59; 27MU 5-1-60; 2FTS/34 24-2-60, recoded 20; 1FTS/30 23-7-69; CWP Leeming 7-71; RAFC/31 6-8-71; **BAC for T Mk.3A** 27-8-74 – 26-11-74; RAFC Cranwell 26-11-74; 1FTS/42 4-12-74 – 4-91; NES and sold 5-91; reg **G-TORE** Butane Buzzard Aviation, North Weald 14-6-91; restored and airworthy by 1992; CofA expired 5-5-95; Richard J. Everett, Sproughton (store) 3-11-00; reg cnx 24-2-04; University of London, Islington (as GI) 23-9-03; Bruntingthorpe 4-10 Stichting International Aircraft Solutions Park, Uithoorn, Neth

XM406 AwCn 11-1-60; 27MU 19-1-60; 2FTS/36 16-2-60, recoded 7; failed to recover from spin and crashed 1m SW Clipstone, Newark 12-11-65; SOC 12-11-65

XM407 AwCn 6-1-60; 27MU 11-1-60; 2FTS/37 29-2-60; 6FTS/27 25-5-62, recoded 21; 27MU 28-11-67; NES 28-3-69; Fire Section Manston 31-10-69 initially for film work; perished 1974

XM408 AwCn 22-1-60; 27MU 4-2-60; 2FTS/38 29-2-60, recoded 28; Free Loan MoA and Hunting 22-10-62 for airframe or engine vibration investigation, (return to 27MU 26-11-62 cnx and loan extended); BAC Warton 27-4-66 for return to service mods; 27MU 18-8-67; 5MU 16-6-72; NES 14-2-73; GI **8333M** but marked as **8233M/222/P** 21-3-73; 1 SoTT Halton 20-11-73; Phoenix Avn Bruntingthorpe/D 1-92 as spares; sold USA and used for fire training at Airport Fire Training, Lafayette, LA, 4-95

XM409 AwCn 22-1-60; 27MU 4-2-60; 2FTS/39 29-2-60, recoded 1; 27MU 23-7-68; NES 28-3-69; GI **8082M** 18-12-69; 1 SoTT Halton/1 13-5-70; for sale 6-89 as spares; Moreton-in-Marsh (fire trg) 4-93; cockpit section to Guernsey Airport 9-95, exchange for Meteor nose section

XM410 AwCn 28-1-60; 27MU 9-2-60; 2FTS/41 8-3-60; 7FTS/48 4-9-62; RAFC/48 21-4-66; 27MU 21-9-66; NES 28-3-69; GI 19-9-69 **8054A/8054M** but marked **MC8054M;** 1 SoTT Halton/C 23-10-69; open store 1-89; Halton hospital gate guard by 2-91; EOD Chattenden as GI 4-92

XM411 AwCn 29-1-60; 27MU 10-2-60; CFS/R-G 22-3-60; FA 3R 29-3-62; ret CFS/73; 27MU 26-8-69; St Athan (hack) 10-11-71; GI **8434M** 16-1-75; 1 SoTT Halton/L 1-7-78; store by 6-91; Otterburn ranges by 12-94; South Yorkshire Aviation Museum, Firbeck 4-99; AeroVenture Museum Doncaster by 1-09

XM412 AwCn 29-1-60; 27MU 5-2-60; 2FTS/40 29-2-60, recoded 3; 3FTS/17 2-10-69; **BAC for T Mk.3A** 18-6-74 – 14-10-74; 3FTS 14-10-74; 1FTS/41 27-11-74; GI **9011M** 24-7-89; 1 SoTT Halton/T; Halton dump 2-93; Witham Special Vehicles, Colsterworth, Leics, 8-1993; Global Aviation Ltd, Binbrook 19-11-93; alloc Lance Tolland Associates, Griffin, GA (stored; not del. 94-95); Richard J. Everett, Sproughton (stored 96-98); Balado Bridge, Perth and Kinross, Scotland for preservation, 2002

XM413 AwCn 26-2-60; 27MU 1-3-60; CFS/R-H 22-3-60, recoded 68; 7FTS/25 21-3-62; 2FTS/24 30-6-66; 27MU 22-7-69; 5MU 22-2-72; NES 19-1-76; Princess Marina College, Arborfield as GI 28-5-76

XM414 AwCn 25-2-60; 27MU 4-3-60; 2FTS/45 22-4-60, recoded 12; RAFC/26 4-9-69; 27MU (store) 17-12-69; St Athan 25-6-70; 6FTS/V 21-10-70; 1FTS/37 6-4-71; **BAC for T Mk.3A** 12-11-74 – 14-2-75; 1FTS/37 14-2-75; 5MU 7-1-77; RAFC/60 3-9-78; 7FTS/101 6-11-79; GI 17-5-89 **8996M,** 1 SoTT Halton; Global Avn Binbrook 19-11-93; Flt Experience Workshop Belfast 3-98; Ulster Aviation Society, Langford Lodge/Long Kesh 23-12-04

XM415 AwCn 25-2-60; 27MU 2-3-60; 2FTS/24 25-3-60, recoded 15; 3FTS/12 28-7-69; 27MU 23-10-69; 5MU 9-2-73; NES 19-1-76; 424 ATC Sqn Southampton 28-5-76; scrapped

XM416 AwCn 26-2-60; 27MU 1-3-60; 2FTS/46 22-4-60; 7FTS/35 18-6-62; 2FTS/ 28-7-66; 6FTS/24 15-9-66; 3FTS/29 5-12-67; 27MU 24-10-69; 5MU 2-2-72; NES 19-1-76; SOC 28-5-76; JATE Sennnybridge as target; destroyed

XM417 AwCn 29-2-60; 27MU 2-3-60; 2FTS/42 7-4-60; 7FTS/38 12-7-62; 6FTS/16 24-6-66; 27MU 28-5-68; NES 28-3-69; GI **8054M** but marked as **8054BM/D** at 1 SoTT Halton 19-9-69; Martin Jones, Hednesford (nose section)

XM418 AwCn 25-3-60; 27MU 28-3-60; 2FTS/49 16-5-60; CFS/S-B 1-3-61; 6FTS/19 14-12-61; 27MU 13-5-63; 6FTS/22 4-1-66; 3FTS/28 8-11-67, Cat 5C engine fire on runway, Leeming 25-3-71; SOC 6-4-71; GI **8593M** Leeming; Fire Section Leeming; scrapped

XM419 AwCn 26-2-60; 27MU 4-3-60; 2FTS/43 21-4-60, recoded 6; RAFC/47 9-5-69; 6FTS/X 17-8-70; RAFC/47 16-3-71; 3 FTS Leeming store 20-3-75; **BAC for T Mk.3A** 13-5-75 – 29-8-75; 3 FTS 29-8-75; CFS/60 14-10-75; RAFC/CFS/54 12-4-76; CFS/3FTS/N 5-9-77; 7FTS/102 30-3-84; GI **8990M** 15-3-89; 4SoTT St Athan 1989; sold 11-05; Newcastle Aviation Academy as GI 2009

XM420 AwCn 7-3-60; 27MU 10-3-60; 2FTS/44 21-4-60; 6FTS/20 25-5-62; 27MU 16-1-68; NES 28-3-69; Fire Section Catterick 18-12-69

XM421 AwCn 11-3-60; 27MU 18-3-60; 2FTS/47 26-4-60; CFS/S-C 1-3-61, recoded 80; 7FTS/47 8-8-62; control lost in cloud and crashed 2m NW Church Fenton 13-12-63; SOC 13-12-63

XM422 AwCn 17-3-60; 27MU 22-3-60; 2FTS/48 26-4-60; CFS/S-D 21-3-61; 6FTS/20 14-12-61; crashed at Acklington during aerobatics (1) 8-5-62; SOC 11-5-62; to scrap compound

XM423 AwCn 15-3-60; 27MU 22-3-60; CFS/R-J 17-5-60; e/f during navex and crashed 3m SE Kidderminster 30-8-61; SOC 31-10-61

XM424 AwCn 25-3-60; 27MU 4-4-60; CFS/R-K 17-5-60, recoded 72; 6FTS/W 20-8-70; RAFC/46 18-3-71; **BAC for T3A** 17-12-74 – 24-3-75; 3 FTS Leeming store 1-4-75; Topcliffe store 12-5-75; Leeming 13-2-76 store; 5MU store 13-2-76; 1FTS/30 31-3-84; Shawbury store 22-7-93; Global Avn Binbrook 19-11-93; reg **G-BWDS** 6-6-95; John Sinclair, North Weald 1-10-98; Military Jet Ltd, North Weald 3-7-03; Area 51 Aviation Services, North Weald 18-8-03; Stephen T. G. Lloyd, Cardiff 18-11-04; Anthony W. Brown/XM424 Group, Manchester 8-1-08; Aviation Heritage Ltd, Coventry 13-10-08; Classic Air Force Museum, Newquay, Cornwall (del 4-3-13 and flew as "XM424"); CAF Coventry, 2014

XM425 AwCn 25-3-60; 27MU 28-3-60; CFS/R-L 24-5-60, recoded 75; **BAC for T Mk.3A** 3-6-75; 3 FTS Leeming store 6-10-75; 5MU 13-10-75; RAFC/54 10-5-78; 1 FTS 2-5-79; 7FTS/88 4-80; GI **8995M** 4-89; 1 SoTT Halton 9-5-89; Phoenix Aviation, Bruntingthorpe 29-3-1995; King's Lynn, Norfolk 13-9-1995; Motor Clinic, Longton, Staffordshire for display coded 88 8-96

XM426 AwCn 29-3-60; 27MU 4-4-60; CFS/R-N 10-6-60; 6FTS/21 11-1-62; 27MU 24-5-63; 2FTS/22 6-4-66; 3FTS 28-7-69; 27MU 23-10-69; 5MU 31-5-72; NES 19-1-76; SOC 28-5-76; RAFEF Abingdon (nose section) and 1151 ATC Sqn Wallsend Tyne and Weir by 6-83; Lutterworth 23-7-88

XM427 AwCn 30-3-60; 27MU 6-4-60; RAFC/12 13-6-60; u/shot night GCA approach and crashed 1m NE Waddington (1) 16-10-62; SOC 18-10-62

XM428 AwCn 31-3-60; 27MU 6-4-60; CFS/R-M 1-6-60; 3FTS/12 13-10-61; m/a/c XN631 1m E Northallerton 20-4-65

XM451 AwCn 31-3-60; 27MU 6-4-60; RAFC/11 9-6-60; 27MU 21-9-66; 5MU 16-6-72; NES 14-2-73; SOC 8-8-74; Kemble dump

XM452 AwCn 12-4-60; 27MU 20-4-60; RAFC/14 13-6-60; stb tip tank struck by lightning and crashed 1m S Rauceby Hospital, Sleaford 5-4-62; SOC 10-4-62

XM453 AwCn 12-4-60; 27MU 20-4-60; RAFC/17 1-7-60; 3FTS/20 1-12-61; 26 Sqn 8-7-74; 3FTS 4-11-74; **BAC for T Mk.3A** 3-12-74 – 11-3-75; 3FTS 11-3-75; 26/Q 11-6-75; 3FTS/Q 3-7-75; 26/Q 4-7-75; 3FTS/Q 13-8-75; 26/Q 5-11-75; 3FTS/Q 8-12-75; 5MU 21-1-76; CFS/G 16-7-81; crashed 2m SE Ribblehead, Yorks 21-11-83

XM454 AwCn 26-4-60; 27MU 27-4-60; RAFC/15 21-6-60; 27MU 21-9-66; 5MU 30-6-72; NES 14-2-73; SOC 8-8-74; Army Apprentices College, Arborfield

XM455 AwCn 22-4-60; 27MU 27-4-60; RAFC/16 20-6-60; 3FTS/14 13-10-61; 26Sqn 8-7-74; 3FTS 24-10-74; **BAC for T Mk.3A** 21-11-74 – 26-2-75; 3FTS/M 26-2-75; 26/M 24-7-75; 3FTS/M 3-10-75; 1FTS/53 13-1-76; CFS/O 21-9-77; GI **8960M** 15-4-88; 2 SoTT Cosford 21-4-88; Global Aviation Ltd, Binbrook 19-11-93; **N455XM** British Warbird Centre Inc, Salt Lake City, UT 30-7-99

XM456 AwCn 25-4-60; 27MU 27-4-60; RAFC/18 26-7-60; Hunting, Luton 19-7-62 for spinning trials; spun into the ground at Girton, Cambs 22-8-62; SOC 19-10-62; 71MU Bicester dump

XM457 AwCn 27-4-60; 27MU 2-5-60; 2FTS/28 28-6-60; 7FTS/34 31-5-62; 1FTS/23 8-4-66; 27MU 12-10-66; 5MU 30-6-72; NES 14-2-73; SOC 8-8-74; Kemble dump

XM458 AwCn 29-4-60; 27MU 2-5-60; RAFC/20 7-7-60; BS Eng Filton 28-3-61 to investigate engine flame-out in stall turns; 3FTS/29 12-3-62 recoded /2; 1FTS (loan) 30-7-74; 3FTS 21-8-74; 26Sqn/H 17-2-75; 3FTS 12-5-75; **BAC for T Mk.3A** 28-5-75 – 22-9-75; 1FTS/51 22-9-75; CFS/P 8-9-77; CFS/3FTS/B 19-9-84; Scampton (store) by 9-89; Otterburn ranges by 10-89; destroyed by 6-99

XM459 AwCn 29-4-60; 27MU 04-05-60; RAFC/19 1-7-60; 3FTS/21 1-12-61; **BAC for T Mk.3A** 28-8-74 – 25-11-74; 3 FTS/N 25-11-74; 26Sqn/N 8-12-75; 3FTS/N 11-2-76; 5MU 13-2-76; 7FTS/104 14-11-84; CFS/3FTS/F by 3-90; 27MU Shawbury 26-10-92; Global Aviation, Binbrook, 13-11-93; exported to San Diego, California, USA, as spares source 2001

XM460 AwCn 17-5-60; 27MU 23-5-60; RAFC/23 19-7-60; CFS/70 1-9-64; o/shot landing, Little Rissington (1) 14-12-64; SOC 15-12-64; 71 MU dump

XM461 AwCn 19-5-61; 27MU 24-5-60; RAFC/21 15-7-60; 3FTS/15 13-10-61, recoded/18 6-67; **BAC for T Mk.3A** 4-8-73; 3FTS/18 15-1-74; CFS/18 19-2-74; 3 FTS/18 31-7-74; 1FTS/11 29-8-74; BAC Warton for trials 12-7-83; 1FTS/11 13-9-83; Global Avn, Binbrook 1991; sold Magnificent Obsessions Ltd, Grimsby 10-91; Lance Toland Associates, Griffin, GA 9-92; reg **N6204H** 6-2-93 on sale to Pike Aviation Inc, Troy, AL; Paul Hunt/Hunt Aviation, Senola GA 2-6-93; Richard D. Ward, Williamson, GA 8-03; David E. Copeland, Mesquite, TX 9-07

XM462 AwCn 17-5-60; 27MU 23-5-60; RAFC/26 26-7-60; 27MU 26-9-66; NES 28-3-69; SOC 18-12-69 to Fire Section Little Rissington

XM463 AwCn 19-5-60; 27MU 24-5-60; RAFC/24 26-7-60; **BAC for T Mk.3A** 19-3-74 – 4-9-74; RAFC 4-9-74; 1FTS/38 11-74; RAF Museum store Cardington 6-3-91; RAF Museum Hendon 1991

XM464 AwCn 26-5-60; 27MU 30-5-60; RAFC/27 26-7-60; 3 FTS Leeming store 20-3-75; **BAC for T Mk.3A** 13-5-75 – 29-8-75;

3 FTS Leeming store 29-8-75; 1FTS/23 9-12-75; 27 MU Shawbury 10-9-92, sold 11-92; Colsterworth, Lincs (store) 20-1-93; sold USA West Texas Airport, El Paso by 2-08; Pima Museum, Tucson, Arizona, 10-09

XM465 AwCn 26-5-60; 27MU 30-5-60; RAFC/28 27-7-60; 1FTS/16 9-9-60; **BAC for T Mk.3A** 7-5-74 – 19-9-74; 1FTS/16 19-9-74; 5MU Kemble 28-1-77; RAFC/53 30-3-78; 7FTS/85 22-6-79; 1FTS/55 1990; St Athan by 6/91; scrapped

XM466 AwCn 31-5-60; 27MU 2-6-60; RAFC/ 15-7-60; 1FTS/14 29-8-60; **BAC for T Mk.3A** 8-10-74 – 24-1-75; 1FTS/14 24-1-75; CFS 21-7-75; 1FTS/14 1-9-75; 5MU 24-10-75; 7FTS/105 7-8-81; 1FTS/31 1-10-84; St Athan by 6-91; sold Magnificent Obsessions Ltd, Grimsby UK 1992; Lance Toland Associates, Griffin GA 2-93 reg **N7075U;** Paul Hunt, Senoia GA, later Memphis TN 2-6-93; James H. Rollison, Vacaville, CA 1-10-96; Steven G. Penning, Santa Rosa, CA 24-4-00; Steven R. Kay, Riverside, CA 29-6-09

XM467 AwCn 31-5-60; 27MU 2-6-60; RAFC/ 26-7-60; 1FTS/15 30-8-60; 6FTS/15 20-9-61; 27MU 28-12-67; NES 28-3-69; GI 8085M 18-12-69; 1 SoTT Halton/6 25-2-70; sunk in Gildenburgh Lake, Whittlesey, Cambridgeshire as a scuba diving feature 1990

XM468 AwCn 3-6-60; 27MU 21-6-60; 1FTS/11 19-8-60; 6FTS/10 26-9-61; 27MU 27-3-68; NES 28-3-69; GI **8081M** 18-12-69; 1 SoTT Halton 6-5-70; 4 SoTT St Athan by 3-90; sfs to Hanningfield Metals, Stock, Essex 30-6-93; nose section transported to Gerry Knowles, King's Lynn 8-93; Terrington Aviation Collection, Terrington St Clement, Norfolk 1996; Wings Museum, Balcombe, W Sussex 23-8-2016

XM469 AwCn 20-6-60; 27MU 22-6-60; 1FTS/12 25-8-60; failed to recover from spin and crashed 5m NE York 5-5-61

XM470 AwCn 20-6-60; 27MU 22-6-60; 1FTS/13 25-8-60; 6FTS/28 7-6-62; 27MU 15-2-63; 2FTS/7 24-11-65; CFS/63 9-5-69; **BAC for T Mk.3A** 01-07-75 – 13-10-75; 3FTS Leeming 13-10-75; 5MU 6-11-75; Shawbury 7-9-82; CFS/M 6-3-85; 1FTS/12 by 7-91; Linton (store) 6-93; 27 MU 22-7-93; tendered 19-11-93; Global Aviation Ltd, Binbrook 21-9-94 and reg **G-BWZZ** 5-9-96; Jet Aviation (Northwest) Ltd, Manchester 7-11-96; Richard J. Schreiber & John P. Trevor, Warrington 9-8-99; Hunter Enterprises Ltd, Leuven, Belgium 19-12-02; North Wales Military

Aviation Services Ltd, Hawarden 17-9-03; sold to South Africa; struck-off reg. 29-6-04 and reg Jet Provost South Africa Pty Ltd, Cape Town 9-7-04 as **ZU-JPR** (ff Cape Town 21-5-04 as RAF "XM470/12"); offered for sale 2-12

XM471 AwCn 22-6-60; 27MU 29-6-60; CFS/R-O 1-9-60; 6FTS/22 11-1-62; RAFC/ 8-4-63; 2FTS/18 20-6-63; 27MU 12-5-69; 3FTS/26 4-2-72; **BAC for T Mk.3A** 9-7-73 – 9-1-74; 3FTS 9-1-74; CFS/26 7-3-74; 1FTS/10 16-7-74; 7FTS/93 26-5-87; GI **8968M** 16-5-88; 2 SoTT Cosford/L/93 16-5-88; Global Avn Binbrook 11-93; sold to an unknown buyer 9-1994 - probably as GI '101' with SOAF

XM472 AwCn 23-6-60; 27MU 28-6-60; CFS/R-P 1-9-60, recoded /81; 7FTS/29 5-6-62; 1FTS/24 21-4-66; CWP Leeming 1-7-71; 3FTS/4 6-8-71; **BAC for T Mk.3A** 4-12-73 – 3-5-74; 3FTS 3-5-74; 1FTS/23 1-10-74; 5MU 21-11-75; 1FTS/22 14-3-79; 7FTS/86 18-6-87; 1FTS/22 1989; GI **9051M** 23-10-1990; nose section to 1005 ATC Sqn, Radcliffe, Manchester

XM473 AwCn 24-6-60; 27MU 28-6-60; 1FTS/10 4-8-60; 3FTS/7 20-9-61; CFS/61 27-8-64; 1FTS/19 6-2-68; **BAC for T Mk.3A** 21-1-75 – 6-5-75; 1FTS/19 6-5-75; 5MU 3-2-77; 1FTS/19 15-6-78; 7FTS/81 5-5-87; GI **8974M** 9-6-88 1SoTT Halton/33; sold Air UK Apprentices School, Norwich Airport 13-6-92; reg **G-TINY** 2-95 ntu; Bedford College, Bedford as GI by 6-99; Everett Aero, Sproughton (store) 2007; Wethersfield, Essex (private) 2011

XM474 AwCn 30-6-60; 27MU 4-7-60; CFS/R-Q 1-9-60; 6FTS/17 14-12-61; declared rogue due spinning problems; MoA/BAC Luton 24-1-64 for spinning investigation; 6FTS/17 1-6-64; 27MU 16-11-67; BS Eng Filton 4-12-67 for wide angle fuel jet spray nozzle evaluation; 27MU 24-4-68; NES 28-3-69; GI **8121M** 10-5-71 to Shrewsbury School CCF; cockpit section to 1330 ATC Sqn, Warrington 4-8-83; South Yorkshire Aviation Museum, Firbeck 1999; 1940 ATC Sqn, Levenshulme, Manchester as GI 7-00; 1804 ATC Sqn, Four Heatons, Stockport

XM475 AwCn 30-6-60; 27MU 4-7-60; 2FTS/20 26-9-60; 7FTS/39 7-6-62; RAFC/50 26-4-66; **BAC for T Mk.3A** 1-4-75; RAFC 15-7-75; TWU/F 7-8-75; RAFC/40 9-1-76; 26 Sqn 12-2-76; RAFC/50 26-2-76; 7FTS/96 21-3-79; 1FTS/44 by 5-90; GI **9112M** 30-7-91; Fire School Manston 14-8-91; scrapped

XM476 AwCn 14-7-60; 27MU 15-7-60; 2FTS/7 23-9-60; 7FTS/37 3-7-62; collided with XN466 on landing, Church Fenton 29-1-63, Cat 5C

XM477 AwCn 13-7-60; 27MU 15-7-60; 1FTS 4-10-60; loss of elevator control and fire warning, crashed 2m S Dishforth 28-3-61; SOC and Bicester dump

XM478 AwCn 15-7-60; 27MU 19-7-60; 1FTS/17 28-9-60; **BAC for T Mk.3A** 22-10-74; 1FTS/17 28-1-75; 5MU 12-12-75; 7FTS/104 22-12-78; 1FTS/33 1-10-84; GI **8983M** 1-2-89; 1SoTT Halton 1989; Global Aviation Ltd, Binbrook 19-11-93; reg **G-BXDL** Transair (UK) Ltd, North Weald 18-3-97; Jet Provost Promotions Ltd, North Weald 23-7-97; Seagull Formation Ltd, North Weald 24-1-00; Gerald P. Williams, Swansea 27-2-02; de Havilland Aviation Ltd, Bournemouth-Hurn 3-3-03 (flew as RAF "XM478"); permit to fly expired 26-4-06; struck-off reg. 28-4-06; **G-BXDL** Noras SRL, Parma, Italy: re-added 16-4-07, (op: Museo dell'Araba Fenice, Reggio Emilia, Italy 7-08); sold to Italy, struck-off UK Register 14-11-08; reg to Noras SRL, Parma, Italy and exported to Reggio nell'Emilia, Italy as **I-PROV** 30-7-2008

159

XM479 AwCn 15-7-60; 27MU 19-7-60; 71MU for BoB Horse Guards Parade 18-8-60; 27MU 26-9-60; RAFC/32 12-12-60; 27MU 26-9-66; 5MU 3-11-72; **BAC for T Mk.3A** 9-2-76; 1FTS/54 30-4-76 (last flew 29-1-93); Global Avn Binbrook 8-7-93; reg **G-BVEZ** 4-8-93; Magnificent Obsessions Ltd, Grimsby 13-10-93; Keith Lister, Newcastle 20-12-95; Newcastle Jet Provost Group, Newcastle 30-8-96; Neil T. McCarthy, Newcastle 12-4-07 (flies as RAF "XM479")

XM480 AwCn 21-7-60; 27MU 22-7-60; 1FTS/21 4-10-60; 6FTS/29 8-6-62; 27MU 1-12-67; NES 28-3-69; GI **8080M** 18-12-69; 1 SoTT Halton/69 21-4-70; Finningley 9-2-94; 4X4 Car Care Centre, Chesterfield by 2-95

XN137 AwCn 15-8-60; 27MU 18-8-60; CFS/R-S 28-9-60, recoded 77; 3FTS/24 10-9-63; 27MU 28-8-69; 5MU 14-1-72; NES

19-1-76; RAF Exhibition Flt Abingdon (nose section) 28-5-76; 1057 ATC Sqn Camberley; Barry Parkhouse Ottershaw 15-11-91; Hands on Aviation, Camberley (marked as 'XN493'); South Molton Devon 2010; Little Addington, Northants for conversion to a simulator 11-2011

XN458 AwCn 26-8-60; 27MU 31-8-60; 1FTS/19 4-10-60; 27MU 28-10-66; 5MU 20-10-72; NES 14-2-73; GI **8234M** and 1SoTT Halton/215/H 14-2-1973 ('8334M' incorrectly issued, ntu); 4 SoTT St Athan 16-5-85; Wales Aircraft Museum, Rhoose by 2-93; Paul Whelland, Ashington, W Sussex 1996 (as 'XN594'); The Standard Public House, Northallerton 8-7-05

160

XN459 AwCn 29-8-60; 27MU 31-8-60; 1FTS/20 3-10-60; **BAC for T Mk.3A** 7-1-75 – 16-4-75; 1FTS/20 16-4-75; MoDPE 24-9-86; 1FTS/20 10-4-87; St Athan store 12-8-87; 1 FTS 10-9-87; CFS/N 9-10-87; 27MU Shawbury 10-6-92; **G-BWOT** 25-3-96 Transair; Quasi Mondi, Epping 20-10-97; Red Pelicans, Staverton 23-4-02; Mohan Soor, Slough 1-5-08; reg cnx 24-10-12; Kennet Avn / TJ Manna, Nth Weald (restoration) 3-12-14

XN460 AwCn 29-8-60; 27MU 31-8-60; 2FTS/26 14-10-60, failed to recover from spin and crashed Castle Bytham, Lincs, 1-2-61; SOC 3-2-61; Global Aviation Ltd, Binbrook 11-93; Lance Tolland Associates, Griffin, GA; reg **N460XN** Mark Johnson, Broomfield, CO 21-6-94

159. Jet Provost T Mk.3A, XM478, preserved in an airworthy condition at Reggio nell'Emilia, Italy, as I-PROV. (Claudio Toselli)

160. First aircraft of the second production order for 100 Jet Provost T Mk.3s, XN458, was delivered to the RAF in August 1960 and spent its entire Service career with No.1 FTS at RAF Linton-on-Ouse. (Hunting via Norman Giffin)

XN461 AwCn 31-8-60; 27MU 5-9-60; 1FTS/22 31-10-60; 7FTS/44 19-7-62; 3FTS/7 8-7-66, recoded K; **BAC for T Mk.3A** 20-5-75; 3FTS/K 25-9-75; 5MU 9-10-75; 1FTS/28 12-10-81 (last flew 29-1-93); sold 8-7-93; reg **G-BVBE** to Eddie Todd, Doncaster 21-7-93; sold to France: struck-off reg. 19-3-97 and reg **F-AZMI** Yves Saunier, Le Havre 2-5-97

XN462 AwCn 27-9-60; 27MU 29-9-60; 1FTS/23 4-11-60; 2FTS/9 9-9-63; CFS/62 31-1-69; **BAC for T Mk.3A** 15-7-75 – 27-10-75; Leeming (store) 27-10-75; 5MU 18-11-75; 3FTS/E 3-11-81; 7FTS/87 30-3-84; CFS/E 2-90; 1FTS/17 17-4-91; 27MU Shawbury 8-9-92; Heli Med (store) Hinckley 12-7-93; FAA Museum Wroughton (store); Fleet Air Arm Museum, Yeovilton, Cobham Hall (store) 23-11-99

XN463 AwCn 27-9-60; A&AEE Boscombe Down / BS Engines Filton (free loan) for battery heating investigation 29-9-60; e/f and crashed on approach at Sutton Mandeville, Wilts 26-10-60; SOC 17-5-61; Hunting Aircraft, Luton; scrapped 4-62

XN464 AwCn 27-9-60; 27MU 29-9-60; CFS/R-T 1-11-60; 6FTS/18 14-12-61; 27MU 14-8-63; NES 28-3-69; SOC to Fire Section Linton 31-7-69

XN465 AwCn 27-9-60; 27MU 29-9-60; CFS/R-U 1-11-60; Cat4Rogue 15-11-61; 27MU 15-11-61; 60MU 27-4-62 for rogue investigation; 27MU 28-11-62; 3FTS/3 6-12-63; failed to recover from spin and crashed 1m N Easingwold 24-2-71; SOC 3-3-71

XN466 AwCn 27-9-60; 27MU 3-10-60; 1FTS/24 4-11-60; 7FTS/26 26-4-62; Cat 3R and 4R collided on r/w with XM476 Church Fenton 29-1-63; Hunting RIW 5-3-63 – 31-10-63; 27MU 5-11-63; 1FTS/29 28-9-65; **BAC for T Mk.3A** 18-2-75 – 6-6-75; 1FTS/29 6-6-75 – 12-91; NES; St Athan by 6-93; No.1005 ATC Sqn, Radcliffe, Manchester (cockpit section); No.184 ATC Sqn, Mauldeth Road West, Manchester by 2007

XN467 Prototype T Mk.4. F/f 15-7-60 during build mods for Viper 11 installation; C(A) 18-7-60 at Hunting; A&AEE Boscombe Down 8-2-61 for aerodynamic handling trials; Hunting, Luton 14-7-61; development work for CA release and spinning with full tip tanks; A&AEE 26-6-63 for checks on the spinning parachute; BAC Warton 13-4-66 for preparation for return to service; 27MU 19-10-67; 5MU 16-6-69; CFS/49 17-9-69; Shawbury 15-6-70; 5MU 23-2-73; NES 20-1-77; SOC as Cat 4GI 1-2-78 **8559M** 1 SoTT Halton; Otterburn ranges 1994

XN468 Second prototype T Mk.4. CS(A) 5-7-60, mods during build for ASV 11 installation; C(A) Hunting 1-9-60; BS Eng Filton 2-12-60 for Viper 11 development flying; Hunting 18-3-61 preparation for A&AEE tests; A&AEE Boscombe Down 27-6-61 for engineering appraisal and engine handling trials; Hunting 18-12-61 for return to service preparation; BS Eng 1-3-62 (cnx); Hunting 19-7-62 for reconditioning to **T Mk.4** standard; AwCn 19-7-63; 1FTS 19-7-63 (not accepted); Hawker Aircraft for refurb 28-1-64; BS Eng 28-1-64; RAFC/67 31-6-65; CFS/41 22-5-66; 27MU 23-10-69; NES 26-1-71; SOC 1-10-71

XN469 AwCn 27-6-60; 27MU 3-10-60; 1FTS/25 8-11-60; Cat4R FA 23-6-70, E/f, force-landed East Moor and u/c collapsed; ReCat 5C 14-8-70; Fire Section Catterick 21-9-70

XN470 AwCn 30-9-60; 27MU 4-10-60; 1FTS/26 8-11-60; **BAC for T Mk.3A** 26-11-74 – 3-3-75; 1FTS/26 3-3-75; 5MU 3-10-75; 7FTS/84 23-10-84; 1FTS/41 by 5-90; 27MU Shawbury; Global Aviation Ltd, Binbrook 19-11-93; reg **G-BXBJ** Global Aviation Ltd, Binbrook 29-1-97; sold to United Arab Emirates, struck-off reg. 25-10-99; Dubai Men's College, Dubai UAE/41 displ. 3-10; Doha airport

XN471 AwCn 30-9-60; 27MU 4-10-60; 1FTS/27 14-11-60; RAFC/21 24-2-65; **BAC for T Mk.3A** 8-4-75 – 16-7-75; RAFC 16-7-75; TWU/L 1-8-75; 3FTS/N 11-2-76; Wyton det/N 31-3-76; 3FTS 21-7-76; Wyton det 26-7-76; 3FTS 4-1-77; RAFC/64 26-1-77; Wyton det 16-2-77; RAFC 11-5-77; Wyton det 29-6-77; RAFC 31-10-77; 1FTS/24 4-6-79; 27 MU Shawbury 25-8-92; Downbird UK Ltd, Stoke-on-Trent; reg **N471XN** Jet Provost Partnership, Aurora, CO 7-7-93; Astre Aire International, Aurora, CO 27-7-95; Craig Wingert, Colorado Springs, CO 14-1-97 (reported to be **XM471**: XN471/XM471 swapped ids during RAF service)

XN472 AwCn 11-10-60; 27MU 13-10-60; CFS/R-V 26-11-60, recoded 78; 1FTS/27 6-8-71; **BAC for T Mk.3A** 22-1-74 – 11-7-74; CFS/78 11-7-74; 5MU 1-12-75; RAFC/47 15-12-77; 7FTS/84 12-7-79; 1FTS/32 1-10-84; GI **8959M** 10-3-88; 2 SoTT Cosford 16-3-88; Global Avn Binbrook 19-11-93; sold USA **N3497N** Biggles Air Inc/J. W. Duff: reg. candidate 16-4-96; J. W. Duff, Denver, CO 24-6-97 as **N69RT;** Richard Jon Todd, Garden Valley, CA 8-97

XN473 AwCn 25-10-60; 27MU 31-10-60; RAFC/22 24-11-60; 27MU 29-9-66; 5MU 19-7-72; **BAC for T Mk.3A** 17-12-75 – 27-4-76; RAFC/58 27-4-76; 7FTS/98 21-3-79; bird strike; abandoned t/o nosewheel collapsed, Cranwell 15-8-84; Cat 5S 20-8-84;

SOC 14-11-84; **8862M** 5-85, nose section to Church Fenton Fire Section 29-5-95

XN492 AwCn 31-10-60; 27MU 7-11-60; RAFC/30 21-12-60; 6FTS/13 13-10-61, recoded 5; 27MU 23-2-68; NES 28-3-69; GI **8079M** 1 SoTT Halton/X/M 18-12-69; Odiham dump by 7-95; Firbeck N. Yorks; 1940 ATC Sqn Levenshulme 12-92; Military A/C Cockpit Collection Welshpool by 10-99; 2434 ATC Sqn Church Fenton 2010; East Midlands Aeropark (cockpit) 2015

XN493 AwCn 24-10-60; 27MU 31-10-60; RAFC/25 24-11-60; 7FTS/30 15-5-62; 3FTS/11 2-8-66; 27MU 12-10-66; 5MU 19-7-72; NES 19-1-76; SOC 28-5-76; nose to Abingdon for exhibition 1976; SOC Cat 5(S) and scrapped 28-5-1976

XN494 AwCn 25-10-60; 27MU 31-10-60; RAFC/28 24-11-60; **BAC for T Mk.3A** 4-9-74 – 4-12-74; RAFC 4-12-74; 1FTS/43 12-12-74; GI **9012M** 16-10-1989; 1 SoTT Halton/43 by 3-90; Middle Wallop for CRT by 7-93; Bruntingthorpe 6-2-98; Crawley Tech College 8-6-98; Gatwick Avn Museum 19-8-08; Cornwall College Camborne, 10-15

XN495 AwCn 31-10-60; 27MU 8-11-60; RAFC/34 20-12-60; 7FTS/31 15-5-62; 2FTS/5 28-3-66; 1FTS/33 9-5-69; **BAC for T Mk.3A** 14-1-75 – 24-4-75; 1FTS/33 24-4-75; 5MU 8-2-77; RAFC/62 3-11-78; 7FTS/102 9-11-79; aborted t/o; belly-landed Elvington 30-8-83; GI **8786M** 1 SoTT Halton 3-10-83; Abingdon BDR 1983; Finningley CRT (nose section), Haydock; Wings Museum, Redhill, Surrey

XN496 AwCn 31-10-60; 27MU 7-11-60; RAFC/31 12-12-60; 27MU 26-9-66; NES 28-3-69; sold Airwork, Christchurch 10-7-69; to GI Saudi Arabia

XN497 AwCn 31-10-60; 27MU 07-11-60; RAFC/29 31-11-60; belly-landed Waddington Cat 3R 14-3-63; Recat 4R 18-3-63; Hunting RIW 18-4-63 – 11-3-64; 27MU 11-3-64; 3FTS/8 3-8-65, recoded P; **BAC for T Mk.3A** 14-10-74 – 29-1-75; Leeming/P (store) 29-1-75; Topcliffe (store) 25-4-75; Leeming; 1FTS/52 8-1-76; St Athan by 6-91; SOC

XN498 AwCn 17-11-60; 27MU 25-11-60; RAFC/33 20-12-60; 27MU 21-9-66; 5MU 3-9-72; **BAC for T Mk.3A** 19-3-76 – 6-7-76; 3 FTS Leeming store/O 6-7-76; 1FTS/16 17-1-77; Shawbury; Global Aviation Ltd, Binbrook 19-11-93; reg **G-BWSH** 13-5-96 (based at Humberside; flew as RAF "XN498"); ptf wfu 8-7-03; Humberside (store)

XN499 AwCn 17-11-60; 27MU 25-11-60; RAFC/35 21-12-60, e/f during landing Cranwell Cat 3R 22-2-62; Recat 4R and Huntings 22-3-62; Huntings RIW 12-4-62 – 24-9-62; RAFC/35 24-9-62; 27MU 10-12-69; 5MU 21-6-72; **BAC for T Mk.3A** 16-2-76 – 2-6-76; 3FTS 2-6-76; 1FTS/19 17-1-77; CFS/L 21-9-77; Shawbury 10-6-92; Global Avn, Binbrook 19-2-93 and reg Lance P. Toland, Griffin, GA as **N7075X** 2-6-93; KW Plastics Inc, Troy, AL; Ronald D. Brooks, Hutchinson, KS 9-05; Henry R. Cutbirth, Monahans, TX 8-12-05

XN500 AwCn 18-11-60; 27MU 25-11-60; RAFC/36 21-12-60; **BAC for T Mk.3A** 3-12-74 – 11-3-75; Leeming (store) /36 11-3-75; Topcliffe 25-4-75, then via Leeming to 26 Sqn/Q 18-12-75; Wyton det 31-3-76; 3FTS/Q 24-4-76; Wyton det 13-5-76; 3FTS/Q 16-11-76; RAFC/63 31-12-76; Wyton det 24-1-77; RAFC/63 29-6-77; JP det 25-7-77; RAFC/63 31-10-77; 7FTS/80 9-8-79; 1FTS/48 5-90; 27MU Shawbury (store) 4-3-92; GI Oxford Air Trg School 15-6-94; Reportedly held at the following locations after 1994: FAST Farnborough 19-4-95; East Midlands Aero Park 9-04; Southampton (store) 30-3-06; Norfolk & Suffolk Avn Museum Flixton 7-10-06

XN501 AwCn 25-11-60; 27MU 1-12-60; 1FTS/28 22-12-60; **BAC for T Mk.3A** 29-5-74 – 2-10-74; 1FTS/28 2-10-74; CFS/S 8-9-77, recoded G; Cat 5S 18-2-88; GI **8958M** 2-3-88; 2 SoTT Cosford 3-3-88; Global Avn Binbrook 19-11-93; exported to Ogden, Utah, USA (store) 1999

XN502 AwCn 25-11-60; 27MU 1-12-60; 1FTS/29 2-1-61; 27MU 20-8-63; 2FTS/4 16-6-66; CFS/66 17-7-69; **BAC for T Mk.3A** 16-8-73 – 6-2-74; CFS/66 6-2-74; 5MU 1-10-75; CFS/N 22-4-83, recoded D; 27 MU Shawbury (store) 4-3-92; Global Aviation Ltd, Binbrook 19-11-93; Biggles Air Inc, New Castle, CO 1994; George Wragg, Gainesville, GA 23-1-95 as **N502GW;** TAG Enterprises Inc, Wilmington, DE 7-10-97; Mark A. Walton, Martinsburg, PA 30-10-01

XN503 AwCn 8-12-60; A&AEE 22-12-60 for battery overheat trial and fuel heating tests in 7-61; 27MU 10-8-61; 6FTS/16 15-11-61 recoded 2; to C(A) and BAC 12-6-68 for TI of a carbon filter and Grimes beacons; 2FTS/ 6-12-68; 4FTS/ 26-2-69; allocated BAC Warton 17-3-69 and loan Min Tech and del Warton 20-3-69 for trial of Cossor SR1600 surveillance radar; AAEE 31-10-69 for CA release of SSR; BAC Warton 11-12-69 for return to service prep; 27MU 16-4-70; BAC

Warton 5-2-71 for TI of Smiths height encoding altimeter; RR Filton 16-7-71 Viper 102 engine vibration trial; 5MU 13-12-72; BAC Warton 9-7-73; 5MU 11-2-74; NES 9-1-76; SOC 28-5-76; nose to Abingdon for exhibition; Bicester; Coventry; Firbeck; 1284 (ATC) Sqn by 4-95; Boscombe Down Avn Collection (nose section) by 2-09

XN504 AwCn 21-12-60; 27MU 2-1-61; 1FTS/34 1-2-61; e/f, crashed Rufforth, Yorks 14-3-63; SOC 18-3-63

XN505 AwCn 30-11-60; 27MU 2-12-60; 1FTS/30 6-1-61; RAFC/29 11-3-65; **BAC for T Mk.3A** 13-3-74 – 18-7-74; RAFC/29 18-7-74; 1FTS/25 6-11-74; 27 MU Shawbury (store) 1-10-92; sold Global Avn Binbrook 1997; Biggles Air, Newcastle 26-5-1993 and exported to the USA as **N374XM** 2001

XN506 AwCn 30-11-60; 27MU 2-12-60; 1FTS/31 24-1-61; 7FTS/42 7-6-62; RAFC/30 8-4-63; 27MU 17-7-63; 3FTS/11 7-7-67; 6FTS/Y 17-8-70; 3FTS/3 1-4-71; 26 Sqn/J 25-10-74; 3FTS/J 11-12-74; 26 Sqn/J 13-1-75; 3 FTS/J 5-2-75; 26 Sqn/J 29-4-75; 3FTS/J 6-5-75; 26 Sqn/J 12-5-75; 3 FTS/J 11-6-75; 26Sqn/J 3-7-75; 3FTS/J 24-7-75; **BAC for T Mk.3A** 19-8-75; CFS/74 12-11-75; RAFC/55 12-4-76; 7FTS/81 27-9-79; 1 FTS 17-10-80; 7FTS/81 3-11-80; 1FTS/19 6-5-87; 27 MU Shawbury (store) 14-4-92; sold to Biggles Air Inc, Newcastle, 15-2-1993; exported to Russ McDonald Field-Herber City Municipal Airport, Utah, USA as **N77506;** Jet Warbirds LLC, Sandy, UT 19-3-96; JAW LMT LC, Sandy, UT 31-12-08

XN507 AwCn 15-12-60; 27MU 8-1-61; 1FTS/33 30-1-61; 27MU 23-9-66; 5MU 3-11-72; NES 14-2-73; SOC 8-8-74; scrapped

XN508 AwCn 15-12-60; 27MU 29-12-60; 1FTS/32 24-1-61; **BAC for T Mk.3A** 13-8-74; 1FTS/33 5-11-74; 5MU 7-2-77; CFS/U 5-2-79; 7FTS/10 10-3-84, recoded 98; 1FTS/47 12-90; DARA St Athan 26-6-93 (cockpit section as GI); scrapped

XN509 AwCn 29-12-60; 27MU 2-1-61; 1FTS/35 1-2-61; 7FTS/27 6-4-62; 27MU 15-8-63; 6FTS/25 13-6-67; 3FTS/27 7-11-67; 6FTS/Z 17-8-70; RAFC/51 31-3-71; **BAC for T Mk.3A** 5-11-74; RAFC 25-2-75; 1FTS/50 6-3-75; 7FTS 29-3-79; 1FTS/50 18-4-79; 27MU Shawbury 5-8-92; Witham Special Vehicles, Colsterworth, Lincs (store) 21-1-93; exported to buyer in Michigan, USA

XN510 AwCn 20-01-61; 27MU 23-01-61; 1FTS/36 28-02-61; 7FTS/28 26-04-62; RAFC/37 10-4-63; 27MU Shawbury 18-7-63; NEA 28-03-69; Shawbury returned effective stock 18-04-69;

5MU 26-01-73; **BAC for T3A** 04-05-76 to 09-08-76; 3 FTS Leeming/R 09-08-76; 1FTS/40 27-01-77; Global Aviation Ltd, Binbrook (store) 19-11-93; reg **G-BXBI** 29-1-97; Everett Aero, Sproughton, Suffolk 24-02-2000; reg cnx 09-12-05; Nafplion, Greece (private; store) 07-08

XN511 AwCn 30-12-60; 27MU 9-1-61; CFS/R-W 27-2-61, recoded 64; 1FTS/ 26-1-68; CFS/64 6-2-68; 27MU 13-10-69; 5MU 2-2-73; NES 19-1-76; SOC 28-5-76 and reduced to a nose section; 2495 ATC Sqn Liversedge; 177 ATC Sqn, Squires Gate, Blackpool 1985; Lutterworth 7-88; Newark Air Museum, Winthorpe 3-89; Robertsbridge Avn Society 1990; AeroVenture, Doncaster, Yorkshire

XN512 AwCn 10-1-61; 27MU 20-1-61; CFS/R-X 27-2-61, recoded 65; 27MU 14-10-69; 4SoTT St Athan 10-11-71; GI 8435M 16-01-75; 1 SoTT Halton/E 6-77; Princess Alexandra Hospital as gate guard 6-93; Phoenix Avn Bruntingthorpe 19-12-95; sold to Kolonien, Belgium for display 10-06; Lommel, Limburg, Belgium (pole mounted)

161

XN547 AwCn 27-1-61; 27MU 1-2-61; RAFC/38 21-3-61; **BAC for T Mk.3A** 22-10-74 – 7-2-75; RAFC 7-2-75; 1FTS/48 14-2-75; control lost in spin and crashed Malton, Yorks 8-3-89

XN548 AwCn 25-1-61; 27MU 1-2-61; CFS/R-Z 7-3-61, recoded 67; **BAC for T Mk.3A** 6-9-73 – 6-2-74; CFS/67 6-2-74; 5MU 21-1-76; RAFC/48 6-1-78; 7FTS/82 4-9-79, recoded 103; Linton (store); GI 25-5-88 as **9014M;** 1 SoTT Halton 7-6-88; sale by tender 3-92; sold USA and reg **N4421B** 9-92; Richard D. Janitell, Colorado Springs, CO 14-4-93; Western Sky Aviation Warbird Museum Inc, St George, UT 2-07

XN549 AwCn 25-1-61; 27MU 1-2-61; CFS/R-Y 27-2-61 recoded 66; 1FTS/30 26-1-68; 27MU 20-6-69; 5MU 5-1-73; NES 14-2-73; GI **8335M** 21-3-73; 1 SoTT Halton/235/R ('8235M' ntu) 13-12-73; 27MU Shawbury 1-3-91 for CRT; Parkhouse Aviation, Booker

3-2-06; Cockpitmania, South Molton, Devon (cockpit section); Warrington (cockpit section; private) by 10-06

XN550 AwCn 31-1-61; 27MU 2-2-61; CFS/S-A 7-3-61, recoded 63; 27MU 30-5-69; 5MU 2-2-73; NES 19-1-76; SOC 28-5-76; 730 ATC Sqn Truro (cockpit section); Watson scrap yard, Stone, Staffs; scrapped 11-06

XN551 AwCn 31-1-61; 27MU 2-2-61; RAFC/37 13-3-61; 6FTS/12 12-10-61; 3FTS/13 1-12-67; **BAC for T Mk.3A** 11-6-74 – 14-10-74; 3FTS 14-10-74; 1FTS/40 4-11-74; 5MU 1-2-77; RAFC/49 14-2-78; 7FTS/100 30-10-79; GI **8984M** 6-2-89; 4 SoTT St Athan 4-89; tendered 11-05; Felton Common, Som, 2-06 (private)

XN552 AwCn 31-1-61; 27MU Shawbury 2-2-61; RAFC/39 21-3-61; Shawbury 26-9-66; 5MU 1-9-72; **BAC for T Mk.3A** 30-1-76 – 29-4-76; RAFC/59 29-4-76; CFS/ I 25-9-79; 5MU 29-5-80; CFS/I 1-7-80; 7FTS/86 12-8-80; 1FTS/32 19-6-87; 27MU Shawbury 22-7-93; Global Aviation Ltd, Binbrook 19-11-93; sold USA & Lance Tolland Associates, Griffin, GA as **N68354** 12-7-94; re-reg **N552XN** to International Jet Centre Inc, Miami, FL 26-2-97

XN553 AwCn 8-2-61; 27MU 13-2-61; RAFC/40 21-3-61; 27MU 7-1-70; 19MU St Athan 1-7-70; 1FTS/34 21-1-71; **BAC for T Mk.3A** 2-4-75 – 15-7-75; 1FTS/34 15-7-75; BAe Warton (loan) spinning trials 26-11-85; 1FTS 30-3-87; St Athan (hack) 29-7-87; Shawbury 23-9-92; Global Avn Binbrook 11-93; sold USA and reg **N57553** Biggles Air Inc, New Castle, CO 26-5-93; Cyndee One Inc, Encino, CA 26-5-93; Van Nuys (store) 2-95; struck-off USCR 14-8-12

XN554 AwCn 10-2-61; 27MU 13-2-61; CFS/S-E 27-3-61 recoded 60; 27MU 30-5-69; 4 SoTT St Athan 17-11-71 as GI; **8436M** 16-1-75; 1SoTT Halton/K 02-77; EOD North Luffenham 4-92; Everett Aero, Sproughton 2003; Gunsmoke Paintball Park, Hadleigh, Suffolk 2007

XN555 AwCn 17-2-61; 27MU 27-2-61; RAFC/41 24-4-61; 27MU 26-9-66; 5MU 29-9-72; NES 14-2-73; SOC 8-8-74; to Fire Section Kemble

XN556 AwCn 22-2-61; 27MU 28-2-61; 1FTS/18 13-4-61; 27MU 4-9-63; 6FTS/1 20-9-63; 1FTS/23 14-6-68; crashed on approach, Linton 17-3-70; Cat 5C and SOC 17-3-70

XN557 AwCn 21-2-61; 27MU 28-2-61; CFS/S-F 14-4-61; 7FTS/46 27-7-62; 2FTS/23 29-6-66; 27MU 13-10-66; 5MU 18-8-72; NES 14-2-73; SOC and scrapped 8-8-74

XN558 AwCn 27-2-61; 27MU 1-3-61; RAFC/42 24-4-61; 27MU 5-1-70; St Athan 1-7-70; 3FTS/4 3-3-71; multiple birdstrike, crashed after crew ejected, Dishforth 29-6-71, Cat 5; SOC 7-7-71

XN559 AwCn 28-2-61; 27MU 2-3-61; RAFC/44 2-5-61; 7FTS/49 18-9-62; RAFC/47 5-4-63; 27MU 18-7-63; NES 28-3-69; 27MU effective stock 18-4-69; 5MU 17-11-72; NES 14-2-73; Fire Section Catterick 1-2-74

XN573 AwCn 28-2-61; 27MU 2-3-61; CFS/S-G 27-4-61 recoded 62; 1FTS/21 3-4-68; 27MU 25-7-69; 5MU 8-12-72; NES 19-1-76; SOC 28-5-76; No.177 ATC Sqn Blackpool Airport (nose section); Newark Air Museum 4-89

XN574 AwCn 15-3-61; Hunting 15-3-61 for final stage development work and C(A) release; 27MU 11-7-61; 3FTS/1 18-8-61; **BAC for T Mk.3A** 18-12-73 – 16-5-74; 3FTS/1 16-5-74; 1FTS/21 16-9-74; 7FTS/92 19-5-87; GI Scampton 27-10-88; tendered 1-89; Simon Richards, Chassey, France 10-89; Aerodrome De Montélimar Museum, France 2014

XN575 AwCn 22-3-61; 27MU 12-4-61; 1FTS/12 16-5-61; 7FTS/45 20-7-62; 3FTS/6 8-7-66; stalled and crashed on t/o Leeming 30-9-69, Cat 5S and SOC 30-9-69

XN576 AwCn 15-3-61; 27MU 16-3-61; CFS/S-H 27-4-61 recoded 79; e/f and abandoned Yanworth, Glos 4-9-69; Cat 5S and SOC 4-9-69; 5MU dump

162

161. In May 1961, the CFS aerobatic display team appeared at the RAFA air show, North Weald, with four aircraft led by Flt Lt Frank Brambley, including XN512. The aircraft had been delivered to the CFS the previous February and was eventually sold to a buyer in Belgium in 2006. (Ray Deacon Collection)

162. Refuelling at the end of the day's flying, Little Rissington, May 1966. The Jet Provost in the foreground suffered an engine failure and crashed at Northleach, Glos, in September 1969. (Author)

XN577 AwCn 17-3-61; 27MU 21-3-61; RAFC/45 2-5-61; Cat 4R heavy landing Cranwell 18-1-62; Hunting 8-2-62; RIW 23-2-62 – 29-6-62; 7FTS/43 6-7-62; 1FTS/18 5-4-66; **BAC for T Mk.3A** 6-8-74 – 12-11-74; 1FTS/18 12-11-74; 7FTS/83 12-5-87; Cat 5 19-2-88; SOC 22-2-88; GI **8956M** 2SoTT Cosford 22-2-88; Global Avn Binbrook (store) 19-11-93; Ogden Municipal Airport, Utah, USA 1999

XN578 AwCn 23-3-61; 27MU 19-4-61; RAFC/48 12-5-61; 6FTS/4 13-4-62; 27MU 18-1-68; NES 28-3-69; Fire Section RAF Valley 18-12-69

XN579 AwCn 28-3-61; 27MU 13-4-61; RAFC/49 16-5-61; TWU/49 25-9-74; RAFC/49 7-8-75; **BAC for T Mk.3A** 3-9-75 – 28-11-75; 1FTS/14 4-12-75; 7FTS 29-3-79; 1FTS/14 23-4-79; 27MU Shawbury 19-11-91; GI **9137M** 5-92; EOD North Luffenham 31-4-92; Everett Aero, Sproughton 2003; Gunsmoke Paintball Park, Hadleigh, Suffolk 2007

XN580 AwCn 28-3-61; 27MU 6-4-61; RAFC/46 2-5-61; abandoned (smoke in cockpit) Scopwick, Lincs 15-6-64; SOC Cat 5C 15-6-64

XN581 AwCn 30-3-61; 27MU 6-4-61; RAFC/47 5-5-61; 7FTS/32 15-5-62; 27MU 16-05-63; 6FTS/7 11-11-65; 3FTS/26 01-11-67; 27MU 24-10-69; CFS/77 29-01-72; **BAC for T3A** 09-09-75 to 13-01-76; CFS/77 13-01-76; RAFC/77 12-04-76 recoded 56; CFS/Q 8-9-77, recoded C; SOC 7-91 Scampton & scrapped

XN582 AwCn 30-03-61; 27MU 24-04-61; RAFC/50 17-5-61; 3FTS/22 12-12-61; **BAC for T Mk.3A** 23-1-74 – 10-7-74; 3 FTS 10-7-74; 1FTS/24 9-10-74; 7FTS/95 22-3-79; 5MU 8-12-80; 7FTS/95 23-1-81; GI **8957M** 2-3-88; 2 SoTT Cosford 11-3-88; Global Aviation, Binbrook 19-11-93; GI Arbury College/Cambridge Regional College, Cambridge 11-3-94; Bruntingthorpe, Leicestershire 21-7-06

XN583 AwCn 19-4-61; 27MU 21-4-61; RAFC/51 17-5-61; 7FTS/33 18-5-62; flew into wood during unauthorised aerobatics, Pannal, Yorks (1) 17-9-64, Cat 5S; SOC 21-9-64

XN584 AwCn 20-4-61; 27MU 24-4-61; RAFC/52 26-5-61; TWU/52 20-9-74; RAFC/52 1-8-75; **BAC for T Mk.3A** 27-8-75 – 28-11-75; CFS/78 28-11-75; CFS/78 12-4-76, recoded 57; CFS/R 18-8-77, recoded E; GI **9014M** 25-10-89; 1SoTT Halton 9-90; Bruntingthorpe, Leics 27-3-95; Univ Sth Wales Aerospace Centre, Treforest, Glam, 2015

XN585 AwCn 20-4-61; 27MU 27-4-61; RAFC/53 29-5-61; **BAC for T3A** 26-11-74; RAFC/53 25-2-75; Leeming (store) 17-3-75; Topcliffe (store) 19-6-75; 1FTS/12 23-2-76; spurious engine fire and crashed 3m W Linton 28-3-79; SOC Cat 5S 28-3-79

XN586 AwCn 27-4-61; 27MU 3-5-61; RAFC/54 29-5-61; Cat 4R13-4-65; BAC RIW 13-10-65 – 16-1-67; 27MU 16-1-67; 2FTS/11 18-7-67; CFS/73 3-10-69; 27MU 22-2-70; St Athan 3-7-70; 1FTS/35 5-3-71; **BAC for T Mk.3A** 17-9-74 – 4-12-74; 1FTS/35 4-12-74; 7FTS/91 27-3-79; GI **9039M** 2 SoTT Cosford 5-90; Global Aviation, Binbrook 19-11-93; Brooklands College, Weybridge, Surrey as GI 8-4-94; Brooklands Museum 2014

XN587 AwCn 27-4-61; 27MU 3-5-61; RAFC/55 5-6-61; 27MU 21-9-66; NES 28-3-69; GI RAF Cranwell 27-12-69 and later scrapped

XN588 AwCn 28-4-61; 27MU 3-5-61; RAFC/43 13-6-61; 27MU 15-8-63; 1FTS/30 15-10-65; dived into the ground near Lundwood, Wharram Le Street, Yorkshire (1) 18-5-67; Cat 5S SOC 19-5-67

XN589 AwCn 28-4-61; 27MU 3-5-61; RAFC/56 9-6-61; **BAC for T Mk.3A** 3-10-74 – 20-12-74; RAFC 7-1-75; 1FTS/46 23-1-75; allocated GI **9143M** 7-5-92; Linton gate 18-3-92

XN590 AwCn 28-4-61; 27MU 3-5-61; 6FTS/1 15-6-61; Cat 4R 6-9-63, nosewheel collapse Acklington; Hunting RIW 28-10-63 – 21-1-65; (BAC 15-1-65 for T I of hydraulic filter); 27MU 21-1-65; RAFC/34 11-5-65; **BAC for T Mk.3A** 4-9-74 – 4-12-74; 1FTS/44 13-12-74; 7FTS/86 29-3-79; multiple birdstrikes and crashed Elvington 31-7-80

XN591 AwCn 1-5-61; 27MU 3-5-61; CFS/S-K 28-6-61, recoded 69; Cat 4R e/f on t/o 10-3-65; DA 26-3-65; BAC Luton 31-3-65; AwCn 30-10-65; 1FTS/ 8-11-65; BS Eng 10-11-66 for Viper flame-out trial; 27MU 7-4-67; NES 28-3-69; SOC 18-3-70 and Army Apprentice College Arborfield as GI; scrapped 1980

XN592 AwCn 12-5-61; 27MU 19-5-61; 6FTS/2 22-6-61; Cat 4R 14-3-65; DA 23-3-65; BAC 8-10-65; 1FTS/11 11-5-66; 2FTS/25 27-7-66; to 27MU 30-7-69; 5MU 22-2-72; NES 19-1-76; SOC 28-5-76; GI Odiham (nose section); scrapped 1991

XN593 AwCn 17-5-61; 27MU 18-5-61; 2FTS/48 29-6-61, recoded 18; Cat 3R and Recat 4R and DA 27-5-63, rear fuselage damage; Hunting RIW 11-7-63 AwCn 24-4-64; 27MU 24-4-64; 1FTS/27 16-9-65; **BAC for T Mk.3A** 11-12-74 – 19-3-75; 1FTS/27 19-3-75;

7 FTS/97 2-6-87; 27MU Shawbury 1989; GI **8988M** 2-3-88; 2 SoTT Cosford/97/Q 5-89; Global Avn Binbrook 19-11-93; sold USA 1999, Salt Lake City, UT (private)

XN594 AwCn 19-5-61; 27MU 25-5-61; 2FTS/31 27-6-61; 7FTS/42 10-6-62; 6FTS/11 24-6-66; 27MU 23-2-68; NES 18-4-69; GI **8077M** 18-12-69; 1 SoTT Halton/M 21-4-70; 2 SoTT Cosford/9/W 2-5-84; France (private)

XN595 AwCn 26-5-61; 27MU 30-5-61; 2FTS/47 27-6-61, recoded 17; CFS/69 17-7-69; **BAC for T Mk.3A** 26-6-75 – 13-10-75; 3FTS 13-10-75; 5MU 4-11-75; 7FTS/81 19-8-80; 1FTS/43 1990; Shawbury 23-4-92; tendered 11-92 and sold Witham Special Vehicles, Colsterworth, Lincs 20-01-93; George F. Davis, New Carlisle IN USA 23-9-98 reg **N4436P;** sold Noblesville, IN 02-13; struck-off register 0-8-13

XN596 AwCn 29-5-61; 27MU 30-5-61; 6FTS/3 11-7-61; 27MU 14-2-68; NES 28-3-69; Airwork, Bournemouth 4-9-69; Singapore AF Seletar as GI **SAFTECH 1**

XN597 AwCn 29-5-61; 27MU 2-6-61; 2FTS/11 7-7-61; Cat 4R 28-6-67, heavy ldg and nosewheel collapsed, Wymeswold; DA 29-6-67; Recat 5C and SOC 12-9-67; broken up by 60MU and nose section as GI **7984M** 12-9-67; 2236 ATC Sqn Beverley, Brencham 1986; Park Avn Faygate 20-2-87; Helicopter Centre, Stoke-on-Trent 1-90; NEAM Sunderland 12-1-91; Sth Yorks Av Museum, Firbeck 12-93; Stamford 9-94; 1940 ATC Sqn, Levenshulme, Greater Manchester 9-95; Sth Yorks Av Museum 12-96; RAF Millom Museum Project, Millom, Cumbria 10-97; sold by auction to Lakes Lightnings, Spark Bridge, Cumbria 27-1-11; Retro Aviation Blackpool Airport (Salop store) 17-2-12

XN598 AwCn 30-5-61; 27MU 5-6-61; RAF Hdlg Sqn 17-7-61; Leeming 18-9-61; 3FTS/5 29-9-61; **BAC for T Mk.3A** 3-10-74 – 9-1-75; 3FTS/O 9-1-75; 1FTS/31 9-2-76; wing struck water and broke up, Gouthwaite reservoir, Yorks (1) 1-6-78; SOC Cat 5S 12-6-78

XN599 AwCn 7-6-61; 27MU 9-6-61; 6FTS/4 17-7-61; Cat 4Prov 27-3-62; Recat 4R 28-3-62 swung off the runway on landing at Acklington, Northumberland, Recat 5C and SOC 28-3-62 to scrap compound

XN600 AwCn 15-6-61; 27MU 16-6-61; 71MU Bicester for BoB exhibition 15-8-61; 27MU 9-10-61; 3FTS/16 2-11-61; 27MU 14-1-63; 5MU 4-3-68; 27MU 25-4-68; 23MU Aldergrove 16-5-68; 27MU 6-8-68; 7 Eng Sqn St Athan 19-6-69; Cat FA 3R 21-1-72, u/shot landing, St Athan; ROS 71MU 21-1-72 to 19-4-72; 7 Eng Sqn; 5MU 7-5-74; NES 19-1-76; SOC Cat 5S 28-5-76; nose section to 168 Sqn ATC Leeds 1987; Yorks A/C Recovery Group 23-7-88 (nose section); Aviodrome Schipol, Lelystad, Neth 13-11-94

XN601 AwCn 19-6-61; 27MU 26-6-61; 6FTS/5 27-7-61; Cat 5S 17-10-62, suffered partial engine failure on take-off from Ouston and struck the ground, pilot attempted to eject when the aircraft cartwheeled but was thrown from the aircraft (1); SOC 19-10-62

XN602 AwCn 19-6-61; 27MU 23-6-61; 6FTS/6 19-7-61; 27MU 21-2-68; NES 28-3-69; **8088M** 26-2-70; Brampton 2-3-70 as gate guard; 1 SoTT Halton as GI 02-8-79; JATE Brize Norton 2-81; Manston Fire School, Kent, 16-4-81

XN603 AwCn 27-6-61; 27MU 28-6-61; 6FTS/7 27-7-61; spurious fire warning, crew ejected and crashed Eshott, 2m SW Acklington 29-7-65; DA Cat 5S and SOC 29-7-65

XN604 AwCn 29-6-61; 27MU 3-7-61; 6FTS/8 1-8-61; spurious fire warning, crew ejected and crashed Felton, Northumberland 9-5-62; Cat 5S and SOC 9-5-62

XN605 AwCn 30-6-61; 27MU 5-7-61; 6FTS/9 4-8-61; 1FTS/31 13-6-68; **BAC for T Mk.3A** 10-9-74 – 5-12-74; 1FTS/31 5-12-74; 5MU 15-1-76; RAFC/52 22-3-78; 3FTS/CFS/T 25-9-79; CFS/J 12-12-85; SOC 10-88 Scampton; tendered 3-89; scrap 8-95

XN606 AwCn 30-6-61; 27MU 5-7-61; 3FTS/2 18-8-61; 27MU 14-1-63; 5MU 4-3-68; 27MU 22-3-68; St Athan 23-6-70; 6FTS/T 20-10-70; 1FTS/36 6-4-71; **BAC for T Mk.3A** 14-5-74 – 2-10-74; 1FTS/36 2-10-74; 7FTS/88 (loan) 2-89; 1FTS/51 20-3-90; **9121M** Brawdy BDRT 17-9-91; tendered and sold to Phoenix Aviation,

163

163. One of the original Jet Provost deliveries to No.3 FTS, XN598, was photographed at Little Rissington in 1961, featuring the unusual positioning of its code letter under the nose. It was written off in a tragic flying accident in June 1978. (Ray Deacon)

Bruntingthorpe 12-92; Rudd Aviation, Basalt, CO USA 5-93 as **N606RA;** Richard D. Janitell, Colorado Springs, CO 6-11-97; James M. Parsons, Harrogate, TN 17-3-05; Tennessee Technology Centre, Morristown, TN 3-5-11

XN607 AwCn 14-7-61; 27MU 18-7-61; 3FTS/4 29-8-61; 27MU 6-8-69; 5MU 2-2-72; NES 19-1-76; SOC 28-5-76 Cat 5S; 168 ATC Sqn, Leeds as GI (nose section); tendered 3-88; North Yorkshire Aircraft Recovery Centre, Chop Gate, Great Ayton 23-7-88; Highland Aviation Museum, Dalcross, 23-6-04

XN629 AwCn 18-7-61; 27MU 19-7-61; 3FTS/3 18-8-61; Cat 3R 14-11-63; Recat 4R e/f; t/o abandoned 18-11-63; Hunting RIW 31-12-63 – 10-2-65; 27MU 10-2-65; RAFC/37 17-6-65; BAC Warton (MoDPE) for avionics refit study 5-1-72; **Prototype T Mk.3A conv;** RAFC 14-12-73; CFS 23-5-74; RAFC/37 2-8-74; 1FTS/39 25-10-74; 7FTS/97 7-89; 1FTS/49 5-90; 27 MU Shawbury 22-4-92; Witham Special Vehicles, Costerworth 20-1-93; reg **G-BVEG** Magnificent Obsessions, Grimsby 19-8-93; Global Avn Binbrook 8-93; Tom Moloney/Transair (UK) Ltd, North Weald 29-3-94; R J Everett Ipswich 19-2-97; re-reg **G-KNOT R** S Partridge-Hicks 9-6-99; reg cnx 21-6-07 and North Weald store; Bentwaters (private; cockpit section) 14-2-10

XN630 AwCn 26-7-61; 27MU 31-7-61; 3FTS/6 18-9-61; RAFC/25 11-3-65; Cat4R 23-7-69, sank back on r/w after t/o, Biggin Hill; Recat 5C 14-8-69; SOC 22-8-69; 71MU dump

XN631 AwCn 31-7-61; 27MU 1-8-61; 3FTS/8 22-9-61; Cat 5S, m/a/c XM428 and crashed 1m E Northallerton 20-4-65; SOC 20-4-65

XN632 AwCn 28-7-61; 27MU 3-8-61; 3FTS/9 22-9-61; 27MU 14-1-63; 5MU 1-12-72; NES 14-2-73; GI 16-7-93 as **8352M;** Civilian Apprentices School, St Athan 30-11-73; Chivenor for CRT 6-12-89; tendered 2-95; Eaglescott, Devon 24-9-95; Graham Revill Collection, Birlingham, Worcs 23-3-96

XN633 AwCn 31-7-61; 27MU 1-8-61; 3FTS/10 27-9-61; 27MU 14-1-63; 5MU 1-12-72; NES 14-2-73; GI as **8353M** 30-11-73; Fire Section Bicester 16-7-73

XN634 AwCn 3-8-61; 27MU 10-8-61; 6FTS/11 11-10-61; Cat 4R 22-10-63 u/shot landing Ouston, Hunting; RIW 26-11-63 – 4-9-64; 27MU 17-9-64; RAFC/30 27-4-65; **BAC for T Mk.3A** 26-3-74 – 30-8-74; RAFC 30-8-74; 1FTS/30 21-10-74; 7FTS/94 22-3-79; 1FTS/53 6-90; tendered at Scampton 12-92; Everett Aero, Sproughton, 5-93; nose section converted to flight simulator with Raven Cockpits, Blackpool; fuselage remained with Everett Aero

XN635 AwCn 28-8-61; RAFC/57 29-8-61; 3FTS/23 12-12-61; 27MU 14-6-63; 5MU 8-12-72; NES 14-2-73; GI Apprentice School/23MU Aldergrove 16-7-73; Fire Section Culdrose 2-77; Predannack fire dump

XN636 AwCn 8-61; RAFC/58 8-9-61; Hunting 23-5-63 to investigate undercarriage defects; RAFC/58 19-7-63; 1FTS/15 1-2-67; **BAC for T3A** 28-1-75 – 14-5-75; 1FTS/15 14-5-75; GI **9045M** 1 SoTT Cosford 26-4-90; tendered 4-93; privately owned and located in the UK

XN637 AwCn 31-8-61; 27MU 7-9-61; 3FTS/13 5-10-61; 27MU 14-1-63; 5MU 1/-11-72; NES 14-2-73; SOC for GI 11-3-74; Sandy Topen/Vintage Aircraft Team, Cranfield 17-2-83 as G-BKOU; Anthony Haig-Thomas, North Weald 26-1-96; Seagull Formation Ltd, North Weald & Cranfield 13-12-99; **G-BKOU** Group, North Weald 10-11-04; G-BKOU/2 Ltd, Dunmow 5-2-09 (flies as RAF "XN637")

XN638 AwCn 31-8-61; 27MU 14-9-61; 6FTS/14 26-10-61; 27MU 20-2-68; NES 28-3-69; Fire Section Church Fenton 18-12-69

XN639 AwCn 31-1-62; 6FTS/24 1-2-62, recoded 8; 27MU 10-4-68; NES 28-3-69; Manston for film purposes 31-11-69; Fire School and burnt by 4-75

XN640 AwCn 31-1-62; 6FTS/25 1-2-62, recoded 5; CFS/74 1-9-64; **BAC for T Mk.3A** 5-8-75 – 10-11-75; Leeming (store) 10-11-75; 5MU 3-12-75; RAFC/51 7-3-78; 7FTS/99 21-3-79; GI **9016MB** 30-11-89; 2 SoTT Cosford 1-90; tendered Global Aviation Ltd, Binbrook 19-11-93; sold to USA as **N640XN** Plane Old PBJ Inc, Bloomfield, CO 21-6-94; James E. Roukema, Pueblo, CO 21-8-98; Defcon Development LLC, Wilmington, DE 4-05; struck-off USCR 11-7-13

XN641 AwCn 1-2-62; 3FTS/26 7-2-62; Cat 3R 10-5-62; Recat 4R 19-6-62; Hunting RIW 24-7-62 – 28-11-62; 27MU 12-12-62; RAFC/45 10-8-65; **BAC for T Mk.3A** 8-10-74 – 21-1-75; RAFC 21-1-75; 1FTS/47 29-1-75; Cat4 o/shot barrier landing Linton-on-Ouse 11-5-84; 27MU Shawbury 10-8-84; GI **8865M** 15-7-85; Fire Section Newton for CRT 26-11-85; perished

XN642 A/C 1-2-62; 3FTS/27 7-2-62 recoded 10; engine failure on t/o; crashed 2m N Leeming (1) 19-2-63; Cat 5S and SOC; remains to 60MU

XN643 AwCn 1-2-62; 3FTS/28 7-2-62; Cat 3R collided XM429 4-9-62; Recat 4R 6-9-62; Hunting RIW 30-10-62 – 14-3-63; CFS 15-3-63; 3FTS/15 30-7-63; 26Sqn 4-11-74; 3FTS/R 13-1-75; 26Sqn/R 5-3-75; 3FTS/R 29-4-75; 26Sqn/R 6-5-75; 3FTS/R 4-7-75; **BAC for T Mk.3A** 12-8-75 – 6-11-75; 1FTS/26 6-11-75; engine failure and crashed 2m N Snainton, N.Yorks 30-7-81; GI **8704M** 17-8-81; RAF Exhibition Abingdon by 1986; nose section to Cranwell by 9-87

JET PROVOST T MK.4

XP547 F/f 4-8-61; AAEE Boscombe Down 11-10-61 for flight checks; Hunting 20-11-61; RAFC/82 22-2-62; BAC Warton 25-1-71 for IFF trial; RAFC/82 25-6-71; CATCS/H 14-10-71; BAC for icing trial 25-10-71; 27MU 14-12-71; CATCS/H 14-12-71; 3FTS/70 9-4-75; TWU/03 4-2-76; 2SoTT Cosford; GI **8992M** 22-3-89; Global Aviation Ltd, Binbrook UK 19-11-93; sold to USA reg **N547XP** 7-97; Renan A. Dieppa, Isla Grande Airport, San Juan, Puerto Rico 12-4-99

164

XP548 AwCn 20-10-61; Hdlg Sqn Boscombe Down 25-10-61; Hunting 29-11-61; RAFC/83 19-2-62; 6FTS/X 16-3-71; Cat 5 Birdstrike, Brawdy 17-1-74; SOC 25-1-74; Brawdy Fire Section as GI **8404M** 25-1-74

XP549 AwCn 23-11-61; CFS/40 23-11-61; CAW/36 18-5-66; 27MU 4-4-67; NES 29-3-68; sfs B. A. Taylor West Bromwich 22-11-68

XP550 AwCn 23-11-61; CFS/41 23-11-61; 2FTS/32 20-5-66; 27MU 1-5-67; NES 29-3-68; sfs B. A. Taylor 22-11-68

XP551 AwCn 30-11-61; CFS/42 11-12-61; CAW/16 18-5-66; 27MU 20-4-67; NES 29-3-68; sfs B. A. Taylor 22-11-68

XP552 AwCn 30-11-61; CFS/43 7-12-61; 3FTS/39 16-5-66; 27MU 21-6-67; NES 26-1-71; sfs 1-10-71 to Staravia, Lasham 1972

XP553 AwCn 30-11-61; CFS/44 11-12-61; 27MU 22-3-67; NES 29-3-68; sfs B. A. Taylor 22-11-68

XP554 AwCn 30-11-61; CFS/45 7-12-61; 27MU 12-4-67; NES 29-3-68; sfs B. A. Taylor 22-11-68

XP555 AwCn 30-11-61; RAFC/70 21-12-61; 27MU 27-7-71; SOC 1-10-71 Fire Section Manby; remains to Staravia Ascot

XP556 AwCn 12-12-61; RAFC/71 21-12-61; 6FTS/Z 31-3-71; 3FTS/70 19-12-75; CATCS/B 21-10-76; 27MU Shawbury (store) 5-7-89; GI **9027M** 15-2-90; 1 SoTT Halton 11-12-90; tendered 6-93; Bruntingthorpe 31-3-95; Cranwell Heritage Centre, Lincolnshire for display 14-2-96

XP557 AwCn 11 1 62; RAFC/72 12-1-62; 6FTS/T 1-4-71; 3FTS/65 12-12-75; 1 SoTT Halton 29-6-76; Cat 5GI **8494M** 13-5-76; SOC 30-6-76; Phoenix Avn Bruntingthorpe 3-92; South Yorkshire Air Museum, Firbeck 29-1-94; Bomber County Aviation Museum, Hemswell 20-1-96; Dumfries and Galloway Aviation Museum, Dumfries, Scotland 25-3-05

XP558 AwCn 23-1-62; RAFC/73 25-1-62; 3 CAACU/Airwork, Exeter 22-1-70; CAW/20 9-7-70; MoDPE Bedford 25-9-73 for nylon net trials; GI **A2628** 13-5-74; SAH Culdrose 22-5-74; 4SoTT St Athan 19-3-79 as **8627M**; CTTCS St Athan 9-88; CCAS St Athan and dumped; tendered 9-97; KLM UK Apprentice Training, Norwich 1997; Everett Aero 4-01; Eckington, Derbyshire (private; cockpit section)

XP559 AwCn 28-1-62; RAFC/74 30-1-62; 27MU 26-11-69 as Cat 5C; NES 28-11-69; SOC 26-1-70 to Lodge Hill Camp for Joint Services Bomb Disposal School, Chattenden; scrapped 1979

XP560 AwCn 28-1-62; RAFC/75 30-1-62; 6FTS/W 18-3-71; SOC 22-12-75 Fire Section Finningley

XP561 AwCn 26-1-62; RAFC/76 30-1-62; 1FTS/51 9-9-66; control lost in cloud and abandoned 15m SW Linton-on-Ouse, Yorks 21-2-68; SOC 22-2-68

XP562 AwCn 19-2-62; RAFC/77 22-2-62; 3FTS/49 20-9-66; 27MU 29-9-69; NES 29-9-69; sfs 18-12-70 B. A. Taylor, West

164. Jet Provost, XP547, was the original production Mk.4 airframe and operated by the Tactical Weapons Unit at Brawdy from February 1976 until the type was withdrawn in March 1989. (Geoff Lee via Bill Perrins)

Bromwich, wings to Staravia, Lasham by 1972, then Staravia, Ascot; scrapped during 1976

XP563 AwCn 26-1-62; RAFC/78 31-1-62; CATCS/L 27-10-71; 6FTS/S 30-9-74; 3FTS/71 19-12-75; CATCS/C 13-10-76; 27MU 7-7-89; GI **9028M** 15-2-90; 1 SoTT Halton 3-4-91; Phoenix Avn Bruntingthorpe 3-95; Witney Technical College, Oxfordshire 8-1-96; Bicester 1998; Everett Aero, Sproughton 7-1-00; Busan City, South Korea (private) 4-07

XP564 AwCn 26-1-62; RAFC/79 31-1-62; 3FTS/61 3-2-70; CATCS/L 29-10-70; 6FTS/Q 22-10-71; CATCS/M 30-11-72; 6FTS/M 5-11-74; TWU/04 12-1-76; crashed into Nant-Y-Moch reservoir near Llandeilo, Dyfed after the crew ejected following throttle failure 22-4-82, Cat 5S 23-4-82; SOC 2 6-83

XP565 AwCn 29-1-62; RAFC/80 1-2-62; 27MU 24-9-71; NES 24-9-71; SOC 8-10-71; Fire Section Shawbury 14-8-72

XP566 AwCn 1-2-62; RAFC/81 2-2-62; crashed 2m N Cranwell while on night approach (1k), Cat 5S 30-4-70; SOC 1-5-70

XP567 AwCn 20-2-62; RAFC/84 22-2-62; 6FTS/R 21-5-71; CATCS/C 21-10-74; Cat 5GI **8510M** 27-3-77; 1 SoTT Halton/23 30-3-77; Richard J. Everett, Ipswich 4-93; sold USA and reg **N8272M** Randall K. Hames, Gaffney SC 8-5-95; Ricky A. Mantei, Columbia, SC, later Zephyr Hills, FL 17-11-97; Mantei & Associates Ltd, Lexington, SC, 26-10-10

XP568 AwCn 15-2-62; RAFC/85 19-2-62; 27MU 23-6-71; NES 23-6-71; Cat 5S 1-10-71; Hatfield Tech College 8-11-71; Park Avn Supply, Faygate (nose section) by 9-83, fuselage to Stratford Aircraft Collection, Long Marston by 7-89; East Midland Aeropark 10-08

XP569 AwCn 22-2-62; RAFC/86 2-3-62; 2FTS/30 15-9-66, spun into the ground at East Drayton near Tuxford, Notts (2) Cat 5S 30-12-66; SOC 30-12-66

XP570 AwCn 28-2-62; CFS/46 13-3-62; RAFC/68 21-4-66; 6FTS/43 19-9-66; 27MU 25-4-67; NES 29-3-68; sfs B. A. Taylor 22-11-68

XP571 AwCn 28-2-62; CFS/47 2-3-62; 6FTS/44 21-5-66; 27MU 9-2-67; NES 29-3-68; sfs B. A. Taylor 22-11-68

XP572 AwCn 7-3-62; CFS/48 13-3-62; 27MU 1-3-67; NES 29-3-68; sfs B. A. Taylor 22-11-68

XP573 AwCn 28-2-62; CFS/49 13-3-62; 1FTS/49 16-5-66; to Min Tech at BS Eng 8-3-67 for fuel system and engine flame-out trials; 27MU 13-11-70; 5MU 16-2-73; NES 20-2-73; Cat 5GI 21-3-73 **8336M**; 1 SoTT Halton 9-8-73 (painted as **8236M**); tendered 6-93; Jersey Airport, Channel Islands for use by Air UK as GI 15-7-94; Fire Section Jersey 1995

165

XP574 AwCn 19-3-62; 3FTS/45 3-4-62; 27MU 14-7-69; NES 14-7-69; sfs Bradbury, Bournemouth 17-2-70

XP575 AwCn 2-3-62; CFS/50 13-3-62; RAFC/92 12-3-65; CAW/33 30-9-66; 27MU 12-5-69; NES 13-5-69; sfs Bradbury 11-11-69

166

XP576 AwCn 22-3-62; 3FTS/42 27-3-62; MoA Luton for wing crack repair 8-1-65 – 21-1-65; 3FTS/42, engine failure while in the circuit and crashed nr Leeming 16-3-70; Cat 5S and SOC

XP577 AwCn 20-3-62; 3FTS/41 26-3-62; 27MU 15-8-69 as NES; sfs B. A. Taylor 18-12-70

XP578 AwCn 20-3-62; 3FTS/40 21-3-62; 27MU 3-6-69 as NES; sfs Bradbury 17-2-70

XP579 AwCn 28-3-62; 3FTS/44 3-4-62; 27MU 27-1-69 as Cat 5C; sfs B. A. Taylor 13-5-69; cockpit section to 27 MU Shawbury Fire Section 6-76

XP580 AwCn 29-3-62; 3FTS/47 6-4-62; 1FTS/ 9-3-65; CAW/34 26-4-65; overstressed on 21-5-68, Cat 4R DA 12-7-68, Recat 5C

9-8-68; 27MU as NES; 431MU RAF Brüggen for camouflage trials 7-1-69, scrapped

XP581 AwCn 27-3-62; 3FTS/43 3-4-62; FACat Prov4R 21-5-64 Recat 3R 13-10-64; RoS 14-10-64 – 30-10-64; 3FTS/43 4-11-64; 27MU 8-5-69; NES 8-5-69; sfs Bradbury, Bournemouth 11-11-69

XP582 AwCn 30-3-62; 3FTS/46 3-4-62; 27MU 26-6-67; NES 29-3-68; sfs B. A. Taylor 22-11-68

XP583 AwCn 30-3-62; RAFC/87 4-4-62; 6FTS/S 26-3-71; CAW/12 2-11-72; 4FTS Valley 27-11-73; SOC 11-1-74 as **8400M** for Crash Rescue Training at Valley; Manston Fire School, Kent 13-11-79

XP584 AwCn 30-3-62; RAFC/88 4-4-62; 27MU 18-12-69; NES 26-1-71; SOC 1-10-71

XP585 AwCn 30-3-62; RAFC/89 4-4-62; 6FTS/45 7-10-66; RAFC/89 24-6-68; 27MU 22-1-70; 5MU 16-2-73; NES 25-6-74; 4 SoTT St Athan 7-10-74 as Cat 5 GI **8407M;** 1 SoTT Halton 4-77; tendered and sold to Phoenix Aviation, Bruntingthorpe 6-93; North East Wales Institute, Wrexham, Wales (renamed as Glyndwr University) 26-10-93

XP586 AwCn 30-3-62; RAFC/90 4-4-62, recoded PCN (Flt Lt P. C. Norris); 27MU 22-9-71; NES 24-9-71; sfs Staravia 14-8-72

XP587 AwCn 6-4-62; 3FTS/48 11-4-62; 27MU 21-11-68; NES 21-11-68; sfs B. A. Taylor 13-5-69

XP588 AwCn 17-4-62; CFS/51 27-4-62; spurious e/fire and abandoned near Chedworth, Glos Cat 5S 2-5-63 and SOC

XP589 AwCn 27-4-62; 1FTS/36 3-5-62; 27MU 18-10-67; NES 4-11-69; sfs B. A. Taylor 18-12-70

XP614 AwCn 30-4-62; 2FTS/41 1-5-62; Cat 3R DA 4-11-69; to 27MU as Cat 5C 12-11-69; NES 28-11-69; sfs B. A. Taylor 18-12-70

XP615 AwCn 26-4-62; 1FTS/35 27-4-62; 27MU 27-2-70; NES 27-2-70; sfs Shackleton 15-2-71

XP616 AwCn 30-4-62; 1FTS/37 3-5-62; flew into hill in bad weather, Newgate Hill, 4m NW Helmsley, Yorks (1k) 14-9-66 and SOC Cat 5S

XP617 AwCn 27-4-62; 3FTS/49 1-5-62; 7FTS/H 17-9-64; 2FTS/49 21-3-66; 27MU 22-12-69; NES 23-12-69; sfs B. A. Taylor 18-12-70

XP618 AwCn 30-4-62; 3FTS/50 2-5-62; 27MU 17-3-70; 27MU and NES 18-3-70; sfs Shackleton 15-2-71

XP619 AwCn 30-4-62; 2FTS/40 1-5-62; 27MU 23-7-69 and NES 24-7-69; sfs Bradbury 17-2-70

XP620 AwCn 18-5-62; 2FTS/43 21-5-62; 27MU 23-12-69; NES 30-4-71; SOC 1-10-71

XP621 AwCn 23-5-62; 1FTS/38 24-5-62; 3FTS/39 11-9-62; Cat 5S 15-11-65 fire wg and abandoned 5m SW Catterick; SOC 17-11-65

XP622 AwCn 18-5-62; 2FTS/45 21-5-62; Cat 5S 20-9-63 engine failure on t/o and crashed Wymeswold, SOC

XP623 AwCn 18-5-62; 2FTS/44 21-5-62; Cat 5S 19-4-63 abandoned in spin, crashed Thrussington, Charnwood, Leics and SOC

XP624 AwCn 21-5-62; 2FTS/48 23-5-62; RAFC/69 13-5-66; 2FTS/31 15-9-66; 27MU 22-12-69; NES 23-12-69; sfs Shackleton 15-2-71

XP625 AwCn 21-5-62; 2FTS/49 23-5-62; CAW/33 31-3-65; Cat 5S 27-7-66 bird strike and crashed nr Nth Frodingham, Yorks; SOC 28-7-66

XP626 AwCn 30-5-62; 1FTS/39 31-5-62; 27MU 25-3-70; NES 26-3-70; sfs 15-2-71 Shackleton

XP627 AwCn 30-5-62; 1FTS/40 31-5-62; 3FTS/60 1-4-70; 6FTS/Q 23-1-71; 27MU 28-5-71; NES 28-5-71; SOC Cat 5S 1-10-71; HSA Hatfield 25-10-71 for structural tests; Mosquito Museum, London Colney 1979; NEAM Sunderland 25-11-80

XP628 AwCn 30-5-62; 2FTS/47 2-6-62; 27MU 22-12-69; NES 23-12-69; sfs B. A. Taylor 18-12-70

XP629 AwCn 31-5-62; 2FTS/46 2-6-62; CAW/26 24-2-65; CATCS/C 14-2-72; 6FTS/R 11-74; 3FTS/66 12-12-75; CATCS/P 22-10-76; 27MU 5-7-89; GI **9026M** 15-2-90; 1 SoTT Halton

165. Following service with the CFS, 1 FTS and engine trials with Bristol Siddeley, Jet Provost T Mk.3, XP573, was relegated as a ground instructional airframe at No.1 SoTT, Halton, as 8336M. It was incorrectly marked as 8236M and is depicted in May 1985. (Gordon Macadie)

166. Seen taxiing out at Bentwaters in May 1967, T Mk.4, XP575, was part of the College of Air Warfare's display team, led by Flt Lt Bill Shrubsole. (Tony Breese Collection)

22-1-91; EODU, North Luffenham 4-92; sold to Everett Aero, Sproughton 2003; Gunsmoke Paintball Park, Hadleigh, Suffolk 2007

XP630 AwCn 31-5-62; 2FTS/50 2-6-62; 27MU 8-12-69; NES 30-4-71; SOC Cat5S 1-10-71

XP631 AwCn 13-6-62; 2FTS/31 15-6-62; Cat 5S 26-5-66 m/a/c XM384 during formation aeros over Woodborough, Notts, and SOC

167

XP632 AwCn 14-6-62; CFS/52 27-6-62; CAW/30 12-3-65; 27MU 25-10-71; NES 26-10-71; SOC Cat 5S 5-11-71; Fire Section Church Fenton 8-5-72

XP633 AwCn 29-6-62; 1FTS/41 9-7-62; 27MU 8-7-70; NES 8-7-70; sfs Blackbushe Engineering Co, Ascot 17-8-71

XP634 AwCn 27-6-62; 6FTS/40 29-6-62; 1FTS/49 20-6-68; 27MU 29-5-70; NES 29-5-70; sfs Blackbushe Eng Co 17-8-71

XP635 AwCn 28-6-62; 6FTS/41 2-7-62; spurious fire wg; abandoned Nether Witton, Morpeth, Northumberland, Cat5S 18-4-63; SOC 22-4-63

XP636 AwCn 29-6-62; 6FTS/43 5-7-62 recoded 42; 3FTS/63 19-6-68; 27MU 23-3-70; NES 23-3-70; sfs Shackleton 15-2-71

XP637 AwCn 29-6-62; 1FTS/42 9-7-62; 27MU 13-5-69; NES 13-5-69; sfs Bradbury's Bournemouth 17-2-70

XP638 AwCn 29-6-72; 6FTS/42 4-7-62; CAW/31 11-3-65; CATCS/K 4-2-72; 5MU 6-6-80; CATCS/K 2-9-80; TWU 9-12-81; CATCS/A 19-3-82; TWU 17-5-83; CATCS/A 20-7-83; 27MU Shawbury 5-7-89; GI **9034M** 15-2-90; 1 SoTT Halton 5-2-91; Waddington BDRF by 1994; tendered 9-97; Ystrad Mynach, Mid Glam 7-2-02 (private); scrapped 9-04

XP639 AwCn 10-7-62; CFS/53 20-7-6; Handling Squadron 28-11-62; CFS/53 19-2-63; Cat 5S 12-3-64 m/a/c XR670 during aeros, Moreton-in-Marsh, Glos; SOC 13-3-64

XP640 AwCn 20-7-62; 3FTS/51 24-7-62; CFS/51 10-4-64; CAW/27 26-2-65; 6FTS/M 6-12-73; CATCS/M 5-11-74; GI 26-8-76 **8501M;** 1 SoTT Halton 13-9-76; tendered 6-93; YAM Elvington, Yorks 27-10-93

XP641 AwCn 19-7-62; CFS/ 20-7-62; 2FTS/34 21-12-62; 27MU 22-12-69; NES 23-12-69; sfs Shackleton 15-2-71

XP642 AwCn 13-7-62; CFS/ 20-7-62; 2FTS/39 21-12-62; 27MU 24-11-69; NES 30-4-71; SOC Cat5S 1-10-71; Scrap at 5MU 14-8-72; to Staravia 19-9-79; Bruntingthorpe 2-9-95; Luton 6-97; Nick Collins, Lavendon, Bucks (nose section); Welshpool, Powys 31-7-11

XP661 AwCn 27-7-62; 6FTS/44 8-8-62; Cat 4R control lost in cloud, overstressed in dive, Acklington 27-3-63; Hunting 4-4-63 and commenced RIW 23-4-63; 60MU 4-6-63 and recat 5GI **7819M** 13-6-63; Linton-on-Ouse Ground School, NEVVA Lambton Hall, Chester-le-Street, alloc **8594M** 9-9-63 by 71MU/RAF Exhibition Flt, Abingdon; scrapped 1980

XP662 AwCn 27-7-62, 6FTS/45 8-8-62, Cat 3R crashed at Ouston 19-11-64, RoS 60MU, Recat 4R 3-12-64, BAC Luton 1-1-65, AwCn 31-8-65, 1FTS/48 8-9-65, 2FTS/ 23-7-69, 1FTS/48 22-9-69, 27MU 24-6-70, NES 24-6-70, Sfs Shackleton 15-2-71

XP663 AwCn 15-8-62; 3FTS/52 21-8-62, recoded 35, recoded 59; 27MU 10-11-70; NES 10-11-70; Cat 5S 1-10-71; Staravia, Lasham

XP664 AwCn 20-8-62; 2FTS/42 20-8-62; 27MU 8-12-69; NES 30-4-71; Cat 5S 1-10-71; Fire Section Warton

XP665 AwCn 30-8-62; 2FTS/38 31-8-62; 27MU 8-10-69; NES 26-1-71; sfs Blackbushe Eng 17-8-71

XP666 AwCn 14-9-62; 7FTS/C 19-9-62; 27MU 29-11-66; to BAC 16-6-67 and sold BAC 30-8-67; conversion at Marshalls/G-27-94 30-8-67; S Yemen AF **105** 31-01-68; Singapore AF **355** 1978; UK/Mike Carlton//Hunter Wing/Jet Heritage as **G-JETP** 13-12-83; Brencham Historic Aircraft 4-6-84; Hunter Promotion Ltd 17-6-85; Hunter One Collection 10-87; LGH Aviation 6-1-88; Hunter Wing 3-5-89; Shadow Valley Investments, Paphos, Cyprus 28-5-93; de-reg 18-3-99 and open store at Paphos, Cyprus

XP667 AwCn 13-9-62; 3FTS/38 14-9-62; RAFC/98 15-3-65; 27MU 15-12-69; NES 16-12-69; sfs Shackleton 15-2-71

XP668 AwCn 31-8-62; 7FTS/A 18-9-62; RAFC/66 23-8-65; 1FTS/50 9-9-66; 27MU 25-6-70; NES 26-6-70; sfs Blackbushe Eng Co 17-8-71

XP669 AwCn 13-9-62; 2FTS/49 17-9-62, recoded 37; 27MU 5-12-69; NES 30-4-71; SOC 1-10-71; 5MU Kemble for Staravia 14-8-72, scrapped

XP670 AwCn 31-8-62; 7FTS/B 10-9-62; failed to recover from spin and abandoned Rayon Bank, Cuxwold, Yorks 5-4-66; SOC 12-4-66

XP671 AwCn 21-9-62; RAFC/91 24-9-62; 1FTS/42 2-12-69; 27MU 8-7-70; NES 8-7-70; sfs Blackbushe Eng Co 17-8-71

XP672 AwCn 28-9-72; 2FTS/36 2-10-62; CAW/25 24-2-65; CATCS/C 4-9-70; CAW/25 15-2-72; 3FTS/65 27-11-73; SOC (GI) 15-1-76 as **8458M;** 1SoTT Halton/C/27 16-1-76; tendered 3-92; reg **G-RAFI** Robert M. Muir, Ramsey, Isle of Man 18-12-92; f/f after restoration 27-2-99; Glenn R. Lacey, Epsom 9-11-98; Richard J. Everett, Ipswich & North Weald 2-11-99 (flew as "XP672"); struck-off register 22-11-10; Bruntingthorpe, Leicestershire (private) 29-7-2011

XP673 AwCn 26-9-62; 3FTS/37 27-9-62, recoded 61; 27MU 4-9-69; NES 4-9-69; sfs B. A. Taylor 18-12-70

XP674 AwCn 28-9-62; 6FTS/46 1-10-62; 3FTS/65 24-6-68; DA 17-4-70; 27MU 29-5-70 as Cat 5; NES 3-6-70; sfs Shackleton 15-2-71

XP675 AwCn 28-9-62; 7FTS/D 3-10-62; 27MU 25-11-66; CFS/48 23-2-67; m/a/c XS229 Little Rissington 26-2-68 as Cat 3R and Recat 4R; Recat 5C 29-3-68; 27MU 8-5-68; NES 8-5-68; sfs B. A. Taylor 22-11-68

XP676 AwCn 11-10-62; 6FTS/47 25-10-62; 3FTS/64 19-6-68; 27MU 17-8-70; NES 24-8-70; sfs Shackleton 15-2-71

XP677 AwCn 10-10-62; 2FTS/35 12-10-62; 27MU 24-11-69; NES 30-4-71; Cat 5S 1-10-71; RAF Exhibition Flt, Bicester/ Abingdon 7-10-71, nose section as GI **8587M;** 2530 ATC Sqn, Headley Court; ATC Sqn, Uckfield 3-10-85; 1643 ATC Sqn, East Grinstead 1994; sold 12-04

XP678 AwCn 16-10-62; 7FTS/E 19-10-62; 27MU 6-11-66; 1FTS/45 17-3-67; 27MU 9-7-70; NES 9-7-70; sfs Blackbushe Eng Co 17-8-71

XP679 AwCn 19-10-62; 7FTS/F 29-10-62; 27MU 8-12-66; CFS/45 11-4-67; 1FTS/36 26-1-68; 3FTS/50 22-4-70; 27MU 14-12-70; NES 21-12-70; sfs Blackbushe Eng Co 17-8-71

XP680 AwCn 30-10-62; 6FTS/48 5-11-62; CAW/N 12-5-64; recoded 23; 6FTS/Q 3-7-73; 4 SoTT St Athan 30-12-75 as GI **8476M;** St Athan dump by 10-92; F&ETC Moreton-in-Marsh 12-93

XP681 AwCn 30-10-62; 7FTS/G 8-11-62; 1FTS/53 25-10-66; 27MU 10-7-70; NES 10-7-70; sfs Shackleton 15-2-71

XP682 AwCn 31-10-62; 7FTS/H 20-11-62; Cat 5S 27-7-64 wire strike and crashed Scotton, Lincs (1); SOC 30-7-64

XP683 AwCn 29-11-62; 6FTS/49 10-12-62; 1FTS/51 20-6-68; 27MU 26-6-70; NES 26-6-70; SOC 1-10-71; sfs Staravia 14-8-72; fuselage to Pinewood Studios for film work, scrapped 1989

XP684 AwCn 21-11-62; 7FTS/J 29-11-62; 27MU 30-11-66; BAC 14-6-67; sold to BAC 30-8-67; Marshalls for conv to T 52 14-6-67; BAC Warton as G-27-93 30-8-67; South Yemen AF as 106 18-12-67

XP685 AwCn 22-11-62; 7FTS/K 29-11-62; 27MU 5-12-66; 2FTS/28 3-3-67; 27MU 23-12-69; NES 30-4-71; SOC 1-10-71; to 5MU for Staravia 14-8-72

XP686 AwCn 30-11-62; 3FTS/35 4-12-62; CAW/32 25-3-65; CATCS/32 24-8-70; CAW/32 2-9-70; 6FTS/S 2-11-72; CATCS/L 30-9-74; 1 SoTT Halton GI **8502M/B/G** 31-8-76; EODU North Luffenham as GI 4-92; Everett Aero, Sproughton 2003; Gunsmoke Paintball Park, Hadleigh, Suffolk, 2007

XP687 AwCn 30-11-62; 3FTS/36 4-12-62 recoded 60; 27MU and Cat 5C 17-2-70; Sfs J Shackleton 15-2-71

XP688 AwCn 30-11-62; RAFC/92 10-12-62; CAW/M 29-4-64, recoded 22; 3FTS/69 11-73; CATCS/E 18-2-74; 27 MU Shawbury (store) 7-7-89; 1 SoTT Halton as GI **9031M** 23-4-91; tendered

167. Wearing the colour scheme and markings of the display team of No.2 FTS, the Vipers, XP630 was operated by the school between June 1962 and December 1969. (Author's Collection)

and to Bruntingthorpe, Leics, 31-10-1993; Botany Bay Village, Chorley,13-2-97; Bolton 12-02; Delph Scuba Diving Centre, Ecclestone and sunk as diving wreck 8-05

XR643 AwCn 20-12-62; 6FTS/50 22-1-63; RAFC/76 8-4-68, recoded DJW (Flt Lt D. J. Willison) 1969; Airwork/3 CAACU (Vampire evaluation) 5-12-69; 5MU Kemble (hack) 10-1-70; 1 SoTT Halton/26 25-5-77; GI **8516M** 12-1-77; sold 7-92; International Air Parts, NSW; Sydney/Bankstown (store) 3-93; stored Bankstown ("RAF 8516M")

168

XR644 AwCn 28-12-62; 6FTS/51 23-1-63; 2FTS/36 25-6-68; 27MU 3-12-69; NES 30-4-71; SOC Cat5S 1-10-71; Fire Section Little Rissington 19-5-72

XR645 AwCn 17-1-63; 7FTS/O 19-1-63, control lost in cloud and abandoned Stellingfleet, Yorks (1) 4-10-66; SOC 5-10-66

XR646 AwCn 23-1-63; 7FTS/P 19-1-63; 27MU 22-11-66; 6FTS/43 26-4-67; 3FTS/68 12-7-68; 6FTS/R 1-2-71; 27MU 28-5-71; NES 28-5-71 SOC Cat 5S 1-10-71; fuselage to HSA, Hatfield, 26-1-72 for structural testing; Halton fire dump

XR647 AwCn 14-1-63; 2FTS/32 30-1-63; CAW/15 5-5-66; 6FTS/25-1-73, m/a/c Jet Provost T4 XS216, during a formation flying exercise and crashed onto a tractor at Norton-Le-Clay, near Boroughbridge, North Yorks, killing two farm hands, the crew ejected safely 7-5-73; Cat 5S and SOC 7-5-73

XR648 AwCn 28-1-63; 2FTS/33 30-1-63; 27MU 22-12-69; NES 23-12-69; sfs B. A. Taylor 18-12-70

XR649 AwCn 12-3-63; 6FTS/53 20-3-63; CAW/11 10-7-68; 27MU 9-9-71; NES 10-9-71; SOC Cat 5S 1-10-71; Fire Section Ouston 14-3-72

XR650 AwCn 13-3-63; 7FTS/L 15-3-63; CAW/24 22-2-66; 3FTS/56 19-2-70; CATCS/P 30-11-70; CAW/11 2-11-72; 3FTS/66

27-11-73; Cat 5GI as **8459M** 19-12-75; 1SoTT Halton /23 21-1-76; dump by 10-92; Boscombe Down /23 by 5-93; Boscombe Down Avn Collection, Old Sarum by 1999

XR651 AwCn 13-3-63; 7FTS/M 15-3-63; 27MU 21-11-66; 3FTS/53 19-4-70; CATCS/M 6-11-70; CAW/19 30-11-72; 3FTS/70 27-11-73; w/up Leeming 11-74; Cat5 GI as **8431M/A** 8-11-74; 1 SoTT Halton 17-1-75; scrapped 7-92

XR652 AwCn 11-3-63; 6FTS/52 22-3-63, FA at Crosby 27-5-65; Recat4R 11-8-65; DA Cat 4R FA 27-8-65; BAC RIW 8-10-65, AwCn 7-12-66; 27MU 12-12-66; BAC Warton 13-6-67 for T 52 conv at Marshalls; G-27-92, to South Yemen AF as **107** 18-12-67

XR653 AwCn 14-3-63; 7FTS/N 22-3-63; 27MU 29-11-66; CAW/16 20-4-67; CATCS/A 24-8-70; CAW/15 25-1-73; 3FTS/68 6-12-73, CATCS/H 9-4-75; 27MU Shawbury 5-7-89; Cat.5 GI **9035M/H** 15-2-90; 1 SoTT Halton 12-3-91; tendered 7-92; International Air Parts, Sydney-Bankstown, NSW, (arr 3-93; store); Nick Costin/ Australian Fighter Flight Centre, Sydney-Bankstown NSW 2001; Australian Aviation Museum, Bankstown, NSW 2001 (loan, displayed in original RAF scheme "XR653/H")

XR654 AwCn 28-3-63; 6FTS/44 2-4-63; RAFC/67 6-5-66; 3FTS/51 30-9-66; CAW/34 15-8-68; 27MU 8-11-71; Cat 5S 25-11-71; Hatfield Tech College 14-2-72; Roger de Clare Adventure Playground, Puckeridge, 8-11-75; Coventry 1977; Bournemouth 1985; Macclesfield Avn Society, Chelford 1988; Barton 13-8-94 (cockpit section); Huntington, Chester 2-99 (cockpit section)

XR655 AwCn 21-3-63; 7FTS/Q 29-3-63; recoded V; 1FTS/52 29-9-66; 27MU 27-11-69; NES 28-11-69; Cat 5S 1-10-71; sfs J. Shackleton & Company, Siddal, Halifax, wings to Staravia at Lasham by 1972

XR656 AwCn 28-3-63; 6FTS/54 2-4-63; RAFC/67 24-6-68; (loan No.228 OCU Coningsby); Airworks (loan) 13-5-69; RAFC/ 28-7-69; 27MU 26-1-70; NES 26-1-71; Cat 5C 1-10-71, sfs B. A. Taylor, West Bromwich

XR657 AwCn 28-3-63; 7FTS/R 2-4-63; 1FTS/37 26-10-66; 27MU 23-6-70; NES 23-6-70; sfs J. Shackleton 15-2-71

XR658 AwCn 29-3-63; 7FTS/S 3-4-63; 27MU 14-12-66; CAW/36 4-4-67; 6FTS/Y 30-3-71; overstressed (10g); canopy shattered, tail and canopy damaged, control lost and crashed near

Gainsborough 26-10-71; SOC Cat 5 GI **8192M** 1-1-72; 6 FTS Finningley as GI; RAF Exhibition Flt, Abingdon by 8-74; Wroughton (store); tendered and sold to the Jet Heritage Centre, Hurn Airport 7-88; exchanged for Swift XF114 at the North East Wales Institute of Higher Education, Connahs Quay, as GI 1-6-90; Holly Farm Garden Centre, Prees, Salop (private) 2016; RAF Manston History Museum, 1-10-16

XR659 AwCn 29-3-63; 6FTS/55 1-4-63; 3FTS/67 14-7-68; 27MU 10-11-70; NES 10-11-70; sfs Blackbushe Eng Co, Ascot 17-8-71

XR660 AwCn 29-3-63; 6FTS/56 2-4-63; CAW/17 27-6-68; CATCS/Q 4-2-72; 4FTS/Q (Fairford det hack) 21-4-72; Cat 3R GA 17-7-72; DA 21-7-72; ROS 71MU 26-7-72; Recat 5 17-8-72; GI **8374M** 15-9-73; Linton-on-Ouse for display 17-8-72; Fire Section 23-12-74; scrapped

XR661 AwCn 29-3-63; 7FTS/T 3-4-63; 27MU 30-11-66; 3FTS/10-5-67; BAC Warton 15-6-67; sold BAC Warton 30-8-67; conv Marshalls as T 52 (G-27-95), South Yemen AF as **108** 31-1-68

XR662 AwCn 29-3-63; 7FTS/U 3-4-63; 27MU 23-11-66; 6FTS/44 9-2-67; CAW/35 3-7-68; RAFC/98 16-2-70; CATCS/B 24-11-71; CAW/24 2-11-72; 3FTS/72 6-12-73; Cat 5 GI **8410M** 23-5-74; 1 SoTT Halton/25 6-6-74; Finningley for fire & rescue 9-2-94; tendered 2-95; Kemble 1997 and sold Delta Jets Kemble as spares, remains to Bicester by 10-1-98; 196 ATC Sqn (Walsall) & Boulton Paul Heritage Centre, Wolverhampton 11-12-99; Baxterley (store) 3-12; Tettenhall Transport Heritage Centre, Wolverhampton

XR663 AwCn 31-3-63; 6FTS/57 23-4-63; Cat FA 3R 25-3-68 overstressed; RoS/60MU 18-4-68; Recat FA 4R 2-7-68; 27MU as Cat 5C 13-7-68; Recat 5C 15-7-68; NES 13-8-68; SOC 6-12-68 to 431MU Brüggen for camouflage trials 6-12-68

XR664 AwCn 18-4-63; 6FTS/41 18-4-63; FA Cat5 30-9-64 bird strike and abandoned 3m NE Jedburgh, Roxborough and SOC; Fire Section Little Rissington

XR665 AwCn 30-4-6; 1FTS/38 2-5-63; 27MU 22-5-70; NES 22-5-70; sfs Shackleton 15-2-71

XR666 AwCn 30-4-63; 6FTS/58 2-5-63; 1FTS/47 5-3-68; 27MU 9-4-70; Cat 5C 9-4-70; NES 10-4-70; sfs Blackbushe Eng Co 17-8-71

XR667 AwCn 30-4-63; 2FTS/44 3-5-63; 3FTS/51 6-10-69; CATCS/F 9-10-70; CAW/16 28-10-71; 6FTS/P 15-3-73; Cat 5C and SOC 12-12-75

XR668 AwCn 31-5-63; 1FTS/45 8-6-63; 27MU 17-3-67; NES 9-10-67; sfs B. A. Taylor 22-11-68

XR669 AwCn 29-5-63; Free Loan MoA 29-5-63 and allocated to Hunting 28-5-63 for TIs and spinning trials; RAE Farnborough 3-12-65 for wind tunnel rain/icing tests; BAC Warton 6-5-66 for development work and TIs then 7-2-68 canopy jettison flight trials and stalling checks against the Mk 5; 27MU 24-3-69; Bristol A/C as BAC 1-11 chase a/c to 27-8-69; 27MU 28-8-69; Cat 5 GI **8062M** 18-11-69; 1 SoTT Halton 26-11-69; reduced to fuselage 26-8-77; SOC and scrapped 7-5-81

169

XR670 AwCn 29-5-63; CFS/51 5-6-63; Cat4R 12-3-64 m/a/c XP639 over Moreton-in-Marsh, Glos; DA 16-3-64; BAC 8-4-64; RIW 23-4-64; 27MU 30-12-64; 7FTS/Y 17-1-66; 2FTS/29 25-11-66; 27MU 9-7-68; 5MU 25-3-69; 1FTS/54 23-4-69; 3FTS/63 5-5-70; CATCS/D 16-10-70; CAW/14 9-3-72; 3FTS/64 26-11-73; Cat 5 GI Halton **8498M** 30-7-76; JATE Brize Norton 1-3-91; Odiham as GI 15-3-91; tendered 9-97; Clacton, Essex 2000; Everett Aero, Sproughton 12-02; Hermeskeil Museum, Germany 4-2003

XR671 AwCn 28-5-63; CFS/54 5-6-63; 2FTS/48 31-5-66; CFS/48 18-2-69; 27MU 14-10-69; NES 14-11-69; sfs B. A. Taylor 18-12-70

168. Former mount of RAF Cranwell's Wright Jubilee Trophy winner in 1969, Jet Provost T Mk.4, XR643, was later operated as a 'hack' with No.5 MU Kemble between January 1970 and May 1977. (BAe Systems Heritage Warton-Percival/Hunting Collection)

169. Initially allocated to Hunting Aircraft for spinning trials, XR669 also acted as a chase aircraft for the BAC 1-11 before being finally scrapped in 1981. The original caption for this image states: 'Tufted for stall warning tests, November 1967'. (BAC via Reg Stock)

XR672 AwCn 31-5-63; 1FTS/43 6-6-63; 3FTS/48 27-2-70; CATCS/H 30-9-70; CAW/11 6-9-71; 6FTS/V 10-11-72; 3FTS/73 19-12-75; Cat 5 GI **8495M** 13-5-76; 1 SoTT Halton/70/50/239 14-6-76; fuselage used as horse jump on a/f 07-92; replaced by XW303 6-3-06; scrapped 2008

XR673 AwCn 18-6-63; 2FTS/30 24-6-63; RAFC/97 15-3-65; 6FTS/V 28-4-71; CATCS/B 10-11-72; 3FTS/75 30-6-75; CATCS/L 12-8-76; 27 MU Shawbury 5-7-89; Cat 5 GI **9032M** 15-2-90; 1 SoTT Halton 3-91; tendered 9-95; Gosh That's Aviation, North Weald 18-12-95, (Howard Rose, North Weald for restoration to airworthiness); reg **G-BXLO** Howard Rose/HCR Aviation Ltd, North Weald 14-8-97; Stewart J. Davies & Shaun Eagle, Sandoft 2-11-04; Century Aviation Ltd, Barnsley 9-6-09 (flies as RAF "XR673"); Century Aviation Ltd, Gamston, 2015

170

XR674 AwCn 31-5-63; 1FTS/44 6-6-63; 3FTS/54 28-4-70; CATCS/B 2-10-70; CAW 8-11-71; CATCS/E 20-3-72; 3FTS/74 18-2-74; CATCS/D 10-3-75; 27 MU Shawbury 5-7-89; GI **9030M** 15-2-90; No.1SoTT Halton/D 25-4-91; tendered 6-93; Gosh That's Aviation Ltd, North Weald 31-8-94 and reg **G-TOMG;** restored to flying condition and ff North Weald 18-9-95 as "XW928"; Kingspride Associates Ltd, Lydd 21-2-97 (flew as RAF "The Swords XW428"), hit ground during low-level steep turn and destroyed, Woolaston, Glos (2) 1-8-99

XR675 AwCn 18-6-63; 6FTS/59 21-6-63; 3FTS/66 24-6-68; RAFC/ 20-5-70; 27MU 29-6-70; NES 29-6-70; sfs Blackbushe Eng Co 17-8-71

XR676 AwCn 19-6-63; 7FTS/W 21-6-63; 3FTS/52 3-11-66; 27MU and Cat strip 28-9-70; NES 23-9-70; sfs Blackbushe Eng Co 17-8-71

XR677 AwCn 19-6-63; 3FTS/34 26-6-63; recoded 58; 27MU 9-9-70; NES 9-9-70; sfs Blackbushe Eng Co 17-8-71

XR678 AwCn 28-6-63; CFS/55 3-7-63; 27MU 4-3-69; NES 4-3-69; sfs Bradbury 11-11-69

XR679 AwCn 28-6-63; RAFC/93 2-7-63; CAW/L 29-4-64, recoded 21; Airwork Exeter 19-2-70; CAW/21 1-5-70; 3FTS/SRF/62 6-12-73; 1 TWU/04 26-4-82; GI **8991M** 22-3-89; 2 SoTT Cosford/04 3-89; tendered and sold Global Avn Binbrook 19-11-93; Jet Provost Club, reg **G-BWGT** 21-8-95; R. E. Todd Doncaster 14-10-96; G. M. Snow Wigan 4-2-08; sold Canada struck-off reg. 4-3-09; re-reg **C-FDJP;** P. G. Rawlinson, Progressive Concepts Inc., Drumbo, Ont, 20-12-12, (operated by Jet Aircraft Museum, London, Ont)

171

XR680 AwCn 28-6-63; 6FTS/60 10-7-63; CFS/45 8-3-68; 27MU 18-3-70; NES 30-4-71; Cat 5S 1-10-71; Fire Section Church Fenton 8-5-72

XR681 AwCn 19-7-63; RAFC/94 19-7-63; 6FTS/Q 12-5-71; CATCS/Q 30-7-71; 27MU 5-8-71; NES 6-8-71; Cat 5S 1-10-71 and b/up; GI **8588M** (nose) RAF Exhibition Flt Bicester 21-9-71; 1349 ATC Sqn, Woking (kept at Odiham) 3-9-85; 1216 ATC Sqn, Newhaven 1993; Robertsbridge Aviation Centre, Mayfield, East Sussex 2002

XR697 AwCn 19-7-63, 3FTS/33 31-7-63, recoded 56; 27MU 2-8-69; NES 12-8-69; sfs B. A. Taylor 18-12-70

XR698 AwCn 31-7-63, 3FTS/32 7-8-63, stalled during a practice forced landing and belly-landed at Leeming, Yorks 3-1-64, Cat 5S; DA & SOC 7-1-64; Fire School Leeming

XR699 AwCn 30-7-63; 1FTS/34 1-8-63; 27MU 25-3-70; NES 26-3-70; sfs Shackleton 15-2-71

XR700 AwCn 31-7-63; 1FTS/46 7-8-63; 3FTS/49 27-2-70; CATCS/N 16-11-70; 27MU 5-8-71; NES 6-8-71; SOC Cat 5S 1-10-71; fuselage to Bicester and reduced to nose section as **8589M** for RAF Exhibition Flt, Abingdon 7-10-71; Belfast Exhibition

Flight, Aldergrove 12-1981; Ulster Avn Society, Long Kesh; No.1137 Sqn ATC, Long Kesh

XR701 AwCn 27-8-63; 1FTS/47 29-8-63, Cat 3R belly-landed, Rufforth 26-5-67; Recat 4R and RoS 60MU 14-6-67; BAC Warton RIW 24-10-67; 27MU 8-8-68; CAW/26 14-2-72; 3FTS/RFS/63 12-73, recoded 70; St Athan 27-10-76; AAEE 29-5-81 for ETPS cont trg and trials support photo; BAC Warton 25-5-84 (TI of ASR.889); CATCS/K 12-10-84; 27 MU Shawbury 8-8-89; GI **9025M** 15-2-90;1 SoTT Halton/K by 2-91; tendered 12-92; Harry Pound Portsmouth 1993; Everett Aero 4-93; sold USA and reg **N8272** W Randall K. Hames, Gaffney, SC 8-5-95; Joni B. Hames, Gaffney, SC 2-1-97; re-reg **N204JP** Richard Griggs, Cheraw, SC 15-5-02; RAF Linton-Texas Squadron LLC, Houston, TX 8-5-11

XR702 AwCn 29-8-63; 3FTS/31 30-8-63, recoded 46; 27MU 30-12-69; NES 31-12-69; sfs B. A. Taylor 18-12-70

XR703 AwCn 29-08-63; 3FTS/30 30-08-63, recoded 57; 27MU 28-04-70; NES 29-04-70; sfs Shackleton 15-02-71

XR704 AwCn 29-8-63; 27MU 13-9-63; CFS/56 16-1-64; CAW/28 26-2-65; Cat 3R 19-9-73; RoS 71MU 25-9-73 – 4-12-73; 6FTS/N 6-12-73; St Athan (hack) 19-12-75; GI 8506M 5-10-76; 1SoTT Halton/30/M 28-3-78; dumped by 10-92; Harry Pound, Portsmouth 1993; R. J. Everett, Ipswich 4-93; sold USA as N8272Y to Randall K. Hames, Gaffney, SC 8-5-95; Joni B. Hames, Gaffney, SC 2-1-97; Airmans Aviation Co, Fort Smith, AR 17-1-01; Bobby R. Young, Burnsville, NC 11-07

XR705 AwCn 12-9-63; 27MU 13-9-63; CFS/57 16-1-64; CAW/29 26-2-65; 27MU 4-11-69; 5MU 9-2-73; NES 14-2-73; SOC 17-10-73 to Fire School Manston

XR706 AwCn 20-9-63; 27MU 25-9-63; 6FTS/62 16-1-64; 2FTS/32 5-7-68; CFS/48 8-10-69; 27MU 22-1-70; NES 26-1-71; SOC 1-10-71 Fire School Catterick

XR707 AwCn 25-9-63; 2FTS/45 2-10-63; RAFC/95 13-10-69; 27MU 7-6-71; NES 7-6-71; Cat 5S 1-10-71; SOC as CAT 5(S) for 2371 ATC Sqn, at Sir William Marteneau School (retained at Cosford) as **8193M** (ntu); Hatfield fire section 12-11-71; burnt by 1975

XS175 AwCn 30-9-63; 27MU 8-10-63; 7FTS/X 16-1-64; 27MU 9-12-66, CFS/44 22-3-67; 27MU 6-11-69; NES 26-1-71; sold BAC

Preston (apprentice trg) 7-7-71; Preston Tech College by 1980; reportedly scrapped by 1986

XS176 AwCn 3-10-63; 27MU 3-10-63; 2FTS/28 10-1-64, recoded 36; 27MU 9-7-68; 5MU 18-10-68; 27MU 1-11-68; 3FTS/47 27-1-69; CATCS/O 24-11-70; CAW/18 28-2-72; 3FTS/73 6-12-73; 5MU 25-2-74; 3FTS/71 26-2-75; CATCS B 30-6-75; GI **8514M** 13-12-76; 1SoTT Halton/M 24-3-77; Halton dump by 2-93; tendered 6-93; Phoenix Avn Bruntingthorpe 27-10-93; Univ of Salford, Gt Manchester 3-11-93; Bruntingthorpe 15-7-99; Alan Bleatman, Salford (nose) 8-99; Highland Avn Museum, Dallachy, Moray 18-6-05

XS177 AwCn 31-10-63; 27MU 11-11-63; RAFC/95 13-1-64; 2FTS/30 13-1-67; 27MU 11-7-68; 5MU 10 1 69; 27MU 30-1-69; Airwork, Exeter 1-4-69; 3FTS/43 8-7-69; CATCS/K 26-10-70; CAW/17 4-2-72; 3FTS/67 26-11-73; TWU (loan; uncoded) 16-2-76; (AAEE 5-9-77 – 7-9-77 as Harrier photo chase); CATCS 17-8-79; TWU 11-2-87; CATCS/N 29-10-87; St Athan (hack) 10-7-89; GI **9044M** 24-4-90; RAF Valley for crash rescue trg 1991; DCAE Cosford as GI 4-02; tendered 10-05; Everett Aero, Sproughton 7-06; Metheringham Aircraft Centre 9-07; Binbrook 9-12; Mount Pleasant Farm, Allensdale, Hexham (private) 7-5-14

172

170. Jet Provost Mk. 4, XR673, of No.2 FTS, RAF Syerston, formates with the camera ship in April 1964. (Canadian Forces Joint Imagery Centre)

171. Wearing the exotic colours of its owner, Eddie Todd, Jet Provost T Mk.4, G-BWGT/XR679, at Linton-on-Ouse in July 1979. It was later sold to a buyer in Canada and operated by Jet Aircraft Museum, Ontario, as C-FDJP. (Roger Lindsay)

172. Jet Provost T Mk.4, XS177, of the CATCS, RAF Shawbury, 1971. It is currently stored at Hexham. (via Claire Williamson)

XS178 AwCn 14-11-63; 27MU 21-11-63; 7FTS/Y 9-1-64; CFS/53 6.4.64; RAFC/99 12-3-65; CATCS/N 26-8-71; 1TWU/05 30-7-79; GI **8994M** 22-3-89; 2SoTT/M Cosford 23-3-89; Global Aviation Ltd, Binbrook 19-11-93; sold Australia (shipped, arr. dismantled Devonport 5-94); Project Jet Provost, Devonport TAS and reg **VH-JPP;** F. Rob Edginton, Launceston TAS 13-2-95; (restored Devonport TAS, ff 3-6-95 as "RAF XS178/05"); wfu, struck-off reg 19-6-03; sold to USA as airworthy and reg **N400KT** Jerry D. Laza, Palestine, TX 7-10-04

XS179 AwCn 31-10-63; 27MU 6-11-63; RAFC/ 10-1-64; CAW/K 29-4-64; recoded 20; 27MU 5-11-69; 5MU 16-3-73; NES 22-3-73 & GI **8337M** (painted as 8237M); 1SoTT Halton 20-8-73; Halton dump by 10-92; tendered 6-93; Phoenix Aviation, Bruntingthorpe 27-10-1993; Univ of Salford, Gtr Manchester 3 11-93; Museum of Science & Technology, Swinton 24-9-03 (store); Secret Nuclear Bunker, Hack Green, Cheshire 15-1-13

XS180 AwCn 31-10-63; 27MU 8-11-63; 6FTS/61 9-1-64; CAW/10 3-7-68; 5MU 27-11-72; NES 14-2-73; GI **8338M** (marked as 8238M) 1SoTT Halton 6-8-73; AR&TF St Athan/21 by 4-93; AR&TF Lyneham by 3-96; AR&TF Fairford by 7-96; AR&TF Lyneham and St Athan by 2000; AR&TF Boscombe Down 2011

XS181 AwCn 31-10-63; 27MU 11-11-63; 3FTS/32 14-1-64; RAFC/96 15-3-65; CATCS/F 14-10-71; Brawdy (loan)10-3-83; CATCS/F 15-4-83; Shawbury (store) 5-7-89; GI **9033M** 15-2-90 and No.1 SoTT Halton; Phoenix Avn Bruntingthorpe 31-3-95; Bucks Aircraft Recovery Group, Bletchley Park (nose) 2-98; 1084 ATC Sqn, Market Harborough, (located at Bruntingthorpe) 2002; Spanhoe Lodge, Northants 6-10; Lakes Lightnings, Spark Bridge, Cumbria 2012

XS182 Hunting 5-11-63 for hydraulic system investigation but not used; AwCn 29-11-63; 27MU 6-12-63; Hunting 6-1-64; CFS/58 3-2-64; RAFC/93 19-3-65; 6FTS/48 19-9-66; 2FTS/29 25-6-68; 3FTS/55 14-4-69; 27MU 10-11-70; NES 10-11-70; Cat 5S 1-10-71 and scrapped

XS183 AwCn 31-12-63; 27MU 6-1-64; 2FTS/46 10-1-64; 27MU Shawbury 17-11-69; NES 30-4-71; Cat 5S 1-10-71; Shawbury dump; wings to Staravia at Lasham 1972, nose section to Plymouth area, Devon

XS184 AwCn 31-12-63; 3FTS/53 13-1-64, recoded 38, recoded 62; 27MU 14-4-70; NES 15-4-70; Cat 5S 1-10-71; remains to Staravia yard, Ascot and scrapped

XS185 AwCn 8-1-64; 3FTS/54 16-1-64; RAFC/ 18-2-70; 27MU 6-5-70; NES 6-5-70; sfs Shackleton 15-2-71

173

XS186 AwCn 30-1-64; CAW/A 10-2-64, recoded 10; 27MU 19-7-68; 5MU 5-3-73; NES 25-6-74; Cat 5GI **8408M** No.4 SoTT St Athan 7-10-74; 1 SoTT Halton as 8408M/M 4-77; EODU, North Luffenham 1992; Everett Aero, Sproughton 2002; Metheringham Aircraft Visitors Centre, Lincs 5-3-04

XS209 AwCn 30-1-64; CAW/B 10-2-64, recoded 11; 27MU 19-7-68; 5MU 5-3-73; NES 25-6-74; Cat 5GI 6-5-74 **8409M;** No.4 SoTT St Athan 7-10-74; No.1 SoTT Halton/29 4-77; Halton dump and tendered 6-93; Tendered again 9-95 and sold to Phoenix Aviation, Bruntingthorpe for export to USA during 1-96 ntu: Kemble 3-98; Delta Jets, Kemble 3-98; Bruntingthorpe 10-5-02; Solway Aviation Museum, Carlisle 24-6-06

XS210 AwCn 30-1-64; CAW/C 10-2-64, recoded 12; 5MU 27-9-72; NES 14-2-73; GI 8339M 21-3-73 (marked as 8239M); No.1 SoTT Halton/22 6-8-73; tendered and sold to International Air Parts, Sydney, NSW 7-92 and stored; Skyline Avn, Devonport 3-97 for restoration

XS211 AwCn 30-1-64; CAW/D 16-2-64, recoded 14; CATCS/D 9-3-72; 3FTS/72 10-3-75; abandoned following engine failure due to fuel starvation during an overshoot at Leeming, 13-2-76 Cat 5S; SOC 13-2-76

XS212 AwCn 19-2-64; CAW/E 4-3-64, recoded 15; CFS/40 28-4-66; 27MU 18-2-70; NES 18-2-70; sfs B. A. Taylor 18-12-70

XS213 AwCn 25-2-64; CAW/F 5-3-64, recoded 16; CFS/46 20-5-66; 27MU 2-12-69; NES 13-2-70; Cat 5 GI **8097M** 5-5-70; sold to Kenya AF as GI 18-6-70

XS214 AwCn 28-2-64; CAW/G 4-3-64, recoded 17; 27MU 19-7-68; 5MU 23-2-73; NES 23-3-73; SOC 11-3-74; Fire Section Cranwell

XS215 AwCn 28-2-64; CAW/H 5-3-64, recoded 18; CATCS/O 18-2-72; 3FTS/69 30-1-75; w/u Leeming 11-76; SOC 15-2-77; GI **8507M** 11-10-76; No.1 SoTT Halton/18 15-2-77; tendered and scrapped 11-93

XS216 AwCn 13-3-64; CAW/I 18-3-64, recoded J by 6-64, recoded 19; 6FTS/Q 30-11-72; m/a/c XR647 during a formation flying ex, Finningley 7-5-73; Cat 5 and SOC 5-6-73; fuselage to Eng Wing Finningley for GI by 4-94; Goole ATC; AeroVenture, Doncaster

XS217 AwCn 26-3-64; 27MU 2-4-64; RAFC/69 6-5-64; CFS/50 22-4-66; 5MU 6-7-72; CATCS 12-6-73; 6FTS 31-8-73 (not accepted); 27MU; 6FTS 1-11-73; 3FTS/73 12-2-74; CATCS/O 30-1-75; 27MU Shawbury 5-7-89; Cat 5 GI **9029M** 15-2-90; No.1 SoTT Halton 4-4-91; tendered and to Bruntingthorpe 29-3-95; Wernigerode, Germany 7-05

XS218 AwCn 3-3-64; 27MU 3-4-64; 3FTS/34 27-4-65, recoded 55; 27MU 11-9-68; CAW/30 8-2-72, recoded 10; 3FTS/61 6-12-73, recoded 72 w/up Leeming early 1977; SOC 23-2-77; GI 11-10-76 **8508M**; No.1 SoTT Halton 23-2-77; reduced to cockpit section and to 1116 ATC Sqn, Woodley, Berkshire by 6-92; 447 ATC Sqn, Henley-on-Thames 1994

XS219 AwCn 13-4-63; 27MU 16-4-64; CAW/35 14-6-65; 27MU 19-7-68; CAW/33 30-5-69; CATCS/E 24-8-70; CAW/29 4-2-72; 3FTS/60 26-11-73; recoded 67; CATCS/A 14-7-76; 1TWU/06 19-3-82; GI 22-3-89 **8993M**; No.2 SoTT Cosford/o 3-89; Global Avn Ltd, Binbrook 19-11-93; sold USA and reg **N219JP** to Biggles Air Inc, New Castle, CO 27-5-94; Airborne Emergency Physicians Inc, San Antonio, TX 13-8-96; Pineus Aloof, Houston, TX 31-10-12

XS220 AwCn 3-4-64; 27MU 7-4-64; 3FTS/47 11-5-65; 27MU 4-9-68; Cat 4R 17-10-69; NES 28-11-69; sfs 18-12-70 B. A. Taylor

XS221 AwCn 23-4-64; 27MU 27-4-64; FEAF 4-8-65; 389/390MU 16-8-65; J P Trials Unit 8-9-65; 389MU 30-11-65; J P Trials Unit 5-2-66; hit trees and cr near Alor Star, Malaya (1) 5-2-66; Cat 5S 10-2-66; SOC 18-2-66

XS222 AwCn 30-4-64; 27MU 13-5-64; RAFC/68 17-6-65; CFS/43 10-5-66; 27MU 15-12-69; NES 26-1-71; Cat 5S 1-10-71

XS223 AwCn 30-4-64; 27MU 5-5-64; FEAF 3-8-65; 389/390MU 14-8-65; J P Trials Unit 11-9-65; 389MU 30-11-65; JP Trials Unit 9-2-66; 389MU 14-3-66; 27MU; issued 23-3-66 (presumably in FEAF for packing) arr 28-4-66; sold BAC Warton 16-1-67 as / becoming G-27-4; to Marshalls for conv to T Mk.52 for Sth Yemen AF as **101** 12-10-67

XS224 AwCn 25-5-64; 27MU 25-5-64; FEAF 3-8-65; 389/390MU 14-8-65; JP Trials Unit 4-9-65; 389MU 30-11-65; JP Trials Unit 5-2-66; 389MU 14-3-66; 27MU 28-4-66; sold BAC Warton 16-1-67; to Marshalls for conv to T Mk.52 G-27-5 for Sth Yemen AF as **102** 12-10-67

XS225 AwCn 29-5-64; 27MU 4-6-64; 1FTS/49 27-10-65; CFS/47 6-5-66; 27MU 18-3-70; NES 26-1-71; Cat 5S 1-10-71; sfs to B. A. Taylor, West Bromwich 7-1-72

XS226 AwCn 29-5-64; 27MU 5-6-64; CAW/36 4-11-65; CFS/42 7-4-66; 27MU 9-12-69; NES 26-1-71; Cat 5S 1-10-71; sfs to B. A. Taylor, West Bromwich 7-1-72

XS227 AwCn 30-6-64; 27MU 7-7-64; sold BAC Warton 18-1-67; Marshalls for conv to T Mk.52 G27-6 Sth Yemen AF as **103** 26-10-67

XS228 AwCn 30-6-64; 27MU 3-7-64; sold BAC Warton 18-1-67; Marshalls for conv to T Mk.52 G-27-7 for Sth Yemen AF as **104** del 26-10-67; sold to Singapore AF 2-75 as **352**; wfu 14-10-81; sold Mike Carlton Hunter One Collection Biggin Hill/Hurn 11-83; reg **G-PROV** to Brencham Historic Aircraft, Hurn 23-8-84 (ff Hurn 23-11-84); Berowell Management Ltd, Biggin Hill 8-11-85; LGH Aviation Ltd, Hurn 1-10-87; Jet Heritage/ Hunter Wing Ltd, Hurn 3-5-89; Rory McCarthy/Bushfire Investments Ltd, North Weald 12-3-93; Donald S. Milne, Stonehaven 8-2-99; Hollytree Management Ltd/ Provost Group, Sutton & North Weald 18-6-01 (repainted North Weald 7-06 as camouflaged South Arabian AF "104")

174

173. Jet Provost T Mk.4, XS185, of No.3 FTS at Lakenheath on 22 May 1965. The aircraft was sold for scrap in 1971. (Jacques Guillem)

174. Jet Provost T Mk.4, XS228, was converted by Marshall's to a T Mk.52 for the South Yemen air force and delivered on 26 October 1967 as '104'. (Jacques Guillem)

XS229 AwCn 30-6-64; 27MU 8-7-64; 3FTS/49 2-12-65; CFS/49 22-4-66; abandoned following m/a/c XP675 during aeros and cr Hawling, Guiting Power, Glos; Cat 5S and SOC 26-2-68

XS230 AwCn 31-8-64; 27MU Shawbury (store) 29-9-64; MoA Air Fleet, BAC Luton 21-3-65; C(A) 13-7-65 for conv to T Mk.5 (Interim); F/f as T Mk.5 28-2-67; A&AEE/ETPS Boscombe Down 14-1-69; BAC Warton 9-5-69; A&AEE (Rebecca fit) 11-8-69; BAC 2-10-69; A&AEE 22-1-70; BAC 6-3-70 (engine bay airflow); R Royce 29-6-70; BAC 17-5-73; A&AEE 4-3-75; BAC 29-5-75; A&AEE 6-6-75; BAC 13-1-76; 5MU 9-2-76; R Royce 6-2-79; sold Transair (UK) Ltd at MoD auction 26-11-94; reg **G-BVWF** Transair (UK) Ltd, North Weald 7-12-94; (del. to North Weald 21-12.94 – op: Transair Pilot Shop, North Weald); reg cnx and re-reg **G-VIVM** Transair (UK) Ltd, North Weald 25-3-96; Gone Flying Ltd, North Weald 16-5-96; Flight Test Associates Ltd, Coventry/Woodford 16-4-98; Ken Lyndon-Dykes/The Sky's The Limited/Swords Aviation, North Weald 21-11-01; Victor Mike Group, Maidstone 25-11-09

175

XS231 F/f 4-12-64; retained by BAC for devt flying on mods to tailplane and engine of BAC-166 fitted with Viper 20 fitted as T Mk.5 (Interim); reg **G-ATAJ** (ntu) 27-1-65; BAC Luton as BAC-166 with c/n **XS231**; F/f Luton as BAC-166 T Mk.5 (interim) 16-3-65; mod to T Mk.5 and trans to Warton on closure of Luton 11-8-66; f/f 7-67; A&AEE 22-1-70 for devt trials; 5MU 9-2-76; RR Filton 6-2-79 for flight & static resonance tests; 5 MU 14-2-81; Scampton 16-3-88 (spares recovery); fuselage sold for spares to Jet Heritage Hurn 3-89; Phoenix Avn Bruntingthorpe (store) 1990; Everett Aero Sproughton 1999; Tim A. Jones, Sth Molton, Devon 9-6-01; Boscombe Down Avn Collection (nose section) 9-09

XW287 F/f 16-7-69; AwCn 31-8-69; CFS/80 3-9-69; Cat 3R 19-9-73; RAFC/74 15-8-74; 3FTS Leeming (store) 1-4-75; **CWP Leeming tip tanks** by 3-10-75 – 5-11-75; 6FTS/P 5-11-75; 27MU Shawbury (store) 21-9-93; tendered and sold to Global Aviation,

Binbrook 19-11-1993; to USA and reg **N4107K** Ted Truman A. Thomas, Cropwell AL 12-7-94; re-reg **N900SA** Truman A. Thomas, Cropwell, AL 8-95; **N287XW** Truman A. Thomas, Cropwell, AL 29-8-95; Southern Aviation Insurance, Birmingham, AL 19-11-96; M. R. Snedeker/G & S Warbird Locators, Bessemer AL, later Pottsboro, TX 9-04

XW288 AwCn 19-9-69; CFS/81 25-9-69; **BAC Conv T Mk.5A** 10-9-74 – 18-11-74; CFS/81 18-11-74; RAFC/29 28-1-76; 1FTS/66 9-3-77; control lost during a barrel roll over the airfield at Linton-on-Ouse while practising for a forthcoming aerobatics competition (1) 18-5-82; Cat 5C, SOC 2-9-82

176

XW289 AwCn 30-9-69; CFS/82 6-10-69; **BAC Conv T Mk.5A** 24-4-74 – 18-9-74; CFS/82 18-9-74; 5MU 14-10-75; RAFC/31 29-4-79; 1FTS/61 21-4-86; RAFC/16 9-11-88; 1FTS/73 7-91; Linton (store) 6-93; Shawbury (store) 30-9-93; tendered 10-93; reg N287XW (ntu); reg **G-BVXT** (cnx 2-95) Global Aviation Ltd, Binbrook, 18-1-95; reg **G-JPVA** 22-2-1995 Tim J. Manna/Kennet Aviation, Cranfield, later North Weald 22-2-95 (flies as RAF "XW289"); Henry Cooke, RNAS Yeovilton 22-11-07; Colin Boyd & Christopher Heames, Stamford 9-7-14; w/o due landing accident, North Weald, 15-6-16 (spares recovery); reg cnx 4-11-16; Horizon Aircraft Services, St Athan 2016

XW290 AwCn 8-10-69; CFS/83 8-10-69; **BAC Conv T Mk.5A** 30-1-75 – 29-4-75; CFS/83 29-4-75; 5MU 8-12-75; RAFC/41 7-7-79; 3FTS/CFS/41; Shawbury (store) 14-10-88; GI **9199M** 6-7-93; 1 SoTT Cosford/MA as GI 20-7-93; (1 SoTT renamed to DCAE Cosford 1-4-04, renamed DSAE 2012)

XW291 AwCn 20-10-69; CFS/84 23-10-69; RAFC 6-9-74; CFS 16-9-74; RAFC/79 3-10-74; 3FTS Leeming (store) 25-3-75; **CWP Leeming tip tanks** 4-11-75; 6FTS/N 4-12-75; Shawbury (store) 13-4-93; sold Global Aviation Ltd, Binbrook 18-1-95 as **G-BWOF;** Transair (UK) Ltd, North Weald 18-3-96 (restored

North Weald, ff 1-97); Techair London Ltd, Bournemouth 3-3-97; Bournemouth Aviation Museum, Hurn (loan) 4-07

XW292 AwCn 13-11-69; CFS/85 14-11-69; **BAC Conv T Mk.5A** 9-4-74; CFS/85 13-9-74; CFS/85; 5MU 18-11-75; RAFC/32 8-5-79; Shawbury (store) 12-9-91; GI 14-10-91 **9128M;** 1SoTT Halton/M 3-12-91; 2SoTT Cosford 9-94 (2 SoTT renamed 1 SoTT on 24-11-1994, then renamed to DCAE Cosford on 1-4-04); tendered 10-05; Astre Air International, Watkins, CO as **N292XW** 11-1-07

XW293 AwCn 13-11-69, CFS/86 13-11-69, 3FTS Leeming (store) 18-4-75 – 23-10-75; **CWP Leeming tip tanks** by 13-11-75; 6FTS/XX 28-11-75, recoded Z; Shawbury store 22-6-93, tendered and sold as **G-BWCS** Colin P. Allen/ Downbird UK Ltd, Stoke-on-Trent, 28-4-95; Permit to fly expired 24-10-96, struck-off reg 3-7-98; Roland E. Todd, Sandtoft: re-added 7-7-99 (flies as RAF "XW293"); John H. Ashcroft/Jet Provost Club, Sandtoft 27-1-07

XW294 AwCn 25-11-69; CFS/87 26-11-69; **BAC Conv T Mk.5A** 9-1-74; CFS/87 16-7-74; 1FTS/66 9-5-75; 5MU 1-3-76; 3FTS/49 19-2-80; RAFC/45 10-11-81; Shawbury (store) 28-10-91; GI **9129M** 14-10-91; No.1 SoTT Halton/45 5-12-91; transferred to 2 SoTT Cosford 9-94 (2 SoTT renamed 1 SoTT on 24-11-1994, then renamed to DCAE Cosford on 1-4-04; tendered 10-05; Astre Air International, Watkins, CO, USA as N294XW 11-1-07; trans Seattle 9-16

XW295 AwCn (undated); CFS/88 9-12-69; **BAC Conv T Mk.5A** 9-1-74; CFS/88 16-7-74; RAFC/64 30-1-75, recoded 19; 1FTS/67 11-5-77; RAFC/29 7-4-86; Shawbury (store) 18-10-91; tendered 7-92; sold to Wessex Aviation and exported to International Air Parts, Bankstown, Sydney, NSW, Australia,14-10-92; (arrived dismantled Sydney-Bankstown "XW295/29" 6-93; Devonport TAS, ex Bankstown 3-97 for restoration; ff Devonport 28-2-99);

Kevin T. Acres, Warrandyte, Vic, as **VH-JPV** 1-5-98; (del. Devonport to Melbourne-Moorabbin 9-3-99 as RAF "XW295"); Hugh Walthro/Airport Facilities Pty Ltd, Melbourne-Essendon, Vic, 11-00; Essendon Executive Pty Ltd, Essendon Airport 1-11-11 (flies as silver "XW295/29")

XW296 AwCn 31-12-69; 1FTS/57 1-1-70; RAFC/64 10-6-74; 3FTS Leeming (store) 14-3-75; **CWP Leeming tip tanks** 3-10-75 – 5-11-75; 6FTS/Q 5-11-75; Shawbury (store) 21-9-93; sold Global Aviation Ltd, Binbrook 19-11-93; sold Lance Toland Associates, Griffin, GA, USA 94; reg **N4107G** Rudy Beaver, Gadsden, AL12-7-94; International Jets Inc, Gadsden AL 22-11-95; Marshall Air Service, Chesterton, IN 29-4-97; Houston, TX (store) 12-03; struck-off register 5-8-13

XW297 AwCn (undated); CFS 15-12-69; 1FTS/59 20-1-70; abandoned in spin and crashed Kiplingcoates, Yorks 17-9-70 Cat 5C; SOC 17-9-70

XW298 AwCn (undated); 1FTS/55 30-12-69; 3FTS Leeming (store) 3-6-75; **CWP Leeming tip tanks** 16-10-75 – 13-11-75; 6FTS/O 13-11-75; BAe/MODPE Warton C(A) release trials 22-12-83; 6FTS/O 22-3-84; Scampton for reduction to spares 28-4-89; Abingdon as GI **9013M** 11-89; Hanningfield Metals, Stock, Essex for scrap 1995

XW299 AwCn (undated); 1FTS/56 30-12-69; **BAC Conv T Mk.5A** 11-3-75 – 20-6-75; 1FTS/56 20-6-75; 5MU 4-11-75; RAFC/40 16-8-79; 1FTS/60 7-10-82; GI **9146M** 18-5-92; No.1 SoTT Halton/60 by 6-92; No.2 SoTT Cosford/MB/60, (2 SoTT

175. Between January 1969 and January 1976, the prototype Jet Provost T Mk.5, XS230, was used by the A&AEE and ETPS until sold to Transair (UK) Ltd and registered as G-BVWF. Later re-registered as G-VIVM, it is now with Swords Aviation at North Weald. (Ray Deacon Collection)

176. Complete with the original fin insignia worn by the Jet Provost T Mk.5 fleet at Little Rissington, XW288 was later upgraded to Mk.5A standard and remained with the CFS until March 1977. It was written off in a tragic flying accident in 1982 whilst with No.1 FTS. (BAe Systems Heritage Warton-Percival/Hunting Collection)

177. The winner of the 1985 Wright Jubilee Trophy was Flt Lt Dave Whittingham of No.1 FTS, whose suitably-adorned Jet Provost, XW295, was noted at RAF Leuchars the following September. (Gordon Macadie)

renamed 1 SoTT on 24-11-1994, then renamed to DCAE Cosford on 1-4-04, renamed DSAE during 2012) 9-94; Jet Art Aviation Ltd 16-1-13; QinetiQ Boscombe Down Apprentice School as GI 28-1-14

XW300 AwCn 31-12-69; 1FTS/58 1-1-70; m/a/c Sea Prince WP315 nr Selby, Yorks (2) Cat 5S 3-3-71; SOC 15-3-71

XW301 AwCn 28-1-70; 1FTS/60 29-1-70; **BAC Conv T Mk.5A** 14-2-75; 1FTS/69 30-5-75; 5MU 30-12-75; 1FTS/63 13-11-79; 7FTS 13-10-80;1FTS/63 3-11-80; GI **9147M** 18-5-92; No.1 SoTT Halton/M 12-6-92; No.2 SoTT Cosford 9-94 /MC/63 (2 SoTT renamed 1 SoTT on 24-11-1994, then renamed to DCAE Cosford on 1-4-04); Jet Art Aviation Ltd 31-1-13; exported to Dronten, Netherlands, and placed on display at Barnveld, Netherlands 17-1-14

XW302 AwCn 30-1-70; 1FTS/61 3-2-70; RAFC/65 20-6-74; 3FTS (store) 21-3-75; **CWP Leeming tip tanks** 3-10-75 – 10-11-75; 6FTS/T12-11-75; Shawbury (store) 20-9-93; tendered 19-11-1993; Global Aviation Ltd, Binbrook 30-9-94; reg **N166A** to Impex Aero Ltd, Wilmington, DE, USA 22-11-95; sold to UK, struck-off US reg on sale to R. Eddie Todd, Sandtoft 23-11-98 as **G-BYED;** David T. Barber, Londonderry 14-12-99; engine failure and forced landing on Lough Foyle mudflats on approach to Eglinton, Northern Ireland 12-2-01 (aircraft submerged by tide, lifted out by RAF Chinook 15-2-01); struck-off reg 28-12-01; M. A. Petrie & J.E. Rowley, Ruthin, for restoration 4-3-02; restoration cnx and struck-off reg 30-12-04; David Ballicki, Sleaford: cockpit as mobile display 2006

XW303 AwCn (undated); 1FTS/64 16-3-70; **BAC Conv T Mk.5A** 14-2-75; 1FTS/64 6-6-75; 5MU 16-2-76; 7FTS/127 7-2-80; 1FTS 19-6-87; 7FTS/127 21-7-87; Shawbury store 23-9-91; GI **9119M** 16-9-91; 1 SoTT Halton/127 15-10-91; 2 SoTT Cosford 3-95 (1 SoTT renamed to DCAE Cosford 1-4-04); fuselage returned Halton, Bucks for use as a horse jump 6-3-06

XW304 AwCn 19-2-70; 1 FTS/62 20-2-70; Leeming (store) 3-7-75; **CWP Leeming tip tanks** 10-75 – 28-11-75; 6 FTS/X 28-11-75; GI **9119M** 16-9-91; 1 SoTT Halton/X 17-12-92; 2 SoTT Cosford/X 4-93 (2 SoTT renamed to DCAE Cosford 1-4-04); tendered and sold to Witham Special Vehicles, Colsterworth, Lincs 2-07; resold to private owner at Brome, Eye, Suffolk

XW305 AwCn 26-2-70; 1FTS/63 27-2-70; **BAC Conv T Mk.5A** 11-3-75 – 30-6-75; 1FTS/63 30-6-75; 5MU 7-1-76; RAFC/42 7-9-79; Shawbury (store) 16-5-91; tendered 19-11-93; Global Aviation Ltd, Binbrook 26-5-1995; Richard J. Everett, Ipswich 9-95; Randall K. Hames, Gaffney, SC, USA 3-4-96 as **N453MS;** Michael Scarks, ME, 26-3-97; Ronald S. Miller, Encino, CA 19-7-00; Charles S. Kennedy, Oceanside, CA, later Staunton, VA 16-1-02; Edward J. Geyman, Wilmington, OH 19-7-13

178

XW306 AwCn (undated), 1FTS/65 16-3-70; 3FTS Leeming (store) 25-7-75; **CWP Leeming tip tanks** 11-75 – 4-12-75; 6FTS/Z 04-12-75, recoded Y; BAe Warton 15-8-81 – 2-9-81 (empennage fatigue loads investigation); 6FTS/Y 3-9-81; 27MU Shawbury 7-9-89; 6FTS/O 7-9-89; Shawbury (store) 13-4-93; Global Avn Binbrook 19-11-93; sold USA to Lance P. Toland Assocs Griffin GA 1995; reg **N313A** 22-11-95; Impex Aero, Wilmington, DE 11-95; Jet Experiences LLC, Missoula, Mt 10-10-95; Nicholas Clinger Sparr, FL 10-8-05; Wing Waxers of South Florida, Lakeland, FL 25-7-12; to Zephyrhills Municipal Airport, FL, 9-16

XW307 AwCn (undated); 1FTS/66 25-3-70; RAFC/60 19-2-74; 3FTS Leeming (store) 24-3-75; **CWP Leeming tip tanks** 10-75 – 13-11-75; 6FTS/S 13-11-75; Shawbury (store) 21-9-93; tendered 19-11-93; Global Aviation Ltd, Binbrook 13-6-94; sold as **N4107U** Jon Galt Bowman, Seattle, WA 12-7-94; Robert D. Kunsak, Leetsdale, PA 6-7-01

XW308 AwCn (undated); 1FTS/67 26-3-70; **BAC Conv T Mk.5A** 18-2-75 – 22-5-75; 1FTS/67 22-5-75; 5MU 19-3-76; 1FTS/65 16-11-79; FA Cat 5 28-10-81; dived out of cloud shortly after take-off and crashed Crumley Hill, Kilmarney 4m W of Leuchars (1), Cat 5S 29-1-81

XW309 AwCn 30-4-70; 1FTS/68 4-5-70; 6FTS/U 16-6-75; **CWP Leeming tip tanks** 24-10-75; 6FTS/V 24-11-75; Shawbury (store) 5-5-93; GI **9197M** 11-3-93; 2 SoTT Cosford/ME/V 27-4-93; (2 SoTT renamed 1 SoTT on 24-11-1994, then renamed to DCAE Cosford on 1-4-04); tendered and sold to Witham Special Vehicles, Colsterworth, Lincs 2-07; Hartlepool Technical School as GI 10-3-07

179

XW310 AwCn 18-5-70; 1FTS/70 19-5-70; **BAC Conv T Mk.5A** 25-3-75 – 8-7-75; mdc fit Leeming 8-7-75 – 5-8-75 then via Linton store to 5MU 1-9-75; 5MU (store) 2-9-75; RAFC/37 12-6-79; BAe 28-7-81 – 8-10-81 (empennage fatigue loads investigation); RAFC/37 18-10-81; Shawbury (store) 30-9-88; sold at MoD auction 8-7-93; sold to Everett Aero, Sproughton 5-5-95; reg **G-BWGS** James S. Everett, Ipswich 18-8-95; Katharina K. Gerstorfer, London 2-5-97; G-BWGS Ltd, North Weald 1-5-03; Mark P. Grimshaw, Norwich 26-8-09

XW311 AwCn 13-5-70; 1FTS/69 14-5-70; Leeming (store) 3-6-75; 6FTS/W 28-11-75; Shawbury (store 29-10-92), GI **9180M** 11-3-93; 2 SoTT Cosford/M/MF/W 5-5-93 (2 SoTT renamed 1 SoTT on 24-11-1994, then renamed to DCAE Cosford on 1-4-04); tendered and sold to Witham Special Vehicles, Colsterworth, Lincs 2-07; Ashclyst Farm, Exeter; Popham Airfield for Sovereign Cars Garage, Whitchurch, Hants 2-08; Kennet Avn, North Weald, Essex 7-1-09 (dumped)

XW312 AwCn 12-6-70; 1FTS/71 16-6-70; **BAC Conv T Mk.5A** 26-2-75; 1FTS/71 12-6-75; 5MU (store) 8-4-76; 1FTS/64 16-11-79; 7FTS (loan) 15-5-80; 1FTS/64 6-6-80; Shawbury (store) 20-8-91; GI **9109M** 8-7-91; 1 SoTT Halton 3-10-91; 2 SoTT Cosford 9-94 (1 SoTT renamed to DCAE Cosford 1-4-04); tendered 10-05; Astre Air International, Watkins, CO, USA 7-06; reg **N312XW** Astre Air International, Watkins, CO 11-1-07; trans Seattle 9-16

XW313 AwCn 30-6-70; 1FTS/72 2-7-70; **BAC Conv T Mk.5A** 24-4-75; 3FTS Leeming (store) 19-8-75; RAFC 30-9-75; 5MU (store) 9-10-75; RAFC/30 28-4-79; 3 FTS/30 16-8-88; 1FTS/85

18-12-91; Linton (store) 6-93; Shawbury (store) 29-9-93; tendered 19-11-93; Global Aviation Ltd, Binbrook 11-93; reg **G-BVTB** Global Aviation Ltd, Binbrook 7-9-94; Richard J. Everett, Ipswich 1995; reg cnx and sold Randall K. Hames, Gaffney, SC, USA 27-6-95 as **N313RH** (dism. Ipswich 6.95 for shipping to USA); struck-off US reg 22-4-13

XW314 AwCn 30-6-70, 60MU Leconfield 3-7-70; A&AEE Boscombe Down 29-7-70, R/T flight trial of ARI 23143; 3FTS/31 25-8-70; 1FTS (loan) 5-2-71; 3FTS/31 26-3-71; **BAC Conv T Mk.5A** 28-8-75; 3FTS Leeming (store) 28-11-75; 5MU (store) 5-1-76; RAFC/28 27-3-79; failed to recover from spin and abandoned near Swinderby, Lincs, 8-5-80

XW315 AwCn 16-7-70; 3FTS/30 1/-/-70, FACat 4R 20-3-72; BAe 5-5-72; RIW 22-8-72; 3FTS/30 17-5-73; **BAC Conv T Mk.5A** 21-1-75; 3FTS Leeming (store) 27-5-75; CFS/83 27-11-75; RAFC/32 12-4-76; CFS/3FTS/63 27-9-7; in flight fire Leeming 5-7-84; Abingdon as GI; SOC 8-5-86 and sfs to Birds of Long Marston; cockpit section to the Stratford Aircraft Collection, Long Marston; M Boulanger, Wolverhampton 1-4-01; sold to a private collector and transported to Preston, Lancashire 27-7-12

XW316 AwCn 28-8-70; 3FTS/32 1-9-70; **BAC Conv T Mk.5A** 11-12-73; 3FTS Leeming (store) 12-6-74; Topcliffe (store) 19-6-75, CFS/82 27-11-75; RAFC/33 12-4-76; CFS/3FTS/64 28-11-77; CFS/52 6-84; 6FTS/K 2-12-85; RAFC/28 8-4-86; 7FTS/135 5-5-88; 3FTS/28 by 9-90; Shawbury (store) 18-10-91; tendered and sold Wessex Avn 15-2-93; Astre Aire, Aurora, CO, USA, as **N316HC** 7-7-93; National Aviation Museum & Foundation of Oklahoma, Tulsa, OK 9-8-01; Resource Financial Holdings, Newark, DE, 26-6-03 (wfu open storage, Melbourne, FL, 3-05)

XW317 AwCn 31-8-70; 3FTS/33 1-9-70; **BAC Conv T Mk.5A** 7-1-74; 3FTS Leeming (store) 21-6-74; RAFC/81 5-11-74 – 11-75, recoded 25; RAE Farnborough 1-3-78 – 30-3-78 (flight test oxygen regulator NBC No.5); RAFC/25 31-3-78; 1FTS/79 25-4-91; Shawbury (store) 14-4-92; tendered 19-11-93; Global Aviation Ltd, Binbrook 11-93; Lance Toland Associates, Griffin, GA, USA

178. Jet Provost T Mk.5A, XW305, depicted with the RAF College at Leeming in June 1980. (Roger Lindsay)

179. Jet Provost T Mk.5, XW309, was fitted with tip tanks in late 1975 for use with No.6 FTS at Finningley. (Author's Collection)

1995; Impex Aero Ltd, Wilmington, DE, reg as **N355A** 22-11-95; Kingsley B. Owen, Hanover, PA 10-97; National Aviation Museum & Foundation of Oklahoma, Tulsa, OK 1-2-01; Resource Financial Holdings, Newark, DE 26-6-03; Camelot Aviation LLC, Wilmington, DE 21-2-14

XW318 AwCn 16-9-70; 3FTS/34 17-9-70; (1FTS loan 5-2-71 – 14-3-71); **BAC Conv T Mk.5A** 15-1-74; 3FTS (store) 14-8-74; Leeming (store) 4-11-74; RAFC/93 16-12-74, recoded 12; 1FTS/78 18-12-91; GI **9190M** 7-6-93; 2 SoTT Cosford 15-6-93 (2 SoTT renamed 1 SoTT on 24-11-1994, then renamed to DCAE Cosford on 1-4-04, renamed DSAE during 2012); Jet Art Aviation Ltd 16-1-2013; sold Netherlands 17-1-14

XW319 AwCn 16-9-70; 3FTS/35 17-9-70; (1FTS loan 3 71); **BAC Conv T Mk.5A** 18-12-73; Leeming (store) 17-6-74; 5MU (hack) 26-9-75; 3 FTS/67 20-12-78; CFS/3FTS/57 4-84; RAFC (loan) 31-1-86, CFS/57 13-3-86; 1FTS/76 1991, tendered 19-11-93; Global Aviation Ltd, Binbrook 28-7-94; Lance Toland Associates, Griffin, GA, 1994; N8087V Impex Aero Ltd, Wilmington, DE, as **N8087V** 7-3-95; struck-off US reg 2-4-13

XW320 AwCn 29-9-70; 3FTS/36 30-9-70; RAFC/62 14-3-74; **BAC Conv T Mk.5A** 6-5-75; 3FTS Leeming (store)/36 4-9-75; 3FTS/50 4-9-75; 1FTS/71 3-12-81; RAFC (loan) 7-2-86; 1FTS/71 17-3-86; 1 SoTT Halton 6-90 as GI **9016M** (incorrectly marked '9015M'); 2 SoTT Cosford as GI 9016M/71

XW321 AwCn 30-9-70; 3FTS/39 1-10-70; 1FTS 21-11-74; 3FTS/39 8-1-75; **BAC Conv T Mk.5A** 24-6-75; 3FTS Leeming (store) 27-10-75; 5MU (store) 10-11-75; RAFC/29 28-3-79; 7FTS/132 27-9-84; 1FTS/62 8-11-90; Shawbury store 5-10-92; GI **9154M**; 2 SoTT Cosford 2-3-93 as 9154M/MH/62

XW322 AwCn 14-12-70; RAFC/1 15-12-70; 5MU 11-4-72; RAFC 'Golden Eagle Flt' 25-9-72; 5MU 7-11-72; (mdc fit Leeming 10-7-75 – 22-8-75); **BAC Conv T Mk.5A** 22-8-75; 5MU 29-1-76; RAFC/1 'Golden Eagle Flt' 16-12-76; 5MU 16-2-77; 6FTS 3-5-77; 5MU 25-8-77; BAe loan 5-4-79; RAFC/43 12-11-79; 1FTS 29-11-79; RAFC 4-2-80; BAe loan (fatigue test) 8-4-83; RAFC 24-5-84; **Scampton conv T Mk.5B** 7-11-88; 6FTS/D 23-11-88; Shawbury (store) 23-6-93; tendered 19-11-93; Global Aviation Ltd, Binbrook 30-9-94; Lance Toland Associates, Griffin, GA, 1994 (shipped to USA ex Binbrook 1994); reg **N8086U** Impex Aero Ltd, Wilmington, DE, 8-3-95; re-reg **N199ER** Impex Aero Ltd, Wilmington, DE, 8-97; Jet Provost Flight, Houston, TX, 19-10-04;

experienced a sudden loss of lift at approx 30 feet AGL during short final landing at Bay City, Tx, crashed and caught fire, 12-6-08; struck-off US reg 7-11-13

XW323 AwCn 11-12-70; RAFC/2 11-12-70; 5MU 29-3-72; RAFC/2 'Golden Eagle Flt' 27-9-72; 5MU 2-11-72; **BAC Conv T Mk.5A** 21-8-75; 5MU 28-1-76; RAFC/2 'Golden Eagle Flt' 31-12-76; 5MU 16-2-77; RAFC/44 1-11-79; 1FTS/86 6-11-91; GI **9166M** 23-10-92; RAF Museum, Hendon 17-11-92

180

XW324 AwCn 30-9-70; 3FTS/38 1-10-70; 1FTS/2 21-2-75; 3FTS Leeming (store)/38 9-5-75; **CWP Leeming fit tip tanks** 3-10-75 – 15-10-75; 6FTS/U 23-10-75; Shawbury (store) 21-7-93; Global Aviation Ltd, Binbrook, 19-11-93; reg **G-BWSG** 13-5-96; reg Adavia Ltd: remained stored Binbrook 18-11-96; Den-Air Aviation Ltd, North Weald 20-8-97: op: Aviators Flight Centre, Southend, del. 22-8-97; Richard M. Kay, Jersey 1-8-00; Jeffery Bell, Nottingham 12-11-07 (flies as RAF "XW324" from EMA)

XW325 AwCn 28-9-70; 3FTS/37 29-9-70; 1FTS/85 17-9-74; 3FTS Leeming (store)/37 27-11-74; **BAC Conv T Mk.5A** 15-1-75; 3FTS Leeming (store)/37 15-4-75; 5MU 26-9-75; RAFC/33 9-5-79; **Scampton for T Mk.5B** 11-88; 6FTS/E 4-89; Shawbury (store) 3-2-93; tendered 19-11-93; Global Aviation Ltd, Binbrook 23-5-95; reg **G-BWGF** 10-8-95; J. W. Cullin/Specialcope Jet Provost Group, Blackpool 21-8-96 (flew as RAF "XW325"); Viper Jet Provost Group Ltd, Carlisle/Exeter/St Athan 25-9-07; Dragonjet Ltd, Cardiff/St Athan 13-5-14; G-JPVA Ltd, North Weald 6-12-16

XW326 AwCn 2-10-70; 3FTS/40 5-10-70; **BAC Conv T Mk.5A** 12-8-75; 3FTS Leeming (store) 24-11-75; 5MU (store) 12-12-75; CFS/3FTS/44 25-1-79; 7FTS/67 5-6-79; 1FTS 20-11-79; 7FTS/120 11-2-80; 1FTS/62 4-86; Shawbury (store) 11-11-88; sold at MoD auction, 8-7-93; Richard J. Everett, Ipswich 20-7-93; (dism. Ipswich for shipping to USA 4-7-95); Randall K. Hames, Gaffney,

SC, 6-12-95 and reg **N326GV**; Gabriel Vidal, San Juan, Puerto Rico 27-1-97; Wings Over Miami Museum, Tamiami, FL, 2004; Aero Consultant Inc, Easley, SC, 7-09; Rafael A. Pesquera, Guaynabo, Puerto Rico 29-8-11

XW327 AwCn 27-10-70; 3FTS/42 28-10-70; **BAC Conv T Mk.5A** 6-11-73; 3FTS Leeming (store)/42 26-4-74; RAFC/92 11-12-74, recoded 28; 1FTS/62 26-1-78; 7FTS 30-6-80; 1FTS/62 30-7-80; 7FTS/134 28-9-84; 6FTS/M 3-12-85; 7FTS/134 4-4-86; CFS/62 8-10-91; Shawbury (store) 4-2-92; 1 SoTT Halton as GI **9130M**/62 27-2-92; 2 SoTT Cosford as GI 9130M/62 3-95

XW328 AwCn 19-10-70; 3FTS/41 20-10-70; **BAC Conv T Mk.5A** 16-11-73; 3FTS Leeming (store)/41 30-4-74; RAFC/80 22-10-74, recoded 22; 1FTS 20-11-79; RAFC/22 30-1-80; 7FTS/128 10-12-87; 3FTS/22 by 6-91, 1FTS/75 8-11-91; 2 SoTT Cosford as **9177M**/MI/75 10-93; sold to Everett Aero, Sproughton, 2014; to Antwerp, Belgium 5-4-2014

XW329 AwCn 29-10-70; 3FTS/43 03-11-70; Leeming (store) by 2-75; **BAC Conv T5A** 28-5-75; 3FTS Leeming (store) 4-9-75; 5MU (store) 24-9-75; 3FTS/48 6-3-79; FA Cat 3 16-6-81, pilot mishandled the aircraft during a simulated engine failure after take-off from Leeming; aircraft stalled while turning back towards the airfield and struck the ground under full power in a nose-up attitude, the crew stayed with the aircraft and were slightly injured; Recat 5GI **8741M** 1-7-82 Church Fenton fire section

XW330 AwCn 30-10-70; 3FTS/44 3-11-70; **BAC Conv T Mk.5A** 23-11-73; 3FTS Leeming (store) 5-6-74; RAFC/91 4-12-74, recoded 23; CFS/3FTS/65 25-10-77; 7FTS/130 30-3-84; RAFC/10 27-8-86; 1FTS/82 1-10-91; GI **9195M** 7-6-93; 2 SoTT Cosford as 9195M/MJ/82; sold Everett Aero, Sproughton 2014; Knutsford, Cheshire (private) 2016

XW331 AwCn 27-11-70, 3FTS/46 30-11-70, FA Cat 4R 11-4-73 heavy landing at Leeming during a simulated flame-out; Recat 5C 11-4-73; Fire School Leeming 16-5-73; North East Aircraft Museum, Usworth, 1976; to Foulness Island during 1979 and presumed scrapped

XW332 AwCn 20-11-70; 3FTS/45 30-11-70; **BAC Conv T Mk.5A** 20-8-75; 3FTS Leeming (store) 24-11-75; 5MU (store) 17-12-75; RAFC/34 7-6-79; Shawbury (store) 16-5-91; tendered and sold Downbird UK Ltd, Stoke-on-Trent 1993; Astre Aire, Aurora, CO, USA 7-93; reg **N332RC** C. Allen/Grand Touring Cars,

Scottsdale, AZ, 12-7-93; Reed L. Dalton, Aurora, CO 18-4-98; (based Denver-Front Range, CO, as "XW332/34")

XW333 AwCn 30-11-70; 3FTS/47 1-12-70; 1FTS/83 8-1-75; Leeming (store)/47 9-5-75; **BAC Conv T Mk.5A** 17-7-75; 3FTS Leeming (store) 10-11-75; 5MU (store) 21-11-75; 3FTS/46 6-3-79; RAFC/36 12-6-79; CFS/61 8-4-86; 1FTS/79 6-92; Shawbury (store) 21-9-93; tendered 19-11-93: Global Aviation Ltd, Binbrook 6-7-94; reg **G-BVTC** Richard Lake/Global Aviation Ltd, Binbrook, later Humberside 7-9-94 (flies as RAF "XW333")

XW334 AwCn 10-12-70; 1FTS/73 11-12-70; BAe 8-1-71, 1FTS/73 2-2-71; **BAC Conv T Mk.5A** 8-4-75; 3FTS Leeming (store) 12-8-75; 5MU (store) 26-9-75; RAFC/39 27-7-79; 7FTS/131 26-9-84; 3FTS/18 16 8 90, Shawbury (store) 21-8-91, tendered and sold Downbird UK Ltd, Stoke-on-Trent 15-2-93; Denver Aerospace Museum, Aurora, CO, 2-93; Astre Aire, Aurora, CO 7-93; reg as **N334XW** C. Allen/Grand Touring Cars, Scottsdale, AZ, 12-7-93; Reed L. Dalton, Aurora, CO, 5-95; Astre Air International, Watkins, CO, 17-5-97 (based Denver-Front Range, CO, as "XW334/18")

181

XW335 AwCn 18-12-70; RAFC/61 21-12-70; **BAC Conv T Mk.5A** 15-8-74; RAFC/61 12-11-74, recoded 27 by 3-76; 5MU (store) 17-3-91; GI **9061M** 1 SoTT Halton/27 10-91; 2 SoTT

180. Complete with the RAF College's 'Ring of Confidence' on the rear fuselages, two Jet Provost T Mk.5As from Cranwell, XW323 and XW435, in March 1982. The former aircraft had earlier been assigned to the 'Golden Eagle Flight' for the training of HRH Charles, Prince of Wales. (Gordon Macadie)

181. Jet Provost T Mk.5, XW334 of No.1 FTS at Topcliffe in May 1972. Formed two years earlier and led by Flt Lt Dave Waddington, the Linton Blades became the first display team from No.1 FTS to be equipped with Jet Provost T Mk.5s. (Roger Lindsay)

Cosford (2 SoTT renamed to DCAE Cosford 1-4-2004); tendered and to Astre Air International, Watkins, CO, 12-06

XW336 AwCn 17-12-70; RAFC/60 17-12-70, recoded 6 and 60 by 3-74; **BAC Conv T Mk.5A** 11-6-74; RAFC 22-10-74, recoded 6; CFS/64 3-90; 1FTS/67 by 4-92; Linton (store) 6-93; Shawbury store 22-9-93; tendered 19-11-93; Global Aviation Ltd, Binbrook, 6-7-94; Lance Toland Associates, Griffin, GA, 1994; reg **N8089U** Impex Aero Ltd, Wilmington, DE, 8-3-95; Plane Old PBJ Partnership, Broomfield, CO, 17-6-98; reg **N78SH** Plane Old PBJ Partnership, Broomfield, CO, 12-5-09

XW351 AwCn 31-12-70; RAFC/63 5-1-71, recoded 3; **BAC Conv T Mk.5A** 17-6-75 – 30-9-75; 1FTS/74 1-10-75; RAFC/31 21-4-86; 5MU (store) 17-3-91; GI **9062M** 28-1-91; 1 SoTT Halton/31 by 10-91; 2 SoTT Cosford 7-95; tendered and sold Astre Air International, Watkins, CO, 12-06

XW352 AwCn 31-12-70; RAFC/62 31-12-70, recoded 3; Leeming (store) 4-4-75; **CWP Leeming fit tip tanks** 14-10-75 – 13-11-75; 6FTS/R 13-11-75; tendered 11-92; sold to Downbird UK, to Tatenhill, Staffs, 6-95; Bruntingthorpe 2-96; Rugby, Warwickshire, 5-96; Everett Aero, Sproughton, Suffolk, 2-98; exported to the USA ca. 1998

XW353 AwCn 13-1-71; RAFC/64 18-1-71, recoded 12; **BAC Conv T Mk.5A** 21-10-75; 3FTS Leeming (store) 2-2-76; BAe Warton (mods) 5-1-82; 5MU (respray) 16-7-82; CFS/3FTS/51 20-8-82; CFS/51 9-3-88; GI Eng Wing, Cranwell/3 as **9090M** 18-2-91; Gate Guard Cranwell 18-7-91

XW354 AwCn 20-10-71; RAFC/65 21-1-71, recoded 7 by 5-72, recoded 65 by 1-74, recoded 7 by 4-74; **BAC Conv T Mk.5A** 20-8-74; RAFC/7 5-11-74; 1FTS 8-7-85; RAFC 5-8-85; 1FTS/70 1-10-91; Linton (store) 6-93; Shawbury (store) 21-9-93; tendered 19-11-93; Global Aviation Ltd, Binbrook, 11.93; Immingham Docks for shipping to Troy, Al, USA, reg as **N300LT** 2-94; Lance P. Toland, Griffin, GA 14-2-94; Wiley Sanders, Troy, AL 1994; Kenneth N. Campbell, Troy, AL 4-94; Tehran Inc, Coos Bay, OR 3-12-97; Walla Walla College, College Place, WA 31-1-01; McCulloh Jet USA Inc, Fort Myers, FL 6-06; WASP Holding Co, Wilmington, DE 16-2-07; Turin Aviation Group, Brandon, FL 5-12-13

XW355 AwCn 26-1-71; RAFC/66 28-1-71; **BAC Conv T Mk.5A** 7-2-74; RAFC/66 20-8-74, recoded 20; JP Det 30-7-78; RAFC 1-4-80; Shawbury (store) 7-10-88; sold Downbird UK Ltd,

Tatenhill 8-7-93; reg **G-JPTV** B. Johansson, Northampton 2-5-96; Robert V. Bowles, Rugby 13-3-98; Mark P. Grimshaw/G-JPTV Group, London 31-12-98; Seagull Formation Ltd, North Weald 24-5-01; Airborne innovations Ltd/ Gower Jets, Swansea 30-7-03; Stewart J. Davies, Doncaster 29-12-03; Century Aviation Ltd. Barnsley 9-6-09 (flies as RAF "XW354"); Century Aviation Ltd, Gamston, 2015

XW356 AwCn (undated); RAFC/67 25-2-71, recoded 8; crashed onto the main railway line at Tupton near Chesterfield, Derbyshire after loss off control, the pilot ejected safely, 12-9-72; Cat 5S and SOC 12-9-72.

XW357 AwCn 12-3-71; RAFC/68 15-3-71, recoded 5; **BAC Conv T Mk.5A** 7-2-74; RAFC/5 27-8-74; Shawbury (store) 9-8-91; tendered and sold to Wessex Aviation and exported to International Air Parts, Bankstown, Sydney, NSW, Australia 14-10-92; (arr. dism. Sydney-Bankstown 3-93, stored Bankstown as "XW357/5"); reg **VH-YZD** Nick Coston/Aerospace Services Group, Sydney, NSW 11-8-03; Joe Demarte, Jandakot, Perth, WA, 4-05 (trucked to Perth ex Bankstown 3.04 for rest. to fly); Giuseppe Demarte, Perth, WA: reg. 21-9-05; sold to NZ: shipped ex Perth 10-11-14; Wanaka Transport & Toy Museum, Wanaka, NZ 12-14

XW358 AwCn 29-3-71; RAFC/73 30-3-71; **BAC Conv T Mk.5A** 18-12-74; RAFC/73 8-4-75, recoded 18; 7FTS/130 18-12-87; CFS/59 22-10-91; Shawbury (store) 14-2-92; GI **9181M** 11-3-93; 2 SoTT Cosford/MK/59 27-4-93; Jet Art Aviation Ltd, Selby, Yorks 16-1-93; CEMAST, Fareham College, Lee-on-the-Solent 7-5-14

XW359 AwCn 30-3-71; RAFC/74 31-3-71, recoded 4 8-72; **BAC Conv T Mk.5A** 7-2-75; RAFC/4 6-5-75; 5MU (store) 25-8-76; 7FTS/128 19-3-80; 1FTS/65 7-4-86; Linton (store) 6-93, Shawbury (store) 28-9-93, tendered 19-11-93; Global Aviation Ltd, Binbrook, 11-93; (Immingham Docks for shipping to USA 10-2-94); reg **N400LT** Lance P. Toland, Griffin, GA 14-2-94; Wiley Sanders, Troy, AL, 1994; Kenneth N. Campbell/KW Plastics, Troy, AL, 4-94; Anthony Schapera, Bishop, CA, 24-7-98

XW360 AwCn 25-3-71; RAFC/69 25-3-71, recoded 1; **BAC Conv T Mk.5A** 7-2-75; RAFC/1 13-5-75; 5MU 19-8-76; 3FTS/47 17-4-80; 7FTS/129 28-7-80; 1FTS/61 8-8-90; GI **9153M** 8-7-92; 2SoTT Cosford/ML/61 15-6-93; Jet Art Aviation Ltd, Selby, Yorks 16-1-13

XW361 AwCn 31-3-71; RAFC/76 1-4-71; **BAC Conv T Mk.5A** 20-5-75 – 28-8-75; 3FTS Leeming (store) 28-8-75; RAFC/21

30-9-75; 7FTS/21 11-6-86; RAFC/21 9-1-87; 1FTS/81 18-12-91; GI **9192M** 7-6-93, 2 SoTT Cosford/81/MM 15-6-93; Jet Art Aviation Ltd, Selby, Yorks 16-1-93; sold Netherlands 17-1-14

XW362 AwCn 19-4-71; RAFC/77 20-4-71; **BAC Conv T Mk.5A** 4-6-74; RAFC/77 14-10-74, recoded 17; 1FTS 6-10-82; RAFC 11-11-82, 3FTS/17; Shawbury (store) 12-9-91; tendered and sold to Wessex Aviation for International Air Parts, Sydney NSW 14-10-92; Top Gun Tasmania Ltd, Brookland Pk, SA, 24-7-98; reg **VH-YZB** Aerospace Services Group, Sydney, NSW, 11-8-03 (stored Bankstown "XW362/17"); Top Gun Tasmania Pty Ltd, Richmond, TAS 27-4-06 (flew in camouflage, spurious Tasmanian AF markings); Top Gun Australia Pty Ltd, Adelaide SA

182

XW363 AwCn 30-4-71; RAFC/79 3-5-71, recoded 2 by 5-72, recoded again to 79 by 1973; **BAC Conv T Mk.5A** 29-8-75; 1FTS/68 2-12-75; 6FTS/G 20-12-85; RAFC/36 8-4-86; 3FTS 20-3-87; sold BAe GI Warton 11-1-91; North West Heritage Group, Warton (loan); Manchester Museum of Science & Industry storage, Swinton, 2007; RAF Millom & Militaria Museum, Haverigg, Cumbria, (loan)10-09; Dumfries & Galloway Museum (loan) 10-10

183

XW364 AwCn 30-4-71; 1FTS/74 3-5-71; **BAC Conv T Mk.5A** 25-3-75 – 17-7-75; 1FTS (store) 8-8-75; 5MU (store) 2-9-75;

3FTS/45 8-2-79; RAFC/35 6-6-79; Shawbury store 10-4-89; GI 5-5-93 **9188M**; 2 SoTT Cosford/MN/35 6-5-93; Halton airfield dump for use by the Recruit Training Sqn 16-10-12

XW365 AwCn 30-4-71; RAFC/71 3-5-71; **BAC Conv T Mk.5A** 6-5-75 – 20-8-75; 3FTS Leeming (store) 20-8-75; 1FTS/73 7-10-75; 3FTS/73 21-3-79, 1FTS/73 5-4-79; 7FTS/73 6-6-80; 1FTS/73 4-7-80; 7FTS/73 24-2-87; 1FTS/73 23-3-87; GI **9018M** 19-12-89; 1 SoTT Halton/73 06-90; 2 SoTT Cosford 27-9-94; tendered 10-05 and sold Astre Air International, Watkins, CO, 12-06

XW366 AwCn 30-4-71; RAFC/72 3-5-71; **BAC Conv T Mk.5A** 7-10-75 – 24-12-75; 3FTS Leeming (store) 6-1-76, 3FTS/52 7-4-76, 1FTS/75 21-12-81, GI **9097M** 7-5-91; 1 SoTT Halton 1990; 2 SoTT Cosford 3-95; tendered 10-05 and sold Astre Air International, Watkins, CO 12-06

XW367 AwCn 19-5-71; RAFC/75 20-5-71; **BAC Conv T Mk.5A** 24-9-74; RAFC/75 17-12-74, recoded 26; 1FTS (loan) 19-9-77, RAFC/26 24-10-77; 1FTS/64 by 12-91; GI **9193M** 7-5-91; 2 SoTT Cosford/64/MO 15-6-93; sold to buyer in Italy

XW368 AwCn 31-8-71; RAFC/86 2-9-71; **BAC Conv T Mk.5A** 19-11-75; RAFC/31 27-2-76; 3FTS/66 5-10-77; CFS/55 19-9-84; 6FTS/L 4-4-86; 1FTS/34 22-1-90, Linton (store) 6-93; Shawbury (store); tendered 19-11-93; Global Aviation Ltd, Binbrook 11-93; sold Lance P. Toland, Griffin, GA, 14-2-94; Wiley Sanders, Troy, AL, 1994; Robert Delvalley, Brooksville, FL 1994; ISRMS, Land-o-Lakes, FL, 27-5-94, reg **N183HJ** (ntu); Hernando Jet Centre, Brooksville, FL, reg **N600LT** 5-11-99; Phantom II Aviation, Scottsdale, AZ, 17-6-03 (flies as RAF "XW368/66"); Bonifey, FL (store)

XW369 AwCn 3-6-71; RAFC/81 4-6-71, recoded 9; **BAC Conv T Mk.5A** 21-5-74; RAFC/9 25-9-74; FA Cat 5S, 5-4-90, failed to get airborne on take-off from Scampton and overshot runway; SOC 5-4-90, Recat 4R and to BAC; Shawbury (store) 29-9-93;

182. Jet Provost T Mk.5, XW362 of the RAF College, Cranwell. It was later sold to a buyer in Australia and is owned by Top Gun Tasmania Pty Ltd, adorned with spurious Tasmanian air force markings. (Author's Collection)

183. Noted on final approach to RAF Abingdon in September 1982, T Mk.5A, XW363 was with No.1 FTS between December 1975 to December 1985. It is currently on loan to the Dumfries and Galloway Museum. (Jerry Hughes)

tendered 19-11-93; Global Aviation Ltd, Binbrook 11-93; Lance P. Toland, Griffin, GA, and reg **N800LT** 14-2-94; David Weininger, Santa Fe, NM, 15-6-95; struck-off US register 4-11-13

XW370 AwCn 2-8-71; 3FTS/49 3-8-71; 1FTS/3 21-2-75; Leeming (store) 22-4-75; **BAC Conv T Mk.5A** 10-7-75 – 22-10-75; 1FTS/72 23-10-75; GI **9196M** 7-6-93; 2 SoTT Cosford/MP/72 15-6-93;

XW371 AwCn 24-6-71; 1FTS/76 25-6-71; **BAC Conv T Mk.5A** 19-3-75; 1FTS/76 25-6-75; 7FTS/59 23-4-79; FA Cat 5 3-7-79, crashed 10m E Lancaster during a low-level navex in bad weather (1k); SOC Cat 5S 09-07-79

XW372 AwCn 28-9 71; RAFC/87 29-9-71; **BAC Conv T Mk.5A** 15-10-75; 1FTS/63 28-1-76; 7FTS/63 18-4-79; 1FTS 13-12-79; 7FTS/121 4-2-80; 6FTS/M 3-4-86; (Finningley store) 22-11-88; 6 FTS/M/121 6-12-88; Shawbury (store) 6-12-88; tendered 19-11-93; Global Aviation Ltd, Binbrook 26-5-95; Everett Aero, Sproughton, Suffolk 9-95; Randall K. Hames, Gaffney, SC, USA as **N372JP** 3-4-96; Joni B. Hames, Rutherfordton, NC, 2-1-97; Walter J. Hester, Marietta, GA, 26-3-01; re-reg **N399PS** Walter J. Hester, Marietta, GA, 15-6-01 (flew as "Wings of the Morning Provost Team"); sale rep., Charleston, SC 6-08; struck-off US register 19-8-13

XW373 AwCn 23-9-71; RAFC/80 24-9-71, recoded 11; **BAC Conv T Mk.5A** 15-4-75; RAFC/11 4-8-75; 3FTS/11; Shawbury (store) 13-8-91; tendered 15-2-93 and sold Downbird UK Ltd, Stoke-on-Trent; C. Allen/Grand Touring Cars and reg **N373XW** 7-7-93; Astre Aire, Aurora, CO, USA 7-93; Jet Provost Partnership, Aurora, CO, 9-8-93; Astre Aire, Aurora, CO, 3-5-95 (based Denver-Front Range, CO as "XW373/11"); struck-off US register 12-9-12

XW374 AwCn 18-6-71; 1FTS/75 21-6-71; **BAC Conv T Mk.5A** 19-3-75; 1FTS/75 27-6-75; 5MU (store) 11-3-76; RAFC/38 6-7-79, unit rena. 3FTS; Shawbury (store) 25-4-91; tendered 7-92; sold to Wessex Aviation 14-10-92; International Air Parts, Sydney, NSW (arr. dism. Sydney-Bankstown 3-93, stored Bankstown assembled 93/97 "XW374/38"); Nick Costin, Sydney-Bankstown, NSW, 3-97; Rodney J. Hall, Port Maquarie NSW 1998/99; reg **VH-JPE** Rodney J. Hall/International Fighter Flight Centre, Port Maquarie, NSW 17-11-99; (civil conv. Bankstown NSW, ff 12-99); Jet Fighter Flight Adventures, Pentland, Qld 16-4-02 (flew as RAF "XW374/38"); Warbird Downunder Holdings, Sale, Vic 22-11-06

XW375 AwCn 25-10-71; RAFC/90 28-10-71, recoded 10; **BAC Conv T Mk.5A** 7-3-75; RAFC/10 17-6-75; 3FTS/10 21-1-80; 6FTS/L 1-1-86; CFS/52 4-4-86; GI **9149M** 7-6-93; 1 SoTT Halton 7-6-93; 2 SoTT Cosford/52 7-95

XW404 AwCn 30-6-71; 1FTS/77 1-7-71; **BAC Conv T Mk.5A** 25-2-75; 1FTS/77 11-6-75; RAFC 7-2-86; 1FTS/77 17-3-86; GI **9049M** 7-6-93; 4 SoTT St Athan 16-8-90; tendered 11-05 and Ashclyst Farm, Exeter, Devon (store); Hartlepool College of Further Education, 15-5-11

XW405 AwCn 9-7-71; RAFC/83 12-7-71; **BAC Conv T Mk.5A** 30-10-75; 1FTS/61 9-2-76; 7FTS 29-5-85; 1FTS/61 24-6-85; 6FTS/J 27-11-85; Shawbury (store) 2-10-89; GI **9187M** 5-5-93; 2 SoTT Cosford 15-5-93; tendered and sold to Witham Special Vehicles, Colsterworth, Lincs 3-07; Ashclyst Farm, Exeter, Devon; Hartlepool College of Further Education 15-5-11 and placed on a plinth in Stockton Street, 11-1-14

XW406 AwCn 7-7-71; 3FTS/48 8-7-71; **BAC Conv T Mk.5A** 6-10-75; 3FTS Leeming (store) 23-12-75; 5MU (store)15-1-76; RAFC/23 21-3-79; 3 FTS/23; Scampton (store & spares recovery) 1991; sold Denver Aerospace Museum, Aurora, CO, USA 5-91

XW407 AwCn 5-8-71; 3FTS/50 9-8-71; **BAC Conv T Mk.5A** 13-10-75; 3FTS/50 21-1-76; 5MU (store) 11-2-76; 3FTS/47 6-3-79; 7FTS/58 31-5-79, recoded 122; m/a/c XW411 when visual contact was lost during a tail chase; despite taking avoiding action he struck and removed the tail section of the two aircraft, abandoned and crashed near Middle Heads Farm, North Yorks, 6-6-86; SOC 27-6-86

XW408 AwCn 9-7-71; RAFC/84 14-7-71; **BAC Conv T Mk.5A** 25-9-74; RAFC/84 17-12-74, recoded 24; Shawbury (store) 12-8-91; tendered and sold to Wessex Aviation 14-10-92; International Air Parts, Sydney NSW (arr. dism. Bankstown 3-93 "XW408/24"); Mike Mathews/Skywise Aviation, Devonport, TAS, 1997 (arr. Devonport ex Sydney-Bankstown 3-97 for rest. to airworthiness); reg **VH-YZC** Aerospace Services Group, Sydney, NSW, 11-8-03; Peter Hanneman, Sydney, NSW, 29-4-07; Michael J. Stoneham, Melbourne, Vic, 1-4-14; Sold?

XW409 AwCn 12-8-71; 1FTS/78 15-8-71; **BAC Conv T Mk.5A** 7-3-75; 1FTS/78 18-6-75; 7FTS/60 4-4-79, recoded 123; GI **9047M** to 4 SoTT/CTTS St Athan 29-6-90; tendered and sold to private owner, Rochdale/Bury area – Hawarden

XW410 AwCn 26-8-71; 3FTS/51 27-8-71; **BAC Conv T Mk.5A** 7-1-74; 5MU 17-6-74; RAFC/90 25-11-74, recoded 14; JP Det 30-1-78; RAFC 10-3-78; 1FTS/80 8-10-82; Shawbury (store) 19-3-92; GI **9125M** 14-10-91; 1 SoTT Cosford/MR 1-3-93; Jet Art Aviation Ltd, Selby, Yorks 16-1-13; Norwich (cockpit section: private) 1-14

XW411 AwCn 19-8-71; RAFC/70 23-8-71; **BAC Conv T Mk.5A** 12-11-75 – 1-3-75; RAFC/70 7-3-75, recoded 16; Wyton Det 1-11-77; RAFC 20-1-78; JP Det 10-3-78; RAFC 30-7-78; JP Det 1-9-78; RAFC 12-78, 1FTS (loan) 20-11-79; RAFC 29-11-79; 7FTS/133 27-9-84; FA Cat 5 6-6-86 m/a/c XW407 2m NW Helmsley and crashed at High Leys Farm, North Yorks; SOC 27-6-86

XW412 AwCn 26-8-71; RAFC/85 27-8-71; **BAC Conv T Mk.5A** 25-6-74; RAFC/85 22-10-74, recoded 15; 1FTS/74 1-10-91; Linton (store) 5-93; Shawbury (store) 22-9-93; tendered 19-11-93; Global Aviation Ltd, Binbrook 1-6-94; Lance Toland Associates, Griffin, GA 1994; reg Impex Aero Ltd, Wilmington, DE, as **N8088V**, 8-3-95; Hampton Air Inc, Griffin, GA 9-8-95; Middle Georgia Technical College Foundation, Warner Robins, GA, as GI 16-7-08; Moneypenny LLC, Peachtree City, GA 6-10-09; PPS Avn LLC (Bruce Wienand), Brakpan, JoBurg, RSA, 8-16 (restoration)

XW413 AwCn 17-9-71; RAFC/89 26-10-71; **BAC Conv T Mk.5A** 23-9-75; 1FTS/69 12-12-75; 3FTS 23-2-79; 1FTS 21-3-79; 7FTS 22-5-80; 1FTS/69 30-6-80; Shawbury (store) 4-2-92; GI **9126M** 14-10-91;1 SoTT Halton 20-2-92; 2 SoTT Cosford 9-94; tendered 7-6 and sold Astre Air International, Watkins, CO 12-06; reg N413XW Astre Air International, Watkins, CO 11-1-07; Craven Community College, New Bern, NC 18-7-12

XW414 AwCn 15-11-71; CFS/89 16-11-71; **BAC Conv T Mk.5A** 10-6-75 – 29-9-75; CFS/89 2-10-75; RAFC/34 12-4-76; 3FTS/67 27-10-77; FA Cat.5S 28-6-78, abandoned after engine failed on final approach and crashed 1m N Dishforth, Yorks; SOC 4-7-78

XW415 AwCn 12-7-72; 5MU (store) 14-7-72; Leeming (store) 15-12-75; **BAC Conv T Mk.5A** 21-1-76; 3FTS Leeming (store) 3-5-76; 3FTS/53 12-5-76; 7FTS 10-11-82; 3FTS 17-2-83; CFS/3FTS 4-84, CFS/53 19-9-84; 1FTS/80 by 25-9-92; Linton (store) 6-93; Shawbury (store); tendered 19-11-93; Global Aviation Ltd, Binbrook, on sale to Lance P. Toland, Griffin, GA 14-2-94, reg **N900LT;** Pike Aviation, Troy, AL, 4-94; Roland Marichal, Miami, FL,18-3-98; Skyline Capital LLC, Fort Wayne, IN, 27-6-07; Mayra Sotero, Miami, FL 24-1-12

XW416 AwCn 13-10-71; RAFC/82 14-10-71; Cat 4R 30-8-72; BAe (repairs) 27-10-72 – 21-12-72; RAFC 19-12-72; **BAC Conv T Mk.5A** 11-11-75; RAFC/30 24-2-76; 1FTS (loan) 19-9-77; RAFC/30 24-10-77, recoded 19 by 7-78; 1FTS/84 11-10-91; GI **9191M** 7-6-93; 2 SoTT/MT Cosford 15-6-93; Everett Aero, Sproughton/Bentwaters 2014

XW417 AwCn 13-10-71; RAFC/88 14-10-71; **BAC Conv T Mk.5A** 31-10-75; 1FTS/64 13-2-76; 7FTS/64 18-4-79, recoded 124; 1FTS 13-12-79; 7FTS 27-2-80; FA Cat.5S 10-12-82, dived into the bank of Thirlmere reservoir, Cumbria after the pilot had become disorientated in bad weather and lost control (1); SOC 5-1-83

XW418 AwCn 16-8-72; 5MU 21-8-72; Leeming 24-11-75 for mdc fit; **BAC Conv T Mk.5A** 16-12-75; 3FTS Leeming (store) 13-4-76; 3FTS/54 29-4-75; CFS/3FTS 9-4-84; CFS/54 19-9-84; 7FTS/126 11-6-86; CFS/60 8-10-91; Shawbury (store) 19-8-92; GI **9173M** 17-12-92; 2 SoTT Cosford/MT 9-03-92; RAF Museum, Cosford; wfu 10-16

XW419 AwCn 21-10-81; RAFC/78 22-10-71; **BAC Conv T Mk.5A** 29-9-75; 1FTS/65 17-12-75; CFS 27-1-78; 1FTS 20-3-78; 7FTS/65 23-4-79, recoded 125; 1FTS 19-6-87; 7FTS 21-7-87; Shawbury (store) 23-9-91; GI **9120M** 16-9-91; 1 SoTT Halton 17-10-91; 1 SoTT Cosford 7-95; tendered 10-95; Wickenby 9-06; Booker 14-10-06; Crondall, Hants (store) 2-07; DHA Bournemouth 3-09; Bruntingthorpe (restoration); Highland Aviation Museum, Tore, Highland (private) 2015

XW420 AwCn 28-10-71; RAFC/91 29-10-91, recoded 8; **BAC Conv T Mk.5A** 14-5-74 – 30-9-74; RAFC/8 11-10-74; 1FTS/83 3-10-91; GI **9194M** 7-6-93; 2 SoTT Cosford/MU/83 15-6-93; Woodvale 25-6-13 for display

XW421 AwCn 30-11-71; CFS/90 6-12-71; **BAC Conv T Mk.5A** 3-6-75; CFS/90 9-9-75; RAFC/35 12-4-76; CFS/3FTS/68 31-10-77; 3FTS 16-6-81; CFS 4-84, CFS/60 19-9-84; Shawbury (store) 29-8-91, GI **9111M** 23-7-91; 1 SoTT Halton 1-10-91; 1 SoTT Cosford 9-94; tendered 9-97 and sold Everett Avn, Sproughton by 7-06; exported to Baarlo, Netherlands 6-09; to Karellas Koropiou, Greece 11-11

XW422 AwCn 23-8-72, 5MU 25-8-72, RAFC/68 21-1-74; **BAC Conv T Mk.5A** 17-12-74; RAFC/3 13-3-75; Shawbury (store) 25-4-91; tendered 19-11-93; Global Aviation Ltd, Binbrook 11-93;

reg **G-BWEB** James S. Everett, Aylesbury/ Ipswich 19-6-95 (op: Bob Thompson/Gosh That's Aviation, North Weald); Clive J. Thompson, Radlett 3-1-96; Douglas W. N. Johnson/Transair Pilot Shop, North Weald 20-10-97; Shaun Patrick/Jet Provost T.5A Group/XW422 Group, Kemble 29-5-03; James Miller, Nailsworth, 20-8-12; Charles O. Kyle & Christopher H. Vaughan, Kemble 16-4-14 (flies as RAF "XW422")

XW423 AwCn 31-8-72; 5MU 6-9-72; Leeming 5-11-75; **BAC Conv T Mk.5A** 25-11-75 – 27-2-76; 3FTS Leeming (store) 2-3-76; 3FTS/55 30-3-76; 1FTS/78 17-3-81; Leeming 14-1-83; RAFC 16-2-83; RAFC/14 16-2-88; Shawbury (store) 12-10-88; Everett Aero, Sproughton 27-4-96; reg **G-BWUW** Russell E. Dagless, Dereham 18-7-96; Lorch Airways (UK) Ltd, Norwich 9-6-98; Tindon Ltd, Little Snoring 20-8-99 (flew as RAF "XW423", Permit to Fly expired 14-2-02); Steve Jackson/North East Wales Institute, Deeside College, Connah's Quay, as GI 25-6-03; struck-off reg. 29-6-06

XW424 AwCn 31-8-72; 5MU (store) 6-9-72; 3FTS/52 25-10-73; 1FTS/4 21-2-75; 3FTS Leeming (store) 14-4-75; **BAC Conv T Mk.5A** 27-10-75; 1FTS/62 29-1-76; FA Cat.5s 30-4-77, crashed at Linton-on-Ouse, Yorks during a solo aerobatic display practice, pilot seriously injured; SOC Cat 5S 10-5-77

XW425 AwCn 23-12-71;BAC Warton 14-8-72 (TI for mdc fit and canopy removal system, loan extended for avionics refit); **T Mk.5A prototype conv** to 31-5-74; loan extended to 21-10-74 for F'boro Air Show; CFS/84 6-6-74; (mdc fit 6-8-75 – 3-9-75); RAFC/36 12-4-76; CFS/3FTS/69 25-10-77; 5MU 13-1-81; 3FTS 31-2-81; CFS 4-84; CFS/61 19-9-84; 6FTS/H 1-1-86; Finningley (store), 9-11-88; Shawbury (store) 23-11-88; GI 9200M 6-7-93; 2 SoTT Cosford/MV/H 20-7-93; Jet Art Aviation Ltd, Selby, Yorks 16-1-13; Dronten; PS Aero Collection, Baarlo, Neth, 2014

XW426 AwCn 25-5-72; 5MU 22-6-72; 3FTS/53 3-1-74; 1FTS/5 21-2-75; 3FTS Leeming (store)/53 15-4-75; **BAC Conv T Mk.5A** 7-11-75; 1FTS/60 27-2-76; FA Cat.5S 23-1-78, crashed at Riggs Farm, Dalby Forest, North Yorks following loss of control in a dive, both crew ejected; Cat 5S and SOC 27-1-78

XW427 AwCn 28-1-72; 5MU 7-2-72; St Athan (hack) 7-5-74; 5MU 9-10-75; Leeming 17-12-75; **BAC Conv T Mk.5A** 21-1-76; 3FTS Leeming (store) 13-4-76; 3FTS/56 12-5-76; 7FTS 10-11-72; 3FTS 17-2-83; CFS 4-84; CFS/56; 1FTS/67 21-1-91; Shawbury (store) 20-1-92; GI **9124M** 14-10-91; 1 SoTT Halton 18-2-92; 2

SoTT Cosford 9-94; tendered 10-05; sold Astre Air International, Watkins, Co, 12-06; reg N427XW Astre Air International, Watkins, Co, 11-1-07

XW428 AwCn 6-7-72; 5MU 11-7-72; 3FTS/54 16-11-73; **BAC Conv T Mk.5A** 5-8-75 – 31-10-75; 1FTS/70 4-11-75; 7FTS 4-7-80; 1FTS 31-7-80; RAFC/39 7-4-86; GI RAE Farnborough 18-6-91; tendered and sold Global Avn, Binbrook 11-93; exported to Randall K. Hames, Cliffside, NC, as **N4311M** 30-12-94; Walter A. Newton, Lenoir, NC, 19-7-95; Vintage Aviation Inc, Leesville, SC, 8-5-12

XW429 AwCn 12-6-72; 5MU 22-6-72; Leeming 3-12-75; **BAC Conv T Mk.5A** 23-12-75; 3FTS Leeming (store) 6-4-76; 3FTS/57 14-4-76; BAC Warton 18-5-77; 3FTS 16-6-77; RAFC/28 13-11-81; 1FTS/66 7-4-86; **Scampton conv T Mk.5B** 27-9-88; 6FTS/C 6-12-88; Shawbury (store) 21-9-93; tendered 19-11-93; Global Aviation Ltd, Binbrook 3-10-94; exported to Impex Aero Inc, Wilmington, DE, and reg **N556A** 21-11-95; All Star Helicopters, Vandalia, OH 21-4-99; Guy B. Williams, Carson City, Nv 19-8-03; Rick Bryant, Springfield, Mo, 4-05; Charles S. Kennedy, Waynesborough, Va 24-2-06; Brian E. Peters, Las Vegas, Nv 25-4-08

XW430 AwCn 25-5-72; 5MU 31-5-72; Leeming 10-11-75; **BAC Conv T Mk.5A** 25-11-75 – 27-2-76; 3FTS Leeming (store) 2-3-76; 3FTS/58 19-3-76; CFS 4-84; CFS/58 19-9-84; 1FTS/77 6-91; 1 SoTT Cosford as GI **9176M**/MW 20-1-93

XW431 AwCn 24-5-72; 5MU 31-5-72; Leeming 11-11-75; **BAC Conv T Mk.5A** 28-11-75; 3FTS Leeming (store) 18-3-76; 3FTS/59 12-4-76; CFS/3FTS/59 8-4-82; CFS/59 19-9-84; **Scampton for T Mk.5B mod** 24-5-88; 6FTS/A 28-9-88; Shawbury (store) 25-5-93; tendered 2-95 and sold Colin P. Allen/ Downbird UK Ltd, Tatenhill and reg **G-BWBS** 13-4-95; Nigel D. Paterson, North Weald 18-4-97 (flew as "XW431/A"); crashed into the North Sea, 1m off Bradwell-on-Sea, Essex, 24-12-98 when control lost during a practice aerobatics at 3,000 ft, pilot ejected but was killed; wreckage to Farnborough for investigation then scrapped by Hanningfield Metals, Stock, Essex

XW432 AwCn 6-6-72; 5MU 8-6-72; Leeming 20-11-75, **BAC conv T Mk.5A** 10-12-75 – 18-3-76; 3FTS Leeming (store) 19-3-76; 3FTS/60 5-4-76; 1FTS/76 26-11-81; 7FTS 24-2-87; 1FTS/76 17-3-87; Shawbury (store) 17-3-92; GI **9127M** 14-10-91; 1 SoTT/76/MX Cosford 09-03-93; Everett Aero, Sproughton/Bentwaters 10-03; Thame, Oxon (private) 6-15

XW433 AwCn 15-6-72; 5MU 30-6-72; Leeming 3-12-75; **BAC Conv T Mk.5A** 6-1-76; 3FTS Leeming (store) 6-4-76; 3FTS/61 27-4-76; 7FTS 10-11-82; 3FTS 17-2-83; 7FTS/124 30-3-84; CFS/124, reno 63; Shawbury (store) 1-5-92; tendered 19-11-93; Global Aviation, Binbrook, 23-5-1995; Ruddington Aviation Ltd, Nottingham 10-8-95 and reg **G-JPRO;** Edwalton Aviation Ltd, Humberside 11-11-99 (flies as RAF "XW433"); Air Atlantique Classic Flight, Coventry 13-7-07; Classic Air Force Museum, Newquay, Cornwall 17-5-13; CAF Coventry, 2014

XW434 AwCn 6-7-72; 5MU 11-7-72; CFS/92 8-8-73; **BAC Conv T Mk.5A** 16-10-73; CFS/92 21-3-74; RAFC/37 12-4-76; 3FTS/CFS/49 17-11-77; 7FTS/57 12-7-79, recoded 126; 5MU 1-10-79; 1FTS/126 23-11-79; 7FTS/126 27-2-80; 1FTS/78 7-4-86; 7FTS 20-10-86; 1FTS/78 7-11-86; 5MU 17-3-91; GI **9091M** 1-3-91; 1 SoTT Halton 10-91; 2 SoTT/MY Cosford 9-94; Jet Art Aviation Ltd, Selby, Yorks 16-1-13; Halfpenny Green Airport, Wolverhampton, for display 30-5-13

XW435 AwCn 12-7-72; 5MU 14-7-72; CFS/93 30-8-73; **BAC Conv T Mk.5A** 23-10-73 – 26-3-74; CFS/93 4-4-74; RAFC/93 12-4-76, recoded 4; Shawbury (store) 18-10-91; tendered 7-92; Wessex Avn 14-10-92; International Air Parts, Sydney, NSW (arr. dism. Sydney-Bankstown "XW435/4" 6-93); Jerry R. Schuster, Taft, Ca, 29-12-98 and reg **N4XW;** Robert A. Stambovsky, Lancaster, Ca 11-05; Turin Aviation Group, Brandon, FL 27-2-14

XW436 AwCn 21-9-72; 5MU 5-10-72; RAFC/69 31-1-74; **BAC Conv T Mk.5A** 23-4-75 – 17-7-75; 3FTS Leeming (store) 30-7-75; 3FTS/62 30-4-76; CFS/62 19-9-84; 1FTS/68 2-91; GI **9148M** 18-5-92; 1 SoTT Halton 18-5-92; 2 SoTT Cosford/69 9-94

XW437 AwCn 27-9-72; 5MU 6-10-72; CFS/91 31-7-73; **BAC Conv T Mk.5A** 4-10-73; CFS/91 21-3-74; RAFC/39 12-4-76, recoded 1; 7FTS 19-11-87; RAFC 11-12-87; 1FTS/71 13-8-91; Linton (store) 5-93; Shawbury (store) 21-9-93; tendered 19-11-93; Global Aviation Ltd, Binbrook, 5-8-94; Lance Toland Associates, Griffin, GA, 1994; Impex Aero Ltd, Wilmington DE and reg **N80873** 8-3-95; Frank C. Waller, Merrimack, NH 15-4-99

XW438 AwCn 28-9-72, 5MU 9-10-72, RAFC/67 13-12-73, **BAC Conv T Mk.5A** 26-11-74; BAC Warton 12-3-75 (TI CL6 compass caging facility); RAFC/67 5-5-75 recoded 2; RAFC/2 29-8-75; **Scampton conv T Mk.5B;** Finningley (store) 5-10-88; 6FTS/B 14-11-88; Shawbury (store) 13-5-93; GI RAFO Technical College, Seeb/Muscat, Oman as **100** 3-10-94

OVERSEAS ORDERS AND INDIVIDUAL HISTORIES

JET PROVOST T MK.51

CJ701 G-23-1 (ex-T Mk.2) del Ceylon 13-12-59; preserved Wirawila AB

CJ702 G-23-5 del Ceylon 13-12-59

CJ703 del Ceylon 13-12-59

CJ704 del Ceylon 13-12-59; abandoned after engine failure, Negombo Lagoon, 1-2-60. Preserved Ratmalana

CJ705 del Ceylon 13-12-59; Viharamahadevi Park, Ratmalana

CJ706 del Ceylon 13-12-59; preserved Batticola AB

CJ707 del Ceylon; Preserved China Bay

CJ708 del Ceylon

CJ709 del Ceylon; preserved Jaffna

CJ710 del Ceylon; gate guard, Anuradhapura AB

CJ711 del Ceylon; Sri Lanka AF Museum, Ratmalana (marked as CJ701)

184

CJ712 del Ceylon 10-12-60; SLAF's Eagles' Lakeside Banquet & Convention Hall, Attidiya

184. Jet Provost T Mk.51 CJ701 (actually CJ711) preserved at the Sri Lanka Museum, Ratmala, 27 February 2014. (Taff Evans)

124 G-23-1 del Sudan 17-10-61; crashed & w/o 13-6-62

139 del Sudan 17-10-61; crashed on take-off at Wadi Sayyidna, near Omdurman, 26-5-62

143 del Sudan 17-10-61; to Nigeria 8-67

157 del Sudan17-10-61; to Nigeria 8-67

101 del Kuwait 1-62; wfu 1970; Kuwait Air Force Collection, Kuwait International Airport (store)

102 del Kuwait 1-62; wfu 1970

103 del Kuwait 1-62; wfu 1970; Museum of Science & Industry, Kuwait City

104 del Kuwait 1962; wfu 1970; Kuwait Air Force Collection, Kuwait International Airport (store)

105 del Kuwait 1962; wfu 1970: Kuwait Air Force Collection, Kuwait International Airport (store)

106 del Kuwait 1962; Kuwait Air Force Collection, Kuwait International Airport (store)

T MK.52

162 del Sudan 28-11-62

173 del Sudan 28-11-62

175 del Sudan 11-11-63

180 del Sudan 11-11-63

181 Originally intended for the Venezuelan air force as E-048; reg G-ASEZ 18-2-63; del Sudan 22-3-63 as 181; crashed in forced landing at Idilidje, Canton de Mangobo whilst on a ferry flight from Fort Lamy to Sudan 7-4-1963; returned HAL 6-63; reg cnx and scrapped 2-1-64

185 del Sudan 23-12-63

190 del Sudan 2-1-64

195 del Sudan 27-1-64

E-040 G-23-1 del Venezuela 2-1963 reno '9385'?; FAV Museum, Maracay

185

E-041 G-23-2 del Venezuela 2-1963 reno '9415'; Maracay/ Mariscal Sucre

E-042 del Venezuela 2-1963 reno '5634'

E-043 del Venezuela 2-1963 reno '4704'

E-044 del Venezuela 2-1963 reno

E-045 del Venezuela 2-1963 reno

E-046 del Venezuela 2-1963 reno

E-047 del Venezuela 2-1963 reno

E-048 del Venezuela 2-1963 reno '5354'

E-049 del Venezuela 2-1963 reno

E-050 del Venezuela 2-1963 reno '3309'

E-051 del Venezuela 2-1963 reno

E-052 del Venezuela 2-1963 reno

E-053 del Venezuela 2-1963 reno

186

E-054 del Venezuela 2-1963 reno

600 del Iraq 31-8-64

601 del Iraq 31-8-64

602 del Iraq 31-8-64

603 del Iraq 16-10-64

604 del Iraq 16-10-64

605 del Iraq 16-10-64

606 del Iraq 12-11-64

607 del Iraq 12-11-64

608 del Iraq 12-11-64

609 del Iraq 9-1-65

610 del Iraq 9-1-65

611 del Iraq 9-1-65

612 del Iraq 15-2-65

613 del Iraq 15-2-65

614 del Iraq 15-2-65

615 del Iraq 25-3-65

616 del Iraq 25-3-65

617 del Iraq 25-3-65

618 del Iraq 28-4-65

619 Del Iraq 28-4-65

JET PROVOST T MK.55

167 G27-106 del Sudan 30-3-69

177 G27-107 del Sudan 30-3-69

187 G27-108 del Sudan 30-3-69

192 G27-109 del Sudan 13-6-69

197 G27-110 del Sudan 13-6-69

STRIKEMASTER PRODUCTION AND HISTORIES

MK.80 SAUDI 901 G27-8 F/f 7-8-80; BAC (devt work); del RSAF 24-9-69

MK.80 SAUDI 902 G27-9 G-AWOR BAC (devt work; Farnboro 9-68) del RSAF 24-9-69

MK.80 SAUDI 903 G27-10 del RSAF 26-8-68; failed to recover from spin 8-12-70

MK.80 SAUDI 904 G27-11 del RSAF 26-8-68

MK.80 SAUDI 905 G27-12 del RSAF 26-8-68

MK.80 SAUDI 906 G27-13 (G-AWOS; FARNBORO 09-68) del RSAF 23-10-68

MK.80 SAUDI 907 G27-14 del RSAF 23-10-68; crashed 26-2-70

MK.80 SAUDI 908 G27-15 del RSAF 26-10-68; crashed 12-8-70

MK.80 SAUDI 909 G27-16 del RSAF 26-10-68; crashed 15-4-70

MK.80 SAUDI 910 G27-17 del RSAF 6-12-68; reno. 1104

MK.80 SAUDI 911 G27-18 del RSAF 6-12-68; RSAF Museum, Riyadh

MK.80 SAUDI 912 G27-19 del RSAF 6-12-68

MK.80 SAUDI 1101 G27-20 del RSAF 5-2-69; GI Riyadh

MK.80 SAUDI 1102 G27-21 to RSAF 5-2-69; Global Aviation Services Ltd, Humberside 10-00; G-BZWL Richard J. Everett/ Everett Aero, Ipswich 22-5-01; sold to USA, struck-off reg.

185. Mounted on a plinth at the Air Force Museum, Aragua, Maracay, Jet Provost T Mk.52, E-040, was delivered to Venezuela in February 1963 and later renumbered as '9385'. (Manuel E. Silva)

186. The first three Jet Provost T Mk.52s (600, 601 & 602) for the Iraqi air force were delivered from Luton to the Rashid air base on 31 August 1964, flown by Reg Stock and two Iraqi pilots, Capt Hakam and Lt Mohammed. (BAC via Reg Stock)

7-7-01; N399WH Wendell Hall, Cheraw, SC 11-7-01; DTK Aviation, Boca Raton, FL 17-6-02; ran off runway, struck fence, Boca Raton, FL 15-5-05; struck-off USCR 12-11-08

MK.80 SAUDI 1103 G27-22 del RSAF 27-3-69; Riyadh store

MK.80 SAUDI 1104 G27-23 del R Saudi AF 27-3-69; Global Aviation Services Ltd, Humberside 10-00; G-SMAS Mk.80(R) A M A Petrie, Hawarden 25-4-05; reg N702MF, Blue Air Training, Las Vegas, NV 11-8-16

MK.80 SAUDI 1105 G27-24 del R Saudi AF 10-2-69; Global Aviation Services Ltd, Humberside 10-00; G-BZYF Richard J. Everett/Everett Aero, Ipswich 3-7-01; sold to USA, struck-off reg. 30-1-02 (stored dism. orig. Saudi scheme, Cheraw, SC 2-02); N156MW Mark Walton, Martinsburg, PA 26-6-02

MK.80 SAUDI 1106 G27-25 del RSAF 9-4-69; Riyadh store

MK.80 SAUDI 1107 G27-26 del RSAF 13-5-69; Sold Australia (?)

MK.80 SAUDI 1108 G27-27 del RSAF 13-5-69; Global Aviation Services Ltd, Humberside 10-00; Richard J. Everett/Everett Aero, Ipswich 2001; Tom Maloney/Transair (UK) Ltd, North Weald 2001 (del. to Duxford 6-01 for civil certification); G-CBPB Transair (UK) Ltd, North Weald 29-5-02 (ff Duxford 14-4-03, del. to Cranwell for repaint as camouflaged FA Ecuador "FAE259"); G-UPPI Transair (UK) Ltd, North Weald 20-5-03; Gower Jets, Swansea 23-1-04; sold to South Africa, struck-off USCR 24-11-05 (noted at Cape Town-Thunder City 12-05 still "FAE259"); ZU-JAK Heriot Aviation, Cape Town 7-9-06 (minor dam. wheels-up landing, Durban-Virginia 28-10-06 (arr. dism. Exeter 5-8-08 for repair); G-UPPI Gerald P. Williams, Swansea 11-12-08; Engine failed and force-landed nr Tiverton, Devon 26-4-09; struck-off reg 14-9-12

MK.80 SAUDI 1109 G27-28 del RSAF 13-6-69; crashed 15-4-79

MK.80 SAUDI 1110 G27-29 del RSAF 13-6-69; "damaged 1983"; RSAF Museum, Riyadh (store)

MK.80 SAUDI 1111 G27-30 del RSAF 13-6-69; Riyadh (store)

MK.80 SAUDI 1112 G27-31 del RSAF 7-7-69; Global Aviation Services Ltd, Humberside 10-00; G-FLYY David. T. Barber, Londonderry, Northern Ireland 3-9-01 underwing drop tanks damaged when landed with undercarriage retracted Kemble (repaired) 7-7-06 (flew in civil scheme "Whitehouse Retail Group"

titles); G-FLYY Strikemaster Ltd, Bath 28-2-12 (flies as Saudi "1112"); Enrico Maranzana & Lorena Pressacco, Kemble 17-3-14; repainted as G-FLYY 2016; Hi G Jets Ltd, Blackpool 9-1-17

MK.80 SAUDI 1113 G27-32 G-BESY BAC Warton; to RSAF 7-7-69; G-BESY BAC 26-4-77; Imperial War Museum, Duxford 13-4-02

187

MK.81 SOUTH YEMEN 501 G27-33 to Sth Yemen AF 6-8-69; to Singapore as 320 1974

MK.81 SOUTH YEMEN 502 G27-34 del Sth Yemen AF 5-8-69; to Singapore as 321 1974

MK.81 SOUTH YEMEN 503 G27-35 G-AXEF BAC Preston 24-4-69 (Paris air show 4-69); to South Yemen AF as 503 5-7-69; to Republic of Singapore AF as 322 1974; International Air Parts, Sydney, NSW 1988; Wally Fisk/Amjet Aircraft Corp, St Paul, MN 1990; N167SM Wally Fisk/Amclyde Engineered Products Inc/Polar Aviation Museum, Anoka County, MN 21-7-93 (rest., CofA 2-2-94, flies as "Kenya AF 322"); Harris Air Inc, Logan, UT 5-5-99; Pacific Coast Air Museum, Santa Rosa, CA 30-7-02; Pacific Rim Aviation, Renton, WA 18-4-08; Dragon Aviation Inc, Wilmington, DE 6-10; crashed into Hudson River, near Kingston, NY 26-2-11 (1k)

MK.81 SOUTH YEMEN 504 G27-36 G-AXFX BAC Preston 21-5-69 (Paris air show); South Yemen AF as 504 7-69; Republic of Singapore AF as 323 1974; International Air Parts, Sydney, NSW 1988; Wally Fisk/Amjet Aircraft Corp, St Paul, MN 1990; N21419 Amclyde Engineered Products Inc, St Paul, MN 6-12-93; Dura Line Corp, Middlesboro, KY 1999; Amjet Services Inc, Blaine, MN 12-2-01 sale rep., Hawarden Airport, UK 5-04; struck-off USCR 30-7-13

MK.82 OMAN 401 G27-102 del Oman as 401 21-1-69; w/o 18-7-71 (1k)

MK.82 OMAN 402 G27-103 del Oman 21-1-69; to Republic of Singapore AF as 327 5-77; International Air Parts, Sydney NSW 1988; Wally Fisk/Amjet Aircraft Corp, St Paul, MN 1990; N2143J Amclyde Engineered Products Inc, St Paul, MN 6-12-93; N167NM Ricky Melton 11-96; North American Aviation Group, Rockford, IL 24-7-98; Baker Aviation, White Bear Lake, MN 20-4-00; JRMC Inc, Chesterton, IN 9-7-01; Courtesy Aircraft Inc, Rockford, IL 1-10-02; Albert V. Mondus, Eagle River, WI 1-04; Time Makers Inc, Bear, DE 20.12-05; Vortek LLC, Redmond, OR 1-08; sold to Canada, struck-off USCR 27-4-11; C-GXDK Danny Richer, Brantford, Ont 5-5-11

MK.82 OMAN 403 G27-104 del Oman 12-3-69; gate guard Thumrait

MK.82 OMAN 404 G27-105 del Oman 12-3-69; to Republic of Singapore AF as 328 5-77; International Air Parts, Sydney NSW 1988; Wally Fisk/Amjet Aircraft Corp, St Paul, MN 1990; N21444 Amclyde Engineered Products Inc, St Paul, MN 6-12-93; Dura Line Corp, Middlesboro, KY 1999; Amjet Services Inc, Blaine, MN 2-2-01; Northwest Helicopters Inc, Olympia, WA 26-1-09

MK.82 OMAN 405 G27-123 del Oman 24-6-69; stalled and crashed on take-off, Bayt al Falaj, 12-4-72

MK.82 OMAN 406 G27-124 del Oman 24-6-69; hit by SAM 7 missile, Sherishitti, 19-8-75

MK.82 OMAN 407 G27-125 del Oman 24-6-69; to Republic of Singapore AF as 329 5-77; International Air Parts, Sydney NSW 1988; Wally Fisk/Amjet Aircraft Corp, St Paul, MN 1990 (noted Chandler Memorial AZ "329" 10-91); N167X David J. Lofstrom, Chandler, AZ 29-4-93; Strikemaster Corp, Dover, DE 5-94; Chris I. Lawry, Cave Creek, AZ 4-3-99; Learning Curve Aviation LLC, Wilmington, DE 16-2-07; Vintage Aviation Inc, Leesville, SC 8-5-12

MK.84 SINGAPORE 300 G27-129 to Republic of Singapore AF 27-10-69

MK.84 SINGAPORE 301 G27-130 to Republic of Singapore AF 6-10-69

MK.84 SINGAPORE 302 G27-131 to Republic of Singapore AF 6-10-69

MK.84 SINGAPORE 303 G27-132 to Republic of Singapore AF 6-10-69; w/o 4-84

MK.84 SINGAPORE 304 G27-133 to Republic of Singapore AF 27-10-69; International Air Parts, Sydney NSW 1988; Wally Fisk/Amjet Aircraft Corp, St Paul, MN 1990; N2145V Amclyde Engineered Products Inc, St Paul, MN 12-93; Hancock Mechanical Services, Louisville, KY 2-2-95 (offered for sale as rest. project 7-03); Robert Lee Gear, Phoenix, AZ 5-2-14

MK.84 SINGAPORE 305 G27-134 to Republic of Singapore AF 27-10-69; International Air Parts, Sydney NSW 1988; Wally Fisk/Amjet Aircraft Corp, St Paul, MN 1990; N21451 Amclyde Engineered Products Inc, St Paul, MN 6-12-93; Northwest Helicopters, White City, OR 11-98; Olympic Jet Inc, Olympia, WA 15-3-01; Amjet Services Inc, St Paul, MN 6-11-01 sale rep., Grass Valley, CA 5-04; struck-off USCR 24-2-05

MK.84 SINGAPORE 306 G27-135 to Republic of Singapore AF 2-3-70; w/o 5-6-73

MK.84 SINGAPORE 307 G27-136 to Republic of Singapore AF 2-3-70; w/o 9-1-74

MK.84 SINGAPORE 308 G27-137 to Republic of Singapore AF 19-3-70; International Air Parts, Sydney NSW 1988; Wally Fisk/Amjet Aircraft Corp, St Paul, MN 1990; N2146G Amclyde Engineered Products Inc, St Paul, MN 6-12-93; Gary Guilliat/Garaire Inc, Incline Village, NV 12-4-00; Strike Master Inc, Batavia, NY 6-08

MK.84 SINGAPORE 309 G27-138 to Republic of Singapore AF 19-3-70; w/o 8-72

MK.84 SINGAPORE 310 G27-139 to Republic of Singapore AF 5-70; International Air Parts, Sydney, NSW 1988; Wally Fisk/Amjet Aircraft Corp, St Paul, MN 1990; N2146J Amclyde Engineered Products Inc, St Paul, MN 6-12-93; Aviation Management Resources Inc, Wilmington, DE 19-9-96; Amjet Aircraft Corp, Blaine, MN 10-1-01 (flies as Singapore AF "310"); Courtesy Aircraft Inc, Rockford, IL 11-04; Vortek LLC, Wilmington, DE 1-06; Dragon Aviation, League City, TX 12-2-08 (flies as Singapore AF "310")

MK.84 SINGAPORE 311 G27-140 to Republic of Singapore AF 5-70; International Air Parts, Sydney, NSW 1988; Wally Fisk/Amjet Aircraft Corp, St Paul, MN 1990; N2146S Amclyde

187. Strikemaster Mk.80, G-BESY/1133, at Le Bourget on 10 June 1975. (Jacques Guillem)

Engineered Products Inc, St Paul, MN 6-12-93; sold to UK, struck-off USCR 12-1-95; G-SARK Adrian Gjertsen/Classic Jets Flying Museum/Sark International Airways Ltd, Bournemouth 13-1-95 (stored at Biggin Hill, 1994-1999); Military Jet Partnership, North Weald 2001 (under rest. to fly, North Weald 2001; ff 1-04); Tubetime Ltd, Biggin Hill 27-6-03; G-MXPH Richard S. Partridge-Hicks, North Weald 4-5-07 (flies as Singapore AF "311")

MK.84 SINGAPORE 312 G27-141 to Republic of Singapore AF 13-7-70; International Air Parts, Sydney NSW 1988; Wally Fisk/Amjet Aircraft Corp, St Paul, MN 1990; N167BC International Jet Centre, Miami, FL 18-7-95; R & M Auto Leasing, Crystal Lake, IL 29-3-00; N1WQ R & M Auto Leasing, Crystal Lake, IL 20-4-05

MK.84 SINGAPORE 313 G27-142 to Republic of Singapore AF 13-7-70; w/o 13-7-82

MK.84 SINGAPORE 314 G27-314 G-AYHS BAC, Warton 22-7-70 (demonstrator Farnborough air show 9-70); to Republic of Singapore AF as 314 28-9-70; International Air Parts, Sydney, NSW 1988; Wally Fisk/Amjet Aircraft Corp, St Paul, MN 1990; N21463 Amclyde Engineered Products Inc, St Paul, MN 6-12-93; Kelly Monroe, St Paul-Anoka County, MN 1995; Thrust Inc, Brooklyn Park, MN 19-7-95 (rest. by Thrust Air at Anoka County, MN, ff 17-10-95); Enrique Robles, Toluca, Mexico 10-95; sold to Mexico, struck-off USCR 8-12-95; XB-GKO Alvarez Robles, Toluca 3-96; N72445 reg. 3-97; Brian Reynolds/Northwest Helicopters, White City, OR 8-11-97 op: Olympic Flight Museum, Olympia, WA 1998; Olympic Jet Inc, Olympia, WA 15-3-01 (flies as polished black, RAF "XR-366"); Blue Air Training, Las Vegas, 20-8-15

MK.84 SINGAPORE 315 G27-315 G-AYHT BAC, Warton 22-7-70 (demonstrator Farnborough air show 9-70); to Republic of Singapore AF as 315 9-10-70; Steve Ferris/International Air Parts, Sydney-Bankstown, NSW 1988; VH-AKY R. Steve Ferris, Sydney-Bankstown, NSW 7-10-92 (rest. Bankstown, ff 10-10-92 as RSAF "315") dam. wheels-up landing, Bankstown (repaired) 26-1-95; Nick Costin/Australian Fighter Flight Centre/Jet Fighter Flights, Sydney-Bankstown, NSW 2001; Aerospace Services Group, Sydney, NSW 26-11-03; broke-up in flight, dest. Bathurst NSW (2k) 5-10-06

MK.82 OMAN 408 G27-146 del Oman 29-12-69; to Republic of Singapore AF as 330 5-77; International Air Parts, Sydney,

NSW 1988; Wally Fisk/Amjet Aircraft Corp, St Paul, MN 1990; N2147S Amclyde Engineered Products Inc, St Paul, MN 6-12-93; Dura Line Corp, Middlesboro, KY 1999; Amjet Services Inc, Blaine, MN 2-2-01; Aero Investments of Minneapolis Inc, Coon Rapids, MN 7-04; Soaring Eagle Southwest LLC, Mesa, AZ 23-3-05; struck-off USCR 31-10-13

MK.82 OMAN 409 G27-147 del Oman 29-12-69; to Republic of Singapore AF as 331 5-77; International Air Parts, Sydney, NSW 1988; Wally Fisk/Amjet Aircraft Corp, St Paul, MN 1990; Michael T. McComsley, Monrovia, CA 1992 (rest. to fly, Avon Park, FL 1992); N331MM Michael T. McComsley, Bellevue, WA 12-7-93; National Aviation Museum, Tulsa, OK 6-11-01; Resource Financial Holdings, Newark, DE 7-7-03; Clark Aircraft Sales, Islamorada, FL 9-05; Douglas V. Lundeen, Jacksonville, FL 2-10

MK.82 OMAN 410 G27-148 del Oman 7-70; hit by ground fire; abandoned 15-9-71

MK.82 OMAN 411 G27-149 del Oman 23-7-70; crashed during practice forced landing near Ghaba, Oman 15-7-84

MK.82 OMAN 412 G27-150 del Oman 20-8-70; damaged 9-7-73; GI AFTC Seeb 4-04

MK.83 KUWAIT 110 G27-151 to Kuwait AF as 110:A 19-3-70; to Warton as ZG805 14-10-86; to Botswana Defence Force as OJ1 22-3-88; G-BXFU Global Aviation Ltd, Binbrook, later Humberside 29-4-97; permit to fly expired 6-8-02, struck-off reg. 17-3-07; to Ecuador as FAE266 17-3-07; AB Manta (store)

MK.83 KUWAIT 111 G27-152 to Kuwait AF as 111:B 19-3-70; to Warton as ZG806 (store) 24-9-86; to Botswana Defence Force as OJ2 22-3-88; G-BXFT Global Avn, Binbrook 29-4-97; N4242T reg. 7-98; Lance P. Toland, Griffin, GA 21-4-99; Impex Aero Ltd, Wilmington, DE 1999; Robert J. Farrell, Sacramento,

188

CA 4-1-05; Jon J. Pelland, Antioch, IL 15-7-14; Attack Aviation Foundation Inc, Las Vegas, NV 21-4-15

MK.83 KUWAIT 112 G27-153 Kuwait AF 112:C 25-6-70; sold BAC 10-86 as ZG807 (store); Botswana Defence Force as OJ5 1-7-88; crashed Gaberone 29-4-89

MK.83 KUWAIT 113 G27-154: to Kuwait AF as 113:D 25-6-70; to Warton as ZG808 (store) 14-10-86; to Botswana Defence Force as OJ6 11-7-88; G-BXFW Global Avn, Binbrook 29-4-97 (arr. Binbrook dism. 7-97, trucked to Humberside 4-10-97 for rest., ff Humberside 12-1-98); ZU-PER Ralph Garlick & James Craven/ Warbird Trust, Newlands, Cape Town 2-3-98 (del. ex Exeter 9-2-98, arr. Cape Town 14-2-98 flies in original camouflage "Botswana DF OJ6"); Test Flying Academy of South Africa 22-4-08

189

MK.83 KUWAIT 114 G27-155 Kuwait AF as 114:E 25-6-70; BAe Warton as ZG809 (store) 14-10-86; to Botswana Defence Force as OJ7 11-7-88; G-BXFX Global Avn, Binbrook 29-4-97; crashed following uncontrollable spin, Welton-Le-Wold, Lincs (1k) 9-12-00

190

MK.83 KUWAIT 115 G27-156 Kuwait as 115:F 25-6-70; BAC Warton as ZG810 (store) 1986; Botswana Defence Force as OJ3 21-3-88; gate guard, Thebe

MK.87 KENYA 601 G27-191 G-AYHR BAC, Warton (Farnborough air show demonstrator); to Kenyan AF as KAF 601 5-2-70; BAe, Warton 1986; to Botswana Defence Force as OJ4 1988; G-AYHR Global Aviation Ltd, Binbrook 29-4-97; McCarthy Aviation/Gone Flying Ltd, North Weald 27-11-97; (to North Weald 14-11-97 ex Binbrook: ff 7-3-98 North Weald as "OJ4/Z2"; G-UNNY McCarthy Aviation/Gone Flying Ltd, North Weald 19-3-98; Tom Moloney/Transair (UK) Ltd, North Weald 24-3-00 op: Aircraft Restoration Co/ARCo, Duxford 2002; Strikemaster Films Ltd, London & Ivory Coast 7-2-03; TU-VRA Strikemaster Films Ltd, Ivory Coast 11-3-03; Force Aérienne de la Côte d'Ivoire as TU-VRA 22-03-03; wfu Abidjan

MK.87 KENYA 602 G27-192 del. 5-2-70; BAe, Warton 1986; to Botswana Defence Force as OJ5 11-7-88; G-BXFP Global Avn, Binbrook 29-4-97; Clive J. Thompson/ McCarthy Aviation, North Weald 11-97 (to North Weald 17-11-97 ex-Binbrook, ff 4-98 as "RNZAF NZ6361"); Strikemaster Films Ltd, London & Ivory Coast 25-2-03; TU-VRB Strikemaster Films Ltd, Ivory Coast: reg. res. 3-03 (impounded at Malta-Luqa 3-03 during del. flight to Côte d'Ivoire as "NZ6361"); British permit to fly expired 4-8-03; Force Aérienne de la Côte d'Ivoire as TU-VRB 21-5-04; struck-off reg. 20-10-04; wfu Abidjan

MK.87 KENYA 603 G27-193 del 9-2-71; crashed nr Meru, Mt Kenya 22-7-74(1k)

MK.87 KENYA 604 G27-194 to Kenyan AF 9-2-71; BAe, Warton 1986; to Botswana Defence Force as OJ9 1988; G-BXFR Global Avn, Binbrook 29-4-97 (OJ9 trucked ex Binbrook to Sproughton 1997 for storage; sold to USA: struck-off reg. 5-8-99

188. The first three Strikemaster Mk.83s were delivered to Kuwait in July 1971. (The Aviation Bookshop via Ray Deacon)

189. Strikemaster Mk. 83, '113' was delivered to the Kuwait air force in June 1970. It was later operated by the Botswana defence force between 1988 and 1997, and is currently with a private owner in South Africa. (BAe Systems Heritage Warton-Percival/Hunting Collection)

190. Strikemaster Mk.83, '114' of the Kuwait air force, Bahrain, on 10 June 1976. It was passed to Botswana in 1988 and sold to Global Aviation in 1997, registered as G-BXFX. Sadly, it was involved in a fatal accident in December 2000. (Jacques Guillem)

MK.87 KENYA 605 G27-195 del. 22-4-71; BAe, Warton 1986; Botswana Defence Force as OJ10 1988; G-BXFS Global Avn, Binbrook 29-4-97; Gone Flying Ltd, North Weald 1-5-98; Richard J. Everett/Everett Aero, Ipswich 17-11-99; G-UVNR Global Aviation Services Ltd, Humberside 4-5-01 (under overhaul at Cape Town-Thunder City 4-06); Gerald P. Williams, Swansea 30-7-09; Petr Turek, Liberec, Czech Republic 25-1-11; de-reg 11-5-16; VH-AGZ Miltek Aviation P/L, Carrum Downs, Vic, Australia 23-12-16

MK.87 KENYA 606 G27-196 del 22-3-71

MK.83 KUWAIT 116 G27-185 Kuwait AF 116:G 2-7-71; W/o 9-11-75

MK.83 KUWAIT 117 G27-186 Kuwait AF 117:H 2-7-71; W/o 13-4-75

MK.83 KUWAIT 118 G127-187 Kuwait AF 118:J 30-5-71 ; W/o 27-7-71

MK.83 KUWAIT 119 G27-188 Kuwait AF 119:K 30-5-71; to Warton as ZG811 (store) 7-10-86; Botswana Defence Force as OJ8 21-9-88; G-BXFV Global Aviation Ltd, Binbrook, later Humberside 29-4-97; permit to fly expired 29-7-04, struck-off reg. 17-3-07; Ecuador as FAE265 17-3-07; Manta (store)

MK.83 KUWAIT 120 G27-189 G-AYVK BAC Warton (Paris air show exhibit 5-4-71); Kuwait AF 120:L 2-7-71; British Aerospace: to Warton as ZG812 7-10-86; stored Samlesbury; Botswana Defence Force as OJ9 21-9-88; crashed on landing, Francistown 21-11-89

MK.83 KUWAIT 121 G27-190 G-AYVL BAC, Warton 5-4-71 (Paris air show 4-71); to Kuwaiti AF as 121:M del. 2-7-71; BAe Warton as ZG813 7-10-86; stored Samlesbury; Botswana Defence Force as OJ4 21-9-88; failed to recover from spin and abandoned, 12m W Francistown 12-12-89

MK.88 NEW ZEALAND NZ6361 G27-197 to RNZAF as NZ6361; Ohakea AB 10-10-72; to Aermacchi 12-92 and sold by tender 3-93; International Air Parts, Sydney NSW 6-93 (arr. dism. Bankstown 7-7-93, stored 7-93); VH-ZEP D. G. Smith/International Air Parts, Narabeen, NSW 9-6-95 (rest. Sydney-Bankstown, ff 1995 as "NZ6361"); Stuart McColl/Australian Indoor Go Kart Centres, Adelaide-Parafield, SA, 1-2-96; Carlowrie Holdings Pty Ltd/Australian Jet Adventures, Newton,

Vic 5-11-99 (flew camouflaged as "RNZAF NZ6361"); sold to USA, assembled at Las Vegas 2013; (US CofA issued 28-3-13); N309JP Attack Aviation Foundation, Las Vegas, NV, 27-10-14; Blue Air Training, Las Vegas

MK.88 NEW ZEALAND NZ6362 G27-198 to RNZAF as NZ6362 Ohakea AB 9-10-72; to Aermacchi 12-92 and sold by tender 3-93; International Air Parts, Sydney, Narabeen, NSW 6-93 (arr. Bankstown dism. 8-7-93); VH-AGI International Air Parts, Sydney-Bankstown NSW 9-9-93; Neville Hyder, Busselton WA 3-94 (rest. Bankstown, ff 28-5-94 as "NZ6362"); Patricia D. Hyder, Busselton WA 19-1-09; ZK-NTY Strikemaster Ltd, Auckland NZ 19-9-14; de-reg 25-1-17; Blue Air Training, Las Vegas, 3-17

MK.88 NEW ZEALAND NZ6363 G27-199 G-AZXJ BAC, Warton; to RNZAF as NZ6363 Ohakea AB 10-7-72; Ohakea storage pending disposal 10-92; International Air Parts, Narabeen, Sydney NSW 6-93 (stored dism. Sydney-Bankstown 1993); VH-JFZ Nick Costin/Aerospace Services Group, Broadway, NSW 21-2-03; Michael Costin, Sydney, later Tocumwal, NSW 5-10-06 (flies in camouflaged Zimbabwe AF scheme)

MK.88 NEW ZEALAND NZ6364 G27-200 G-AZXK BAC, Warton (Farnborough air show 9-72) to RNZAF as NZ6364 8-11-72; Ohakea AB wfu stored 1993; to Aermacchi 12-92 and sold by tender 3-93; International Air Parts, Sydney, NSW 6-93 (arr. Sydney-Bankstown dism. 7-7-93 ex NZ; repacked 23-9-93 for shipping to USA); N6364Z Falcon Helicopter Inc, Lees Summit, MO 1-3-95; Tri-State Warbird Museum, Batavia, OH 15-4-08; Dragon Aviation Inc, Wilmington, DE 26-5-1; Blue Air Training, Las Vegas

MK.88 NEW ZEALAND NZ6365 G27-201 G-AZYN BAC, Warton (static display at Farnborough 9-72); to RNZAF as NZ6365 8-11-72; GI 4 TTS Woodbourne 1990

MK.88 NEW ZEALAND NZ6366 G27-202 to RNZAF as NZ6366 9-72; GI 4 TTS Woodbourne 4-93

MK.88 NEW ZEALAND NZ6367 G27-203 to RNZAF as NZ6367 10-72; hit power lines during low-level exercise and crashed into hillside at Waiau, Nth Canterbury, 3-7-85

MK.88 NEW ZEALAND NZ6368 G27-204 to RNZAF as NZ6368 10-72; failed to recover from spin, Pahiatua, 27-10-92

MK.88 NEW ZEALAND NZ6369 G27-205 to RNZAF as NZ6369 11-72; failed to recover from aerobatic manoeuvre and crashed into forest near Taupo (1k) 20-11-91.

MK.88 NEW ZEALAND NZ6370 G27-206 to RNZAF as NZ6370 11-72; to Aermacchi (storage) 11-92 and sold 3-93; International Air Parts, Sydney, NSW 6-93 (arr. dism. Bankstown 8-7-93, stored); VH-RBA Michael Broadbent, Southport, Qld 12-95 (under rest. Sydney-Bankstown NSW 1995); Hastings Valley Machinery, Port Macquarie NSW 30-11-00; Rod Hall/North Coast Breast Centre, Port Macquarie, NSW 25-2-04 (flew as RNZAF "NZ6370"); sold to NZ, struck-off Australian reg 18-1-11 ZK-STR Strikemaster Ltd, Auckland 11-4-12 (flies as camouflaged RNZAF "NZ6370"); de-reg 25-10-17; Blue Air Training, Las Vegas, 2-17

MK.89 ECUADOR FAE243-T43 G27-207 G-AZXL BAC, Warton 28-6-72; del 4-12-72; Esc 2113; e/f and crashed on take-off 14-10-81

MK.89 ECUADOR FAE244-T44 G27-208 del 4-12-72

MK.89 ECUADOR FAE245-T45 G27-209 del 4-12-72; W/o 20-9-73

MK.89 ECUADOR FAE246-T46 G27-210 del 4-12-72; pres Museo Aereo de la Fuerza Aerea Ecuatoriana, Quito 3-14

MK.89 ECUADOR FAE247-T47 G27-211 del 4-12-72; Esc 2113 crashed after engine failure on take-off, 4-8-80, pilot ejected.

MK.89 ECUADOR FAE248-T48 G27-212 del 4-12-72; Esc 2113 crashed at Manta, Ecuador 10-11-75

MK.89 ECUADOR FAE249-T49 G27-213 del 4-12-72; W/o 22-11-73

MK.89 ECUADOR FAE250-T50 G27-214 del 4-12-72; W/o 16-6-75

MK.82A OMAN 413 G27-215 del Oman as 413 5-3-73; shot down by ground fire (1k) 9-7-73

MK.82A OMAN 414 G27-216 del Oman as 414 5-3-73; preserved Masirah

MK.82A OMAN 415 G27-217 del Oman as 415 10-4-73; GI AFTC Seeb

MK.82A OMAN 416 G27-218 del Oman as 416 10-4-73; cr during air test, Bid Bid, 20-3-76

MK.82A OMAN 417 G27-219 G-BAWE BAC Warton (Paris air show 4-73) 18-4-73; del Oman as 417 8-6-73; preserved Salalah

MK.82A OMAN 418 G27-220 G-BAWF BAC Warton (Paris air show 4-73) 18-4-73; del Oman as 418 8-6-73; preserved Al Ansab, Oman

MK.82A OMAN 419 G27-221 del Oman as 419 18-7-73; hit by SAM-7 and SOC 29-9-75; nose section as GI, Masirah

MK.82A OMAN 420 G27-222 del Oman as 420 18-7-73; preserved Galla, Oman

MK.80A SAUDI 1114 G27-225 del RSAF 2-11-73; Global Avn, Humberside 2000; G-BZYH Richard J. Everett/Everett Aero, Ipswich 3-7-01; sold to USA, struck-off reg. 30-1-02; N605GV Gabriel Vidal, Miami, FL 5-2-02; Attack Aviation Foundation Inc, Las Vegas, NV 14-5-14; Blue Air Training, Las Vegas

MK.80A SAUDI 1115 G27-226 del RSAF 2-11-73; Global Avn, Humberside 2000; Richard J. Everett/Everett Aero, Ipswich 2001 (stored Humberside 2002); BAe Humberside Airport

MK.80A SAUDI 1116 G27-227 del RSAF 11-12-73; preserved Dhahran

MK.80A SAUDI 1117 G27-228 del RSAF 11-12-73; w/o 16.2.76

MK.80A SAUDI 1118 G27-229 del RSAF 7-2-74; Riyadh (store)

MK.80A SAUDI 1119 G27-230 del RSAF 7-2-74; w/o 11-5-75

MK.80A SAUDI 1120 G27-231 del RSAF 4-4-74; Global Avn, Humberside 2000; Richard J. Everett/Everett Aero, Ipswich 2001 (stored Humberside 2002); G-RSAF M. A. Petrie and John E. Rowley, Hawarden 8-4-05; North Wales Military Aviation Services Ltd, Hawarden 10-3-08; M A Petrie, Hawarden 16-7-08; Viper Classics Ltd, London 20-11-09; M. A. Petrie, Hawarden 4-2-16 (repainted in Omani colour scheme 417 2-16)

MK.80A SAUDI 1121 G27-232 to R Saudi AF 4-4-74; Global Avn, Humberside 2000; Richard J. Everett/Everett Aero, Ipswich 2001 (stored North Weald 2002); G-CCAI Richard J. Everett, Sproughton 28-1-03; N799PS Walker J. Hester, Marietta, GA 7-2-03; sale rep., Angleton, TX 6-08; Sabre Aviation

Services, Lake Jackson, TX 5-09; Marine Military Academy Air Wing, Harlingen, TX 7-3-12; MD Aviation Ltd, Rockaway, NJ 10-4-15

MK.80A SAUDI 1122 G27-233 del RSAF 6-6-74; w/o to Riyadh dump

MK.80A SAUDI 1123 G27-234 del RSAF 6-6-74; RSAF Museum, Riyadh

MK.89 ECUADOR FAE251-T51 G27-235 del 5-76

MK.89 ECUADOR FAE252-T52 G27-236 del 5-76; pres Salinas/BA Ulpiano Paez 10-14

MK.89 ECUADOR FAE253-T53 G27-237 del 5-76; W/o 27-12-76

MK.89 ECUADOR FAE254-T54 G27-238 del 5-76

MK.88 NEW ZEALAND NZ6371 G27-240 TO RNZAF as NZ6371 3-75; to Aermacchi (store) 12-92; sold 3-93; International Air Parts, Sydney NSW: dism. 6-93 (arr. dism. Bankstown 7-7-93, stored 1993); reg VH-ONP International Air Parts, Narabeen, Sydney, NSW 20-12-95 (rest. to fly, Bendigo Vic 1996); Nick Costin/Aerospace Services Group Pty Ltd/Australian Fighter Flight Centre, Georges Hall, Sydney, NSW 18-2-99; Michael Costin, Sydney, later Tocumwal NSW 5-10-06

MK.88 NEW ZEALAND NZ6372 G27-241 to RNZAF as NZ6372 4-75; to Aermacchi (store) 12-92; sold 3-93; International Air Parts, Sydney, NSW 6-93 (arr. Dism. Sydney-Bankstown 8-7-93); John Pierce, Watchem, Vic 11-93 (trucked to Bendigo ex Bankstown 11-93 for rest.); reg VH-LLD John Pierce, Bendigo, Vic 22-11-94; Robert A. Douglas, Coolangatta, Qld 1-6-00; Peter O'Halloran, Watchem, Vic 10-4-01 (flew as camouflaged "RNZAF NZ6372"); Hastings Valley Machinery, Port Macquarie, NSW 10-9-03; Rod Hall/Hastings Fighter Flight, Port MacQuarie, NSW 24-6-06; retired, struck-off reg 22-11-12; ZK-BAC RNZAF Strikemaster Ltd, Lower Hutt, NZ 17-3-14

MK.88 NEW ZEALAND NZ6373 G27-242 to RNZAF as NZ6373 4-75; RNZAF Museum, Wigram (preserved)

MK.88 NEW ZEALAND NZ6374 G27-243 to RNZAF as NZ6374 5-75; RNZAF Museum, Ohakea Wing 1992; loan to Wanaka Warbirds & Wheels, Wanaka Airport

MK.88 NEW ZEALAND NZ6375 G27-244 (Paris air show 5-75); to RNZAF as NZ6375 5-75; withdrawn 1991; 4 TTS Woodbourne as GI 7-91

MK.88 NEW ZEALAND NZ6376 G27-245 to RNZAF as NZ6376 6-75; 4TTS Woodbourne as GI 4-93

MK.82A Oman 421 G27-250 del Oman as 421 1-9-76; GI AFTC Seeb

MK.82A OMAN 422 G27-251 del Oman as 422 1-9-76; wfu Masirah (store) 2-12

MK.82A OMAN 423 G27-252 del Oman as 423 13-7-76; Sultan's Armed Forces Museum, Muscat

MK.82A OMAN 424 G27-253 del Oman as 424 13-7-76; GI AFTC Seeb

MK.89 ECUADOR FAE255-T55 G27-246 del 5-76; Esc 2113 Crashed after engine fire 27-1-79, pilots ejected

MK.89 ECUADOR FAE256-T56 G27-247 del 5-76; Esc 2113 Crashed after engine failure 23-11-79

MK.89 ECUADOR FAE257-T57 G27-248 del 5-76

MK.89 ECUADOR FAE258-T58 G27-249 del 5-76; W/o 18-10-76

MK.80A SAUDI 1124 G27-290 G-BECI BAC, Warton 27-7-76 (demonstrator at Farnborough 9-76); del RSAF 22-9-76; RSAF Museum, Riyadh

MK.80A SAUDI 1125 G27-291 del RSAF 22-9-76; Global Avn, Humberside 2000; G-CFBK Trans Holdings Ltd, Shoreham 12-2-08; James S. Everett, Ipswich 24-7-12; Trans Holdings Ltd, Shoreham 7-10-14; de-reg 24-6-15; to Australia 6-15; reg VH-AOE; Miltek Avn, Carrum Downs, Vic 27-10-16

MK.80A SAUDI 1126 G27-292 del RSAF 22-9-76; GI Tech College, Dhahran

MK.80A SAUDI 1127 G27-293 del RSAF 23-11-76; RSAF Museum Riyadh

MK.80A SAUDI 1128 G27-294 del RSAF 23-11-76; w/o 9-86; Dhahran dump

MK.80A SAUDI 1129 G27-295 del RSAF 14-12-76; Global Avn, Humberside, store; BAe Humberside Airport

MK.80A SAUDI 1130 G27-296 del RSAF 14-12-76; Global Avn, Humberside 2000; Richard J. Everett/Everett Aero, Ipswich 2001; G-CDHB Christopher C. Hudson, Bromley 31-1-05; Stewart J. Davies, Sandtoft 21-11-05; G-VPER David Davidson/Team Viper Jet Formation Team 14-5-09; ZK-VPR Brian D. Hall, Christchurch 11-5-11; arr. by road at Christchurch Airport 7-7-11, (flies as "R Saudi AF 1130")

MK.80A SAUDI 1131 G27-297 del RSAF 25-1-77

MK.80A SAUDI 1132 G27-298 del RSAF 25-1-77; GI Tech College Dhahran

MK.80A SAUDI 1133 G27-299 G-BESY BAC, Warton 26-4-77; del RSAF 7-7-77; wfu 1997; Imperial War Museum, Duxford 4-02

MK.80A SAUDI 1134 G27-300 G-BESZ BAC, Warton 26-4-77; del R Saudi AF 12-7 77; GI Tech College, Dhahran

MK.80A SAUDI 1135 G27-312 G-BFOO BAe, Warton 22-3-78; del RSAF 2-5-78; GI Tech College, Dhahran

MK.89 PS.367 ECUADOR FAE259-T59 G16-26 G-BIDB F/f 7-8-80; civil reg. 15-9-80 – 11-8-87; ZG621 del 11-87; engine failure on approach, Taura AB, 10-3-01, both pilots ejected

MK.89 PS.368 ECUADOR FAE260-T60 G16-27 G-BHIZ F/f 23-10-80; ZG622 civil reg. 5-2-81 – 5-8-87; del Ecuador 11-87; crashed Lago Agrio, 122m E of Quito, 25-3-09, both pilots ejected (1k)

MK.90 PS.369 SUDAN 141 G16-28 del 19-11-83

MK.90 PS.370 SUDAN 142 G16-29 del 19-11-83

MK.90 PS.371 SUDAN 144 G16-30 del 30-11-83

MK.89 PS.372 ECUADOR FAE261-T61 G16-31 del 21-10-88; w/o as overstressed, Eloy Alfaro AB 11-3-97; stored Manta

MK.89 PS.373 ECUADOR FAE262-T62 G16- del 21-10-88; pres Bahia

MK.89 PS.374 ECUADOR FAE263-T63 G16- del 21-10-88; pres Manta

MK.89 PS.375 ECUADOR FAE264-T64 G16- del 21-10-88

MK.82A PS.376 OMAN 425 G27-405 del Oman 25-9-86; Seeb AB, Oman: inst airframe 2000; G-SOAF M. A. Petrie & J. E. Rowley, Hawarden 21-2-05; Strikemaster Flying Club, Hawarden 21-12-07

RAF MAINTENANCE AIRFRAMES

Following the end of their operational careers, a large number of Jet Provost airframes were relegated for ground training purposes with various RAF Technical Training Schools and Air Training Corps squadrons; many were later displayed at Service establishments as gate guardians or employed for fire, crash and rescue training. From October 1956, 174 Jet Provosts were allocated for use as maintenance airframes and renumbered in a numerical series suffixed by the letter 'M'. The majority of the airframes were issued to RAF Halton, Cosford and the Defence College of Aeronautical Engineering (DCAE) at St Athan and retained in ground running condition as training aids for flight-line personnel or for instructional purposes. A number were resold to private buyers following their disposal.

The following is a list of instructional airframe serials, previous identities and dates allocated.

JET PROVOST T MK.1 7369M/XD692 (10-56) ntu; 7570M/XD674 (4-58)

JET PROVOST T MK.3 / T MK.3A / T MK.4 7726M/XM373 (7-61); 7819M/XP661 (9-63); 7984M/XN597 (9-67); 8054AM/XM410 (9-69); 8054AM/XM410 (9-69); 8054M/XM417 (9-69); 8055AM/XM402 (9-69); 8055BM/XM404 (9-69); 8062M/XR669 (11-69); 8070M/XM351(12-69); 8076M/XM386 (12-69); 8077M/XN594 (12-69); 8078M/XM351 (12-69); 8079M/XM492 (12-69); 8080M/XM480 (12-69); 8081M/XM468 (12-69); 8082M/XM409 (12-69); 8083M/XM367 (12-69); 8084M/XM369 (12-69); 8085M/XM467 (12-69); 8088M/XN602 (2-70); 8097M/XS213 (5-70); 8121M/XM474 (12-70); 8192M/XR658 (12-71); 8193M/XR707 (1-72); 8229M/XM355 (3-73); 8230M/XM362 (3-73); 8231M/XM375 (3-73); 8232M/XM381 (3-73); 8233M/XM408 (3-73); 8234M/XN458 (3-73); 8235M/XN549 (3-73); 8236M/XP573 (3-73); 8237M/XS179 (3-73); 8238M/XS180 (3-73); 8239M/XS210

(3-73); 8352M/XN632 (7-73); 8353M/XN633 (7-73); XN635 (7-73); 8374M/XR660 (9-73); 8400M/XP583 (1-74); 8401M/XP686 (1-74); 8404M/XP548 (1-74) ntu; 8407M/XP585 (5-74); 8408M/XS186 (5-74); 8409M/XS209 (5-74); 8410M/XR662 (5-74); 8434M/XM411 (1-75); 8435M/XN512 (1-75); 8436M/XN554 (1-75); 8458M/XP672 (12-75); 8459M/XR650 (12-75); 8460M/XP680 (12-75); 8494M/XP557 (5-76); 8495M/XR672 (5-76); 8498M/XR670 (7-76); 8501M/XP640 (8-76); 8502M/XP686 (8-76); 8506M/XR704 (10-76); 8507M/XS215 (10-76); 8508M/XS218 (10-76); 8510M/XP567 (10-76); 8514M/XS176 (12-76); 8516M/XR643 (1-77); 8559M/XN467 (8-77); 8587M/XP677 (undated); 8588M/XR681 (undated); 8589M/XR700 (undated); 8593M/XM418 (undated); 8594M/XP661 (9-63); *8627M/XP558 (1-79); 8704M/XN643 (8-81); 8786M/XN495 (10-83); 8862M/XN473 (5-85); 8865M/XN641 (7-85); 8917M/XM372 (10-86); 8956M/XN577 (2-88); 8957M/XN582 (3-88); 8958M/XN501 (3-88); 8959M/XN472 (3-88); 8960M/XM455 (4-88); 8962M/XM371 (4-88); 8968M/XM471 (5-88); 8971M/XN548 (5-88); 8974M/XM473 (6-88); 8983M/XM478 (2-89); 8984M/XN551 (2-89); 8987M/XM358 (3-89); 8990M/XM419 (3-89); 8991M/XR679 (3-89); 8992M/XP547 (3-89); 8993M/XS219 (3-89); 8994M/XS178 (3-89); 8995M/XM425 (4-89); 8996M/XM414 (5-89); 9011M/XM412 (7-89); 9012M/XN494 (10-89); 9014M/XN584 (10-89); 9016MB/XN640 (11-89); 9025M/XR701 (2-90); 9026M/XP629 (2-90); 9027M/XP556 (2-90); 9028M/XP563 (2-90); 9029M/XS217 (2-90); 9030M/XR674 (2-90); 9031M/XP688 (4-91); 9032M/XR673 (2-90); 9033M/XS181 (2-90); 9034M/XP638 (2-90); 9035M/XR653 (2-90); 9036M/XM350 (3-90); 9039M/XN586 (5-90); 9045M/XN636 (4-90); 9046M/XM349 (6-90); 9048M/XM403 (9-84); 9051M/XM472 (10-90); 9112M/XM475 (7-90); 9121M/XN606 (9-91); 9044M/XS177 (4-90); 9137M/XN579 (5-92); 9143M/XN589 (5-92)

JET PROVOST T MK.5/5A 8741M/XW329 (7-82); 9013M/XW298 (11-89); 9016M/XW320 (6-90); 9018M/XW365 (6-90); 9047M/XW409 (6-90); 9049M/XW404 (6-93); 9061M/XW335 (10-91); 9062M/XW351 (10-91); 9090M/XW353 (2-91); 9091M/XW434 (3-91); 9097M/XW366 (5-91); 9109M/XW312 (7-91); 9111M/XW421 (7-91); 9119M/XW303 (9-91); 9120M/XW419 (9-91); 9124M/XW427 (10-91); 9125M/XW410 (10-91); 9126M/XW413 (10-91); 9127M/XW432 (10-91); 9128M/XW292 (10-91); 9129M/XW294 (10-91); 9130M/XW327 (2-92); 9146M/XW299 (5-92); 9147M/XW301 (5-92); 9148M/XW436 (5-92); 9149M/XW375 (6-93); 9153M/XW360 (7-92); 9154M/XW321 (3-93); 9166M/XW323 (10-92); 9172M/XW304 (9-91); 9173M/XW418 (12-92); 9176M/XW430 (1-93); 9177M/XW328 (10-93); 9179M/XW309 (3-93); 9180M/XW311 (3-93); 9181M/XW358 (3-93); 9187M/XW405 (5-93); 9188M/XW364 (5-93); 9190M/XW318 (6-93); 9191M/XW416 (6-93); 9192M/XW361 (6-93); 9193M/XW367 (5-91); 9194M/XW420 (6-93); 9195M/XW330 (6-93); 9196M/XW370 (6-93); 9199M/XW290 (7-93); 9200M/XW425 (7-93)

The Defence College of Aeronautical Engineering (DCAE) was The Defence College established on 1 April 2004 following the Defence College of Aero training Review (DTR).

* Formerly allocated A2628 while GI with SAH, RNAS Culdrose, 5-74 to 3-79

ABBREVIATIONS

A&AEE	Aeroplane & Armament Establishment
AWCN	Awaiting Collection
AFT(S)	Advanced Flying Training (School)
BAC	British Aircraft Corporation
BAE	British Aerospace
BDR	Battle Damage Repair
BFT(S)	Basic Flying Training (School)
BS	Bristol Siddeley
CA	Controller Air
CAACU	Civilian Anti-Aircraft Co-operation Unit
CNX	Cancelled
CWP	Contractor's Working Party
DA	Deposit Account
DARA	Defence Aviation Repair Agency
(D)CFI	(Deputy) Chief Flying Instructor
DSAE	Defence School of Aeronautical Engineering
EOD	Explosive Ordnance Disposal
ETPS	Empire Test Pilots School
F/F	First flight
GCA	Ground Control Approach
IRE	Instrument Rating Examiner
JATE	Joint Air Transport Establishment
MOS	Ministry of Supply
MU	Maintenance Unit
NAVEX	Navigation Exercise
NES	Non Effective Stock
NTU	Not Taken Up
QFI	Qualified Flying Instructor
RAE	Royal Aircraft Establishment
RAFEF	Royal Air Force Exhibition Flight
RIW	Repair In Work
ROS	Repair on Site
RR	Rolls-Royce
SAH	School of Aircraft Handling
SFS	Sold for Scrap
SOAF	Sultan of Oman's Air Force
SOC	Struck off Charge
SOTT	School of Technical Training
TI	Trial Installation
TRE	Telecommunications Radar (Research) Establishment
TTE	Technical Training School

BIBLIOGRAPHY

BAGSHAW, ROY ET AL., *RAF Little Rissington: the Central Flying School years 1946-1976,* Pen & Sword, 2006

HAIG-THOMAS, ANTHONY, *Fall Out: Roman Catholics and Jews,* Old Forge Publishing, 2008

MCCLOSKEY, KEITH, *Airwork: A History,* The History Press, 2012

MCDONALD, PAUL, *Winged Warriors: the Cold War from the cockpit,* Pen & Sword, 2012

RICHARDSON, COLIN, *Masirah: Tales from a Desert Island,* Pentland Press, 2001

ROBINSON AFC*, JOHN B., *Life of Flying,* Self-Published

WHITE, ROWLAND, *Storm Front,* Corgi Books, 2012

INDEX

FROM JET PROVOST TO STRIKEMASTER

OVERSEAS AIR FORCES

MILITARY OPERATORS

OTHER OPERATORS